ADMINISTRATIVE TRIBUNALS AND ADJUDICATION

Among the many constitutional developments of the past century or so, one of the most significant has been the creation and proliferation of institutions that perform functions similar to those performed by courts but which are considered to be, and in some ways are, different and distinct from courts as traditionally conceived. In much of the common law world, such institutions are called 'administrative tribunals'. Their main function is to adjudicate disputes between citizens and the state by decisions of government agencies – a function also performed by courts in 'judicial review' proceedings and appeals. Although tribunals in aggregate adjudicate many more such disputes than courts, tribunals and their role as dispensers of 'administrative justice' receive relatively little scholarly attention.

This, the first wide-ranging book-length treatment of the subject for many years, compares tribunals in three major jurisdictions: Australia, the UK and the US. It analyses and offers an account of the concept of 'administrative adjudication', and traces its historical development from the earliest periods of the common law to the twenty-first century. There are chapters dealing with the design of tribunals and tribunal systems and with what tribunals do, what they are for and how they interact with their users. The book ends with a discussion of the place of tribunals in the 'administrative justice system' and speculation about possible future developments.

Administrative Tribunals and Adjudication fills a significant gap in the literature and will be of great value to public lawyers and others interested in government accountability.

Administrative Tribunals and Adjudication

Peter Cane

·HART·
PUBLISHING

OXFORD AND PORTLAND, OREGON
2009

Published in North America (US and Canada) by
Hart Publishing
c/o International Specialized Book Services
920 NE 58th Avenue, Suite 300
Portland, OR 97213–3786
USA
Tel: +1 503 287 3093 or toll-free: (1) 800 944 6190
Fax: +1 503 280 8832
E-mail: orders@isbs.com
Website: http://www.isbs.com

Hart Publishing Ltd, 16C Worcester Place, Oxford, OX1 2JW
Telephone: +44 (0)1865 517530 Fax: +44 (0)1865 510710
E-mail: mail@hartpub.co.uk
Website: http://www.hartpub.co.uk

British Library Cataloguing in Publication Data

Data Available

ISBN: 978-1-84113-009-5

Typeset by Columns Design Ltd, Reading
Printed and bound in Great Britain by
TJ International Ltd, Padstow, Cornwall

For Mike Taggart

Inspiring colleague, firm friend, outstanding scholar

Preface

This book is the main fruit of a major research project generously funded by the Australian Research Council (Discovery Project DP0558688). The project presented me with significant challenges. My undergraduate study of administrative in law at Sydney University pre-dated the major reforms initiated by the publication in Australia of the Report of the Kerr Committee (the Commonwealth Administrative Review Committee) in 1971, which took effect in the mid–late 1970s. Public law played no part in my graduate legal studies at Oxford. Nevertheless, I started teaching both administrative law and constitutional law to Oxford undergraduates in 1978 and did so until the mid-1990s. I was dimly aware in that period of developments in Australia but paid them little attention. By the time I returned to Australia in 1997 I had forgotten most of the Australian constitutional law I had learnt as a student, and I knew almost nothing about the dramatic changes in the law and institutions of administrative adjudication that had taken place in Australia during my absence and which are commonly referred as the 'new administrative law' or the 'federal administrative law package'.

In 2000 I organised a colloquium entitled 'Administrative Law in a Federal System' in honour of Sir Anthony Mason,[1] whose term as a National Fellow of the Australian National University had recently ended. A National Fellowship is the most prestigious visiting academic post at the ANU, and in that capacity Sir Anthony had been attached to the Law Program in the Research School of Social Sciences, of which I was at that time the Head. Honouring Sir Anthony in this way was particularly appropriate. As Solicitor-General of the Commonwealth of Australia in the late 1960s he was instrumental in the establishment of the Commonwealth Administrative Review Committee (of which he was a member). As Justice and then Chief Justice of the High Court of Australia in the 1980s and 1990s, Sir Anthony played a central role in judicial development of administrative law in a critical period of creative energy. Extra-judicially, he has also written extensively on public law in general and administrative law in particular.[2] With the hubris of the neophyte, and in a blissful state of ignorance, I contributed to the Colloquium an essay[3] that made a radical and heterodox argument about the

---

[1] Papers given at the Colloquium were published in the *Federal Law Review* (Vol 28, No 2).
[2] A selection of these writings can be found in G Lindell (ed), *The Mason Papers: Selected Articles and Speeches by Sir Anthony Mason AC, KBE* (Sydney, The Federation Press, 2007).
[3] 'Merits Review and Judicial Review: The AAT as Trojan Horse' (2000) 28 *Federal Law Review* 213.

relationship between judicial review and merits review, and the role of the Administrative Appeals Tribunal, which Sir Anthony thought (and, I gather, still thinks) seriously wrong-headed.

In 2003, when I was casting around for a project that might prove attractive to the Australian Research Council, I hit upon the idea of studying merits review and the peak federal merits review tribunals – the Administrative Appeals Tribunal (AAT) – in much greater detail, partly with the objective of determining whether my earlier speculations on the subject would withstand closer and more sustained analysis. As would be expected, there is a very large Australian literature concerned with merits review and tribunals (the AAT in particular), but much of it is quite practical and institutional in approach. At the time I began thinking about writing my grant proposal there was no book-length academic account that tried to make sense of what had happened on the tribunal front since 1971. The first edition of my colleague, Dennis Pearce's invaluable book, *The Administrative Appeals Tribunal* was published in 2003,[4] and I have relied on it much more heavily than is indicated by the frequency of citation of the second edition in this volume. Without it, coming to terms with the complex technical law of merits review would have been a mammoth task.

As originally conceived, the project had an analytical and an empirical component. The former focused on the principles, theory and practice of merits review, and the latter was concerned with the dissemination of knowledge about merits review and the AAT within four government agencies that together account for about 90 per cent of the AAT's caseload. In the event, for various logistical reasons the empirical component had to be abandoned. In the attempt to turn a problem into an opportunity (and to justify the money and effort already expended on the project), I decided to supplement my research and re-orient the project as a study of administrative adjudication with the AAT at its centre, but moving out from there in historical and comparative directions. This book is the product of that re-orientation. I was relieved to discover that my basic instincts about merits review and the AAT were broadly correct, although the lack of sophistication and nuance in my earlier efforts now make me cringe.

One of the aims of this book is to introduce to a wider audience in the common-law world some of the distinctive features of Australian public law and legal institutions. Although it has often been observed that the federal administrative law package was unique and extremely innovative, it is relatively little known or understood outside Australia. Although Australian public law is built on solid British foundations, at federal level it is also significantly informed by American ideas, and this dual heritage makes it a particularly fascinating and fruitful topic for study not only conceptually but also institutionally, historically and comparatively. For many academic administrative lawyers, tribunals are of only peripheral interest. This, I have come to appreciate after many years of ignoring them as much as I could, is a blinkered point of view and an extremely

---

[4] The second edition appeared in 2007: D Pearce, *The Administrative Appeals Tribunal*, 2nd edn (Australia, LexisNexis Butterworths, 2007).

unsatisfactory state of affairs. It was not until I started to study Australian public law in earnest and to think about administrative adjudication historically[5] and comparatively that I began to value tribunals not only for their practical importance but also for their theoretical and constitutional significance. This process has required me to negotiate some very steep learning curves.

Although this book is relatively short, it is based on a very great deal of research, much of it invisible beneath the surface of the text. In doing that research I have been greatly assisted by a succession of fine, young scholars: Zoë Guest, Tal Karp, David Ananian-Cooper, Glyn Watson, Wendy Kukulies-Smith and Yee Fui Ng. I owe large debts to many academic colleagues, and in particular to John Allison, John Bell, Carol Harlow, Leighton McDonald, Jerry Mashaw, Genevra Richardson, Mike Taggart and Nick Wikeley not only for their help with this project but also for many years of stimulating intellectual interchange, and warm friendship and support. I am grateful to an anonymous reviewer for many perceptive and constructive comments. I remain, of course, responsible for all errors of fact, emphasis and interpretation, and for all infelicities of expression.

Finally, I want to pay special tribute and convey warm thanks to all those at Hart Publishing who have been involved in various ways with the production of this book. I have known Richard Hart and Jane Parker as close friends for more than 20 years, and this is the third of my books that their press has graciously agreed to publish. It is a delight to me to observe the success of Hart Publishing as it goes from strength to strength. The service that Richard has done for the legal profession generally and for legal scholars in particular is inestimable. Long may it continue!

Peter Cane
Canberra
5 January 2009

---

[5] In this respect, I was extremely fortunate that Chantal Stebbings' excellent book, *Legal Foundations of Tribunals in Nineteenth Century England* (Cambridge, Cambridge University Press, 2006) had been published before I decided to broaden my historical canvas.

Contents

Contents

Abbreviations

AAR	Administrative Appeal Reports
AAT	Administrative Appeals Tribunal
AAT Act	Administrative Appeals Tribunal Act 1975 (Cth)
ABA	American Bar Association
ACUS	Administrative Conference of the United States
ADJR Act	Administrative Decisions (Judicial Review) Act 1977 (Cth)
ADR	alternative dispute resolution
ADT	Administrative Decisions Tribunal (NSW)
AIT	Asylum and Immigration Tribunal
AJ	administrative judge
AJTC	Administrative Justice and Tribunals Council
ALD	Administrative Law Decisions
ALJ	administrative law judge
APA	Administrative Procedure Act 1946 (US)
ARC	Administrative Review Council
ART	Administrative Review Tribunal
CCCA	Commonwealth Court of Conciliation and Arbitration
CO	Commonwealth Ombudsman
ECHR	European Convention on Human Rights
FIADRWG	Federal Interagency Alternative Dispute Resolution Working Group
FTC	Federal Trade Commission
ICC	Interstate Commerce Commission
JAC	Judicial Appointments Commission
JP	Justice of the Peace
MRT	Migration Review Tribunal
MSPB	Merit Systems Protection Board
OPM	Office of Personnel Management
PDR	proportionate dispute resolution
PHSO	Parliamentary and Health Service Ombudsman
RRT	Refugee Review Tribunal
SAT	State Administrative Tribunal (WA)
SSAT	Social Security Appeals Tribunal
SSCSC	Social Security and Child Support Commissioners
TCE Act	Tribunals, Courts and Enforcement Act 2007 (UK)
UK	United Kingdom
US	United States
VCAT	Victorian Civil and Administrative Tribunal
VRB	Veterans' Review Board

Table Of Cases

Australia

Table Of Cases

United Kingdom

United States of America

Table of Legislation

Australia

Canada

United Kingdom

United States of America

Council of Europe

1

Survey

1.1 The Project

ONE OF THE most significant, large-scale and enduring constitutional developments of the past 150 years has been the creation of a set of governmental institutions known, in major common law jurisdictions outside the United States, as 'tribunals'. This book is about a subset of that set of institutions. It is the main fruit[1] of a project that started out as a theoretically and temporally contextualised study of the Australian Administrative Appeals Tribunal (AAT). As the project developed, I came to the conclusion that it in order properly to understand the AAT and its place in the governmental system it would be necessary to broaden the study in three directions: first, institutionally – to cover not only the AAT but a larger set of institutions that I will refer to as 'administrative tribunals'; secondly, comparatively – to take in the United Kingdom[2] and the United States of America (and, to a lesser extent, France) in addition to Australia; and thirdly, historically – attempting to dig more deeply than I had originally intended into the antecedents of the 'modern' administrative tribunal. The choice of the UK and the US as the main comparator jurisdictions was made easy by the fact that the Australian federal constitutional system[3] (as we will see in more detail later) has a dual heritage, partly British and partly American.

---

[1] Other produce can be found in P Cane and L McDonald, *Principles of Administrative Law: Legal Regulation of Governance* (Melbourne, OUP, 2008) ch 8; 'Understanding Administrative Adjudication' in L Pearson, C Harlow and M Taggart, *Administrative Law in a Changing State: Essays in Honour of Mark Aronson* (Oxford, Hart Publishing, 2008); 'Judicial Review in the Age of Tribunals' [2009] *Public Law* 479; 'Judicial Review and Merits Review: Comparing Administrative Adjudication by Tribunals and Courts (available on request).

[2] Technically, 'United Kingdom' refers collectively to the three legal systems of England and Wales (which together constitute a single system), Scotland and Northern Ireland. 'Great Britain' (or 'Britain') refers collectively to England and Wales, and Scotland. 'England' is commonly used to refer to England and Wales. In this book, 'United Kingdom' will be used to refer indiscriminately to each and all of these entities unless greater precision is required or appropriate.

[3] Australia is a federation. The federal entity is called 'the Commonwealth (of Australia)' and the constituent regional governmental entities are the six states (New South Wales, Queensland, South Australia, Tasmania, Victoria and Western Australia) and the two mainland self-governing Territories

An important aim of the project is to increase knowledge and understanding of the AAT outside Australia. This explains why – despite the broadening of focus I have just described – the AAT plays a more prominent part in the analysis than any other single institution. The AAT deserves this special position for various reasons. First, in terms of subject matter, its jurisdiction is very wide; secondly, it reviews decisions at both first-instance ('first tier') and appellate ('second tier') levels; thirdly, it has generated (and continues to generate) a large body of reported case law; fourthly, it occupies a markedly distinctive niche in the constitutional structure of Australian federal government; fifthly, its characteristic function is to engage in 'merits review' – a concept which, in the Australian context, has acquired a technical meaning that deserves careful analysis for the light it can throw on the functions of tribunals more generally; sixthly, the creation and operation of the AAT have led to important further developments in the design of institutions of governance at both state and federal levels in Australia; and finally, Australian practice in this area has significantly influenced recent and ongoing re-organisation of the tribunal system in the UK.[4]

1.2 Administrative Tribunals and Administrative Adjudication

Whereas I originally intended the AAT to be the centre and main subject of attention, broadening the project in the way I have described led me to think of it instead as a sort of lens that could be used to sharpen analysis and refine understanding of a particular set of governmental institutions. A common feature of contributions to the literature on 'tribunals' is an initial, somewhat despairing observation that the term 'tribunal' is used to refer to many different types of institutions, followed by a discussion that fails to realise the implicit promise of definitional sensitivity. One way of dealing with this unsatisfactory

(the Australian Capital Territory – which is the seat of the Commonwealth government – and the Northern Territory). The constitutional position of the territories is different in various ways from that of the States; but for the purposes of this book, these differences are irrelevant.

[4] *Tribunals for Users: One System, One Service* (Report of the Review of Tribunals chaired by Sir Andrew Leggatt, TSO, 2001) 206–10. Ironically, however, the new structure (described in more detail in 2.3.1 and 3.1 below) bears more similarity to highly controversial proposals for an Administrative Review Tribunal, which were defeated in the Australian Senate in 2001 and have not been revived (see 2.3.3). As already noted, the 'UK' terminology is not entirely accurate. There are some tribunals that operate on a UK-wide basis, but others that operate only within Scotland (see Scottish Consumer Council, *Options for the Future Administration and Supervision of Tribunals in Scotland: A Report by the Administrative Justice Steering Group*, Sept 2008) or Northern Ireland (see L Allamby, 'Northern Ireland Administrative Justice Reform: Government Timetable Awaited', (July 2007) <http://www. council-on-tribunals.gov.uk/adjust/item/comment_nireform.htm> accessed 16 October 2008). The discussion in this book refers primarily to UK-wide tribunals.

situation would be to attempt a mapping exercise designed to develop a taxonomy of the various agencies to which the term 'tribunal' is applied. However, such an approach is unlikely to be particularly interesting or illuminating. Instead, the strategy of this book is to focus on institutions – 'administrative tribunals' – that share certain basic characteristics with the AAT and to sideline other types of institution to which the term 'tribunal' is applied.

For this purpose, three distinctive features of the AAT may be singled out: its institutional nature, its characteristic function and its jurisdiction.

1.2.1 The AAT is not a court

First, the AAT is not a court. This statement can be explained quite precisely because in Australian federal law, the word 'court' has a technical constitutional meaning, namely a body established under Chapter III of the Constitution, the judges of which are appointed in accordance with section 72 of the Constitution (with security of tenure and salary protection) and the predominant function of which is the exercise of federal judicial power. Under Australian federal constitutional law, non-judicial functions may not be conferred on federal courts unless they are incidental to the exercise of judicial power. As will be explained in much more detail later, the characteristic function of the AAT – 'merits review' – is non-judicial and so cannot be conferred on a federal court. For this reason, the AAT was deliberately created as a non-court. In terms of the formal separation of powers embodied in the first three Chapters of the Australian Constitution – which respectively confer legislative power on the legislature (Chapter I), executive power on the executive (Chapter II) and judicial power on the judiciary (Chapter III) – the AAT belongs to the executive branch of government, not the judicial. Being a non-court, the AAT is staffed by 'members', not 'judges' or 'justices'.

In constitutional systems, such as those of the UK and the Australian states, which do not embody a formal separation of powers, the terminological distinction between 'tribunals' and 'courts' lacks the constitutional significance it has in the Australian federal system. In Australian federal constitutional law, all judges of federal courts must be appointed in accordance with the provisions of section 72 of the Constitution. By contrast, in systems such as those of the UK and the Australian states, while judges of superior courts typically enjoy security of tenure and salary protection similar to that conferred on judges of Australian federal courts by section 72 of the Constitution, judges of inferior courts may not. Furthermore, in such systems there is no formal constitutional distinction between judicial and non-judicial power and no prohibition of the conferral on courts of functions that would be classified as non-judicial in Australian federal law. As a result, in such systems, agencies of the type that provide the focus of this study may not be called 'tribunals'. For instance, the New South Wales Land and Environment Court has the power, in some areas of its jurisdiction, to engage in merits review; but it also exercises functions that in federal law would be classified as judicial. By reason of the constitutional prohibitions of conferring non-judicial power on a court and of conferring both judicial and non-judicial power on the same body (whether a court or a non-court), the federal Parliament could not create such a body. Again, just as in such systems bodies called 'courts' may function as tribunals, so bodies called 'tribunals' may be courts. For instance, the Upper Tribunal established by the Tribunals, Courts and Enforcement Act 2007 (UK) ('TCE Act') is a 'superior court of record'.

Because the distinction between courts and tribunals is less formally and sharply drawn in the law of the UK and the Australian states than in Australian federal law, the meaning of the statement, that a tribunal is not a court, is less clear in such systems than it is in the Australian federal system. Nevertheless, the distinction between tribunals and courts is recognised and clearly drawn even in systems that lack formal separation of powers; and in such contexts, discussion of the differences between and the relative strengths of 'tribunals' and 'courts' is a staple of the literature on 'tribunals'. As we will see in 2.2, this may be explicable historically: at least since Montesquieu's exposition in the 18th century, in accounts of the concept of separation of powers the judicial branch has typically been identified with superior central courts, which can be most easily contrasted with tribunals, largely ignoring inferior and local courts which may bear more similarity to tribunals than to superior courts. Moreover, in the UK at least, an important strand in the history of the development of tribunals was dissatisfaction with and a desire to create alternatives to the superior central courts. Thus, whereas, in Australian federal law, the contrast between tribunals and courts has constitutional significance, in systems that lack formal separation of powers its significance comes, partly at least, from a relatively narrow understanding of the institution of a court that conceals the diversity amongst entities referred to by that name.

The situation is different again in the US. As in the case of Australia, the analysis will focus on US federal law and the federal governmental system. In the US, the term 'tribunal' is rarely used to describe institutions of the type on which this book concentrates or, indeed, to describe any of the types of agency that are commonly referred to as tribunals in other major common law jurisdictions. In an early article in the *Harvard Law Review* WH Pillsbury used the term 'administrative tribunal' in a sense reasonably close to that adopted here.[5] But in his famous book, *The Administrative Process*,[6] JM Landis used the phrase to refer to multi-functional regulatory agencies, and to the extent that the term is used in the US literature, this is the meaning it typically bears. There is a tendency, especially in the older English and Australian literature, to use the term to refer both to administrative tribunals in the sense adopted in this book and to bodies

---

[5] 'Administrative Tribunals' (1922–23) 36 *Harvard Law Review* 405 and 583.
[6] New Haven and London, Yale University Press, 1938.

that perform regulatory functions, such as licensing;[7] and this is one reason why (as noted earlier) many discussions of tribunals begin with an expression of definitional despair.

Like the first three Chapters of the Australian Constitution, the first three Articles of the US Constitution embody a formal separation of powers: Article I deals with the legislature and legislative power, Article II with the executive and executive power and Article III with the judiciary and judicial power. However, as will be explained in more detail in 3.2, the US Supreme Court has not interpreted the US Constitution as requiring such a sharp distinction between courts and non-courts as the Australian High Court has read out of (or into) the Australian Constitution. Put crudely, the Supreme Court has recognised that Congress may confer judicial power on bodies that are not Article III courts provided that in doing so, it does not undermine the values protected by separation of powers (namely prevention of undue concentrations of power and conflicts of interest, and protection of individual rights) and provided it makes adequate provision for review by a Chapter III court of the exercise of judicial power by such bodies. There are two categories of such bodies: so-called 'Article I courts' and agencies that belong to the executive branch. Within agencies, judicial power is exercised by officials called 'administrative law judges' (ALJs, who are appointed under the provisions of the Administrative Procedure Act 1946) and 'administrative judges' (AJs, who are not so appointed).[8] ALJs and AJs are the closest US equivalents to administrative tribunals in the sense adopted in this book, and unless the context indicates otherwise, the term 'tribunal' will generally be used to include such officials. A significant difference between Article I courts and ALJs/AJs is that the latter are typically embedded within government agencies whereas the former are not.

In the US, therefore, the term 'court' is not confined to bodies established under Article III of the Constitution; but the word is not used to describe officials within agencies that perform judicial functions even though such officials are called 'judges'. Nor is the term 'tribunal' normally applied to them. Nevertheless, debates that are conducted in Australia and the UK in terms of tribunals on the one hand and courts on the other are also carried on in the US. For instance, the *modus operandi* of ALJs and AJs is often compared and contrasted with that of 'courts' understood in terms of a relatively narrow, traditional paradigm of the superior central court; and since the 1930s in the US proposals have often been made for the establishment of an administrative 'court' in the sense of a free-standing agency that would employ ALJs and AJs, who would cease to be embedded within agencies.

---

[7] eg JA Farmer, *Tribunals and Government* (London, Weidenfeld and Nicolson, 1974).
[8] AJs are sometimes referred to as 'hearing examiners'.

In summary, although the word 'court' is understood in various ways and with varying degrees of precision in different jurisdictions, tribunals are recognised in our three main comparator jurisdictions as being, in some sense, not courts.

1.2.2 The AAT reviews decisions

The second noteworthy feature of the AAT is its characteristic function, namely that of reviewing decisions. Although the AAT's name suggests that it conducts 'appeals', the Administrative Appeals Tribunal Act 1975 – the AAT's constitutive legislation – gives it the function of 'reviewing' decisions. Indeed, a replacement for the AAT, proposed in the late 1990s but never brought into existence, was to be called the 'Administrative Review Tribunal'. As we have already noted, this characteristic function of the AAT is commonly described as 'merits review', a non-judicial task that cannot be conferred on a federal court. Merits review can be contrasted with 'judicial review', an analogous but significantly different judicial function that cannot be conferred on a federal tribunal. For present purposes, we can ignore the distinction between these two forms of review (it is discussed in detail in Chapter 5) and concentrate on the concept of 'review' itself.

The linguistic instability in descriptions of the AAT ('appeal' or 'review'?) is significant. There is a well-recognised distinction in administrative law theory between 'appeal' and 'review'. This distinction has two dimensions, one concerned with the powers of the court or tribunal (in particular whether the court of tribunal can make a substitute decision) and the other concerned with available grounds for adjudicatory intervention (for instance, error of law, error of fact and so on). In the term 'judicial review', the word 'review' indicates that the court may upset decisions only on relatively narrow grounds and that it lacks the power to make substitute decisions. Conversely, use of the term 'appeal' in relation to the AAT reflects the fact that it has the power (amongst others) to make substitute decisions and that the basis on which it can make such a decision – that the primary decision was not the 'correct or preferable' one – is broad. On the other hand, use of the term 'review' in relation to the AAT serves to emphasise the fact that although the AAT's characteristic function of merits review approximates to a *de novo* rehearing and that the AAT has power to make decisions, the AAT is not a primary decision-maker but a maker of 'substitute' decisions. The AAT, we might say, has power to supervise the *making* of decisions by *reviewing* and, in appropriate cases, by *re-making* decisions.

For the sake of clarity, it is important at this point to say a word about the use throughout this book of the word 'review' (and the cognate term 'reviewer'). In particular, the word 'review' is not used in contrast to the word 'appeal'. So, for instance, UK readers should not read the word 'review' as a shorthand for 'judicial review' (as opposed to an appeal). Rather, (unless the context indicates otherwise), the word 'review', without any adjective, is used to refer to what administrative tribunals characteristically do (however that may be understood).

6

Review by courts will normally be referred to as 'judicial review'. For clarity's sake, what tribunals do will sometimes be referred to as 'non-judicial review', and this term should be understood as synonymous with 'review' without any adjectival qualification. The term 'merits review' will be used (only) to refer to the Australian concept elaborated in Chapter 5, which is a mode of 'review'. In the UK, the term typically used to describe what tribunals do is 'appeal', and this may be contrasted with 'judicial review'. In my terms, 'appeal' used in this way is a mode of 'review' (without adjectival qualification), and an 'appellate tribunal' is a species of 'reviewer'. An aim of Chapter 5 is to compare and contrast the various understandings of what tribunals do in our comparator jurisdictions with the Australian concept of merits review. One of the issues for consideration will concern similarities and differences between the UK concept of 'appeal' (understood as a mode of 'review') and the Australian concept of 'merits review'.

How should we understand the AAT's characteristic function of reviewing primary decision-making?[9] First, note that the word 'review' is used not only in the terms 'judicial review' and 'merits review' but also in the term 'internal review'. Internal review can be distinguished from 'external' review. This distinction is partly a function of institutional structure. Adopting a spatial metaphor, review is internal if it takes place within the institution in which the original decision-maker was located at the time the decision was made, but external if it takes place within a different institution. For instance, a primary decision to refuse a social security benefit to a claimant, made by an officer of a social security agency, may be internally reviewed by a more senior official within the agency and externally reviewed by an administrative tribunal institutionally separate from the agency. In terms of this distinction, the AAT reviews decisions externally. Adopting a different metaphor, the distinction between internal and external review concerns the 'distance' between the decision-maker and the reviewer. In these terms, the distinction may be understood as a matter of degree depending on various aspects of the relationship between the decision-maker and the reviewer, including their respective institutional locations. This latter way of thinking about the internal/external distinction may be particularly useful in understanding bodies, such as the Refugee Review Tribunal (RRT) and the Migration Review Tribunal (MRT) in Australia,[10] and officials such as ALJs and AJs in the US, that occupy a somewhat equivocal position vis-à-vis the relevant decision-making agency.

Internal review may be contrasted not only with external review but also with 'reconsideration' of a decision. Reconsideration and internal review are typically similar processes, the difference between them being that reconsideration is undertaken by the original decision-maker whereas internal review is conducted

---

[9] The Franks Committee expressed the distinction I have in mind here as that between 'decisions' and 'further decisions': Report of the Committee on Administrative Tribunals and Enquiries, 1959 (Cmnd 218) [7]–[8].

[10] For further discussion see 5.4, n 151.

by a different official. All of these processes – reconsideration, internal and external review, and judicial and merits review – may be contrasted with the handling of complaints – a contrast which, like that between internal and external review, will receive more attention in Chapter 7. 'Handling complaints' is a broader concept than 'reviewing decisions' in the sense that a complaint may or may not concern a decision and may or may not lead to the review of a decision. Typically, the tasks of reviewing decisions and handling complaints will be allocated to different (types of) institutions. A common way of providing for the handling of citizens' complaints about government activity is to create an office of ombudsman.[11] The processes for and outcomes of dealing with complaints tend to be significantly different from those associated with reviewing decisions. Nevertheless, these two phenomena share at least one important characteristic, namely that they are typically initiated by an applicant (a person, corporation or group) who claims to be adversely affected in some relevant way by a decision or action of a government agency that falls within the jurisdiction of the reviewer or complaint-handler. This focus of reviews and complaint-handling on what we might call the 'individualised' impact of decisions distinguishes the prime task of reviewers and complaint-handlers from that of agencies such as auditors and inspectors. Auditing and inspection processes are often not initiated by individuals; and they typically focus on systems – which are the product of large sets of decisions and actions, and their impact on the public as a whole or significant sections of the public – rather than on one or more particular decisions and their impact on individual persons, corporations and discrete groups.

With these preliminaries out of the way, we can return to our initial question of how we might understand the characteristic function of the AAT, namely reviewing decisions externally. When a decision made by a government agency is challenged or disputed, a common pattern is for the decision first to be reconsidered by the original decision-maker. If the decision-maker affirms the original decision or varies it in a way that does not satisfy the affected party, the original decision may be internally reviewed. If neither reconsideration nor internal review resolves the affected party's grievance, that party may seek external review of the decision by a court or a tribunal.

One way of understanding these various processes is in terms of a stylised model of legal decision-making that involves the application of general rules in three steps: identification of an individual's conduct or circumstances; identification of a social objective expressed in a rule (or 'norm'); and regulation of the individual's conduct or circumstances in accordance with, and in order to promote the social objective of, the rule. In more traditional terminology, these three steps involve respectively finding facts, ascertaining law and applying the law as ascertained to the facts as found. For our purposes, the word 'law' in the

---

[11] Or 'ombuds', as the office is sometimes described in the US. See eg, Special Feature, 'Ombuds Standards' (2002) 54 *Administrative Law Review* 535. The office originated in Sweden, and 'ombudsman' is a gender-neutral word in the Swedish language. It is widely so used in English as well.

traditional formulation needs to be understood broadly to include not only 'hard law' – rules made by legislatures and courts that have the quality of 'bindingness', but also 'soft law' – rules that govern decision-making in a less rigid way by providing 'relevant considerations' to be taken into account in making individual decisions rather than peremptory instructions about how individual cases are to be dealt with. Soft law (often called 'policy') plays an extremely important part in structuring and guiding the making of decisions of the sort that administrative tribunals review, which are (perhaps typically) based on a combination of hard law and soft law criteria. The basic rule is that soft law norms must be applied flexibly with due regard to the circumstances of the individual(s) affected by the decision in question. It does not follow, of course, that individual circumstances can be ignored when hard law norms are applied, but only that individual circumstances are not an independent variable (as it were); rather their significance is determined by the formulation and interpretation of the norm to be applied. Understood in the way just described, it is very difficult to distinguish making, reconsidering, and internally reviewing decisions on the one hand from external review on the other because both involve a similar three-step reasoning process.

Another possible way to think about external review of decisions would be to associate it with adjudication of disputes. The most famous modern discussion of the concept of adjudication is that of Lon Fuller.[12] Fuller described the 'settling of disputes and controversies' as the 'most obvious aspect' of adjudication; but he identified its characteristic feature as 'the mode of participation of the affected party'. Fuller contrasted adjudication, as a mode of decision-making, with elections and contracting. He argued that the characteristic mode of participation in elections is voting and that the characteristic mode of participation in contracting is negotiation. The characteristic feature of adjudication he described as 'an institutionally defined and assured opportunity for presentation of proofs and reasoned arguments' by the disputing parties to a neutral third party – in other words, a hearing. Does either of these features – dispute and hearing before a neutral third party – distinguish external review by the AAT from the making, reconsideration and internal review of decisions?

Obviously the element of dispute is lacking from the process of primary decision-making. Primary decision-making is typically a non-adversarial, non-competitive process of regulating individuals' conduct and circumstances in accordance with policies embodied in rules. Although the primary decision-maker has an interest in the outcome, that interest is institutional. The job of the decision-maker is not to assert a social (let alone a personal) interest against the interests of the affected party but rather to promote a social interest consistently with respecting relevant interests of the affected party. On the other hand,

---

[12] LL Fuller, 'The Forms and Limits of Adjudication' (1978) 92 *Harvard Law Review* 353; this article circulated widely in draft form for about 20 years before being published posthumously.

reconsideration, internal review and external review are all typically triggered when an affected party disputes a primary decision; but for this very reason, the element of dispute does not enable us to distinguish between these three processes.

What about the element of a hearing before a neutral third party? Certainly, application for external review of a decision typically involves transformation of the decision-making process from a two-party to a three-party affair. It may also involve a shift from a non-adversarial ('inquisitorial') mode of decision-making in which the decision-maker is actively involved in collecting the (factual and legal) material on which the decision will be based, to an adversarial mode in which the parties are primarily responsible for collecting and presenting such material to the third party. Furthermore, it may involve a change in the role of the party supporting the decision from one of promoting a social interest consistently with respecting the interests of the affected individual to one of defending the correctness of the decision against that person's interests. Such shifts characterise judicial review, but they are not necessarily a feature of non-judicial external review of the type conducted by the AAT. Non-judicial external reviewers may take a more active role in the process of collecting relevant material than is typical of courts, and the role of the party representing the decision-maker may be to assist the reviewer to decide whether the decision ought to be affirmed, varied or replaced by a substitute decision rather than to convince the reviewer that the decision under review ought to be affirmed. Nevertheless, either way, the role of the third party will be to decide neutrally and impartially whether or not the decision should be affirmed, varied or replaced by a substitute decision. Review by the AAT and, typically, external review more generally involve the transformation of the decision-making process from a two-party to a three-party affair by the insertion of a neutral third party.

Even so, is the element of a *hearing* before such a neutral third party characteristic of external review in the way, according to Fuller, that it is characteristic of adjudication? This is a difficult question to answer. Fuller apparently thought that adversarial presentation of proofs and arguments on behalf of the affected parties is an 'indispensable part' of the adjudicatory mode of decision-making.[13] His model of adjudicatory decision-making appears to be the civil or criminal trial. If, with Fuller, we understand a hearing to involve adversarial presentation of proofs and arguments, external review may provide a hearing, but equally it may not, depending on the respective roles of the reviewer and the decision-maker. On the other hand, if we understand a hearing, without any adversarial connotation, to involve the opportunity to present proofs and arguments to a decision-maker, the element of a hearing may not serve to

---

[13] n 12 above, 382–84. In this passage, Fuller focuses on the role of the advocate in ensuring adversary presentation. 'But', he says, '…the true significance of partisan advocacy lies deeper. It is only through the advocate's participation that the hearing may remain in fact what it purports to be in theory: a public trial of facts and issues.' (383).

distinguish external review from making, reconsideration or internal review of decisions. In making decisions, reliance is often placed on the affected party to provide relevant factual (and perhaps even legal) material, and the affected party may be under an obligation to provide such information. The affected party may also be given the opportunity to make an oral presentation to the decision-maker, or may be required to attend an interview with the decision-maker. Reconsideration and internal review will typically be based on the same material as the primary decision; but the affected party may be given an opportunity to present new material. External review will typically provide affected parties with an opportunity to make a case to the third party, but it will not necessarily provide an opportunity to present new material.

The position we have reached is that the clearest distinction between making, reconsideration and internal review of decisions on the one hand, and external (non-judicial) review of decisions on the other, is that the former involve two parties whereas the latter typically involves three. External review, like reconsideration and internal review, is triggered by dispute; and all of these modes of decision-making may provide affected parties with the opportunity to be heard and to present arguments and proofs. External review, like Fullerian adjudication, provides the opportunity for a hearing before a neutral third party; but unlike Fullerian adjudication, external review may not involve adversarial presentation of arguments and proofs. We may capture both points by referring to the characteristic review function of the AAT as 'administrative adjudication'. The word 'adjudication' marks the similarity between external review and Fullerian adjudication and the word 'administrative' marks the contrast between the adversarial civil or criminal trial, on which Fuller's analysis is based, and external review, which may or may not be conducted adversarially.

There is another significant difference between making, reconsidering and internally reviewing decisions on the one hand, and administrative adjudication (external review of decisions) on the other. To understand this difference we need to go back to the three-part reasoning process involved in all of these modes of decision-making: finding facts, identifying relevant law (general rules) and applying the law as identified to the facts as found. Even subject to the qualification stated earlier about the concept of 'law' in this formulation, the traditional terminology fails to bring out clearly a significant feature of the process of applying general rules. General rules provide an instrument for promoting social goals by aggregate regulation of the conduct and circumstances of individuals. Used in this way, rules establish a relationship and, potentially at least, create conflict between the interests of society on the one hand and of its individual members on the other. This relationship (and possible conflict) between the social and the individual is given concrete expression when rules are applied in particular cases.

The contrast between the general and the particular, the social and the individual, is central to the concept of (general) rules and to the process of their application. General rules and their application may set up a creative tension

11

between social objectives and individual interests. Moreover, I would argue, a significant contrast between administrative adjudication on the one hand and the other modes of decision-making (which, for convenience, I shall refer to generically as 'implementation') on the other can be found in the fact that the potential tension between the general and the particular, the social and the individual, which lies at the heart of all the modes of decision-making, can be resolved in various ways; or, in other words, that the balance between the general and the particular, the social and the individual, can be struck in various ways.

One thing the legal realists (and especially Jerome Frank)[14] taught us is that 'finding facts' is only partly a matter of discovery, observation and description of data about the world: it is also partly a matter of analysis, classification and interpretation. Another lesson from the legal realists is that for various reasons (including the indeterminacy of language and uncertainty about the future) 'identifying relevant law' and, thereby, identifying relevant social objectives may require discrimination and judgment. This is so even if the rule does not (as it may) delegate to the decision-maker a measure of discretion or choice in defining social objectives.[15] Decision-makers sometimes (perhaps often or even usually) may and must exercise at least judgment and discrimination, if not discretion and choice, in regulating individual conduct and circumstances in accordance with rules. Because general rules set up a tension between social objectives and individual interests, decision-makers, in exercising judgment and discretion, are in a position to resolve this tension in various different ways, favouring either the social objective of the rule on the one hand, or the interests of the affected individual on the other. In cases of conflict between social objectives and individual interests, decision-makers must choose between promoting social objectives at the expense of individual interests and vice versa.

An illuminating approach to understanding implementation on the one hand and administrative adjudication on the other is in terms of these two broadly different ways of resolving conflicts – between social objectives and individual interests – that arise in the process of regulating the conduct and circumstances of individuals by the use of general rules. We can usefully associate the resolution of such conflicts in favour of social objectives with implementation, and the resolution of such conflicts in favour of individual interests with administrative adjudication.[16] Whereas the basic purpose of implementation is to promote

---

[14] J Frank, *Law and the Modern Mind* (Gloucester, Mass, Peter Smith, 1970) – originally published in 1930; *Courts on Trial: Myth and Reality in American Justice* (Princeton, NJ, Princeton University Press, 1973) – first published in 1949.

[15] Such delegation may be either express, or implied by the deliberate use of widely open-textured language.

[16] Jerry Mashaw makes an analogous argument when he claims that by reason of their differing institutional responsibilities, agencies in the course of implementing statutes, and courts in the course of reviewing agency decisions, are likely to approach statutory interpretation differently: JL Mashaw, 'Norms, Practices and the Paradox of Deference: A Preliminary Investigation into Agency Statutory Interpretation' (2005) 57 *Administrative Law Review* 501; 'Agency-Centered or Court-Centered Administrative Law? A Dialogue with Richard Pierce on Agency Statutory Interpretation' (2007) 59

social goals consistently with according due respect to individual interests, the basic purpose of administrative adjudication is to protect the interests of individuals without unduly hindering the promotion of social goals. Institutions charged respectively with implementation and adjudication – we might say – have different institutional orientations. It must be stressed, however, that both implementation and adjudication are concerned both with social objectives and with individual interests, the difference between them lying in the way that conflicts between the two are resolved: implementation tends to favour the promotion of social objectives whereas adjudication tends to favour the promotion of individual interests.

The distinction between implementation and adjudication should not be understood in terms of accounts of separation of powers that divide the institutions of government into three 'branches' – the legislature, the executive and the judiciary – and allocate respectively to each branch as its characteristic task one of three types of functions – legislative, executive and judicial. In particular, implementation should not be thought of as an administrative function of the executive, and adjudication should not be thought of as a judicial function of the judiciary. There are several reasons to resist this way of thinking about administrative tribunals. First, although we recognise sets of governmental institutions called respectively the legislature, the executive and the judiciary, it is widely accepted that not every governmental agency can be fitted neatly into one or other of these three branches. Thus, we might want to resist the straightforward allocation of administrative tribunals to either the executive or the judicial branch of government as traditionally conceived. Secondly, it is now recognised that all agencies thought of as belonging to one or other of the three 'core' branches of government perform a complex mix of functions that may defy easy classification in terms of the traditional tripartite division.

Perhaps most importantly of all, it is now widely agreed that the terms 'legislative', 'administrative' and 'judicial', when used to describe and differentiate governmental functions, are vague and imprecise. The problem is sometimes signalled by the use of the prefix 'quasi' to describe a function, performed by an agency allocated by separation theory to one of the core branches of government, which is essentially similar to a function attributed by separation theory to one of the other branches: 'quasi-legislative', 'quasi-judicial'. Consider rule-making, for instance. It is now universally accepted that (appellate) courts may make general

---

Administrative Law Review 889. For a different approach see RJ Pierce Jr, 'How Agencies Should Give Meaning to the Statutes They Administer: A Response to Mashaw and Strauss' (2007) 59 *Administrative Law Review* 197. For the suggestion that resolving conflicts in favour of social interests is an 'endemic sin' of government administration see GDS Taylor, 'May Judicial Review Become a Backwater?' in M Taggart (ed), *Judicial Review of Administrative Action in the 1980s: Problems and Prospects* (Auckland, OUP, 1986) 153, 154. For an acknowledgment of the distinction in terms of 'bureaucratic administration' on the one hand and 'administrative justice' on the other together with a rejection of the way the distinction is used here see D Galligan, *Due Process and Fair Procedures: A Study of Administrative Procedures* (Oxford, Clarendon Press, 1996) 237–40.

rules incidentally to adjudicating individual cases. Nothing much is to be gained by debating whether, in so doing, a court is performing a 'legislative' function or a 'judicial' function, or by branding judicial law-making 'quasi-legislative'. It is more illuminating to analyse the ways in which rule-making by courts differs from rule-making by other governmental institutions. So, for instance, whereas general rules that are a by-product of adjudication ('adjudicative rules') typically have retrospective operation, general rules that are not ('legislative rules')[17] typically have only prospective operation. For this reason, and because adjudicative rules (unlike legislative rules) are provisional in the sense of formally being open to modification (and not merely interpretation) at the point of application, adjudicative rule-making is typically more constrained than legislative rule-making by requirements of consistency and coherence with the pre-existing body of rules. For this reason, too, legal training is typically considered to be a more important qualification for being an adjudicator than for being a legislator because a major element of legal education involves acquisition of an appreciation for the values of coherence and consistency, and transmission of knowledge of the existing body of legal materials.

One way of accommodating these various insights about the idea and ideal of separation of powers might be to recognise one or more additional branches of government. For instance, in the US independent regulatory agencies have been described as a 'fourth' branch of government;[18] and some Australian writers have recently argued for the identification of a (fourth) 'integrity' or 'accountability' branch.[19] Although such an approach may avoid some of the analytical defects of the traditional account of separation of powers, it is not clear that it addresses its underlying theoretical shortcomings. A very different response is to abandon the metaphor of branches in favour of some concept of governmental 'networks' to be elaborated through a process of 'micro-analysis' of governmental institutions and their various inter-relationships and interactions.[20] However attractive such a radical approach might be in theory, it is not a helpful place to start in seeking to understand current arrangements because the idea of separation of powers has deeply influenced the development of administrative tribunals and is still central

---

[17] Which may take the form, for instance, of primary (Parliamentary or Congressional) legislation ('statutes'), secondary or 'delegated' legislation ('regulations', 'order', 'byelaws' etc) and 'soft law' ('codes', 'directives', 'manuals', 'instructions', 'policies' etc). Note that 'legislative' is being used here in a different sense from that which it bears in the legislative-executive-judicial trichotomy. For more discussion of the distinction see P Cane, 'Taking Disagreement Seriously: Courts, Legislatures and the Reform of Tort Law' (2005) 25 *Oxford Journal of Legal Studies* 393.

[18] Notoriously accused of being 'headless' by the US President's Committee on Administrative Management: *Report of the President's Committee on Administrative Management* (Washington, 1937) 40.

[19] J McMillan, 'The Ombudsman and the Rule of Law' (2005) 44 *Australian Institute of Administrative Law Forum* 1; J Spigelman, 'The Integrity Branch of Government' (2004) *Australian Institute of Administrative Law National Lecture Series on Administrative Law*, No 2, 2.

[20] EL Rubin, *Beyond Camelot: Rethinking Politics and Law for the Modern State* (Princeton and Oxford, Princeton University Press, 2005).

to the way we think about the structure and design of governmental institutions. Anyway, we must be careful not to throw the baby out with the bathwater. As a normative aspiration, separation of powers expresses the abiding value of avoiding excessive concentration of governmental power in individual agencies, avoiding combinations in one and the same agency of governmental tasks (such as prosecution and adjudication) that potentially create conflicts of interest, and subjecting agencies that exercise governmental power to external supervision.

Nevertheless, the traditional tripartite division of governmental institutions and functions – legislature/legislative, executive/executive, judiciary/judicial – is neither necessary nor particularly effective for promoting this aspiration and these values. As a general principle, it may be efficient for a governmental institution to specialise in the performance of one task as its characteristic function; but there is no reason to think that allowing an agency to perform more than one type of function will necessarily lead to undue concentration of power or conflicts of interest. So, for instance, provided certain constraints are observed, the functions of making rules and adjudicating disputes about their implementation can be and are combined in one and the same institution without thereby unduly concentrating power or creating potential conflicts of interest. Similarly, it is possible to combine the functions of making rules and implementing them in one and the same institution without unduly concentrating power, provided the activities of the institution are subject to adequate external scrutiny. On the other hand, the general view is that combining the power to prosecute offences and to try offenders in one and the same body would unduly concentrate power in that body and potentially generate conflicts of interest.

Similarly, there is good reason to think that combining in one and the same body the two functions of implementing rules and adjudicating disputes about their implementation would unduly concentrate power because these two functions are incompatible in the sense that they involve resolution of conflicts between social and individual interests in different ways. The basic role responsibility of the implementer of rules is to promote the social objectives of the rule compatibly with respecting the interests of affected individuals whereas the basic role responsibility of the adjudicator is to protect the interests of individuals compatibly with promoting the social objectives of the rule. Of course, so understood, there is no bright-line distinction between implementation and adjudication because conflicts between individual and social interests can typically be resolved in various ways that favour one or other interest to varying degrees. Rather the distinction is one of focus and emphasis: the prime responsibility of the implementer is to the rule and its social objectives whereas the prime responsibility of the adjudicator is to the individual and their personal interests.

The distinction between implementation and adjudication throws considerable light on the nature and functions of administrative tribunals. For instance, the fundamental similarity of the reasoning processes involved in the two activities helps to explain why the distinction between the 'administrative' function of implementing rules and the 'judicial' function of adjudicating disputes about the implementation of rules has always been found so difficult to draw analytically. Implementation and adjudication are not two different types of function but essentially the same function performed to different ends and with a different point. On the other hand, the difference of purpose and emphasis between the two functions helps to explain why adjudicatory procedure tends to focus on and protect the individual to a greater extent than 'administrative procedure', and why individualising the focus of administrative procedure is often disapprovingly described in terms of 'judicialising the administrative process'. Noting the difference between implementation and adjudication also helps to explain the high value attached to the independence of officials, whose job is to resolve disputes between citizen (and, in some contexts, non-citizen) and government about the implementation of rules, from influence and control by officials responsible for implementation.

At this point, a second terminological caveat is in order. As we will see in 3.2, in the US, the term 'adjudication' is typically distinguished not from what I am calling 'implementation' but from 'rule-making'. Moreover, in the US a distinction is drawn between 'formal' and 'informal' adjudication. One way of understanding this latter distinction is that formal adjudication involves 'some kind of hearing' whereas informal adjudication takes place in settings that are 'non-confrontational and often not even face-to-face', and is undertaken by '"non-hearing" deciders'.[21] In this sense, 'informal adjudication' may be equivalent to what I am calling 'implementation' undertaken by primary decision-makers. Similarly in the UK, in some contexts primary bureaucratic decision-makers may be called 'adjudicators'. It is important to bear in mind throughout that by 'adjudication' I mean external review of primary decision-making by courts and tribunals. Such terminological complexities are a hazard and an inevitable price of comparative analysis.

1.2.3 The AAT's jurisdiction

Administrative tribunals such as the AAT are, in some sense, not courts. Their characteristic function is administrative adjudication – ie, externally reviewing disputed decisions. The third feature of the AAT that I want to emphasise concerns its jurisdiction. The AAT's jurisdiction is defined in terms of reviewing decisions made in exercise of (specified) statutory decision-making powers (decisions made 'under an enactment').[22] In fact, all of these powers are conferred on government officials or agencies, but this feature is not an element of

---

[21] PR Verkuil, 'Reflections upon the Federal Administrative Judiciary' (1991–92) 39 *UCLA Law Review* 1341, 1342.

[22] In the Australian system (as in the UK) the legal powers of government come from two sources: statute and common (ie, judge-made) law. Largely for historical reasons, powers of the latter type are sometimes called 'prerogative', although there is debate about whether all non-statutory governmental powers are prerogative in a technical sense. For present purposes we can ignore this debate.

the specification of the AAT's jurisdiction: the jurisdiction of the AAT is defined in terms of the source of the power to make decisions rather than the identity of the decision-maker.

Government can be understood both as a set of institutions and as a set of functions. The word 'governance' may be used to refer to the functional understanding, leaving the word 'government' to refer to the institutional understanding. It is now widely accepted that not all of the activities of government institutions involve the performance of governance (or 'public') functions. For instance, when governments employ cleaners or buy paper-clips they are typically considered to be engaging in ('private') activities no different from those that citizens and non-governmental organisations engage in when they employ cleaners or buy paper clips, even if they are empowered to undertake these activities by statute. Conversely, it is now widely accepted that non-governmental entities sometimes perform governance ('public') functions (such as social or economic regulation) typically in exercise of statutory powers.

As previously noted, all of the categories of statutory decisions that the AAT has jurisdiction to review are made by governmental officials and agencies. In theory, however, the AAT could be given power to review a decision made by a non-governmental entity in exercise of a statutory power. Conversely, many – perhaps most – of the sorts of statutory decisions the AAT has jurisdiction to review are made in exercise of public functions; but some arguably are not. For instance, a significant proportion of the AAT's workload involves review of decisions by a statutory agency about the award of statutory workers' compensation benefits to federal government employees: the workers' compensation system applies to non-governmental and governmental employers and employees alike.

Nevertheless, the AAT – an administrative tribunal – can be contrasted with what are sometimes called 'party-and-party' tribunals. Examples of the latter are employment tribunals in the UK, which deal with 'private' disputes between employers (including government agencies) and employees. Some adjudicatory bodies operate both as administrative tribunals and party-and-party tribunals. For instance, the Victorian Civil and Administrative Tribunal (VCAT) in Australia has jurisdiction both to review statutory decisions concerned, for example, with the licensing of businesses and land-use planning, and to deal with matters arising, for example, from disputes between landlords and tenants, and between vendors and purchasers of goods and services. The characteristic function of party-and-party tribunals is not to review decisions made by government agencies, nor to review decisions made in exercise of statutory powers or decisions made in performance of public functions. Rather their characteristic function is to resolve disputes about the conduct of private activities whether by governmental or non-governmental entities and regardless of whether one or other of the parties was empowered to engage in the activity by a statutory provision.

Another way of describing the difference between administrative tribunals and party-and-party tribunals is in terms of the distinction between administrative adjudication and Fullerian adjudication. Because party-and-party tribunals resolve private disputes, the model underlying their operation is adversarial. By contrast, because administrative tribunals review public decisions made under statute, the model underlying their operation may not be adversarial. Party-and-party tribunals, we may say, belong to the 'civil justice system' whereas administrative tribunals belong to the 'administrative justice system'.[23] In the legal systems with which we are primarily concerned, the basic model of civil justice is adversarial whereas administrative justice may or may not be delivered through adversarial processes.

In summary: administrative tribunals as understood in this book are non-courts the characteristic function of which is external review of public decisions, most commonly decisions made in exercise of statutory powers. More neatly, we may say that the characteristic function of administrative tribunals is administrative adjudication.

1.3 The Plan of the Book

This first chapter has explained in broad terms what the book is about: administrative adjudication by administrative tribunals. Chapter 2 explores the history of administrative adjudication and administrative tribunals. This exploration is in no sense incidental to an account of what we might call the 'administrative tribunal phenomenon'. On the contrary, it is impossible to understand the nature and role of administrative tribunals without having a clear sense of their historical development and that of their ancestors.

The historical discussion in Chapter 2 necessarily introduces a comparative element into the account of administrative tribunals. As soon as I broadened the scope of the project beyond the AAT I realised the importance, in seeking to understand the administrative tribunal phenomenon, of locating these institutions within a broader institutional and constitutional landscape. In the Australian context, this broadening of perspective inevitably leads to comparative analysis, not only because the Australian constitutional and governmental system has a mixed heritage (partly British and partly American) but also because Australia is a federation. The British and American systems represent two quite distinctive constitutional paradigms, while the Australian system represents a complex and fascinating hybrid of those two basic paradigms. The Australian system's mixed heritage is manifested primarily in the Australian Constitution – ie, the Constitution of the Commonwealth of Australia. By contrast, the constitutions of the Australian states are essentially British in origin and design; and

---

[23] A third mode of justice is 'criminal justice'. Even in systems that lack formal separation of powers, there is great reluctance to confer criminal jurisdiction on non-courts.

they lack the elements of the Australian Constitution that are attributable to American influence. The AAT is part of the federal system, and much of its distinctiveness is explicable by reference to features of the Australian Constitution. Because the constitutional system of the Commonwealth of Australia is significantly different in certain basic respects from the constitutional systems of the Australian states, even a study of the administrative tribunal phenomenon as manifested in Australia alone must have a comparative element.

Comparative analysis is a dangerous activity, and I need to say something about my approach to this exercise. Even in discussing the law and legal institutions of one jurisdiction, choices constantly have to be made about how much detail and which details to include. Include too much detail and the analysis becomes tedious and irrelevant; include too little detail or the wrong details and the argument risks appearing (and being) ungrounded. These risks are even greater when the aim is to compare the law and legal institutions of several jurisdictions, even if the analyst conducting the comparison (unlike me) is equally well-versed in the laws and legal systems of the various jurisdictions. However despite the dangers, comparison is worthwhile if it sharpens our understanding and appreciation of the systems being compared and provides those who are expert in a particular system a fresh perspective on its detailed operation. I believe that comparative analysis of the law and institutions of administrative adjudication can improve overall understanding of the broader phenomenon as well as its particular manifestation in the various jurisdictions being compared. The comparative analysis pursued in this book is conducted at a relatively high level of generality. This methodology may give those with detailed knowledge and understanding of the law and legal systems of the various jurisdictions being compared cause for frustration and dissatisfaction as they detect inaccuracies, half-truths and defects of description, explanation and emphasis. All I ask of such readers is that they suppress their annoyance with minor failures of detailed execution sufficiently to allow them to focus on the larger picture. If the big picture brings some of the details into sharper focus, this book's aim will have been achieved.

It is possible to tell a common historical story about administrative tribunals in our three comparator systems up until about the end of the 18th century. From that point on, the historical stream divides as the American and Australian systems split off from their common English parent and develop in quite distinct directions. The result is three sets of diverse institutional arrangements. Careful analysis of these various institutional arrangements and their respective histories in turn highlights various aspects of the administrative tribunal phenomenon that enable us to detect both similarities amongst and differences between the jurisdictions.

On the basis of the historical account in Chapter 2, Chapter 3 describes four models of administrative tribunals and administrative adjudication. For reasons already explained, the first three models – the UK, US and Australian models – are discussed at greater length than the fourth, French model. However, the

French model deserves some attention because it represents an approach distinctly different from that found in any of the major common-law jurisdictions. Chapter 4 provides, as it were, a guided tour of the models pointing out common structural elements – membership, independence, specialisation and supervision – and also some of the differences in design of those elements in the various systems. These two chapters offer what we might call a horizontal cross-section, concerned with the relationships and interactions between governmental institutions. At least since the 18th century, separation of powers has provided the dominant framework for thinking about the institutional structure of government and for this reason it has an important place in these chapters.

In Chapter 5 we move from structure to function. Here, once again, the focus is on understanding the functions of tribunals in relation to the functions of other governmental institutions, most notably courts. It is in this Chapter that the AAT will figure most prominently, primarily because the distinction between judicial and non-judicial functions – which dominates the Australian version of separation of powers – provided the fundamental constitutional rationale for its establishment. The concept of merits review – the characteristic (non-judicial) function of the AAT and of other federal tribunals – has been elaborated in great detail and provides a firm foundation for understanding what administrative tribunals do. Also prominent in thinking about the AAT from its very inception has been that it performs the 'normative' function of improving the quality of primary governmental decision-making. On closer inspection, this apparently simple idea turns out to be complex and problematic.

In Chapter 6 attention shifts from form and function to purpose. At the same time the analysis moves from the horizontal plane of institutional relationships to the vertical plane of the interaction between tribunals and their 'users'. Vis-à-vis their users, the purpose of tribunals is increasingly described in terms of 'administrative justice' – tribunals, we are told, are part of a system the overall purpose of which is to deliver administrative justice to individuals. One aim of Chapter 6 is to unpack this complex and ubiquitous idea and to examine various aspects of the operation of tribunals that constitute strands of the concept of administrative justice: access to tribunals; the scope of their jurisdiction; rules of procedure and evidence; and issues of cost and timeliness. The AAT will be used as a point of departure for the discussion of these various issues.

Finally, Chapter 7 attempts to locate administrative tribunals in a wider landscape of institutions of 'accountability'. What we might call 'the accountability sector' has become large and diverse in the past 50 years. This has raised many new questions about the relationship between its various components; and changes in the nature and operation of tribunals and courts have posed afresh old questions about how these two traditional elements of the sector interact. Other developments, too, offer new perspectives on old controversies. For instance, the exponential growth of internal review mechanisms leads us to reflect again on debates of the 1920s and 1930s in the UK about the relationship between administrative adjudicators and government agencies. Indeed, it may lead us to reflect on the very distinction between internal and external review, especially in the light of the institutional structure of administrative adjudication in the US.

1.4 Conclusion

As a general topic, administrative tribunals receive relatively little attention in the mainstream literature of administrative law. A great deal is written on courts and judicial review, much of it highly sophisticated historically, comparatively and theoretically. By comparison, the literature on administrative tribunals and on the juridical nature of what they do is slight and under-developed. Much of the most innovative writing on administrative adjudication by tribunals dates from their infancy and adolescence. Outside the US, at least, much of the literature on administrative tribunals produced in the past 30 or 40 years has had a practical and pragmatic focus; in-depth and book-length analysis of tribunals has been noticeable by its absence.

This is noteworthy for several reasons. First, it is widely understood that in aggregate, administrative tribunals deal with many more disputes between citizen and government than do courts. A citizen in dispute with government is very much more likely to have 'their day' in a tribunal than in a court.[24] In each of our comparator jurisdictions, the body of officials who sit on tribunals is very much larger than the cadre of traditional judges who specialise in dealing with disputes between citizen and government. Administrative tribunals, it is sometimes said, provide 'mass justice'. Secondly, the issues of institutional design raised by administrative tribunals and their place in systems of government are at least as interesting and important as those on which students of courts focus. Consider, for instance, the fact that there are areas of the law of fundamental importance to the daily lives of many people – such as immigration and social security – with which courts have very little involvement and which are almost completely the province of tribunals. Thirdly, a new emphasis on and concern with 'administrative justice' – especially in the UK – has highlighted the importance of understanding the interrelationships between and the respective roles of all the various institutions, including tribunals, which constitute the 'administrative justice system'.

It is not the main aim or aspiration of this book to convince the reader of the importance of administrative tribunals, still less to fill the gap in the academic literature – it will take much more than this work to do that. For reasons that will become obvious, Australian public lawyers probably need less convincing than

---

[24] Judicial review may be relatively more important in the US than in either the UK or Australia because of the large and active part played by courts in supervising executive rule-making.

most of the significance of tribunals; but even in Australia administrative tribunals, relative to courts and judicial review, attract less attention in the academy and the classroom than they deserve. Rather, my prime purpose is to make a contribution to the process of understanding, in contemporary terms, the nature and role of administrative tribunals and what they do, with special reference to the Australian system of federal 'merits review' tribunals. There is a lot more that could be said, of course. In particular, this book does not provide a detailed description of the tribunals that exist in the various comparator jurisdictions, or systematic statistics about staffing, caseload, resources, performance and so on. It should not be inferred from this that I consider such matters to be unimportant but only that they are not central to the predominantly analytical and conceptual focus of this book.

Administrative tribunals and the environment in which they exist and operate have changed greatly in recent times, and tribunals themselves have reached adulthood. Now is an opportune time to re-connect with some of the big issues from the past as well as to engage anew with the contemporary world of administrative adjudication and tribunals. Doing that is the broad purpose of this book.

2

History

2.1 Introduction

ADMINISTRATIVE TRIBUNALS (sometimes with the added adjective 'modern') are often said to be a product of social, economic and political developments of the 19th and 20th centuries. In the UK, 1911 is considered an important date because it witnessed the establishment, under Part II of the National Insurance Act, of a non-judicial system for reviewing decisions about entitlement to unemployment insurance payments.[1] In the US, a commonly cited date is 1887, the year in which the Interstate Commerce Commission (ICC) was established.[2] However, these supposedly paradigmatic institutions did not, of course, appear out of the blue. For instance, the income tax commissioners that were created at the very end of the 18th century in England have be seen as significant precursors of, or even the first, administrative tribunals;[3] and in an important study Chantal Stebbings traces their antecedents back to the third decade of the 19th century.[4] Various writers have suggested analogies between administrative tribunals and the so-called 'conciliar courts' that flourished in the 16th and 17th centuries in England, especially the Court of Star Chamber; and even between administrative tribunals and the Court of Chancery in the earlier centuries of its operation. Again, in the US, the earliest predecessors of the ICC have been found in bodies created in the first session of the First Congress in 1789.[5]

More importantly, however, the nature, functions and constitutional significance of administrative tribunals as we understand them today cannot be

---

[1] RE Wraith and PG Hutchesson, *Administrative Tribunals* (London, George Allen and Unwin, 1973) 17, 33–37 (hereafter 'Wraith and Hutchesson')

[2] J M Landis, *The Administrative Process* (New Haven and London, Yale University Press, 1938) 9–10.

[3] Wraith and Hutchesson, 24–25. Stebbings describes the General Commissioners of Taxation as 'the oldest extant tribunal': C Stebbings. *Legal Foundations of Tribunals in Nineteenth Century England* (Cambridge, CUP, 2006) (hereafter 'Stebbings') 2.

[4] Stebbings.

[5] *Final Report of the Attorney-General's Committee on Administrative Procedure* (Washington, 1941) 8.

appreciated in terms of an historical account[6] that focuses only on specific institutions. It is just as important to pay attention to the development of the political ideas and constitutional theories that underpinned the creation and operation of relevant institutional structures. Of such ideas and theories, separation of powers is undoubtedly the most significant. One of the aims of this chapter is to explore the interaction between concept-formation and institution-building in the development of administrative adjudication.

The other main aim of the chapter is to tell a – not 'the' – story of the development of tribunals in the three jurisdictions that provide the focus of this study: the UK, the US and Australia. The first section of the chapter traces the common lineage of tribunals in each of these jurisdictions starting from the birth of the English legal system; and the second section continues the story in each of the jurisdictions in turn. Although writers on administrative tribunals not-uncommonly refer to events as far back as the 17th century, it is not normal to delve any deeper into the history of the English legal system. Nevertheless, it is valuable to do so (if only very briefly) because patterns of institutional creation and transformation that characterise the more recent history of administrative adjudication can be found at the very dawn of the English legal system. Although the circumstances and forms of administrative adjudication have changed dramatically in the past millennium, the basic phenomenon has not. Casting the historical net widely sharpens our appreciation of fundamental issues in the design and operation of adjudicatory institutions.

2.2 1066 to 1800

We can begin the historical story of administrative tribunals in England in 1066. William the Conqueror inherited from his predecessors a relatively unified and centralised kingdom.[7] In any state, one of the main roles of government and one of the most important techniques for maintaining peace and order (as well as power) is to provide facilities for handling citizens' grievances and resolving disputes between citizens and government. At first, the royal officers responsible for this function – the judges – were members of the King's inner circle of advisers and counsellors – the royal court.[8] When the King went on progress around the country, so did the judges. Gradually, however, the dispute-resolution function was separated off from the other activities of the king's council (*'curia Regis'*). The Courts of King's Bench and Common Pleas – the 'common law

---

[6] For discussion of historical approaches to constitutional issues see JWF Allison, *The English Constitution: Continuity, Change and Legal Effects* (Cambridge, CUP, 2007) esp ch 2.

[7] JH Baker, *An Introduction to English Legal History*, 4th edn (UK, Butterworths LexisNexis, 2002) ch 1 (hereafter 'Baker').

[8] Baker, 17–22.

courts' – were established and assumed a fixed abode in London. A similar story of institutional separation of the judicial function from the general flow of government business can be told about the Chancery Court.[9] Despite this institutional separation, the central courts[10] remained associated with the Monarch. They administered royal justice on behalf and in the name of the Monarch. The King hired and fired the judges. In the 16th and 17th centuries certain institutions – the conciliar courts[11] – were more closely identified with the Monarch and the Council than either the common law courts or the Chancery Court.[12] They played an important part in handling disputes in which the Monarch was involved or had a special interest.

In this early period (roughly from the Norman Conquest to the English Revolution) the distinction between 'administering justice' and governing the country was less sharply drawn than it is now. The relationship between the central courts and the executive at this time can perhaps be captured by saying that 'doing justice' was understood as a mode or task of governance, and courts were understood as instruments of governance. By contrast, today we think of courts, vis-à-vis the executive, primarily as instruments of accountability, for the supervision of government activity rather than performance of a governmental task.

The association at the central level between the executive (ie, the Monarch and Council) and the courts had its counterpart at the local level in the role of Justices of the Peace.[13] JPs ('magistrates') were the representatives of the Monarch in the shires, and by the 18th century (which is sometimes described as the heyday of the JP), they had many, diverse administrative responsibilities, both regulatory and welfare-related.[14] The primary mode[15] of exercising their administrative functions was judicial.[16] It was through proceedings initiated by complaints,

---

[9] Baker, 99–105.

[10] There were also, of course, many local courts associated, for instance, with boroughs and manors: Baker, 22–27.

[11] Baker, ch 7

[12] In the 19th century, the term 'star chamber' was applied to some tribunals as a term of abuse: Stebbings 317.

[13] See generally CA Beard, *The Office of Justice of the Peace in England in its Origin and Development* (New York, Burt Franklin, 1904); T Skyrme, *History of the Justices of the Peace, Vols I and II* (Chichester, Barry Rose, 1991). For a brief account of local government before 1832 see KB Smellie, *A History of Local Government*, rev edn (London, Unwin University Books, 1968) ch 1.

[14] 'By 1833 the JPs were the true rulers of the country': D Roberts, *Victorian Origins of the British Welfare State* (Handen, Conn, Archon Books, 1969) 9.

[15] Skyrme, n 13 above, *Vol I*, 135–38; JP Dawson, *A History of Lay Judges* (Cambridge, Mass, Harvard University Press, 1960) 139–40. However, 'courts of the justices of the peace, like other medieval courts, had not drawn sharp lines between adjudication, executive action and rule-making' and in the 18th century the justices increasingly engaged in administration and rule-making outside the judicial context: Dawson, ibid 143–44.

[16] Theoretical complexities underlie this statement, which rests on a distinction between functions and procedures. Vile's view is that the distinction between different government functions (legislative, executive, judicial) is based on a distinction between different decision-making procedures: MJC Vile, *Constitutionalism and the Separation of Powers* (Oxford, Clarendon Press, 1967)

presentments and indictments, and conducted in Petty Sessions and Quarter Sessions that the JPs performed many of their formal administrative tasks.

The 17th century witnessed a major change in the relationship between the monarchical executive and the central courts. The conciliar courts were abolished and, as a result of the triumph of Parliament over the Monarch, the central courts came to be understood no longer as participants in the royal project of governance but as instruments of Parliamentary will, expressed in statutes.[17] In its mature form, this new relationship was most famously expounded by AV Dicey (in *An Introduction to the Study of the Law of the Constitution*, first published in 1885)[18] in terms of the principle of Parliamentary sovereignty (or 'supremacy'). The new role of the courts, vis-à-vis the executive was to ensure its conformity to the will of Parliament. The independence of the judges of central courts from royal control was reinforced in the Act of Settlement of 1701, which transferred from the Monarch to Parliament the power to fire judges,[19] limited the grounds on which a judge could be removed from office, and guaranteed judicial remuneration.[20] As a result of these developments, Dicey was eventually able to paint the relationship between the courts and the executive in terms of the rule of law – the idea that the government, like its citizens, is answerable in the courts – thus completing the transformation of courts from instruments of governance into instruments for holding the government accountable to the citizenry.

The English governmental system as it existed in the first half of the 18th century provided the inspiration for the famous proposal of Charles de Secondat, the Baron Montesquieu – contained in Book XI, Chapter 6 of *L'Esprit des Lois*, first published in 1748 – that government be understood in terms of a tripartite division of institutions: the legislature, the executive and the judiciary; and a threefold, and corresponding, division of functions: legislative, executive and judicial. Although it is often said[21] that Montesquieu was not a very acute

---

346–48. This helps to explain why the judicial function is often defined in terms of a particular (adversarial) procedural paradigm. See further 5.2.

[17] Wraith and Hutchesson, 22–23.

[18] The standard modern edition is the 10th, with an Introduction by ECS Wade (London, Macmillan, 1959). The last edition produced by Dicey was the 8th, published in 1914.

[19] However, until 1760, all judicial commissions lapsed on the death of the Monarch, thus providing an opportunity for selective renewal of commissions.

[20] '[B]e it hereby enacted that … judges commissions be made *quamdiu se bene gesserint* [so long as they are of good behaviour], and their salaries ascertained and established; but upon the address of both Houses of Parliament it may be lawful to remove them'. However, in England the power to hire judges remained entirely with the government until the recent creation of the independent Judicial Appointments Commission. It is still a purely executive function in Australia but without the oversight exercised by the legislature in the US.

[21] Most famously by Dicey, *Introduction to the Study of the Law of the Constitution*, 337–38. It has been argued that the criticism is based on a misreading of Montesquieu who (it is suggested) understood the British system not in terms of separation of powers but as a balanced constitution: I Stewart, 'Men of Class: Aristotle, Montesquieu and Dicey on "Separation of Powers" and "The Rule of Law"' (2004) 4 *Macquarie Law Journal* 187.

observer, his proposal did neatly encapsulate the results of the major constitutional re-alignments of the 17th century, which saw the Monarch stripped of the
power to legislate and adjudicate in favour respectively of Parliament and the
common law and Chancery courts (in the latter case at the expense of the
conciliar courts, the abolition of which ended the close association of the
Monarch and the executive with adjudication of disputes). But at the time
Montesquieu was writing, executive power still resided formally and, to a
significant extent effectively, in the Monarch. Later in the 18th century royal
influence over the affairs of Parliament and the running of the country waned as
more and more of the Monarch's personal powers were in practice transferred to
ministers, and control over those ministers shifted from the Monarch to Parliament. Finally, in the 19th century, with extension of the franchise and reform of
the electoral system, ultimate sovereignty shifted from the Monarch to the
citizenry, thus creating the so-called 'constitutional monarchy' that the UK now
possesses. These developments also ushered in the era of 'responsible government' and formulation of the doctrine of ministerial responsibility according to
which members of the political executive belong and are directly answerable to
the legislature. With the development of modern political parties from the late
19th onwards, the separation of executive and legislature, which had been so
hard-won in the upheavals of the 17th century, was effectively reversed.

At the time Montesquieu was writing (and for half a century or more
afterwards) the tasks of central government were more-or-less limited to the
administration of justice (through the central courts), waging war – either for
defence of the realm or for territorial aggrandisement – and the associated
activities of diplomacy (ie, conducting foreign affairs) and taxation. The two
other major activities of government – regulation and welfare – were organised
locally, not centrally; and this local governmental activity was subject to relatively
little central control, especially after the abolition of the conciliar courts.[22] In the
17th century the Court of King's Bench had developed techniques (utilising the
prerogative writs of certiorari, prohibition and mandamus) for exercising some
control over local administration,[23] but such control (like judicial review today)
was necessarily piecemeal, sporadic and unsystematic.[24] Nor did Parliament or
the executive exercise significant oversight of local administration.

---

[22] JWFAllison, *A Continental Distinction in the Common Law: A Historical and Comparative Perspective on English Public Law* (Oxford, Clarendon Press, 1996) 153; Beard, *The Office of Justice of the Peace in England,* 118–24.

[23] EG Henderson, *Foundations of English Administrative Law: Certiorari and Mandamus in the Seventeenth Century* (Cambridge, Mass, Harvard University Press, 1963); SA de Smith, *Judicial Review of Administrative Action*, 3rd edn (London, Stevens, 1973) App 1; Baker, ch 9.

[24] According to Roberts (*Victorian Origins of the British Welfare State*, 17) in 1833 the central courts gave judgment in only 60 cases 'concerning the duties of magistrates and parishes'.

Two other points should be made about Montesquieu's account. The first is that Montesquieu[25] conceived of the judicial function primarily, if not solely, in terms of investigation and finding of facts and the mechanical application of pre-existing rules to facts. Apparently, he did not appreciate either the dynamic, law-generating nature of the common law method or the complexities of statutory interpretation and the creativity it allows and requires. Before the dramatic growth in the volume of legislation in the 19th century, judge-made common law was the most important source of legal rules. In modern terms, the dominant mode of rule-making was adjudicatory, not legislative. The transformation of courts after the English Revolution involved not only their distancing from the executive but also their decline as a source of law.[26] This decline continued apace in the 20th century, and has been only partially reversed by the increasing role of courts in enforcing constitutionally entrenched bills of rights. As instruments of governance, courts had for centuries been important not only as administrators but also as legislators. In the modern period, both of these functions are subsidiary to the main adjudicatory role of courts.

Secondly, Montesquieu did not take account of the role of judicial processes in local administration. In his exposition of separation of powers, the judicial branch of government seems to be identified with central courts; and ever since, in discussions of separation of powers, it has been understood as consisting not of all courts, but only of institutions that occupy a position in the constitutional structure analogous to that of the English central courts of the mid-18th century. Montesquieu effectively ignored what Stebbings calls the 'pragmatic and amorphous mass of inferior dispute-resolution bodies of limited jurisdiction'.[27] Similarly, the office of judge has been identified primarily with adjudicators who enjoy the sort of independence that was secured for the judges of English central courts by the Act of Settlement.

Nevertheless, whatever Montesquieu's efforts lacked in analytical rigour they more than made up for in impact. Montesquieu's ideas were highly influential both in North America and in France in the late 18th century,[28] not only on thinking about the nature of government, but also on the drafting of constitutional documents. In practical terms, separation of powers has proved to be

[25] As Lawrence Claus has convincingly argued: 'Montesquieu's Mistakes and the True Meaning of Separation' (2005) 25 *Oxford Journal of Legal Studies* 419. See also MJC Vile, *Constitutionalism and the Separation of Powers*, 89–90; Stewart, n 21 above, 198; L Heuschling, 'Why Should Judges be Independent? Reflections on Coke, Montesquieu and the French Tradition of Judicial Dependence' in KS Ziegler, D Baranger and AW Bradley (eds), *Constitutionalism and the Role of Parliaments* (Oxford, Hart Publishing, 2007).
[26] For an illuminating comparative account of the role of judge-made law in constitutional debates in the 17th century see RC van Caenegam, *Legal History: A European Perspective* (London, Hambledon Press, 1991) ch 8.
[27] Stebbings 295. See also HW Arthurs, *Without the Law: Administrative Justice and Legal Pluralism in Nineteenth-Century England* (Toronto, University of Toronto Press, 1985).
[28] Vile, *Constitutionalism and the Separation of Powers*, 77–78, 85–86, 122, 129–31, Ch VII. Concerning France see Allison, *A Continental Distinction in the Common Law*, 16–18, 137–52.

probably the most powerful constitutional idea ever conceived. One version – sometimes called 'pure' – is embodied in French constitutional arrangements.[29] Under this version, for instance, the 'ordinary courts' may not review government activity or declare legislation invalid. A different, 'flexible' (or 'partial'), checks-and-balances version underpins US constitutional arrangements and the architecture of the first three Articles of the US Constitution itself. In important ways, the US Constitution influenced the drafting of the Australian Constitution, the first three Chapters of which have a design similar to that of the first three Articles of the US document. Independence of the judiciary is universally accepted to be a necessary condition of good government and freedom of the individual regardless of the details of other constitutional arrangements.[30] This is particularly true in Westminster parliamentary systems, where the main significance of separation of powers lies in the independence of the judiciary. Indeed, when Blackstone 'domesticated'[31] Montesquieu for an English audience, it was security of judicial tenure that he emphasised.[32] These various institutional arrangements are widely considered to be more-or-less essential for avoiding excessive concentration of power, for avoiding conflicts of interest and for protecting the rights of the individual.

By the end of the 18th century, then, much constitutional thinking was dominated by concepts of separation of powers based on interpretations of Montesquieu's account of the institutions of English central government. The idea of separation of powers summed up a long period of institutional development that ended with the Monarch being deprived of the power to legislate without the cooperation of Parliament and being prevented not only from administering justice but also from directly influencing its administration by the central courts. This framework of constitutional thought sets the scene for the major developments that were to take place in the 19th and 20th centuries.

---

[29] See 3.4.

[30] Although in practice, it is not always honoured as such: witness events in Pakistan in 2007, which show that the judiciary is unlikely to be left alone if courts can be and are used as weapons in political power struggles.

[31] Allison, *A Continental Distinction in the Common Law*, 156; *The English Historical Constitution*, 75.

[32] Judicial independence and the separation of judicial power constitute the dominant strand in English thinking about institutional design: J Allison, 'The Separation of Powers in the Modern Period on England: Constitutional Principle or Customary Practice?' in H Van Goethem (ed), *Iuris Scripta Historica XVI: Gewoonte en Recht* (Brussel, Wetenschappelijk Comité voor Rechtsgeschiedenis, Koninklijke Vlaamse Academie van België voor Wetenschappen en Kunsten, 2002). According to this approach, separation of judicial power promotes the rule of law. It is interestingly reflected in the Constitutional Reform Act 2005 which, in s 1, Delphically reasserts 'the rule of law' and, in s 3, 'independence of the judiciary'. See also Allison, *The English Historical Constitution*, ch 4.

2.3 19th and 20th Centuries

2.3.1 The UK

From about the 1830s in Britain, social and economic problems associated with the Industrial Revolution brought about two major changes in the role and nature of government. The first involved centralisation of governmental power and responsibility.[33] Centralisation had two aspects – transfer of governmental functions from numerous local authorities to a single central authority, and increased control by a central authority of the performance of governmental functions at local level. Many of the administrative functions formerly performed by Justices of the Peace were transferred to central government agencies, and the 19th century witnessed the creation of multi-functional local authorities over which central government assumed more and more control.[34] The second major change involved increasing assumption by central government of new regulatory and welfare responsibilities in addition to the more traditional concerns of national security and taxation.

As we have seen, the period between the Conquest and the beginning of the 18th century witnessed a gradual process of separation of the executive and the judiciary accompanied by an increasing differentiation of functions. In particular, in terms of their relationship with the executive, the central courts, from being part of the machinery of government, came to be understood primarily as machinery for holding the executive accountable. An important institutional form through which centralisation and proliferation of government activities were initially effected involved a reversion of sorts to older practices. In response to various social and economic problems of the day, Parliament created non-departmental 'multi-functional' executive agencies with names such as 'board' and 'commission'. To such agencies was committed the task of managing a particular statutory scheme by the exercise of 'an admixture of legislative, administrative, ministerial and judicial functions'.[35] The relative importance of judicial work in the overall workload of these bodies varied from one agency to another; but in general we might say that the performance of judicial functions in such agencies was 'embedded' within the larger statutory task with which the agency was charged. Arrangements for the performance of embedded judicial

---

[33] For a useful general account see Roberts, *Victorian Origins of the British Welfare State*, chs 3 and 10. See also MW Thomas, 'The Origins of Administrative Centralisation' (1950) 3 *Current Legal Problems* 214. The main concern here is with centralisation of administrative functions. However, the 19th century also witnessed a process of rationalisation of the judicial system designed to reduce the number of local and specialised courts. This process provides important context for understanding the development of adjudicatory institutions distinct from courts.

[34] Smellie, *A History of Local Government*, chs 2 and 3, n 13 above.

[35] Stebbings 8

functions varied between agencies. In some, adjudication of disputes was under-taken by the very same officials who made the disputed decisions; in others, there was an internal separation of functions, primary decision-making and review of primary decision-making being allocated to different officials.

There were various reasons why resolution of disputes arising out of the management of new statutory regimes was typically embedded within managing agencies. For Victorian policy makers, 'effective dispute-resolution was not the only, or even the principal requirement'.[36] Dispute-resolution was regarded 'as no more than an element … in a wider administrative process'.[37] The 'flexibility, continuity and relative political neutrality' of non-departmental agencies made them 'ideally constituted for the specialised purposes of dispute-resolution'.[38] Moreover, 'dispute-resolution through the implementing administrative body would … serve to preserve central control over the entire administration of the law.'[39] Embedded adjudication was seen as an important element of the centrali-sation that was considered essential to tackle the social problems that industriali-sation was bringing in its wake.

> The debate was not … primarily as to how disputes should be resolved, but as to how the centralising legislation could be administered in the cheapest, most efficient and most effective way.[40]

In the course of the 19th century, as the principle of ministerial responsibility to Parliament for the conduct of government business became firmly established, as central government departments grew in size and capacity, and as government sought more continuity in and control over policy-making, multi-functional, non-departmental agencies fell out of favour, and their non-judicial tasks were progressively transferred to departments and departmental agencies.[41] As a result, non-departmental, multi-functional agencies that performed both judicial and non-judicial functions were transformed into mono-functional agencies the characteristic task of which was adjudication of disputes arising out of the management of a particular statutory regime by a departmental agency. By the early 20th century, the free-standing mono-functional adjudicatory agency had emerged, and the term 'tribunal' – which, according to Stebbings, was consciously not applied to multi-functional agencies[42] – came into common usage.

Understood in this way, the history of the development of the 'modern' administrative tribunal in England bears significant similarities to the history of the development of (central) courts. Both types of institution have their origins

---

[36] ibid 62.
[37] ibid.
[38] ibid 63.
[39] ibid.
[40] ibid.
[41] HWR Wade, *Towards Administrative Justice* (Ann Arbor, University of Michigan Press, 1963) ch II and 52–55.
[42] Stebbings 70–71

31

in the practice of embedded adjudication of disputes and gradually emerge as free-standing, mono-functional adjudicatory agencies. When multi-functional agencies were first established in the 19th century, embedded adjudication of disputes between citizen and government was understood as an aspect of the administrative process. It was only when such agencies were stripped of their non-adjudicatory functions and transformed into mono-functional adjudicatory agencies that the similarity between their basic function and that of courts was clearly discerned. Once that happened, however, administrative tribunals came to be seen as more-or-less problematic because, although their function was understood to be essentially similar to that of courts, they did not belong to the judicial branch of government and they were not staffed by judges who enjoyed guaranteed security of tenure and salary protection.[43]

This 'problem of tribunals' was a product of the institutional aspect of separation of powers – the idea that government is composed of three branches each of which is exercises a distinct governmental function.[44] If that doctrine had been understood as being essentially concerned with avoidance of undue concentrations of power and conflicts of interest resulting from admixture of functions, and with promotion of independent scrutiny of the exercise of power, the creation of non-court adjudicatory bodies would not, in itself, have been problematic. However, separation of powers was also understood to stand for the proposition that each of the three functions of government identified by Montesquieu should be allocated to a different institution or set of institutions. The idea that the judicial function should be allocated to judicial institutions, coupled with a narrow understanding of judicial institutions in terms of the superior central courts, was what generated the problem of tribunals.

The early decades of the 20th century witnessed the establishment of many free-standing, mono-functional tribunals. Although not embedded within agencies, such tribunals, like their 19th-century forebears, were 'specialist' in the sense that they were created to adjudicate disputes arising out of the implementation of a specific statutory regime. One result of their specialist nature was that they were linked in various ways to the department responsible for implementing the relevant statutory regime. Indeed, typically the Minister of the relevant department had the power to appoint the members of the tribunal; and tribunals were typically dependent on the department for staff and resources. The issue of the 'independence' of tribunals from their sponsoring departments was destined to remain a cause of much contention for the rest of the century.

Moreover, embedded adjudication did not disappear overnight. In 1929 the Lord Chief Justice of England, Lord Hewart published a book provocatively

---

[43] Stebbings 105–09.
[44] NW Barber, 'Prelude to the Separation of Powers' (2001) 60 *Cambridge Law Journal* 59; EL Rubin, *Beyond Camelot: Rethinking Politics and Law for the Modern State* (Princeton, Princeton University Press, 2005) ch 2.

entitled *The New Despotism*.[45] The longest chapters of the book are concerned with administrative (ie, executive, delegated) legislation and with the threat to judicial independence posed, in his opinion, by proposals to abolish the office of Lord Chancellor. Hewart's main preoccupation was with unaccountable executive power. He graphically describes statutory provisions, allowing Ministers to amend statutes by executive order and preventing the courts from reviewing executive action, as the 'ingenious and adventurous' employment of parliamentary supremacy to 'defeat' the rule of law.[46] Concerning administrative adjudication, Hewart's main objection was to arrangements under which (in his view) anonymous non-independent civil servants employed within government departments and acting in the name of Ministers, were able to perform judicial functions behind closed doors, on the basis of no or inadequate evidence, and without giving the affected person a hearing or providing reasons for their decisions.[47] Hewart's worry was not that Ministers and their civil servants exercised judicial power but that they did so 'lawlessly'. Nevertheless, he made no proposals for institutional reform.

Much more significant for our purposes is a book by WA Robson, first published in 1928, entitled *Justice and Administrative Law*.[48] Robson was just as critical as Hewart of English arrangements for adjudication of disputes between citizen and government, especially of the embedded variety. Like Hewart[49] (but at much greater length), Robson argued that it was essential for non-judicial adjudicators to bring a 'judicial mind' (or 'spirit') to the performance of their adjudicatory tasks. Indeed, Robson opined, '[w]ithout a judicial mind to apply it, our body of law would disintegrate in a year, and society relapse into savagery'(!)[50] He also stressed that adjudicators should be structurally independent; that they should act personally and not through (anonymous) delegates, in public, on the basis of evidence given at a proper hearing, and consistently; and that they should give reasons for their decisions. Unlike Hewart, Robson discussed and made concrete proposals about the design of institutions for adjudication of disputes between citizen and government. He was opposed to embedded adjudication:

---

[45] London, Ernest Benn, 1929. For background see M Taggart, 'From "Parliamentary Powers" to Privatization: The Chequered History of Delegated Legislation in the Twentieth Century' (2005) 55 *University of Toronto Law Journal*, 575, esp 576–80.

[46] *The New Despotism*, 17.

[47] ibid 46–52.

[48] London, Macmillan, 1928. A second edition appeared in 1947 and a third in 1951.

[49] *The New Despotism*, 46.

[50] *Justice and Administrative Law*, 1st edn, above n 48, 35–36. For this reason, Robson believed that 'lawyers should not be barred from appearing before any Administrative Tribunal whatsoever': ibid 282.

Administrative justice should in all cases be carried on by definite tribunals. ... In no circumstances should judicial functions be left to remain in hotchpot with the ordinary executive duties of a central department.[51]

He proposed that in appropriate cases there should be an appeal from an administrative tribunal to a 'superior Administrative Appeal Tribunal, whose decision should be final'.[52] There should, he said, be no appeal from a tribunal to a court; but he believed that tribunals should act 'judicially' and that the appropriate way of enforcing this obligation was through judicial review by a court.[53]

Robson's approach was particularly significant because, by expressly proposing a system of administrative tribunals that were relatively immune from judicial control, he raised the issue of how the jurisdiction of such tribunals should be determined. Hitherto, non-judicial institutions for administrative adjudication had been created pragmatically and on a piecemeal basis. Robson argued that the main reason for their creation was the need to break away from the individualistic, property-and-contract-based ideology of the courts and the common law in order to achieve the objectives of statutory programmes of regulation and welfare.[54] He also cited a number of subsidiary reasons such as a desire for adjudication that was cheaper and quicker than that provided by courts (better 'access to justice' in the modern jargon), resistance to increasing the size of the judiciary[55] and the need for expertise in adjudication of disputes in new areas of government activity. On the basis of these reasons, Robson proposed that adjudication should be committed to an administrative tribunal where:

— 'a new policy of social improvement is to be carried out ... of a kind which involves interference with private rights of property or personal freedom';
— 'it is desired to create new standards rapidly in a hitherto unexplored field';
— 'new or existing standards are to be applied or extended throughout the country';
— 'the correctness of a decision must depend to an appreciable extent on special knowledge'.[56]

However, Robson said, tribunals should not be given jurisdiction merely to provide cheaper or quicker adjudication, and they should not normally be given

---

[51] ibid 319.

[52] ibid 321; see also 91.

[53] ibid 236–37, 321.

[54] It has also been argued that in some contexts, at least, judges were thought to suffer from class bias: H Genn, 'Tribunal Review of Administrative Decision-Making' in G Richardson and H Genn (eds), *Administrative Law and Government Action* (Oxford, Clarendon Press, 1994) 252–53.

[55] See also Genn, n 54 above, 254–56.

[56] ibid 315–16. Robson apparently thought that the first criterion defined the proper function of tribunals. Whether he considered the other criteria essential or optional, cumulative or alternative, is unclear.

jurisdiction over matters already dealt with by courts, but only over matters 'in which the State has intervened in some way or other, either by way of regulation or the provision of a service'.[57]

By 1929, public debate about delegated legislation and administrative adjudication had reached such a level that the government felt the need to create a committee – the Committee on Ministers Powers, chaired (briefly) by the Earl of Donoughmore, by whose name it is colloquially known and the appointment of which was announced just before the launch of Hewart's book – to consider legislation and adjudication by Ministers and their appointees. Concerning administrative adjudication, the Committee's terms of reference instructed it to consider powers to make 'judicial or quasi-judicial decisions' and to 'report what safeguards are desirable or necessary to secure the constitutional principles of the sovereignty of Parliament and the supremacy of Law'. Perhaps in response to the distinction between judicial and quasi-judicial decisions, the Committee itself threw separation of powers into the mix, saying that although it was impossible absolutely to separate legislative, executive and judicial powers, the distinction between them 'is none the less real, and for our purposes significant'.[58] The Committee identified the main problem about administrative adjudication as being the existence of statutory powers to make judicial and quasi-judicial decisions 'against which there is no appeal' to a court.[59]

Faced with terms of reference littered with metaphysical concepts and resembling a question in an advanced constitutional theory examination, the Donoughmore Committee made three moves. First, reflecting concerns expressed by the likes of Hewart and Robson, it stressed the importance of fair procedure in the performance of adjudicatory functions by Ministers and their appointees. Secondly, in the name of the rule of law, it invented and then manipulated distinctions between administrative, quasi-judicial and judicial functions to justify a conclusion that there was nothing basically wrong with the existing allocation of adjudicatory powers between the courts, Ministers and free-standing administrative tribunals. It also enunciated criteria, for future allocation of these various types of functions to institutions, which were incapable of being, and never were, applied in practice.[60] Thirdly, it rejected Robson's

---

[57] ibid 317.

[58] Report of the Committee on Ministers' Powers, 1932 (Cmd 4060) 4

[59] ibid 2.

[60] The Committee's basic idea was that 'judicial' functions (involving the application of law) should be allocated to courts, and only exceptionally to tribunals; and that 'administrative' functions (involving the exercise of policy discretions) should be allocated to ministers. It understood 'quasi-judicial' functions to involve a mix of judicial and administrative elements; 'they naturally fall to Ministers', the Committee said (ibid 116). But in exceptional cases in which the two elements of such a function could be separated, the judicial element might be allocated to a 'Ministerial Tribunal'. Allocation of discretionary policy decisions to ministers was justified in terms of ministerial responsibility. 45 years later Tony Prosser was to argue that tribunals had been established to review certain welfare benefit decisions not as an alternative to allocating the function to a court but rather to make unpopular policies more palatable and protect ministers from responsibility for individual

proposal for a relatively self-contained system of free-standing administrative tribunals in favour of preserving the existing pragmatic and piecemeal approach to the design of administrative adjudicatory institutions, maintaining the judicial review jurisdiction of the courts over such institutions and recommending a universal right of appeal on points of law from administrative adjudicators to a court under a uniform and simple procedure.

In a comment on the Report, Robson dramatically pronounced that the Donoughmore Committee, saddled with tendentious terms of reference that directed it to consider the demands of both parliamentary supremacy and the rule of law, had 'started life with the dead hand of Dicey lying frozen on its neck'.[61] Robson's assessment of Dicey's significance in the modern history of administrative adjudication has been highly influential. Indeed, English administrative law in the first half of the 20th century is often depicted as an ideological battleground between the followers of Dicey (notably Hewart) on the one side and Robson and his like-minded colleagues at the London School of Economics (such as Harold Laski) on the other.[62] The standard criticism is that Dicey's views and influence 'undermined'[63] non-judicial administrative adjudication and delayed the development of English 'administrative law'[64] by at least 50 years. This accusation is based mainly on Dicey's argument that the 'rule of law' as understood in England requires that citizens should have access to the 'ordinary

benefit decisions: T Prosser, 'Poverty, Ideology and Legality: Supplementary Benefit Appeal Tribunals and Their Predecessors' (1977) 4 *British Journal of Law and Society* 59. In a 2004 government White Paper – *Transforming Public Services: Complaints, Redress and Tribunals* (London, HMSO, 2004) it was accepted that tribunals had the *effect* 'of diverting responsibility away from Ministers' (para 3.24). Prosser's argument implausibly assumes that the typical individual welfare benefit decision involves the exercise of policy discretion. In high-volume jurisdictions such as social security it is unrealistic and undesirable to expect ministers to take responsibility for individual decisions. What they must be responsible for are the general norms – hard and soft law – according to which individual cases are decided. In this regard – as we will see in 5.3.2.2 – the critical question concerns the powers of tribunals in relation to soft law.

[61] WA Robson, 'The Report of the Committee on Ministers' Powers' (1932) *Political Quarterly* 346, 351.

[62] Although interestingly, Laski was a (non-dissenting) member of the Donoughmore Committee.

[63] Stebbings 108.

[64] The question, 'Is there such a thing as administrative law in England?' was a staple of academic debate in the early 20th century. Unfortunately, the term 'administrative law' was used in various senses. Often it was used to refer to arrangements like the French system of *droit administratif*, at other times the question was taken to be asking whether or not informal administrative rules (what we would now call 'soft law' and what Jerry Mashaw calls 'the internal law of the administration': JL Mashaw, *Bureaucratic Justice: Managing Social Security Disability Claims* (New Haven and London, Yale University Press, 1983)) were 'law'. In the more recent literature, the question is often rephrased to ask whether English law recognises a distinction between public law and private law. Dicey's views are hard to discern partly because he said very little about what we would now call 'administrative law'. The only aspect of judicial review he discussed at length was *habeas corpus*, which many modern writers (following his lead) treat as part of constitutional law.

courts' for adjudication of disputes with government. In order properly to assess this criticism we need to put Dicey's account of the rule of law in historical perspective.

Reflecting the outcome of the constitutional upheavals of the 17th century, Dicey argued that the English constitution was founded on the principles of the supremacy of Parliament and the rule of law. The former principle encapsulated the transfer of legislative power from the Monarch to the legislature, while the latter encapsulated the re-alignment of the courts with Parliament, the exclusion of the Monarch from the exercise of judicial power and the protection of judges from interference by the provisions of the Act of Settlement. Understood in this way, the idea that citizens should have access to the courts for the resolution of disputes with the government is primarily concerned to ensure the enforcement of the will of Parliament (expressed in statutory law) against the executive (still, at the end of the 17th century, significantly under the control of the Monarch) by a judiciary whose independence from the executive was protected by security of tenure and salary. In Dicey's scheme the prime importance of the rule of law lay in the principle that government officials should be ultimately answerable for the exercise of power to a set of institutions staffed by judges whose independence from executive government was guaranteed by statute (reflecting basic constitutional principles).

An implication of the standard criticism of Dicey is that he thought that the ('ordinary') courts (and the 'ordinary' law they administered) should have an adjudicative monopoly over disputes between citizen and government as well as over disputes between citizen and citizen. This conclusion is questionable for at least two reasons. First, although Dicey may have been the most influential writer on English public law in the late 19th and early 20th centuries,[65] his views had no discernible effect on the growth of administrative tribunals. It is true that the Donoughmore Committee adopted Dicey's account of the rule of law, describing it as '[t]he best exposition of the modern doctrine';[66] but as we have seen, the Committee found nothing wrong with then-existing structural arrangements for administrative adjudication. To the extent that Dicey's views hindered the growth of administrative adjudication, their restraining effect was perhaps shown in an unwillingness on the part of courts (until the 1960s) to engage in aggressive judicial review, not in hindering the development of non-judicial review by tribunals.[67]

---

[65] 'It is not too much to say that "Dicey on the Constitution" dominated political and legal thought among educated Englishmen … for more than thirty years': WA Robson, 'The Report of the Committee on Ministers' Powers' (1932) *Political Quarterly* 346, 347. His influence, though indirect, is undiminished.

[66] 1932 (Cmd 4060) 72.

[67] This effect on the development of judicial review was apparently the result of the view attributed to Dicey that English law did not contain rules imposing on officials obligations that it did not impose on citizens. For an argument that the standard view – that in the 1960s courts became much more active in controlling the executive than they had been earlier in the century –

Secondly, in *An Introduction to the Study of the Law of the Constitution*, first published in 1885 and revised by him for the last time in the 8th edition, published 1914, Dicey does not mention multi-functional or mono-functional non-judicial institutions of administrative adjudication. Commonly, this glaring omission is taken as evidence of the incompatibility of such institutions with his view of the constitution. However, if Dicey did consider the English institutions of non-judicial administrative adjudication that existed in his day to be a constitutional monstrosity, it is surprising he did not say so. Instead of railing against such institutions, Dicey focused his critical gaze on the French system of *droit administratif*. As he understood it, the central institutional feature of the French system (which he contrasted with the English 'rule of law') was the existence of two systems of courts, civil courts for dealing with disputes between citizens and administrative courts for dealing with disputes between citizen and government. The relationship between the two sets of courts was regulated by a rule that prohibited the civil courts from adjudicating disputes between citizens and government, over which the administrative courts had exclusive jurisdiction. Dicey traced the history of this system from the beginning of the 19th century and concluded that many of the objections that could be made to its original manifestation were no longer valid by the end of the century.[68] However (he observed), despite all the changes, the French system retained its central institutional feature. Dicey was right to maintain that the English system was basically different from the French in this respect; and despite finding significant merit in the latter,[69] he obviously considered the former to be preferable.

Dicey framed the difference between the two systems in terms of whether the 'ordinary courts' (administering 'ordinary' law) had jurisdiction over disputes between citizen and government. This language is unfortunate because Dicey's contrast between the English and French systems depends on the fact that in the former, there is only one relevant type of court (and only one relevant category of

---

oversimplifies a more complex reality, see S Sterett, *Creating Contstitutionalism? The Politics of Legal Expertise and Administrative Law in England and Wales* (Ann Arbor, University of Michigan Press, 1997).

[68] This historically-based, positive assessment of the French system appeared for the first time in the 6th edn, 1902: FH Lawson, 'Dicey Revisited I' (1959) 7 *Political Studies* 109, 111. For a modern French assessment of Dicey see R Errera, 'Dicey and French Administrative Law: A Missed Encounter' [1985] *Public Law* 695.

[69] *An Introduction to the Study of the Law of the Constitution*, above n 18, 398–401. Hewart who, like Dicey, located the foundational principles of the English constitution in supremacy of Parliament and the rule of law is commonly demonised as Dicey's most enthusiastic disciple in opposing administrative tribunals and in criticising the French *droit administratif*. In fact, however, like Dicey, he says nothing about administrative tribunals. Stebbings' suggestion to the contrary (Stebbings 330) is an artefact of quotation out of context. Far from attacking *droit administratif* he contrasts it favourably with the English position, crediting it with qualities of systematicity and legality lacking in local arrangements, which he considered 'lawless' by comparison: 'the "administrative tribunals" of the Continent are real Courts, and what they administer is law, though a different law from ordinary law.': *The New Despotism*, 45.

law).[70] Where there are two mutually independent species of the genus (administering two distinct categories of law), neither subordinate to the other but each coordinate with the other, the idea that one is 'ordinary' and the other is special makes little sense.[71] In fact, in Dicey's scheme the adjective 'ordinary' is redundant. His basic normative point was that disputes between citizen and government should fall within the jurisdiction of (and therefore be subject to law administered by) courts staffed by judges enjoying security of tenure and salary protection. The critical question is whether the rule of law, so understood, required the adjudicative jurisdiction of the courts over disputes between citizen and government (or, for that matter, between citizen and citizen) to be exclusive and monopolistic or whether, on the contrary, it required only that all adjudicatory bodies should be arranged in a hierarchical system with the 'courts' – ie, the central courts of common law and equity – at the top, and in which all inferior adjudicators were ultimately controllable by and answerable to the superior central courts. The former we might call the 'judicial monopoly' interpretation of the rule of law and the latter the 'judicial supervision' interpretation.

In my judgment, the judicial supervision interpretation is at least as plausible as the judicial monopoly interpretation. Dicey would clearly have insisted upon judicial review of non-judicial administrative adjudication; and he would, no doubt, have been a vigorous opponent of statutory provisions purporting to exclude judicial review of administrative tribunals. He would definitely have favoured appeals on points of law from non-judicial adjudicators to courts.[72] The Donoughmore Committee clearly considered its unequivocal adoption of the Diceyan analysis to be compatible with its sanguine approach to administrative adjudication. The Committee's recommendation that the making of 'judicial' decisions should be allocated to non-judicial bodies only in exceptional circumstances was, no doubt, partly a product of its Diceyanism; but it bore no fruit. More important was its insistence that non-judicial administrative adjudicative decisions should be subject to both judicial review and appeal to a court on points of law. For all his professed anti-Diceyanism, Robson also supported judicial review; but he thought that appeals (covering law, fact and policy) should (in 'important' cases)[73] go to an appeal tribunal from which there would be no

---

[70] On the importance of legal categories see Allison, *A Continental Distinction in the Common Law*, ch 6. Robson interpreted Dicey's assertion that citizen and official alike are subject to the ordinary law as meaning that they are subject in all respects to the same laws: *Justice and Administrative Law*, 3rd edn, 438–40. This was clearly not the case in Dicey's day, and he did not maintain that it was (*An Introduction to the Law of the Constitution*, 194); although he did downplay the amount of what he called 'official law'.

[71] Similarly: M Weston, *An English Reader's Guide to the French Legal System* (New York, Berg, 1991) 68–69.

[72] Concerning judicial supervision of non-judicial adjudication in the 19th century, see Stebbings ch 6.

[73] *Justice and Administrative Law*, 3rd edn (London, Stevens & Sons Ltd, 1951) 459. The Donoughmore Committee was also prepared to contemplate an appeal to an appeal tribunal on issues of fact in exceptional cases: 1932 (Cmd 4060) 117.

further appeal to a court. In the end, then, the substantial difference between the Diceyans[74] and their detractors concerned the destination of appeals on points of law from non-judicial administrative adjudicators: no-one, it seems, argued for a fully bifurcated system of adjudicatory institutions along French lines. The significance of the difference between the two camps depends on unstable and manipulable distinctions between appeal and review, and between law on the one hand and fact and policy on the other.[75] However, both sides obviously assumed that in practice as well as in theory, appeals on points of law gave courts considerably more scope than judicial review for supervision of administrative adjudication.

The issue of judicial appeals played an important part in debates about administrative adjudication throughout the 20th century. We might understand this issue ideologically in terms of the distinction drawn in 1.2.2 between implementation and adjudication. That distinction, it will be recalled, turns on the balance, in applying rules and principles to individual cases, between individual and social interests. We may speculate that the anti-Diceyans opposed judicial appeals partly because they feared that appellate courts would strike this balance too heavily in favour of the individual and against society, and upset the different balance struck by non-judicial adjudicators. Conversely, the Diceyans favoured judicial appeals partly and precisely because they saw them as a means of protecting individual interests against undue encroachment, in the name of the public interest, by rule-implementers and non-judicial administrative adjudicators.

Late in his career, in 1915, Dicey wrote a short article[76] commenting on two decisions of the House of Lords dealing with administrative adjudication: *Board of Education v Rice*[77] and *Local Government Board v Arlidge*.[78] This article can be read as evidence of a partial recantation of his supposed repudiation of non-judicial adjudication. However, if we abandon the assumption that – despite his silence about them – Dicey considered non-judicial adjudicatory bodies to be a constitutional monstrosity, the article takes on a different complexion. *Board of Education v Rice*, Dicey says, merely illustrates the well-established principle that statutory authorities (including non-judicial adjudicators) must act in strict conformity with their empowering statutes and that any action which does not so conform 'should be treated by a court of law as invalid'. The basic issue in the

---

[74] Although some of the more enthusiastic, such as CK Allen in his marvellously titled book, *Bureaucracy Triumphant* (London, OUP, 1931), favoured expansion of the court system rather than creation of more tribunals (ibid 66–68). On the other hand, Allen (like Hewart – see n 69 above) thought that the French system as it existed in his day was a truer embodiment of the rule of law than the English (ibid 99).

[75] Robson himself said of the phrase 'point of law' that it 'means in practice finding grounds of objection to the decision to which the court will listen': WA Robson, 'Administrative Justice and Injustice: A Commentary on the Franks Report' [1958] *Public Law* 12, 18.

[76] 'The Development of Administrative Law in England' (1915) 31 *Law Quarterly Review* 148.

[77] [1911] AC 179.

[78] [1915] AC 120.

Arlidge case was whether non-judicial administrative adjudicators should be required to follow judicial (ie, court-like) procedures. The Court of Appeal said 'yes' and the House of Lords 'no'. Dicey commented: 'There is a great deal to be said in favour of each view'. Dicey's final conclusion was that although there had been a large growth in conferral of 'judicial or quasi-judicial authority' on non-judicial bodies, 'the fact that law courts can deal with any actual or provable breach of the law committed by any servant of the Crown still preserves the rule of law.' It is impossible to tell to what extent this conclusion represents an about-face on Dicey's part because his original account of the rule of law (contained more-or-less unchanged in Chapter IV of every edition since the 3rd, published in 1889) was consistent with both the judicial monopoly and the judicial supervision approaches.

If I am right in suggesting that Dicey's understanding of the rule of law was not inconsistent with non-judicial administrative adjudication,[79] how might we explain his silence on this topic? One possibility is that he deeply regretted the growth of non-judicial adjudication and wished that it would disappear. Dicey was ideologically opposed to the increasing involvement of central government in social and economic life.[80] To the extent that courts and the 'ordinary law' were identified with individualistic and laissez-faire ideological premises, and non-judicial adjudicatory bodies were associated with increasing governmental activity and power, he would have objected to the increasing use of institutions of the latter sort. However, the view that courts should, *as a matter of constitutional principle*, have a monopoly of adjudicatory power – as opposed to an ultimate supervisory role – does not follow from a political and ideological objection to non-judicial adjudication. It is worth remembering, too, that Robson's strong advocacy of administrative tribunals that would be largely independent of both the executive and the courts was based primarily on the conviction that judges and courts could not be trusted to promote the ideology and programmes of the welfare and regulatory state[81] and secondarily on certain supposed practical advantages of tribunals over courts (such as cheapness and speed). There is no reason to think that Robson thought tribunals superior to courts as a matter of constitutional principle.

Unsurprisingly, given the blandness of its conclusions and the impracticability of many of its recommendations, the Report of the Donoughmore Committee

---

[79] This conclusion forms the basis of the argument in a frequently cited early US book on administrative adjudication: J Dickinson, *Administrative Justice and the Supremacy of Law in the United States* (New York, Russell and Russell, 1927) esp ch II. Dickinson used 'supremacy of law' more-or-less synonymously with 'rule of law'.

[80] RA Cosgrove, *The Rule of Law: Albert Venn Dicey, Victorian Jurist* (London, Macmillan, 1980) chs 8 and 9.

[81] Curiously, however, from the 3rd edn of *Justice and Administrative Law* (428–29) we learn that Robson proposed to the Donoughmore Committee that whereas tribunals should deal with disputes arising out of 'service functions' of the state, disputes in connection with 'regulatory functions' would remain with the courts. Distrust of judicial ideology also lay behind Robson's preference for a general appeal tribunal as opposed to an Administrative Court (ibid 462).

had no discernible impact except, perhaps, to encourage maintenance of the status quo. It raised but did not resolve three basic issues about administrative tribunals: systematisation, procedure, and appeals. As to the first, the number of administrative tribunals continued to increase, especially after the Second World War, in the same pragmatic and piecemeal way as hitherto.[82] Despite its rejection of Robson's vision of parallel judicial and non-judicial adjudicative institutions, the Donoughmore Committee clearly viewed tribunals as different from courts both in nature and function; but it apparently did not contemplate that there might be a tribunal 'system' analogous to the court system that had been constructed in the 19th century. Concerning tribunal procedure, the US Congress – as we will see – gave some attention to the general issue in the Administrative Procedure Act 1946; but there was no equivalent legislation in the UK and procedures varied considerably from one tribunal to another.

Arrangements for appeals continued to be chaotic. In some cases, there was no appeal from the decision of a non-judicial administrative adjudicator; in others there was an appeal to another non-judicial adjudicator (an appeal tribunal or a Minister); and in yet others, there was an appeal on points of law to a court. This variability of practice provides reason to doubt that Dicey's practical influence was anything like as powerful as his detractors alleged. On the other hand, it enabled Diceyan sympathisers, such as HWR Wade (writing in 1981) to imply that the anti-Diceyan (and particularly Robsonian) prejudice against judicial appeals had been the dominant influence on the development of supervision arrangements from the early 20th century.[83] At all events, by mid-century a tide of opinion in favour of judicial supervision began to rise. In 1951, in an attempt to plug gaps in statutory provision for judicial appeals on points of law, 'error of law on the face of the record' was re-invented as a ground of judicial review,[84] and subsequently the definition of 'the record' was significantly expanded.

In 1955 the government set up a Committee on Tribunals and Enquiries chaired by Sir Oliver Franks to consider, amongst other things, the 'constitution and workings of tribunals other than ordinary courts of law'.[85] Robson and

---

[82] See, eg, CK Allen, 'Administrative Jurisdiction' [1956] *Public Law* 13. Kathleen Bell argues that the Donoughmore Committee intended to discourage the establishment of more tribunals but that its refusal – following Dicey – to contemplate the establishment of a 'separate system of administrative courts' encouraged their proliferation: K Bell, *Tribunals in the Social Services* (London, Routledge & Kegan Paul, 1969) 9. Bell calls tribunals a 'compromise': ibid 20.

[83] HWR Wade, 'Administrative Tribunals and Administrative Justice' (1981) 55 *Australian Law Journal* 374.

[84] *R v Northumberland Compensation Appeal Tribunal, ex p Shaw* [1952] 1 KB 338, described by Wade and Forsyth as 'one of Lord Denning's most celebrated judgments': HWR Wade and CF Forsyth, *Administrative Law*, 8th edn (Oxford, OUP, 2000) 276.

[85] Report of Committee on Administrative Tribunals and Enquiries, 1957 (Cmnd 218) iii. Ironically, the immediate catalyst for the establishment of the Committee was the notorious 'Crichel Down' affair (see JAG Griffith, 'The Crichel Down Affair' (1955) 18 *Modern Law Review* 557), which arose out of the decision-making activities of government officials, not tribunals. The Committee's terms of reference did not explicitly cover such decision-making, and the Committee interpreted them narrowly in this regard: 1957 (Cmnd 218) 3. Thus, whereas the Committee had much to say

others argued before the Committee for amalgamation or grouping[86] of tribunals so as to inject some order into the diverse and unruly collection of individual bodies, but in response the Committee made only one minor recommendation along these lines. The Franks Committee's major contribution to systematisation was its recommendation for the establishment of a Council on Tribunals to 'keep the constitution and working of tribunals under continuous review'.[87]

Much more important was the approach of the Committee to tribunal procedure and supervision. Unlike the Donoughmore Committee, the Franks Committee paid no express homage to the Diceyan legacy; but its report was arguably more Diceyan in spirit than that of its predecessor in its promotion of a judicialised model of non-judicial administrative adjudication. 'We consider', the Committee said, 'that tribunals should properly be regarded as machinery ... for adjudication rather than as part of the machinery of administration.'[88] Furthermore, 'as a matter of general principle ... a decision should be entrusted to a court rather than to a tribunal in the absence of considerations which make a tribunal more suitable'.[89] The Committee enunciated the famous trio of (essentially judicial) procedural ideals for tribunals: openness, fairness and impartiality; and they recommended that tribunals should give reasons for their decisions.[90] It did not, however, suggest that these ideals should be embodied in a set of common procedural rules for tribunals. Concerning supervision of tribunals, the Committee rejected proposals for a general administrative appeals tribunal and for an administrative division of the High Court.[91] It considered the 'ideal' arrangement to be a 'general appeal' on 'fact, law or merits' from a first-instance

---

about decision-making procedure in the 'formal' context of tribunals (and public inquiries), it had nothing to say about procedure in the 'informal' bureaucratic context. It was left to the courts to push the law forward in this area: *Ridge v Baldwin* [1964] AC 40. The US Administrative Procedure Act 1946 similarly deals only with 'formal adjudication' (the equivalent of tribunal decision-making) and not with 'informal adjudication' (the equivalent of bureaucratic decision-making). This distinction between 'due process' in formal decision-making and due process in informal decision-making cuts across that between what are sometimes called 'pre-decision hearings' and 'post-decision hearings'. For instance, the public inquiry is a formal, pre-decision process.

[86] Robson favoured grouping of distinct tribunals because he feared that integration of diverse jurisdictions into a single body would result in a loss of expertise. For more on amalgamation see 4.3.1.

[87] 1957 (Cmnd 218) para 43.

[88] ibid para 40.

[89] ibid para 38. This principle represented a complete reversal of the 19th century approach of entrusting adjudication of disputes arising under new statutory schemes to non-judicial bodies.

[90] ibid paras 23–25; although it has to be conceded that if there was one thing about which Dicey's supporters and his detractors had always been in agreement it was that tribunals should 'act judicially' both in terms of procedure and by bringing a 'judicial mind' to bear on disputes.

[91] 1957 (Cmnd 218) paras 120–26. The Administrative Court – an element of the High Court – was established in 2000. This should not be seen as marking the final defeat of a Diceyan prejudice against special administrative courts because the Administrative Court is not a special administrative court in the relevant sense. Its prime function is judicial review, and it is not an appeal tribunal either in theory or in practice. The Committee's main argument against establishing an administrative court was that it would have involved an appeal from a specialised tribunal to a generalist court.

tribunal to an appellate tribunal, combined with an appeal to a court on points of law (regardless of the availability of judicial review).[92]

Whereas the Donoughmore Committee (reflecting its terms of reference) understood non-judicial adjudication to be qualitatively different from judicial adjudication, the Franks Committee conceptualised tribunals as essentially the same as courts ('court substitutes') but with certain practical – and contingent – advantages that made them preferable to courts in exceptional cases.[93] For this reason, the Franks Committee Report may be considered a watershed in thinking about administrative adjudication. How might we explain this significant shift of attitude? One possibility may be a change in the British political climate between the 1920s and the 1950s. The Donoughmore Committee operated in the shadow of the ideological struggles of the 19th century between laissez-faire individualism and government interventionism. Influential figures, such as Hewart and Robson, associated non-judicial adjudication with interventionism and judicial adjudication with individualism. This way of thinking about adjudication was reflected in the framing of the Donoughmore Committee's terms of reference and report around a distinction between judicial and non-judicial functions. By the 1950s, significant government involvement in welfare and regulation had become firmly established and more widely accepted; and the ideological divide between individualists and 'socialists' may, perhaps, have narrowed somewhat. Courts may have come to be seen as less antipathetic to the welfare and regulatory state than they were perceived to be a century earlier. As a result, in understanding the relationship between courts and tribunals, more weight may have been placed on the practical and contingent differences between them (cheapness, speed, informality, procedural flexibility, specialist expertise), and these differences may have seemed too flimsy to support a strong distinction between the two types of adjudicatory institution.

Another factor that may have cleared the way for closer identification of tribunals with courts was the distinction in the Franks Committee's terms of reference between tribunals and public inquiries. The latter, which are of most practical significance in the context of land-use planning, involve a form of embedded adjudication: a departmental 'inspector' conducts a hearing and either makes a decision subject to an appeal to the Minister, or makes a report on the basis of which the Minister prepares the decision. It was the extra-departmental tribunal that the Committee classified as part of the judicial system, not the public inquiry, which it apparently treated as an administrative, not a judicial institution. In the 1920s embedded adjudication was considered to be a major

---

[92] ibid paras 104–19.
[93] Whereas the Donoughmore Committee had preferred both ministers and courts to tribunals in their respectively appropriate spheres, Franks 'preferred tribunals to ministers and courts to tribunals' as administrative adjudicators: Committee of the Justice-All Souls Review of Administrative Law in the United Kingdom, *Administrative Justice: Some Necessary Reforms* (Oxford, Clarendon Press, 1988) 213.

problem to which free-standing, extra-departmental tribunals were a possible solution. By contrast, the Franks Committee did not consider the public inquiry problematic, provided fair procedures were followed.

Recommendations of the Franks Committee were quickly enacted in the Tribunals and Inquiries Act 1958 (although the Act applied to only a limited number of specified tribunals). The Act created the Council on Tribunals, lightly regulated the appointment and removal of chairs and members of tribunals, made general provision for appeals on points of law and for the giving of reasons for decisions on request, and limited the effect of privative (or 'ouster') clauses enacted before the date of the Act's commencement.[94] The judicialisation of tribunals, for which the Committee had laid a firm foundation, was taken an important step further by the House of Lords in its 1969 decision in *Anisminic v Foreign Compensation Commission*.[95] For our purposes, the decision is significant for two main reasons. First, the court construed a statutory ouster clause very narrowly, thus establishing a general principle of strict interpretation of such provisions and increasing the opportunities for judicial supervision of tribunals. Secondly, it expanded the scope of judicial review by broadening the concept of 'jurisdictional error', thus significantly narrowing the distinction between judicial review and appeal on a point of law on which so much turned in earlier debates about supervision. Around this time the courts also began to increase the potential for judicial supervision of tribunals by progressively widening the concept of 'error of law'. Judicial review for error of law on the face of the record was reinforced by a provision of the 1958 Act making reasons, required to be given on request, part of the 'record' of the tribunal proceedings.

Of the three issues left unresolved by the Donoughmore Committee, the only one on which the Franks Committee made a major impact was procedure. Advising and making recommendations on procedural rules was an important part of the statutory remit of the Council on Tribunals, which promoted the Franks criteria of openness, fairness and impartiality. Because the Tribunals and Inquiries Act applied only to certain tribunals, arrangements for appeals remained a 'hotchpotch'.[96] However, undoubtedly the main item of business left unfinished by the Franks Committee was systematisation. In the late 20th century, significant steps towards the creation of a tribunal system were taken in the area of social security. The caseload of social security tribunals represented a third of the total caseload of all tribunals combined. By the beginning of the 21st century the so-called Appeals Service, into which five sets of welfare tribunals were amalgamated, consisted of a hierarchy of more than 2,000 full-time and part-time sitting members headed by a President and six regional Chairmen. The

[94] The legislation was consolidated and re-enacted in 1971 and 1992, but the temporal reach of the provision about privative clauses was not changed.
[95] [1969] 2 AC 147.
[96] H Woolf, 'A Hotchpotch of Appeals – The Need for a Blender' (1988) 7 *Civil Justice Quarterly* 44.

social security tribunals followed common procedures; there was a single internal appeals structure and a unified administrative support agency. But outside this area, the picture was one of a disparate and diverse collection of largely self-contained tribunals operating without common procedures or administrative arrangements.

Social security tribunals in particular had, since the late 1960s, been the subject of a great deal of research and commentary, by both academics and practitioners, dealing with issues such as flexibility and informality of procedure; evidence gathering; funding of applications and representation of applicants; the role and performance of tribunal members, both lawyers and non-lawyers; and experiences and attitudes of tribunal users.[97] In *Justice and Administrative Law* Robson had discussed in some detail the practical advantages that tribunals were said to enjoy over courts and optimistically concluded (although without empirical support) that these advantages were realised in practice. 50 years later the results of empirical studies increasingly cast doubt on this conclusion and led to criticism of the tendency to slip from statements of aspiration to statements of reality when talking about tribunals.[98] We noted earlier that for the Franks Committee, the supposed practical advantages of tribunals were what distinguished them from courts. Questioning of the superiority of tribunals in these respects further undermined the rationale of the institutional distinction between tribunals and courts.

In 2000 the government set up a Review of Tribunals chaired by Sir Andrew Leggatt. Instead of the Franks ideals of openness, fairness and impartiality, the 2001 Review Report – *Tribunals for Users: One System, One Service* – aimed to promote a more 'independent, coherent and user-friendly' tribunal *system*. The Review's detailed proposals met some resistance in government, and legislation – the TCE Act – did not reach the statute book until 2007, although by that time a new administrative support agency – The Tribunals Service – (which needed no statutory authorisation) had already been established.

---

[97]   eg K Bell, *Tribunals in the Social Services*; K Bell, P Collison, S Turner and S Webber, 'National Insurance Local Tribunals' (1974) 3 *Journal of Social Policy* 289, (1975) 4 *Journal of Social Policy* 1; J Fulbrook, *The Appellant and His Case: The Appellant's View of Supplementary Benefit Appeals Tribunals* (London, Child Poverty Action Group, 1973); M Herman, *Administrative Justice and Supplementary Benefits* (London, G Bell & Sons, 1972); Wraith and Hutchesson (1973); R Lister, *Justice for the Claimant: A Study of Supplementary Benefit Appeal Tribunals* (London, Child Poverty Action Group, 1974); M Adler and A Bradley (eds), *Justice, Discretion and Poverty: Supplementary Benefit Appeal Tribunals in Britain* (London, Professional Books, 1975); A Frost and C Howard, *Representation and Administrative Tribunals* (London, Routledge, 1977); H Genn and Y Genn, *The Effectiveness of Representation at Tribunals* (London, Lord Chancellor's Department, 1989); J Peay, *Tribunals on Trial: A Study of Decision-Making under the Mental Health Act 1983* (Oxford, Clarendon Press, 1989); J Baldwin, N Wikeley and R Young, *Judging Social Security: The Adjudication of Claims for Benefit in Britain* (Oxford, OUP, 1992). See generally R Rawlings, *Greivance Procedure and Administrative Justice: A Review of Socio-Legal Research* (Economic and Social Research Council, 1987) ch 2.

[98]   H Genn, 'Tribunals and Informal Justice' (1993) 56 *Modern Law Review* 393; n 54 above.

For present purposes, the chief importance of these developments is that they represent a major step forward in the judicialisation of tribunals. The Tribunals Service – like its judicial counterpart, the Courts Service – is an executive agency of the Ministry of Justice, thus breaking the long-standing pattern of dependence of tribunals for staffing and resources on the very departments whose decisions they had jurisdiction to review. Under the provisions of the 2007 Act, legally qualified members of tribunals are called 'judges' even if they do not hold judicial office in the traditional sense;[99] and the 'guarantee of judicial independence', contained in section 3 of the Constitutional Reform Act 2005, applies to the 'tribunal judiciary' as well as to the 'court judiciary'.[100] Tribunals that adjudicate disputes between citizen and government[101] are organised in a two-tier, trial ('First-tier Tribunal') and appellate ('Upper Tribunal') structure, with appeals on points of law from the Upper Tribunal to the Court of Appeal.[102] In England, court judges can sit as Judges of the Upper Tribunal, and the Senior President of the Tribunal Service is a Lord Justice of Appeal (a judge of the Court of Appeal). Tribunal Judges and Members of the First-tier Tribunal and Members of the Upper Tribunal are appointed by the Lord Chancellor. Tribunal Judges of the Upper Tribunal (like court Judges) are appointed by the Queen on the advice of the Lord Chancellor. Tribunal Judges and Members may be removed from office by the Lord Chancellor with the concurrence of the Lord Chief Justice but only on the ground of inability or misbehaviour. The independent Judicial Appointments Commission plays a central role in the appointment not only of court Judges but also of tribunal Judges and Members of the First-tier and Upper Tribunals.[103] The Upper Tribunal has been given limited judicial review jurisdiction – a jurisdiction formerly exercisable in England only by the High Court and in Scotland by the Court of Session.

It is anticipated that the Tribunal Procedure Committee will, in due course, develop a common core of Tribunal Procedure Rules analogous to (but perhaps

---

[99] Because the term 'describes exactly what the post holders … do … [t]hey make decisions about people's rights and about Government responsibilities': Vera Baird QC, House of Commons Public Bill Committee, 15 March 2007.

[100] Tribunals, Courts and Enforcement Act 2007 s 1. The informal designations 'tribunal judge' and 'court judge' are useful.

[101] And, in the case of immigration tribunals, non-citizen and government. Initially the Asylum and Immigration Tribunal was to be left outside the new system. However, following a consultation exercise in 2008, the Justice Minister announced on 8 May 2009 that the AIT will be replaced by Chambers of the First-tier and Upper Tribunals in 2010. The prime motivations for this somewhat surprising change of policy are to relieve the courts of an increasing burden of immigration cases and to reintroduce a two-tier system of non-judicial review of immigration decisions in place of the single-tier AIT.

[102] The Review, we are told (*Tribunals for Users*, (Norwich, Stationery Office, 2001) 207–10), was informed by the Australian system, and in particular the Administrative Appeals Tribunal. Ironically, however, the English structure bears more similarity to highly controversial proposals for an Administrative Review Tribunal, which were defeated in the Australian Senate in 2001 and have not been revived. See 2.3.3.

[103] The role of the JAC in relation to non-judicial Members of tribunals is regulated by Sch 14 of the Constitutional Reform Act 2005.

less comprehensive and prescriptive than) the Civil Procedure Rules, which regulate the operation of the civil courts. The principles and values that underpin the structure and operation of the tribunal system – independence, accessibility, efficiency, an appropriate level of procedural (in)formality, appropriate use of modes of 'alternative dispute resolution' (ADR), appropriate speed and an appropriate mix of legal and non-legal expertise – are precisely the same as those that underpin the structure and operation of the court system. The Council on Tribunals – established, it will be recalled, to give effect to a recommendation of the Franks Committee – has been replaced by the Administrative Justice and Tribunals Council, the remit of which covers the whole 'administrative justice system'.

Despite these developments, it is unlikely, in the foreseeable future, that the distinction between courts and tribunals will be abolished in the UK. The more likely result is effective recognition of a branch of government the prime function of which is adjudication (the adjudicatory branch as opposed to the judicial branch) consisting of two separate adjudicatory hierarchies (of courts and tribunals), differentiated primarily in terms of their respective areas of jurisdiction, running in parallel but converging at the appellate level and sharing the two highest appellate bodies: the Court of Appeal and the UK Supreme Court (formerly the House of Lords). In this dispensation, it will be possible to describe tribunals as a type of court and courts as a type of tribunal; or, more accurately, courts and tribunals as species of adjudicative institution. It seems no exaggeration to say that the UK administrative justice system is now closer to the Diceyan ideal of the rule of law than at any time since its modern history began in the 1830s. In the words of the first Senior President of Tribunals, the reforms brought about by the TCE Act represent a 'profound constitutional change, completing the process of embedding the tribunal judiciary in the judicial system'.[104]

2.3.2 The US

The US element of this book focuses on federal law, and this section will be concerned with the historical background to the development of administrative adjudication at that level of the US polity. We noted earlier that the establishment of the ICC in 1887 is commonly considered to mark the birth of administrative law in the US. However, according to Mashaw,

---

[104] Senior President of Tribunals, *Second Implementation Review*, October 2008, <http://www.tribunals.gov.uk/Tribunals/Documents/Publications/SecondIR(psrc301008)final.pdf>, para 11 accessed 30 March 2009.

From the earliest days of the Republic, Congress delegated broad authority to administrators, armed them with extrajudicial coercive powers, created systems of administrative adjudication, and provided for judicial review of administrative action. And the first independent agency at the national level was not the ICC, but the Patent Office, created ninety-seven years earlier.[105]

The ICC did not represent

some fall from a state of separation of powers grace in the early Republic. Early Congresses ... combined policymaking, enforcement, and adjudication in the same administrative hands, [and] created administrative bodies outside of executive departments.[106]

Mashaw also finds instances of courts being co-opted as part of an administrative decision-making process to provide 'late eighteenth-century Americans with trial-type process for presenting factual claims'; and he sees in this practice a foreshadowing of embedded adjudication within multi-functional, administrative agencies.[107] Even so, the creation of the ICC was significant because, like analogous bodies in the UK – in particular, the Railway Commission established in 1873 – it was set up to address major economic and social problems caused by rapid industrialisation. As in the UK, new types of public institution were considered necessary to deal adequately with new problems;[108] and as in the UK debates of the period, agencies were also seen as preferable to courts because courts and the common law they made and applied, were considered to be ideologically in conflict with the aims of the programmes that agencies were established to administer.

Under Montesquieu's influence the United States Constitution embodies a separation of powers: legislative power is allocated to Congress (Article I), executive power to the President (Article II), and judicial power to the Supreme Court and other courts created by Congress (Article III). Although Article III provides that the 'judicial power of the United States shall be vested' in courts staffed by judges who enjoy constitutionally entrenched security of tenure and salary protection, as early as 1828 the Supreme Court held that Congress may confer what is, in effect, judicial power on 'legislative' (or 'Article I') courts, staffed by judges who need not enjoy the constitutional protections afforded to

---

[105] JL Mashaw, 'Recovering American Administrative Law: Federalist Foundations, 1787–1801' (2006) 115 *Yale Law Journal* 1256, 1260. Concerning the Patent Office see ibid 1302. See also JL Mashaw, 'Reluctant Nationalists: Federal Administration and Administrative Law in the Republican Era, 1801–1829' (2007) 116 *Yale Law Journal* 1636.

[106] 'Recovering American Administrative Law', 1268.

[107] ibid 1331–32.

[108] A classic statement of this view is found in JM Landis, *The Administrative Process* (New Haven and London, Yale University Press, 1938). Landis's basic argument was that the task of agencies was not merely to regulate behaviour in a negative sense but also positively to promote economic and social well-being.

Article III judges.[109] Just as Congress can delegate legislative power to executive agencies on which the text of the Constitution does not expressly confer such power,[110] so it can also delegate judicial power to bodies on which the text of the Constitution does not expressly confer it.[111] Such a body may be a free-standing mono-functional adjudicator – in which case it may be thought of and styled a 'court' (although not all such bodies are so called); or it may be multi-functional, in which case it will probably be thought of as an administrative agency, whether departmental or non-departmental (ie, whether directly responsible to the President or 'independent' in the sense that the President has limited power to dismiss its members).[112] Since the mid-19th century, the Supreme Court has developed various juridical techniques to prevent Congress unacceptably undermining the separation of judicial power established by the Constitution. Simplifying somewhat, the position it has eventually reached is that Congress can confer judicial power on bodies that are not Article III courts provided their decisions are appropriately subject to review by an Article III court and that the conferral of judicial power does not unacceptably undermine the values protected by separation of powers (primarily protection of individual rights and avoidance of excessive concentrations of governmental power).[113]

For our purposes, the significance of the ICC lies not in its multi-functionality or its independent status but rather in the working methods it developed. The ICC was established to regulate the railways. To this end, various functions – legislative, administrative and judicial – were conferred on the Commissioners. Like English JPs, the ICC performed regulatory functions (such as licensing, policing and enforcement) on a case-by-case basis. Because of the large volume of work, the Commissioners delegated to 'hearing examiners' the task of finding relevant facts ('conducting an evidentiary hearing') and generating a 'record' that could form the basis of the Commissioners' decision.[114] However, this delegation

---

[109] *American Insurance Co v Canter* (1828) 1 Pet 511; 7 L Ed 242. Section 8.6 of Article I confers on Congress the power 'to constitute Tribunals inferior to the supreme Court'. The common view is that such tribunals exercise judicial power and that they are, in this respect, indistinguishable from inferior federal courts created under Section 1 of Article III. For a contrary argument see JE Pfander, 'Article I Tribunals, Article III Courts, and the Judicial Power of the United States' (2004–05) 118 *Harvard Law Review* 643.

[110] The constitutionality of Congressional delegation of legislative power to executive bodies was established by the early 20th century: SG Breyer, RB Stewart, CR Sunstein and A Vermeule, *Administrative Law and Regulatory Policy: Problems, Text and Cases*, 6th edn (New York, Aspen Publishers, 2006) 32–33.

[111] According to the US Supreme Court, when an executive agency adjudicates, it exercises 'judicial power', even if not 'the judicial power of the United States': *Federal Maritime Commission v South Carolina Ports Authority* (2002) 535 US 743; 122 S Ct 1864.

[112] The Supreme Court held such limitations to be constitutional in *Humphrey's Executor v United States* (1935) 295 US 602 (see Breyer et al, *Administrative Law and Regulatory Policy*, 74–83). For an argument about the similarities between courts and agencies see M Shapiro, *The Supreme Court and Administrative Agencies* (New York, The Free Press, 1968) ch 1.

[113] For a little more discussion see 3.3.

[114] The ICC was given statutory power to appoint examiners in 1906. The Attorney-General's Committee on Administrative Procedure (hereafter 'CAP') analogised this practice to that 'common

did not affect the power of the Commissioners to deal with the case *de novo* if they chose; and at first, hearing examiners played little part in making final decisions. But gradually their role became more significant: they started making recommended decisions and the Commissioners became increasingly willing to accept such decisions as those of the Commission. Nevertheless, the decision-making power remained in the Commission, and the effect to be given to the work of hearing examiners was a matter of internal practice.[115] This working pattern of delegating finding of facts and making of recommendations was well established by 1914 when the Federal Trade Commission (FTC) was created.[116]

The practice of the agency with the power of final decision delegating part of the decision-making process to officials (hearing examiners) within the agency obviously raises questions about the degree to which the final decision is and should be constrained by the record generated by the hearing examiner. In *Morgan v United States*[117] the Supreme Court laid down the general principle that 'the one who decides must hear', thus imposing (imprecise) limits on the capacity of agencies to divide the decision-making function into component parts and to allocate some of those parts to hearing examiners. Uncertainty about the precise role of hearing examiners in the decision-making process and about how and by whom the final decision was made lay at the heart of much of the opposition to agencies at this time.

President Franklin D Roosevelt's New Deal programmes of the 1930s involved a very significant increase in federal government activity in areas of regulation and welfare, and the creation of 14 new administrative agencies as well as expansion of two others. The ICC and the FTC provided the model. Roosevelt was deeply suspicious of lawyers and judges, and viewed the common law and the courts as a serious obstacle to solving the economic and social problems associated with the Depression, which he thought required decisive, coordinated and expert executive action. As in England around this time, the growth of the administration became increasingly controversial in the US.[118] Lord Hewart's *The New Despotism* and CK Allen's *Bureaucracy Triumphant* found their US counterpart in JM Beck's *Our Wonderland of Bureaucracy* published in 1932.[119] Opposition to administrative agencies provided a focus both for those who were ideologically and

---

in equity courts, of appointing a special master to hear the evidence and report his findings and conclusions': *Report of the Attorney-General's Committee on Administrative* Procedure (Washington, 1941) (hereafter '*RCAP*') 24.

[115] The CAP found practice to be variable in this regard: *RACP* 44.

[116] For a brief discussion of the early operation of these and other agencies see RE Cushman, 'The Problem of the Independent Regulatory Commissions' in *Report of the President's Committee on Administrative Management* (Washington, 1937) 209–14; and for more detail Cushman's classic, *The Independent Regulatory Commissions* (New York, OUP, 1941).

[117] (1936) 298 US 468.

[118] H Burstein, 'The Development of the Administrative Process: 1932–1940' (1945) 5 *Law Guild Review* 172.

[119] New York, Macmillan Co. Beck was a former Republican Solicitor-General. The book is subtitled *A Study of the Growth of Bureaucracy in the Federal Government, and Its Destructive Effect on*

strategically opposed to the growth of government ('big business', as Roosevelt called them) and for groups, most notably the American Bar Association (ABA), which (for both principled and self-interested reasons) championed traditional legal protections for individual rights such as judicial review, separation of powers and 'the rule of law'.[120] Particularly controversial was that many agencies had the power both to investigate and prosecute regulatory infractions and to decide whether the facts supported the prosecution. Many people thought that the combination of these conflicting functions in the one body was contrary to the constitutional requirement of separation of powers, and favoured the abolition of multi-functional agencies and the establishment of mono-functional, free-standing agencies to conduct administrative hearings.

Another of the concerns of both supporters and opponents of the New Deal was that the growth of the administration and of independent agencies had been undesirably rapid, reactive and unplanned. To address this concern, in 1936 Roosevelt set up a Committee on Administrative Management to investigate the operations of the executive branch of government. In its 1937 Report the Committee memorably described 'independent regulatory commissions' as

> miniature independent governments set up to deal with the railroad problem, the banking problem, or the radio problem. They constitute a headless fourth branch of Government, a haphazard deposit of independent agencies and uncoordinated powers. They do violence to the basic theory of the American Constitution that there should be three major branches of the Government and only three. The Congress has found no effective way of supervising them, they cannot be controlled by the President, and they are answerable to the courts only in respect of the legality of their activities.[121]

The independent regulatory commissions, the Committee said, 'suffer from an internal inconsistency':[122] they are entrusted with policy-making functions for the performance of which they should be responsible to the President, but also with judicial functions in relation to which they should be independent. The

---

the Constitution. Ch XII, 'Bureaucracy as Prosecutor, Jury and Judge', draws heavily on Hewart. As a celebration of the growth of new institutions of government involvement in social and economic life, Landis's *The Administrative Process* may be cited as a US counterpart of Robson's *Justice and Administrative Law.* For a more recent, positive assessment of the US administrative process see JO Freedman, *Crisis and Legitimacy: The Administrative Process and American Government* (Cambridge, CUP, 1978). Of course, the US literature is primarily concerned with multi-functional agencies and with adjudication as one of those functions, whereas the English literature contributes primarily to debates about mono-functional bodies.

[120] A major account of the relevant events is GB Shepherd, 'Fierce Compromise: The Administrative Procedure Act Emerges from New Deal Politics' (1995–96) 90 *Northwestern University Law Review* 1557. See also J Grisinger, 'Law in Action: The Attorney-General's Committee on Administrative Procedure' (2008) 20 *The Journal of Policy History* 379.

[121] *Report of the President's Committee on Administrative Management,* 39–40.

[122] ibid 40.

combination in agencies of functions of policy-making, prosecution and adjudication was (the Committee said) 'unwholesome'.[123] What was needed was a structure that would restore appropriate control to the President while preserving appropriate independence to agencies.

The Committee proposed that the independent commissions should be absorbed into executive departments of government and restructured so that their policy-making functions would be performed by an administrative section and their judicial functions by a judicial section 'wholly independent' (except organisationally)[124] from the department and the President.[125] The implementation of such a restructuring would obviously have led to a major strengthening of the power and 'status'[126] of the President – which, no doubt, partly explains why the President described the Report as 'a great document of permanent importance'[127] – and why the Committee's proposals, which would have required Congressional action for their execution, were never implemented.

In the early years of the New Deal, the fight against agencies was primarily waged, with considerable success, in the courts. In 1933 the ABA established a Special Committee on Administrative Law, and in the following years the Committee made various proposals for the establishment of a specialist administrative court that would take over the functions of hearing examiners within agencies. In 1937, however, the balance of power on the Supreme Court shifted decisively in the government's favour, and the battle against the agencies moved from the courts to the legislature. The ABA's Special Committee abandoned its proposal for an administrative court in favour of a plan to reform agency procedure and strengthen judicial review of agency decisions, and in 1938 it submitted a reform bill to Congress (which became known as the Walter-Logan Bill) designed to regulate and constrain the conduct of agencies in various ways. In 1939, the President responded to the increased momentum for procedural reform by establishing the Attorney-General's Committee on Administrative Procedure with a view to formulating less radical reform proposals and defeating the Walter-Logan Bill.

Before the Committee on Administrative Procedure could report, in 1940 Congress passed the Walter-Logan Bill. Because the Bill imposed on agencies much more severe restrictions than Roosevelt was prepared to accept, the President vetoed the Bill; and a Congressional attempt to override the veto was narrowly defeated.[128] The Committee's Report, which was based on empirical

---

[123] ibid.

[124] ibid 41.

[125] These proposals were based on Cushman's 'special study' for the Committee: *Report of the President's Committee on Administrative Management*, 203–43.

[126] ibid 41.

[127] ibid iii.

[128] For savage criticism of Roosevelt's veto message by one of the architects of the Walter-Logan Bill see R Pound, 'The Place of the Judiciary in a Democratic Polity: An Examination of the Walter-Logan Bill Veto Message' (1941) 27 *American Bar Association Journal* 133. Pound was not alone

studies of the operations of 27 (mostly regulatory) federal agencies, has become a foundational document in US administrative law.

At first, the Second World War pushed administrative reform off the political agenda. But the large role played by the agencies in the war effort emphasised both their importance and their defects. Movement towards reform began again, this time with a new spirit of compromise that led eventually to the enactment in 1946 of the Administrative Procedure Act (APA), which was based on a draft bill included in the Report of the Committee on Administrative Procedure.[129] In its essentials, the Act remains unchanged to this day. Michael Asimow neatly summarises what the supporters of the New Deal got out of the compromise: multi-functional agencies survived; hearing examiners remained within agencies and the final power of decision remained with the agency; and only a very small proportion of agency hearings were formally subjected to the provisions of the APA. On the other hand, the APA was good for opponents of the New Deal in that it imposed various procedural requirements on the conduct of hearings; it created an internal separation of the fact-finding function of hearing examiners from the tasks of investigation and prosecution undertaken by other agency officials;[130] and it protected the position of adjudicators vis-à-vis agencies in various ways, raising their status and giving them a distinct identity within the agency.[131] Asimow goes so far as to describe the APA as 'the Magna Charta for the administrative state'.[132] The APA represented a fundamental shift from thinking about administrative adjudication constitutionally (in terms of separation of powers) to thinking about it in terms of procedural fairness and due process. As we have seen, the Report of the Franks Committee represented a similar shift to procedural thinking in the UK; and as we will see in the next section, this focus on procedure at the expense of separation of powers distinguishes both the US and the UK from Australia.

The provisions of the APA apply both to 'independent', non-departmental agencies and to 'executive', departmental agencies. At the heart of the APA lies a distinction between 'rule-making' and 'adjudication'.[133] It is the provisions on adjudication that are of concern here. 'Adjudication' is defined very broadly in the

---

in seeing the issues in terms of democracy versus absolutism. Accusations of Marxism, nazism and fascism abounded and in retrospect, it seems extraordinary that debates about public administration became so ideologically charged. Pound's argument is thoroughly Diceyan (ibid 135–36): democracy requires that the administration be subject to (the rule of) law and this requires (traditional) judges to enforce the law against the administration. The picture he paints of administrative lawlessness is reminiscent of Hewart's *The New Despotism*.

[129] B Schwartz, 'The American Administrative Procedure Act, 1946' (1947) *Law Quarterly Review* 43.

[130] For a useful discussion see LL Jaffe, 'Basic Issues: An Analysis' (1955) 30 *New York University Law Review* 1273, 1278–83.

[131] M Asimow, 'The Administrative Judiciary: ALJs in Historical Perspective' (2000) 20 *Journal of the National Association of Administrative Law Judges* 157.

[132] ibid 163.

[133] See 3.2 for more discussion of this distinction.

APA as 'process for the formulation of an order'. 'Order' is defined as 'the whole or a part of a final disposition … in a matter other than a rule but including licensing'. In other words, adjudication embraces all decisions except rule-making. The Act applies only to cases where another statute requires an adjudication to 'be determined on the record after an opportunity for an agency hearing'. This creates a distinction between 'formal' adjudication, which requires a hearing on the record conducted by an ALJ, and 'informal' adjudication, which does not.[134]

Formal, on-the-record hearings are conducted either by (members of) the agency or (typically) by an 'ALJ' (formerly a 'hearing examiner': the name was changed in 1972 in order to raise the status of the office; and the change has been seen as part of a process of 'judicialisation' of administrative adjudication).[135] ALJs are appointed by individual agencies on the basis of a competitive process conducted by the Office of Personnel Management (itself an independent agency). Appointments are effectively permanent, and an ALJ may not be removed, suspended, or suffer a reduction of grade or salary except for 'good cause established and determined by' the (independent) Merit Systems Protection Board (MSPB) after a hearing on the record.[136] Cases must be allocated to ALJs by rotation. ALJs may not 'perform duties inconsistent with their duties and responsibilities as administrative law judges' and may not be 'responsible to or subject to the supervision or direction of an employee or agent engaged in the performance of investigative or prosecuting functions for an agency';[137] and such

---

[134] Confusingly, the term 'informal adjudication' is used in a broader and a narrower sense. In the narrower sense, it refers to hearings conducted by AJs (as opposed to ALJs) that need not comply with the procedural requirements of the APA. See generally JH Frye III, 'Survey of Non-ALJ Hearing Programs in the Federal Government' (1992) 44 *Administrative Law Review* 262; PR Verkuil, 'Reflections Upon the Federal Administrative Judiciary' (1991–92) 39 *UCLA Law Review* 1341. The largest single group of AJs is employed to decide immigration cases. Some commentators argue that the APA should be amended to cover some informal hearings: eg, M Asimow, 'The Spreading Umbrella: Extending The APA's Adjudication Provisions to All Evidentiary Hearings Required by Statute' (2004) 56 *Administrative Law Review* 1003; CR Howarth Jr, 'Restoring the Applicability of the APAs Adjudicatory Procedures' (2004) 65 *Administrative Law Review* 1043. In its broader sense, 'informal adjudication' refers to administrative decision-making regardless of whether it is (or, perhaps, which is not) preceded by a hearing before a third party. The CAP defined informal adjudication as involving decision-making following 'inspections, conferences and negotiations' as opposed to 'formal hearings': *RCAP*, 5. The CAP observed that most decisions by agencies are made informally: *RCAP*, 35. Concerning procedural requirements for informal decision-making see RJ Krotoszynski Jr, 'Taming the Tail that Wages the Dog: Ex Post and Ex Ante Constraints on Informal Adjudication' (2004) 56 *Administrative Law Review* 1057; PL Strauss, *Administrative Justice in the United States*, 2nd edn (Durham, NC, Carolina Academic Press, 2002) 210–12.

[135] F Davis, 'Judicialization of Administrative Law: The Trial-Type Hearing and the Changing Status of the Hearing Officer [1977] *Duke Law Journal* 390. In 1947, Schwartz described the APA as evidence of a 'tendency in America … towards the judicialisation of … new forces of social control': n 129 above, 63.

[136] The CAP's aim was to bring about 'a more uniformly high quality of hearing officers': *RACP*, 6. See further 4.1.2 below.

[137] The CAP expressly rejected a proposal for the establishment of free-standing 'tribunals' in favour of internal separation of functions within agencies: *RCAP*, 55–60.

employees and agents may not participate in a hearing except as witness or counsel. These various provisions are designed to ensure that although ALJs are formally employed by and perform their functions within agencies, in conducting hearings they are free from control by members and employees of the agency.

Typically, the decision of the ALJ is final, subject to a *de novo* appeal to or review by the agency itself.[138] Thus while the ALJ, although embedded within the agency, operates independently, the outcome of hearings can in principle be reversed by a multi-functional entity – the agency – whose combined powers may give rise to the sorts of conflict of interest from which the APA seeks to insulate ALJs.[139] Moreover, on appeal or review the agency has all the powers it would have if it were making the initial decision. External review is provided in the form of judicial review, which is available, on various grounds listed in the APA, to 'a person adversely affected or aggrieved'. Technically, it is action of the 'agency' that is amenable to judicial review, not decisions of ALJs; but unless the decision of an ALJ is appealed to or reviewed by the agency, the ALJ's decision will be the agency's decision. Commenting in 1947, Bernard Schwartz stressed the breadth of judicial review in the US as compared with the position in England at that time. He argued that 'provisions for the finality of administrative action' would be unconstitutional in the US,[140] but the validity of this argument is doubtful.[141] In 1967 the Supreme Court held that there was a 'presumption in favour of judicial review of agency action,[142] although it is unclear how strongly this protects against exclusion of review.[143]

The APA regulates the procedure for formal hearings in various respects according to a judicial model. Thus parties are entitled to be represented at hearings; normally, the 'proponent of an order' bears the burden of proof; parties are entitled to present evidence orally and to cross-examine witnesses; and the 'record' of the hearing must include a statement of the ALJ's reasons. Writing in 1947, Schwartz considered the APA to be a major step forward in ensuring the 'fundamentals of just procedure' in the administrative process, although he was not prepared to say that 'a detailed code of administrative procedure is desirable or even feasible'.[144] The issue of a general code of administrative procedure is a matter of continuing debate about which more will be said later.[145]

---

[138] In some agencies, an appeal board is interposed between ALJs and the agency: RA Cass, 'Allocation of Authority Within Bureaucracies: Empirical Evidence and Normative Analysis (1986) 66 *Boston University Law Review* 1; JO Freedman, 'Review Boards in the Administrative Process' (1968–69) 117 *University of Pennsylvania Law Review* 547; RL Weaver, 'Appellate Review in Executive Departments and Agencies' (1996) 48 *Administrative Law Review* 251. See further 4.3.2 below.

[139] The APA specifically states that the provisions designed to separate adjudication from investigation and prosecution do not apply to decision-making by the agency.

[140] n 129 above, 60–61.

[141] S Breyer et al, *Administrative Law and Regulatory Policy*, 808–11.

[142] *Abbott Laboratories v Gardner* (1967) 387 US 136.

[143] See further 4.3.2.

[144] n 129 above, 62–63.

[145] See 6.5.1.

In 1955 the (second) Hoover Commission on Organisation of the Executive Branch of Government (which was appointed by President Eisenhower to review the operation of the administrative process) proposed that the adjudicatory functions of certain agencies be vested in a new administrative court.[146] In 1971 the President's Advisory Council on Executive Organisation (the 'Ash Council'), appointed by President Nixon, recommended that an administrative court should be established to review decisions of the major regulatory agencies.[147] Despite these and various other proposals for radical structural changes to the administrative process since the enactment of the APA in 1946,[148] there have been no major structural amendments of the regime established by the APA. On the other hand, there have been significant changes in public administration that have had an impact on the application of the provisions of the APA that regulate the activities of ALJs. These changes are further discussed in 3.2.

2.3.3 Australia

The Australian element of this book focuses on the Administrative Appeals Tribunal in particular and the system of federal 'merits review tribunals' in general; and this section will be mainly concerned with the historical background to and development of federal tribunals. The Australian federal legal system came into existence with the creation of the Commonwealth of Australia in 1901.

We may begin with a multi-functional agency called the Inter-State Commission which, like the US Interstate Commerce Commission, was originally conceived in the late 19th century as a railway regulator. Despite the fact that section 101 of the Australian Constitution provides that 'there shall be an Inter-State Commission with such powers of adjudication and administration as the Parliament deems necessary for the execution and maintenance ... of the provisions of this Constitution relating to trade and commerce', such a body has existed for a total of only about 20 years in the period since 1901. Section 101 sits in Chapter IV of the Constitution, which deals with 'finance and trade'. Chapters I–III (which are modelled on Articles I–III of the US Constitution) relate, respectively, to the legislature (on which legislative power is conferred), the executive (on

---

[146] *Report on Legal Services and Procedure*, 61–62; discussed CB Nutting, 'The Administrative Court' (1955) 30 *New York University Law Review* 1384; LL Jaffe, 'Basic Issues: An Analysis' (1955) 30 *New York University Law Review* 1273, 1283–89.

[147] The President's Advisory Council on Executive Organization, *A New Regulatory Framework: Report on Selected Independent Regulatory Agencies*. See NL Nathanson, 'The Administrative Court Proposal' (1971) 57 *Virginia Law Review* 996.

[148] See eg, NL Nathanson, 'Proposals for an Administrative Appellate Court' (1973) 25 *Administrative Law Review* 85; R Marquadt and EM Wheat, 'The Developing Concept of an Administrative Court' (1981) 33 *Administrative Law Review* 301; KY Kauper, 'Protecting the Independence of Administrative Law Judges: A Model Administrative Law Judge Corps Statute' (1984–85) *U of Michigan Journal of Law Reform* 537; PW Parmele, 'Preserving the Judicial Independence of Federal Administrative Law Judges: Are Existing Protections Sufficient?' (1987–88) *Journal of Law and Policy* 207.

which executive power is conferred) and the judiciary (on which judicial power is conferred); and this injects into the Australian constitutional system an element of separation of powers lacking in the systems of the UK and the Australian states. Under section 103, members of the Commission hold office for a period of seven years whereas under section 72, judges of Chapter III courts were originally appointed for life (now until the age of 70). As in the case of Chapter III judges, the salary of members of the Commission is guaranteed, and they can be removed only on an address of both Houses of Parliament for misbehaviour or incapacity.

This constitutional scheme could be interpreted as indicating that the regime of separated powers should be applied only to institutions established under Chapters I–III and not to the Inter-State Commission. Apparently adopting this interpretation, Parliament conferred judicial power on the first Inter-State Commission, which operated between 1913 and 1920. However, in 1915 the High Court held that because the Inter-State Commission, not having been established in accordance with the provisions of Chapter III, was not a 'court', it could not be given the (judicial) power to issue an injunction.[149]

As we saw in 2.3.2, multi-functional agencies were constitutionally controversial in the US for many years, but the opposition was eventually bought off by the enactment of the APA in 1946. In Australia, by contrast, the 'dominant principle of demarcation'[150] that Parliament cannot confer judicial power on non-judicial bodies – which arguably reflects the importance of judicial independence and the separation of judicial power in the British version of separation of powers, and which was first enunciated by the High Court in 1909[151] – has effectively prevented the creation of multi-functional agencies of the sort that proliferated in the UK in the 19th century and that are a basic feature of public administration in the US. As a result, embedded adjudication is unknown in Australia.

However, the principle that judicial power cannot be conferred on non-judicial bodies not only presented an obstacle to the creation of multi-functional agencies. It also threatened to pose problems for governments wishing to create free-standing, mono-functional administrative tribunals of the type that came to characterise administrative adjudication in the UK in the first half of the 20th

---

[149] *New South Wales v The Commonwealth* (1915) 20 CLR 54 (the '*Wheat* case'). The US Interstate Commerce Commission originally lacked the power to make coercive orders and had to apply to a court for such an order. However, it was given this power in 1906 and in the US, no constitutional barrier has been erected preventing conferral of such powers on administrative agencies. However, agencies cannot punish for disobedience of their coercive orders – only a court can do that. A corollary of the power to make coercive orders is that decisions of the agency are immediately enforceable subject to appeal or review. In *Brandy v Human Rights and Equal Opportunity Commission* (1995) 183 CLR 245 the High Court of Australia held that the power to make immediately enforceable decisions subject to appeal or review was a judicial function which could not be conferred on a body that was not a Chapter III court.

[150] *Wheat* case, 90 (Isaacs J).

[151] *Huddart Parker & Co Pty Ltd v Moorhead* (1909) 8 CLR 330, 355 (Griffith CJ).

century.[152] In 1925 the High Court held that the federal system for adjudication of taxation disputes was unconstitutional on the ground that it involved the exercise of judicial power by a review tribunal, which was not a Chapter III court.[153] The main problems identified by the Court were that decisions of the tribunal on questions of fact were expressed to be final and conclusive, and that there was a right of appeal on questions of law from the tribunal to the High Court in its appellate, as opposed to its original, jurisdiction. In reaction to the Court's decision the legislation was amended in various respects, and it was provided that in reviewing decisions, the tribunal 'shall have all the powers and functions' of the original decision-maker, and that the decision of the tribunal was to be deemed to be that of the original decision-maker.[154] The High Court dismissed a challenge to the amended legislation,[155] being motivated to do so, it seems, at least partly by perceived advantages of tribunals over courts but also by the need to supplement the inadequate judicial resources for administrative adjudication then available in the federal system.[156]

As in the UK, free-standing, mono-functional administrative tribunals proliferated at both the federal and the state levels in Australia in the first half of the 20th century. However, the next important episode in our story did not arise out of the operation of a tribunal that adjudicated disputes between citizen and government but rather from the federal system for the resolution of industrial disputes between employers and employees. In 1956 the High Court was presented with a case involving a challenge to the constitutionality of conferral on the Commonwealth Court of Conciliation and Arbitration (CCCA) (an industrial relations body) of the power to issue orders of compliance with its awards and to punish, as contempt of court, disobedience of such orders. The High Court controversially decided that the constitutional principle of separation of judicial power required not only that judicial functions could not validly be conferred on non-judicial bodies, but also that non-judicial functions could not validly be conferred on judicial bodies (unless incidental to judicial functions).[157] A majority of the High Court held that the primary functions of the CCCA were arbitral and non-judicial, and consequently that conferral on it of the judicial power of making enforceable orders was unlawful because the Constitution prevented the conferral of both judicial and non-judicial powers on the same

---

[152] In addition, it also hindered the use of tribunals to adjudicate disputes between citizens.

[153] *British Imperial Oil Co Ltd v Federal Commissioner of Taxation* (1925) 35 CLR 422.

[154] Income Tax Assessment Act 1992–95 s 44(1). Such provisions were foreshadowed by Isaacs J: (1925) 35 CLR 422, 435.

[155] *Federal Commissioner of Taxation v Munro* (1926) 38 CLR 153; affirmed by the Privy Council in *Shell Co of Australia Ltd v Federal Commissioner of Taxation* (1930) 44 CLR 530.

[156] See particularly the judgment of Isaacs J in *Federal Commissioner of Taxation v Munro* (1926) 38 CLR 153. Ironically, Isaacs J was the chief architect of the principle that judicial power could not be conferred on non-judicial bodies. But he also realised that it would cause great inconvenience if applied to prevent the development of non-judicial administrative tribunals.

[157] *R v Kirby, ex p Boilermakers' Society of Australia* (1956) 94 CLR 254; affirmed on appeal by the Privy Council: *A-G (Commonwealth) v R, ex p Boilermakers' Society of Australia* (1957) 95 CLR 529.

institution. It followed from this reasoning not only that judicial powers could not be conferred on non-judicial bodies but also that non-judicial powers could not be conferred on judicial bodies. The Court rejected an alternative approach (espoused by the minority) under which non-judicial power (such as the arbitral power) could validly be conferred on a body properly constituted as a court (such as the CCCA) provided the non-judicial power was not inconsistent with the proper constitutional role of courts.[158]

The relevance of the decision in the *Boilermakers'* case to administrative adjudication by tribunals did not become clear until 1971, which saw the publication of the report of a committee appointed by the federal government (the Commonwealth Administrative Review Committee, commonly known as the Kerr Committee).[159] Ironically, the focus of the Committee's terms of reference was on a proposal to establish a new federal court to review 'administrative decisions'. Arrangements for non-judicial administrative adjudication were not explicitly mentioned, although the Committee was instructed to consider 'the desirability of introducing legislation along the lines of the United Kingdom Tribunals and Inquiries Act 1958'. Dissatisfaction with what were seen as the technicality, defects and inadequacies of the inherited English system of judicial review based on the common law prerogative writs became acute in the 1950s and 1960s in Australia, and Australian lawyers no doubt observed moves by English courts in that period to exercise their review powers more aggressively. In this regard, the work of the Kerr Committee led to the creation (by the Administrative Decisions (Judicial Review) Act 1977) of a statutory regime of judicial review built on conceptual foundations very different from those of the common law,[160] and to the establishment of the Federal Court of Australia, which is now the most important federal forum for judicial review and which has since been supplemented by the Federal Magistrates Court.

Concerning administrative tribunals, the situation at the federal level in Australia appears to have been rather different from that which confronted the Franks Committee in England. The system of federal administrative tribunals was apparently not as large or diverse as the English tribunal system, and in Australia there appears not to have been the high level of concern about the processes and procedures of administrative adjudication that existed in England

---

[158] However, this alternative approach is used to determine when individual Chapter III judges may perform non-judicial functions: L Zines, *The High Court and the Constitution*, 5th edn (Sydney, The Federation Press, 2008) 262–67; K Walker, 'Persona Designata, Incompatibility and the Separation of Powers' (1997) 8 *Public Law Review* 153; F Wheeler, 'Federal Judges as Holders of Non-Judicial Office' in B Opeskin and F Wheeler (eds), *The Australian Federal System* (Melbourne, Melbourne University Press, 2000). It is the basis on which the appointment of a Chapter III judge as President of the Administrative Appeals Tribunal was held valid in *Drake v Minister for Immigration and Ethnic Affairs* (1979) 24 ALR 577.

[159] Report of the Commonwealth Administrative Review Committee (Parliamentary Paper No 144 of 1971) (hereafter 'Kerr Committee Report').

[160] See P Cane and L McDonald, *Principles of Administrative Law: Legal Regulation of Governance* (Melbourne, OUP, 2008) chs 3–5.

and the US as far back as the 1920s. In 1968 the Victorian Statute Law Revision Committee had recommended the creation of a general Administrative Appeals Tribunal in the State of Victoria.[161] However, the main catalyst for this proposal appears to have been a perception that judicial review was an inadequate mechanism for challenging government decisions. This emphasis on the need to supplement judicial review (and also, as we have already noted, to simplify its grounds and procedures) was also central to the Kerr Committee's approach. By contrast, the Donoughmore and Franks Committees had both been established to address concerns about administrative decision-making, not judicial review.

The Kerr Committee noted the rejection by the Franks Committee of proposals for the establishment of a general administrative appeals tribunal or an administrative court.[162] This issue of the choice between tribunals with wide and diverse jurisdiction and tribunals with narrow and specialised jurisdiction was central to the thinking of the Kerr Committee. Even more important, however, was the introduction at the very beginning of the Report of a concept that does not appear in the terms of reference and which was, apparently, an invention of the legal imagination of the members of the Committee: review of decisions 'on the merits'. The system of common law judicial review, the Committee said, 'cannot provide an adequate review of administrative decisions'[163] and needs to be supplemented by review on the merits. Moreover, the Committee noted, no provision was then made for reviewing the merits of the bulk of federal government decisions; and so new arrangements were needed for reviewing government decisions on the merits. This conclusion, the Committee said, raises the further questions of whether the power to review on the merits should be conferred on a court or on 'some other tribunal'; and if on the latter, whether review should be conducted by a single tribunal with wide and diverse jurisdiction or by a number of tribunals with narrow, specialised jurisdiction. In short, the Kerr Committee posed a question that had never hitherto been asked: what is the best arrangement for providing 'merits review' of 'administrative decisions'?

The Kerr Committee's recommendation for the establishment of a 'general Administrative Review Tribunal'[164] was based on pragmatic considerations and on a constitutional argument which went roughly as follows: (1) reviewing the merits of government decisions is a non-judicial function because it typically involves the resolution of 'non-justiciable' issues;[165] (2) because it involves a

---

[161] Kerr Committee Report, paras 76–82.

[162] Kerr Committee Report, paras 142–43. Similarly, the Committee interpreted its term of reference relating to the Tribunals and Inquiries Act 1958 primarily as concerning the choice between a general tribunal and a set of specialist tribunals, and the related question of the role of an advisory body to oversee the tribunal system: Kerr Committee Report, ch 13.

[163] Kerr Committee Report, para 5.

[164] Kerr Committee Report, para 291.

[165] This pivotal argument is difficult and weak: P Cane, 'Merits Review and Judicial Review: The AAT as Trojan Horse' (2000) 28 *Federal Law Review* 213, 215–17. It seems to rest on foundations similar to those of the distinction between judicial and quasi-judicial functions associated with the Donoughmore Committee on Ministers' Powers. See further 5.3.2.1.

non-judicial function, merits review jurisdiction cannot be conferred on a court; (3) it is desirable to make general provision for review of the merits of government decisions; (4) to this end, therefore, it is necessary to create a non-judicial body with wide merits review jurisdiction. This argument is obviously based on the understanding of the principle of separation of judicial power that underpins the decision in the *Boilermakers'* case. So understood, *Boilermakers'* fundamentally changed the significance of separation of powers for administrative adjudication. In the taxation cases, non-judicial administrative tribunals were conceptualised as a pragmatically necessary supplement to courts. By contrast, the Kerr Committee's use of the *Boilermaker's* principle turned tribunals into constitutionally necessary alternatives to courts. It also established that there are two distinct species of administrative adjudication: judicial review (a judicial function of courts) and merits review (a non-judicial function of tribunals), although the Kerr Committee said very little about the nature of merits review and its relationship to judicial review. These issues are dealt with in detail in Chapter 5 below.

The Administrative Appeals Tribunal (AAT) was created to give effect to the Kerr Committee's recommendation for the establishment of a general administrative review tribunal. In the Australian federal system, it is the peak 'merits review tribunal', as this type of body is commonly called. It now has jurisdiction to review decisions made under more than 400 provisions in federal statutes covering a diverse set of governmental activities. In some areas (such as tax and workers' compensation) the AAT operates as a first-tier external reviewer, and in others (such as social security and veterans' benefits) as a second-tier external reviewer. In reviewing decisions, the AAT 'may exercise all the powers and discretions that are conferred by any relevant enactment on the person who made the decision'. This formula was based on the wording approved by the High Court in 1926 in relation to review of taxation decisions. The AAT may affirm or vary the decision under review or set it aside and make a substitute decision or remit the matter to the decision-maker for reconsideration.[166] These provisions contain the core of the concept of 'merits review'. In one of the first cases arising out of the work of the AAT, its task was described as being to ensure that the 'correct or preferable' decision was made.[167] This phrase, along with the idea that the AAT 'stands in the shoes of the decision-maker', informally encapsulates the effect of the statutory specification of the AAT's role. Indeed, in its 1995 Review of Commonwealth Merits Review Tribunals, *Better Decisions*,[168] the Administrative Review Council (ARC) said that the 'overall objective of the merits review

---

[166] Administrative Appeals Tribunal Act 1975 s 43.
[167] *Drake v Minister for Immigration and Ethnic Affairs* (1979) 2 ALD 60, 68 (Bowen CJ and Deane J).
[168] Administrative Research Council Report No 39 (Canberra, Australian Government Publishing Service, 1995) (hereafter '*Better Decisions*'), vii. For a critical analysis of the report see J Disney,

system is to ensure that all administrative decisions are correct and preferable'. The ARC is an advisory body, created as a result of a recommendation of the Kerr Committee, with a watching brief over the whole of the administrative justice system.

Although the Kerr Committee recommended the creation of a 'general' (ie, non-specialist) tribunal, it also contemplated that existing specialist tribunals might continue to operate and that new specialist tribunals might be created 'in special circumstances'.[169] One of the areas in which the AAT was given jurisdiction was deportation following conviction of an immigrant for a criminal offence. Because of the political sensitivity of this area of policy, the AAT did not initially have the power to make a decision in substitution for the decision under review but only to make recommendations to the Minister. Even so, successive governments found the AAT's activities in this area irksome, and this partly explains the establishment of specialist, first-tier immigration tribunals – now the Migration Review Tribunal and the Refugee Review Tribunal – from the decisions of which there is no appeal to the AAT.[170] Other high-volume, specialist, first-tier tribunals are the Social Security Appeals Tribunal and the Veterans' Review Board. The AAT can review decisions of both of these tribunals. Decisions of the AAT (and of other merits review tribunals) are subject to judicial review (unless such review is excluded by a statutory privative clause);[171] and there is a right of appeal from decisions of the AAT to the Federal Court on questions of law.

Although the AAT was expressly established as a non-court, it has always been seen as an essentially judicial institution, at least in the sense that its procedures are basically judicial and its members understand their task in judicial terms (as being to 'act judicially');[172] and this despite the fact that a committee, appointed in the wake of the Kerr Committee to advise which administrative decisions should be subject to merits review, expressed the opinion that it was 'desirable

'Reforming the Administrative Review System: For Better or For Worse? For Richer or For Poorer?' in J McMillan (ed), *The AAT – Twenty Years Forward* (Canberra, Australian Institute of Administrative Law, 1998).

[169] Kerr Report, para 280. See also Final Report of the Committee on Administrative Discretions (1973) ('Bland Committee Report') paras 185–90.

[170] The Principal Member of the MRT and RRT may, under certain circumstances, refer decisions to the AAT, but this power has been exercised only once.

[171] Such a clause cannot exclude the judicial review jurisdiction of the High Court of Australia under s 75(v) of the Constitution. See generally Cane and McDonald, *Principles of Administrative Law*, ch 7 and 4.3.2.2(i) below.

[172] 'The legislature clearly contemplated that the Tribunal, though exercising administrative power, should be constituted upon the judicial model, separate from, and independent of, the Executive': *Re Becker and Minister for Immigration and Ethnic Affairs* (1977) 1 ALD 158, 161 (Brennan J). See also *Re Tam Anh Le and Secretary, Department of Education, Science and Training* (2006) 90 ALD 83, [24]–[29]. '[S]uch independence ... is essential to the compatibility of performing a non-judicial function with the holding of office as a Ch III judge': *Wilson v Minister for Aboriginal and Torres Strait Islander Affairs* (1996) 189 CLR 1, 18 (Brennan CJ, Dawson, Toohey, McHugh and Gummow JJ).

that the community should recognise... [t]ribunals for what they are – not courts but tribunals whose major activities are the review of decisions under administrative discretions, sometimes with mere recommendatory functions, and, themselves, in much of their jurisdiction, an extension of the total administrative process'.[173]

The first large-scale public review of merits review tribunals did not take place until the 1990s. In its 1995 *Better Decisions* report the ARC focused on the AAT and the high-volume first-tier merits review tribunals in the areas of immigration, social security and veterans' benefits. The Council made various somewhat bland recommendations for promoting the accessibility and user-friendliness of merits review tribunals. It took a pluralistic, laissez-faire attitude to procedure, considering 'that it would not be useful to be overly prescriptive in relation to tribunal styles and levels of formality'[174] and encouraging each tribunal to adopt procedures appropriate to the nature of its jurisdiction. However, the Council did express the opinion that courts 'will always remain more formal than tribunals need be, and are unlikely to provide an appropriate procedural model for tribunals'.[175] A major theme of *Better Decisions* concerned the so-called 'normative function' of merits review. One of the implications of the ARC's understanding of the function of merits review – 'to ensure that *all* administrative decisions are correct and preferable'[176] – is that the task of a merits review tribunal is not confined to ensuring that the individual decisions it reviews are correct or preferable but extends to making a contribution towards raising the general standard of administrative decision-making so as to reduce the incidence of (successful) applications for external review. The ARC made various suggestions about ways in which agencies could promote realisation of the normative goal of merits review. This topic is discussed in more detail in 5.5.

Undoubtedly the most significant and radical of the ARC's recommendations concerned the structure of the tribunal system. As we have noted, both the Kerr Committee and Bland Committee contemplated the continued existence of specialist tribunals alongside the general tribunal. However, developments since the 1970s were seen by the ARC as having produced a system that lacked the coherence contemplated by these Committees; and it took upon itself the task of proposing a restructuring of the tribunal system 'to create a whole that is greater than the sum of its constituent parts'.[177] It recommended the creation of a two-tier Administrative Review Tribunal (ART) into which the AAT, and the four first-tier merits review tribunals which were the subject of the ARC's report, were to be amalgamated. The lower tier, which would operate in subject-specific divisions, was to provide external merits review as of right from decisions of

---

[173] Bland Committee Report, para 171.
[174] *Better Decisions*, 28.
[175] *Better Decisions*, 30.
[176] *Better Decisions*, vii (emphasis added).
[177] *Better Decisions*, x.

government officials and internal, departmental reviewers. The upper tier was to provide a further review, by leave, in cases raising matters of general significance (such as issues of statutory interpretation), or in which the decision of the lower tier arguably 'involved a manifest error of fact or ... law that is likely to have materially affected the decision',[178] or in which new relevant information has come to light that could not reasonably have been discovered prior to the finalisation of the case in the lower tier. Although review by a 'review panel' in the upper tier was to be available only on these grounds, the function of the review panel was to be 'to conduct merits review of the entire decision'.[179] Decisions of both tiers were to be subject to statutory judicial review by the Federal Court, but the ARC made no recommendation for appeals from the ART to the Federal Court. As for membership of the ART, the ARC recommended that only the President should be required to have legal qualifications and that no member should be required to be a judge.

Criticism of the ARC's approach focused on two main issues. One was diversity. Commentators worried that amalgamation of diverse specialist tribunals into a single body would – despite the divisional structure of the lower tier – lead to an undesirable degree of uniformity in the handling of different types of case.[180] Some detected in the somewhat ambivalent tone of the ARC's discussion of the constitution of tribunals[181] a risk that the operation of the lower tier of the ART would involve greater use of single-member panels, and that this would favour appointment of lawyers, thus reducing the range of experience and expertise represented amongst the membership of the ART.[182] By contrast, the second main point of criticism rested on a fear that on balance, the ARC's proposals would shift the AAT in particular and the tribunal system in general from a judicial to an administrative model both in terms of membership and procedures. It is not surprising that the ARC's proposals for a single tribunal generated conflicting reactions because the underlying aim was to reap the benefits of both generalism and specialism in the one institution. Generalism tends to favour an emphasis on legal skills and relative procedural formality whereas specialism tends to favour an emphasis on non-legal skills and relative procedural informality. The ARC's proposals were insufficiently detailed or elaborated to enable observers to assess with confidence the chance that they would achieve what each considered to be the ideal mix of generalism and specialism. Indeed, *Better Decisions* is permeated by an ambivalent failure

---

[178]   *Better Decisions*, 149.
[179]   *Better Decisions*, 152.
[180]   eg R Bacon, 'Are the Babies Being Thrown Out with the Bathwater?: Retaining the Benefits of Specialist Tribunals within the ART' in C Finn (ed), *Administrative Law for the New Millennium* (Canberra, Australian Institute of Administrative Law, 2000) 150.
[181]   *Better Decisions*, 35–39.
[182]   Disney, n 168 above, 349–50.

adequately to resolve the tension between the contrasting demands of generalism and specialism, uniformity and diversity, legal and non-legal values.[183]

In March 1997 the Government announced that it had accepted in principle the ARC's proposal for a new Administrative Review Tribunal amalgamating the AAT and the other major merits review tribunals. In the event, however, the Government decided to leave the Veterans' Review Board (VRB) out of the proposed ART structure, thus casting doubt on the rationale for major structural change. The Government's announced objectives in accepting the ARC's proposal were to reduce the number of applications for review and the cost of the system, and to make tribunal procedure more flexible and less formal – a programme unlikely to win over many doubters.[184] So vocal was the opposition to the March announcement that in July 1997 the Government made a second announcement to reassure critics that the ART proposals would not undermine tribunal 'independence'.[185] However, implementing legislation introduced to Parliament in 2000 only served to increase the level of opposition to the amalgamation plan.[186] The views of many had been succinctly stated in 1998 by the then-President of the AAT, Justice Jane Matthews: 'The proposed amalgamation constitute[s] such a downgrading of the merits review system as to fundamentally threaten the quality and independence of external merits review.'[187]

The ART legislation was eventually defeated in the Australian Senate, and in February 2003 the Attorney-General announced that the Government would not pursue amalgamation. Instead, it settled for amending the AAT legislation to achieve some of the objectives of the ARC's proposals in *Better Decisions*. Amongst other things, the amending legislation aimed to increase the use of ADR techniques by the AAT. It also empowered the AAT to determine the scope of its review of a decision by limiting 'the questions of fact, the evidence and the issues that it considers';[188] it allowed multi-member panels of the AAT to be constituted entirely by the lowest grade of AAT member; and it slightly increased the power of the Federal Court when hearing appeals from the AAT – although appeals can relate only to a point of law, the Federal Court can now, in certain circumstances, make findings of fact instead of remitting the case back to the AAT.

For the moment, then, the federal tribunal system remains rather fragmented. The AAT exercises a mix of first-tier and second-tier external review jurisdiction

---

[183] RD Nicholson, 'Better Decisions: Commonwealth Administrative Review at the Crossroads' in McMillan, (ed) *The AAT – Twenty Years Forward* (Canberra, Australian Institute of Administrative Law, 1998).

[184] See eg, R Bacon, 'Tribunals in Australia – Recent Developments' (2000) 7 *Australian Journal of Administrative Law* 69, 71–75; 'A Study in Tribunal Amalgamation: The Importance of a Principled Approach' (2005) 12 *Journal of Social Security Law* 81, 94–95.

[185] R Creyke, 'Whither the Review System' in R Creyke and M Sassella (eds), *Targeting Accountability and Review: Current Issues in Income Support Law* (Canberra, Australian Institute of Administrative Law, 1998) 128–29.

[186] See eg, R Creyke, 'Tribunals: Divergence and Loss' (2001) 29 *Federal Law Review* 403.

[187] Cited in Bacon, 'Tribunals in Australia', n 184 above, 75.

[188] US agencies have a similar power under the APA in relation to appeals from decisions of ALJs.

but cannot review decisions of first-tier immigration tribunals. By contrast, three of the Australian states – New South Wales, Victoria and Western Australia – have successfully pursued tribunal amalgamation to a greater or lesser extent. Ironically, too, the federal experience was part of the inspiration for the amalgamation process currently underway in the UK. The potential benefits of amalgamation remain unclear. Nevertheless, debates about amalgamation raise some of the most basic questions about tribunals: specialism versus generalism, formality versus informality, legal versus non-legal expertise, and so on. Australia is a rich source of data about such issues, which are discussed at greater length in 4.3.1.

2.4 Conclusion

The discussion in this chapter has shown how the development of tribunals in three jurisdictions that share a common history for about 800 years has diverged in significant and immediately obvious ways. It has also shown how that divergence is intimately related to local economic, political and social circumstances as well as to distinctive ideas about public administration and distinctive theories of constitutional and institutional design. In the next chapter I will draw out of this historical account three models of administrative adjudication and administrative tribunals each based on one of the three jurisdictions on which this book focuses. A fourth, 'French' model will be briefly sketched as a counterpoint to the other three. The historical analysis in this chapter and the models that will be described in the next chapter will provide much of the raw material for the discussion in the rest of the book of a series of generic questions and issues to which administrative adjudication gives rise.

3

Models

I N THIS CHAPTER I elaborate four models of administrative adjudication, three based on the historical account in Chapter 2. By way of counterpoint, I will also say something about a fourth, French model. There are three main reasons for extending the analysis in this chapter to the French system. The first is that the French model is distinctively different from the other three. A second is that the distinctiveness of French model derives from a distinctive interpretation of that most central of constitutional ideas, the separation of powers; and as we will see, the differences between the other three models can also be understood in terms of different interpretations of that doctrine. Thirdly, the French model played a significant part, especially in England, in modern discussions and analyses of administrative adjudication and administrative tribunals, for some as a comparator and for others as an inspiration. These four models, together with the historical account in Chapter 2, will provide background and raw material for the analysis in the rest of the book of various features of administrative adjudication and administrative tribunals.

3.1 The UK Model

The two most distinctive characteristics of administrative tribunals in the UK system are that they are free-standing, mono-functional adjudicatory institutions and that they are understood as being 'court substitutes'. In historical terms, tribunals are often analogised to courts that were relatively closely associated with the executive and through which the Monarch could participate in or at least influence the adjudicatory process, especially in cases that were of particular interest to the government. In the period between the abolition of the last of such courts in the middle of the 17th century and the creation in the 19th century of multi-functional, non-departmental, central administrative agencies, central government was little involved in adjudication of disputes between citizen and government, which was largely undertaken by Justices of the Peace at local level.

Administrative adjudication embedded within multi-functional, non-departmental agencies was a short-lived phenomenon in England partly because of the development of ministerial responsibility and partly because of the strength of the principle of judicial independence. A corollary of the principle of ministerial responsibility is that policy-making and policy-implementation should be undertaken primarily by political heads of government departments (Ministers) and by officials who are directly answerable to them. Hence, in the course of the 19th century, multi-functional agencies were stripped of their functions of making and implementing policy and left only with an adjudicatory function. Once this happened, and as a result of the similarity of the function of agencies to that of courts, similar ideas of separation and independence were applied to tribunals as had been developed in relation to courts in the 17th century. Thus, by the third decade of the 20th century it was widely agreed that if there were to be administrative tribunals, they should be separate from and in some sense 'independent' of the departments whose decisions they reviewed. However, the precise requirements of the ideal of independence remained contested throughout the 20th century. It was not until the turn of the 21st century that institutional arrangements for non-judicial administrative adjudication were firmly based on the principle not only that tribunals should be free-standing rather than embedded but also that they should not be organisationally linked to the departments responsible for making the decisions which they had jurisdiction to review, either in terms of appointment of their members or the provision of staff and resources, or supervision and monitoring of day-to-day operations.

By contrast with the position in the UK, in the US – where the executive and the legislature are separated rather than integrated – creation of multi-functional agencies, endowed with a mix of legislative, executive and judicial powers, which were not part of the departmental structure of government, and so were not directly answerable to the President, provided a technique by which Congress could limit the control of the Chief Executive over the day-to-day running of government and the regulation of economic and social life. Moreover, because the Supreme Court never interpreted the Constitution as prohibiting the delegation of either legislative or judicial power by Congress to such independent agencies, ideas of separation of powers did not, ironically, exert as much pressure as they did in England for the separation and independence of adjudicators from policy-makers and implementers.

Conceptualising mono-functional administrative tribunals as being similar to courts in nature and function obviously raises the question of why it is necessary or desirable to have two different types of adjudicatory body. So long as administrative adjudication was embedded within multi-functional agencies, the question did not present itself in this stark form because although such agencies might perform functions similar to those performed by courts, they did much else besides. Multi-functional agencies were so different from courts that it was clear why there was room for both. But once the difference between agencies and courts diminished, the issue of redundancy became more pressing. Note that the question here is not why it is desirable to make provision for adjudication of disputes between citizen and government. That question might be answered in terms, for instance, of providing citizens with an avenue for redress of grievances, bolstering the legitimacy of government decision-making and improving its quality. Rather the question is why, since the early 19th century, when confronted with a choice between allocating jurisdiction to review a particular category of government decisions to a court or to some other type of adjudicatory body, UK legislatures have commonly chosen to allocate the jurisdiction to a tribunal rather than a court. Historically, the standard explanation was that by comparison with courts and judicial adjudication, tribunals and non-judicial adjudication were quicker, cheaper, more accessible and user-friendly, more expert and specialised, and more empathetic to the ideology of welfare and regulation.[1] The received wisdom until the middle of the 20th century was that although non-judicial adjudication was essentially similar in nature to judicial adjudication, tribunals were better administrative adjudicators than courts in various ways. In order to maintain this approach convincingly, it was necessary to draw quite a sharp distinction between tribunals and courts – and this is what the Donoughmore Committee did.

The received wisdom was dealt a serious blow by the Franks Committee, which made the important ideological move of associating tribunals with courts ('judicialising' them, we might say). Matters got worse in the following decades as researchers began increasingly to question whether tribunals actually realised the advantages attributed to them, and as various changes to the procedures and operations of courts began to reduce the apparent differences between judicial and non-judicial adjudicatory institutions – at least some judicial institutions began to look and behave more like tribunals than like paradigm courts. These developments raised an uncomfortable question: if there were no major ideological or pragmatic reasons for having two types of adjudicatory institutions, why not amalgamate them into a single adjudicatory branch of government? The case for amalgamation was strengthened by the unsystematic structure of the tribunal sector. The unplanned growth of tribunals had been a matter of comment for most of the 20th century. Now that the court and tribunal sectors are being integrated into a single, twin-track system of adjudicatory institutions headed by

---

[1] It is a striking feature of the history of tribunals in the UK that, despite their supposed, and widely accepted, practical advantages over courts, they have always been considered in some sense inferior. Thus, the Donoughmore Committee thought they should be used only exceptionally as an alternative either to a court or an executive decision-making process, and the Franks Committee thought that while they were preferable to executive decision-makers, they should be used only exceptionally as an alternative to a court. This schizophrenia about tribunals is well illustrated in Harry Street's Hamlyn Lectures, *Justice in the Welfare State* (London, Stevens & Sons, 1975) 2–10. On the one hand, he unfavourably compares tribunals to courts by likening the latter to a Rolls-Royce and the former to a Mini Minor; while on the other he provides a lengthy, eight-point analysis of the defects of courts that explain why tribunals have been preferred as reviewers of decisions about welfare benefits. However, in doing so he is not, he tells us, 'passing strictures on the courts'. Then, as if to damn tribunals with faint praise, he observes that judges are not hostile to tribunals but 'accept them as a necessity' while insisting that disputes 'ordinarily ought to be tried in the courts' unless there is a 'powerful case' to prefer a tribunal.

the two highest central courts, it is difficult to see what the theoretical or constitutional significance of the distinction between them might be.

The distinction between courts and tribunals becomes even more puzzling when we observe that perhaps because tribunals were, indirectly at least, a product of centralisation of governmental functions, they are typically compared with the superior central courts. Dissatisfaction with central courts and their processes was a significant factor in the development of embedded administrative adjudication in the 19th century, and it is these courts that have always occupied centre stage in constitutional theorising, even if not in constitutional history. In the new integrated adjudicative sector, it is easy to think of the First-tier and Upper Tribunals as part of the machinery of centralised justice. This is partly because the statutory statement of the principle of judicial independence, which covers the tribunal judiciary as well as the court judiciary, was developed in relation to, and has its prime application to, judges of the central courts. If we imagine tribunals in this sort of framework, it is natural to emphasise the difference between them and courts even if they are understood to be performing an essentially similar function. One reason is that, whereas judges of superior courts are lawyers, tribunal 'members' (as opposed to tribunal 'judges') are not. Another is that the procedures of superior courts tend to sit at the formal end of the spectrum of adjudicatory processes, whereas the procedures of many tribunals are at the informal end. However, if we compare tribunals with magistrates courts (which have a more local flavour and orientation), they may appear to be more court-like than such bodies because many tribunal members are legally qualified whereas magistrates typically are not. Again, if we compare tribunals with small claims courts and the like, and if proper account is taken of the constant pressure to de-formalise court procedure, the tendency of tribunals to relative procedural informality may look less distinctive.

Administrative tribunals, as understood in this book, have often been called 'court-substitutes'. In the light of the foregoing analysis, there seems little reason not to call them simply 'courts'. Tribunals appear to be significantly different from courts only when courts are equated with a particular subset of the institutions that bear the name and only when insufficient attention is paid to the considerable diversity amongst courts in terms of membership and procedure. In the UK model, then administrative tribunals are best understood not as substitutes for courts but rather as a species of court.

3.2 The US Model

Central to the analysis in this book is the distinction between adjudication and implementation (1.2.2). As we saw in 2.3.2, the regime of the APA 1946 (APA) is based on a different distinction between adjudication (which is defined as 'process for the formulation of an order') and rule-making: adjudication is any and every decision-making process other than rule-making.[2] Adjudication in this sense may be formal – conducted by an ALJ under the provisions of the APA, or informal. By far the bulk of government decision-making, other than rule-making, is informal.[3] The APA regulates informal rule-making but not informal adjudication. Understanding the US model of administrative adjudication requires an explanation of the relationship between these two different concepts of adjudication – adjudication as contrasted with implementation and adjudication as contrasted with rule-making.

As contrasted with implementation, adjudication (it will be recalled) involves review of disputed primary decisions made in implementation of general rules. In this 'review model' adjudication, like implementation, may involve more-or-less mechanical application of norms to facts; but it (and implementation) may also involve creative interpretation of norms or require 'discretionary' creation of norms within parameters set by the terms of the norm being implemented. On the other hand, as contrasted with rule-making, while adjudication encompasses review of primary decisions, it may also be part of a process of (or a procedure for) making a primary decision. It is the latter 'primary decision model' of adjudication that appears chiefly to have been in the minds of the drafters of the APA, even though its provisions are not limited to adjudication in the primary decision-making context. Adjudication in the primary-decision sense, like adjudication in the review sense, may involve more-or-less mechanical application of norms; but it may also involve creative interpretation of norms or require 'discretionary' creation of norms within parameters set by the terms of a norm binding on the primary decision-maker. Indeed, in the US secondary literature, adjudication in the primary decision sense tends to be understood predominantly as a mode of norm-creation (or 'policy-making' as it is often called).

So understood, adjudication – unlike rule-making – involves norm-creation in the context of the consideration of individual cases and the consequent formulation of an order (as opposed to a rule). The decision-making model originally developed in the regulatory context by the ICC and adopted by other regulatory agencies, such as the FTC (established in 1914) and the New Deal agencies set up in the 1930s, involved policy-making in the context, for instance, of consideration of individual applications for licences and of enforcement measures taken against individuals for failure to comply with regulatory norms. Norms created through adjudication are analogous to judge-made common law norms while norms created through rule-making are analogous to legislative norms.

---

[2] For qualifications to this statement see M Asimow (ed), *A Guide to Federal Agency Adjudication* (Chicago, American Bar Association, 2003) 5–8.

[3] See further 2.3.2 n 134.

What explains the identification of adjudication, in the primary decision sense, as a mode of norm-creation? Technically, in a multi-functional regulatory agency the power to perform all of the various tasks involved in regulatory activities such as licensing and enforcement belongs to the agency itself – ie, to the individual or small group of individuals that constitute the agency in the formal sense, analogous to the political head of a government department. This we might refer to as a model of 'integrated' decision-making. From this technical starting point, the ICC developed what we might call a model of 'split' decision-making based on a distinction between 'policy-making' and 'fact-finding'. Under the split model, the task of fact-finding was allocated to officials of the agency originally called 'hearing examiners' (now 'administrative law judges' (ALJs) and 'administrative judges' (AJs)). The basic idea was that the facts as found by the hearing examiner would provide the empirical basis for policy-making by the agency. As we saw earlier, hearing examiners were at first not much involved in 'making the decision' – ie, in the policy-making phase of the process of formulating orders. Gradually, however, the role of the hearing examiner increased to the point where many decisions were effectively – although not technically – made by hearing examiners subject to review by or appeal to the agency. This development re-integrated the decision-making process but at the same time effectively relocated decision-making power in the hearing examiner as opposed to the agency itself. In 1935 the Supreme Court disapproved this re-location of decision-making power by informal delegation to hearing examiners when it enunciated the principle that 'the one who decides must hear', presenting agencies with serious challenges of time and resource management.[4]

The split decision-making model developed in US agencies is analogous to the public inquiry system of land use planning in the UK under which the 'decision' is technically made by the Minister on the basis of a report prepared by an inspector who inquires into the circumstances of the land use application. As in the US, the split system in the UK has developed into an integrated system: in the majority of cases, the decision is made by the inspector subject to an appeal to the Minister. Re-integration of split decision-making systems and consequent re-location of effective decision-making power caused much controversy in the US in the 1930s. Opponents of the New Deal and its agencies wanted the fact-finding process to be separated from the policy-making process, allocated to a free-standing agency independent of the policy-makers, and conducted according to a formal judicial model of evidence-gathering and fact-finding. Supporters of the New Deal, by contrast, wanted fact-finding and policy-making to remain as integrated as possible, and they favoured more informal and less judicialised modes of evidence-gathering and fact-finding.

---

[4] *Morgan v US* (1936) 298 US 468. For discussion see SG Breyer, RB Stewart, CR Sunstein and A Vermeule, *Administrative Law and Regulatory Policy: Problems, Text and Cases*, 6th edn (New York, Aspen Publishers, 2006) 734–38.

The APA represented a compromise between these two extremes. The integrated model was re-affirmed: typically the hearing examiner was to make the decision subject to review by or appeal to the agency. Procedure for hearings was formalised and judicialised in various respects. A Chinese wall was constructed within agencies between hearing examiners and other officials, and hearing examiners were accorded various protections, related to appointment, dismissal and salary, to bolster their independence from control or influence by the agency and its officers. These separation-of-functions provisions were particularly significant in relation to regulatory enforcement activities to prevent those responsible for policing compliance, and investigating and prosecuting non-compliers, from judging their own cause in what was, effectively, a quasi-criminal proceeding.[5]

At the time the APA was negotiated and enacted, consideration of individual cases (adjudication) was the dominant mode of policy-making in federal regulatory agencies and more significant than rule-making.[6] Moreover, in the minds of both supporters and opponents of the New Deal, regulation was the dominant mode of governmental involvement in economic and social life.[7] The first Social Security Act was passed in 1935, but no payments were made until 1940 and administration of social security was more-or-less ignored in the debates leading up to the enactment of the APA.[8] It was not until 1956 that the disability programme, which has provided the focus of scholarly discussion of social security administration in the US, was established.[9] In 1946 the majority of hearing examiners were employed in regulatory agencies and the majority of hearings were related to regulation. By the late 20th century the balance had

---

[5] By contrast, in *Richardson v Perales* (1971) 402 US 389 the Supreme Court held, in effect, that the system of social security benefit appeal hearings before ALJs, in which the agency did not appear at the hearing and the claimant was not represented, was not inconsistent with the separation-of-functions provisions of the APA.

[6] In a much-cited discussion of this distinction (RA Cass, 'Models of Administrative Action' (1986) 72 *Virginia Law Review* 363) Cass frames the distinction in terms respectively of 'incremental' and 'comprehensive' modes of decision-making and argues that analysis of the administrative process would be improved by cross-correlating that distinction with one between 'political' and 'apolitical' decision-making. In those terms, we can describe the APA's provisions about adjudication as a compromise between the political and the apolitical.

[7] 'American administrative lawyers have concentrated primarily upon the regulatory agency – for the natural reason that it serves to restrict private rights': B Schwartz and HWR Wade, *Legal Control of Government: Administrative Law in Britain and the United States* (Oxford, Clarendon Press, 1972) 27.

[8] The Attorney-General's Committee on Administrative Procedure concerned itself only with benefit agencies 'which disburse benefits after there has been an opportunity for some type of hearing' as opposed to those that ascertain entitlement to benefits by informal processes: *Final Report of the Attorney-General's Committee on Administrative Procedure* (Washington, 1941) 263.

[9] The seminal work is JL Mashaw, *Bureaucratic Justice: Managing Social Security Disability Claims* (New Haven and London, Yale University Press, 1983). Social security benefits paid in 1940 totalled $35 million; in 1950 the figure had grown to $961 million and by 1960 the total was $11.2 billion.

changed dramatically. Now, by far the majority of ALJs are employed in benefit agencies, and the majority of hearings are benefit-related.[10]

There has been another significant change in public administration in the US since the 1940s: rule-making has become the dominant mode of policy-making by both welfare and regulatory agencies.[11] As one commentator says, 'Since the explosion of environmental, health and safety regulation in the late '60s and early '70s, rulemaking has become the pre-eminent administrative activity in the United States'.[12] But the problems that led to the change were being discussed a decade earlier. In a 1960 report, JM Landis was highly critical of the emphasis on adjudication in the regulatory process with consequent delay and inefficiency, and of the failure of agencies to utilise rule-making to 'develop broad policies'.[13] Agencies themselves also began to appreciate the practical advantages of rule-making over adjudication as a way of making policy:[14] particularly in relation to programmes that affect large numbers of individuals and require the making of large numbers of individual decisions, rule-making enables policy-makers to delegate the processing of individual cases to relatively low-grade officials and makes it easier for policy-makers to influence and exercise control over the resolution of individual claims and disputes. In the welfare context, greater use of rules, rather than marking a retreat from policy-making by case-by-case adjudication, reflected a shift from an understanding of welfare as charity to welfare as a right and an associated desire to reduce the discretionary element in primary decision-making.[15]

Inevitably, the formal hearing by an independent hearing officer (ALJ) plays a different role in a system in which policy is made by rules than in a system in which policy is made by consideration of individual cases. The efficiency gains of

---

[10] DJ Gifford, 'Adjudication in Independent Tribunals: The Role of an Alternative Agency Structure' (1990–91) 66 *Notre Dame Law Review* 965; 'Federal Administrative Law Judges: The Relevance of Past Choices to Future Directions' (1997) 49 *Administrative Law Review* 2.

[11] For instance, the Federal Trade Commission, established in 1914, issued its first regulatory rule in 1964, and power to make rules was formally conferred on it by Congress in 1975. Many of the agencies established in the 1960s and 1970s were expressly given rule-making power. The modern law of judicial review in the US has been predominantly made in the context of control of agency rule-making. For a useful overview in the regulatory context see DJ Gifford, 'The New Deal Regulatory Model: A History of Criticisms and Refinements' (1983–84) 68 *Minnesota Law Review* 299, 316–23.

[12] PL Strauss, *Administrative Justice in the United States*, 2nd edn (Durham, NC, Carolina Academic Press, 2002) 226. But contrast SP Croley, *Regulation and Public Interests: The Possibility of Good Regulatory Governance* (Princeton and Oxford, Princeton University Press, 2007) 110: 'most independent [regulatory] agencies rely heavily on formal adjudication ... [and] employ informal adjudication processes to conduct regulatory business'.

[13] JM Landis, *Report on Regulatory Agencies to the President-Elect, Submitted by the Chairman of the Subcommittee on Administrative Practice and Procedure to the Committee on the Judiciary of the United States* (Washington, 1960) 22. See also LJ Hector, 'Problems of the CAB and the Independent Regulatory Commissions' (1960) 68 *Yale LJ* 931.

[14] Breyer et al, *Administrative Law and Regulatory Policy*, 499–514.

[15] The classic analytical account of the foundations of the welfare rights movement is CA Reich, 'The New Property' (1964) 73 *Yale Law Journal* 733–87. The shift also had a profound effect on the law of administrative procedure.

rule-making are achieved in part by simplifying the factual basis of individual decisions and thus reducing the need for difficult and time-consuming collection and interpretation of large amounts of evidence. Whereas policy-making by consideration of individual cases typically involves an elaborate evidence-gathering phase before the decision is made, when policy is made by rules, decisions based on the application of such rules in individual cases are typically preceded by a less elaborate and less time-consuming evidence-gathering exercise undertaken by the decision-maker. In such an environment primary decisions are typically not made by ALJs and are not made under the provisions of the APA – in other words, they are made by informal adjudication (in the primary decision-making sense). Moreover, when policy is made by a rule-maker, the basic task of officials charged with making decisions in individual cases is to apply the rule (although this may, of course, require creative interpretation of the rule or even incremental, gap-filling rule-creation). In other words, where decisions in individual cases are based on the application of rules, such decision-making involves implementation of norms in the sense of that term explained in 1.2.2.

In a system in which making primary decisions in individual cases basically involves implementation of rules not made by the decision-maker, what is the role of judicialised, formal, evidentiary hearings of the sort conducted by ALJs? Whereas the role of the ALJ, in a system where policy is made by considering individual cases, is to participate in the making of, or to make, primary decisions, in a system in which implementation is the mode of primary decision-making the role of the ALJ is to review primary decisions that are challenged by affected individual(s). In other words, the role of the ALJ is to adjudicate in the sense in which that term was explained in 1.2.2 – adjudication as opposed to implementation: ie, application of norms to facts in the context of reviewing a decision involving the application of norms to facts. Put another way, the shift from policy-making by considering individual cases to policy-making by rules transforms the role of the adjudicator from something analogous to that of the inspector in the UK public inquiry system (a maker of primary decisions subject to review by or appeal to a policy-maker) to that of a 'tribunal' in the English sense of an adjudicator of disputes between citizen and government.[16]

If this analysis is correct, the most obvious differences between English tribunals and ALJs that review decisions are that ALJs are embedded within the agencies that make the decisions that ALJs review, whereas English tribunals are free-standing agencies; and that ALJs sit alone whereas English tribunals are

---

[16] In 1955 the Hoover Commission on Organization of the Executive Branch of Government proposed transfer of the functions of hearing examiners to an administrative court partly on the ground that once agency policy becomes crystallized into rules, it is appropriate for the application of those rules to be committed to a fully independent body. See CB Nutting, 'The Administrative Court' (1955) 30 *New York University Law Review* 1384, 1387; LL Jaffe, 'Basic Issues: An Analysis' (1955) 30 *New York University Law Review* 1273, 1284–85.

commonly multi-membered.[17] It is worth noting that despite the change in the role of ALJs associated with the shift from policy-making by consideration of individual cases to policy-making by rules, the provisions of the APA have remained more-or-less unchanged even though its provisions were drafted against the background of a model of policy-making by consideration of individual cases. This has created tension. In a system of policy-making by consideration of individual cases, provision for review of or appeal from primary decisions of ALJs to the agency, which is ultimately responsible for policy-making, seems a reasonable mechanism for enabling the agency to influence and control development of policy. By contrast, in a system of policy-making by rules in which the role of ALJs is to review decisions by implementers, allowing an appeal from the ALJ to the rule-maker may be thought to create a conflict of interest.

The justification for this conclusion lies in the distinction between implementation and adjudication. In applying norms to facts, the prime task of the implementer is to give effect, in an individual case, to the social policy embodied in the norm and, within acceptable limits, to give preference to that policy in resolving conflicts between social interests and the interests of the affected individual. By contrast, the prime task of the adjudicator is to focus on the interests of the affected individual and, within acceptable limits, to give them preference when they conflict with the social interests promoted by the norm. In this light, to allow reviews by or appeals to the rule-maker would be to give the rule-maker a second bite at the cherry, as it were: once by making the rule and thereby controlling the decision of the implementer, and again by having the power to modify the decision of the adjudicator.

Despite the fact that under the APA the power of final decision technically resides in the agency, in high-volume, rule-based programmes it is typically not efficient for the agency to attempt to control decision-making by ALJs by reviewing individual decisions. This is partly because of the very large number of individual decisions made by a large corps of ALJs, and partly because the law of judicial review effectively requires agencies to defer to findings of fact by ALJs.[18] In some cases, there may be an appeal from the ALJ to a multi-member review board within the agency, but typically the agency itself does not attempt to control policy by reviewing decisions of such an appeal board. Instead, management techniques may be employed to regulate the output of ALJs without seeking to control the outcome of individual cases. The use of such techniques has been challenged in the courts on the ground of inconsistency with the provisions of

---

[17] Internal appeal bodies within agencies may be multi-membered. One of the reasons for multi-membership of tribunals is to allow for the participation of non-lawyers in the decision-making process. In the US, ALJs are trained lawyers appointed as the result of a competitive exercise. See further 4.1.3 below.

[18] *Universal Camera Corp v National Labour Relations Board* (1951) 340 US 474. See also 4.3.2.2 (i), n 136 and text; 5.7.2, nn 237–40 and text.

the APA that protect the independence of ALJs, but with only limited success.[19] The result has been a long-term stand-off between agencies (especially the Social Security Administration) and the association that represents ALJs (The National Association of Administrative Law Judges). One way of resolving this situation would be to remove ALJs from agencies and locate them in a free-standing adjudicatory institution subject to supervision by the courts. Such a development would bring the US model of administrative adjudication more into line with the UK and Australian models. The repeated failure of various proposals along these lines[20] is perhaps partly a function of the continued hold of the APA model in which agencies retain – even if only in theory – the ultimate power to control ALJ decision-making. Resistance to a free-standing adjudicatory agency is also based on the diversity of tasks performed by ALJs in various agencies and on a fear of loss of expertise.

The distinctiveness of the US model of embedded administrative adjudication (in the review sense) reflects its origin as a mode of primary regulatory decision-making and the dominance of the regulatory model until the second half of the 20th century.[21] In the UK, by contrast, the dominant context of administrative adjudication in the 20th century was welfare rather than regulation; and this environment was more suited to the development of free-standing administrative tribunals. It will also be recalled that the emergence of the free-standing administrative tribunal in the UK in the late 19th and early 20th centuries was in part a result of the growth in the number and size of government departments and the consequent demise of multi-functional agencies. In the US, by contrast, especially in the 1930s, the non-departmental administrative sector (in the form of 'independent agencies') grew much faster than the departmental sector (including 'executive agencies').[22] The focus on regulation and the importance of independent agencies in the US has produced a system of embedded administrative adjudication (ie, adjudication in the review, not the primary decision, sense) that

---

[19] VG Rosenblum, 'Contexts and Contents of "Good Cause" as Criterion for Removal of Administrative Law Judges: Legal and Policy Factors' (1983–84) 6 *Western New England Law* 593; HH Bruff, 'Specialized Courts in Administrative Law' (1991) 43 *Administrative Law Review* 329, 345–52; DJ Gifford, 'Adjudication in Independent Tribunals: The Role of an Alternative Agency Structure' (1990–91) 66 *Notre Dame Law Review* 965, 1005–19; PL Strauss and others (eds), *Gellhorn and Byse's Administrative Law: Cases and Comments*, 9th edn (Westbury, NY, Foundation Press 1995) 958–78; JS Wolfe, 'Are You Willing to Make the Commitment in Writing? The APA, ALJs, and SSA' (2002) 55 *Oklahoma Law Review* 204.

[20] Such a proposal was expressly rejected by the Attorney-General's Committee on Administrative Procedure. In 1955 the Hoover Commission on Organization of the Executive Branch of Government in its *Report on Legal Services and Procedure* proposed the creation of a new administrative court as did President Nixon's Advisory Council on Executive Organization in 1971. Many States have created free-standing agencies for administrative adjudication. See further 4.3.1 below.

[21] DJ Gifford, 'Federal Administrative Law Judges: The Relevance of Past Choices to Future Directions' (1997) 49 *Administrative Law Review* 1.

[22] The US preference for non-departmental agencies may reflect a greater faith in (supposedly) apolitical expertise and specialisation than exists in the UK.

straddles regulation and welfare, and departmental and non-departmental agencies. In Britain, by contrast, the focus on welfare and the importance of the departmental system of public administration has produced a system of free-standing administrative adjudication that straddles regulation and welfare, and departmental and non-departmental agencies.

The discussion so far in this section can be summarised by saying that the APA rubric of 'adjudication' covers two different models of decision-making, which we might for convenience call the 'primary decision' model and the 'review' model respectively.[23] Under the review model the function of the decision-maker is adjudication in the sense explained in 1.2.2 – ie, review of disputed decisions made, in implementation of norms, by officials other than the reviewer. The implementation of norms requires the identification of an applicable norm, and this may involve interpretation and – at least at the margin – even creation of norms. Norm implementation is not necessarily a mechanical process. Under the primary-decision model, the decision-maker is a participant in the making of an primary decision. Adjudication in this sense is typically described as a mode of 'policy-making' – ie, norm-creation; but like implementation, it may involve norm-creation only at the margin or interstitially depending on how much discretion the agency has to make policy under its empowering statute.

The concern in this book is with the review model of adjudication. The distinction between the two models may have implications for various aspects of the administrative process. For instance, the formal, judicial model of procedure embodied in the APA may be thought more appropriate to the review model than to the primary decision model, especially if the latter is understood chiefly in terms of policy-making rather than rule-implementation.[24] In fact, the vast bulk of primary decision-making in the US, other than rule-making, is conducted neither by ALJs nor under the provisions of the APA. Again, the relationship between the policy-maker and the adjudicator might be thought appropriately to differ according to whether adjudication is part of a primary decision-making process or, on the contrary, a mechanism for reviewing primary decisions; and proposals for the creation of a separate administrative court or corps of ALJs might take on a different complexion depending on how the role of such a body is understood.

The distinctive feature of the US (review) model of administrative adjudication is that the adjudicator is embedded within a specialised government agency. US administrative adjudicators perform similar functions to both Article I and Article III courts, but because they are not free-standing, they are not understood

---

[23] Michael Asimow describes them respectively as the institutionalist and judicialist models: 'The Administrative Judiciary: ALJs in Historical Perspective' (2000) 20 *Journal of the National Association of Administrative Law Judges* 157, 160.

[24] eg GM Pops, 'The Judicialization of Federal Administrative Law Judges: Implications for Policymaking' (1978–79) 81 *West Virginia Law Review* 169. Pops calls the two models 'judicial' and 'administrative' respectively.

to be courts. Unlike UK administrative tribunals, which are connected with the court system both by appeals and judicial review, appeals from US embedded adjudicators typically lie to the agency whose decisions the adjudicator reviews. Court supervision primarily takes the form of judicial review. Superficially, the main significance of the distinction between the UK model of free-standing administrative adjudication and the US model of embedded administrative adjudication would seem to lie in the issue of independence – that is, the relationship between the maker of primary decisions and the reviewer of those decisions. Certainly, independence of ALJs in the Social Security Administration has been a matter of long-term and often acrimonious controversy, and it is perhaps significant in this respect that the largest single group of non-ALJ adjudicators review decisions about immigration – an area in which governments typically want to retain considerable control over resolution of individual disputes. On the other hand, 'independence' is not easily measured, and it is not clear that the independence of ALJs would be greatly enhanced by replacing the current system of internal separation of the adjudicatory function within agencies with a free-standing, cross-agency administrative tribunal or court.[25]

Whereas the development of the UK model of administrative adjudication can be understood conceptually in terms of the principles of ministerial responsibility and judicial independence, the development of the US model can perhaps be explained in terms of institutional balance. In England, judicial independence developed out of the struggle for power between the Monarch (the executive) and Parliament: Parliament asserted itself partly by detaching the administration of justice from the executive and transforming courts from being instruments of executive governance to being supervisors of the executive. The integration of the executive and the legislature in the 19th century and the development of judicially enforced human rights in the 21st have reinforced the role of the judicial branch as an external check on the other branches. Isolating adjudication of disputes between citizen and government from other government activities is seen as critical to preserving the rights of the individual against encroachment by the executive and, increasingly, by the legislature as well. Separation of powers, being understood primarily in terms of judicial independence, focuses on the relationship between the individual and the state.

In the US, by contrast, while maintaining the liberty of the individual is seen as the ultimate reason for separation of powers, the means to that end is the creation of tension between the three branches of government by an elaborate system of checks and balances. In this arrangement, less weight falls on, and less value is attached to, isolation and independence of the judiciary than in the UK. Because the legislature and the executive are not integrated, the legislature can exercise more control over the executive than is possible in the UK and,

---

[25] PL Strauss, *Administrative Justice in the United States*, 2nd edn (Durham, NC, Carolina Academic Press, 2002) 139.

conversely, the executive exercises less control over the legislature. For both reasons, judicial control of the executive is less important than in the UK. Furthermore, the judiciary has more power over the legislature than in the UK system, and the legislature plays a more active part in judicial appointments. Isolation of the judiciary from the politics is less important in the US than in the UK. Whereas in the UK the judiciary is seen as a counterweight to the other branches from which, therefore, it needs to be strongly isolated, in the US isolation is less important because the judiciary is just one element in a complex web of institutional interactions. Independence of the judiciary does not have the talismanic quality in the US system that it enjoys in the UK set-up.[26]

This checks-and-balances approach to separation of powers can be seen at work in multi-functional agencies, which can be understood (in the words of the President's Committee on Administrative Management) as 'miniature ... governments'.[27] Instead of isolating administrative adjudicators from makers and implementers of policy, the various elements of the agency are set in a state of tension. Thus, ALJs are appointed by agencies but as a result of an independently-run competitive process; and they can be dismissed by agencies, but only after a formal hearing before an independent adjudicator. ALJs operate within the agency but behind a Chinese Wall; and their decisions are subject to appeal or review by the agency but the decision of the agency is subject to external (judicial) review. Despite being embedded within an administrative process, the procedure for formal administrative adjudication is based on the model of the civil court trial, and there must be a 'record' (transcript) of the proceedings. ALJs are all trained lawyers.

We may conclude, therefore, that the fundamental difference between the UK and the US models – the difference between embedded and free-standing administrative adjudication – is a function of different understandings of separation of powers.

3.3 The Australian Model

In both the UK and the US models administrative tribunals are, if not institutions of the same species, at least different species of the same genus. By contrast, in the Australian model, tribunals and courts do not belong to the same genus. This is surprising considering that Australian constitutional arrangements are an amalgam of those in the UK and the US. Once again, the explanation lies in a distinctive interpretation of separation of powers.

In Australia, the executive and the legislature are integrated in much the same way as in the UK. The major qualification is that because the Australian Senate is

---

[26] See further 7.1.
[27] Report of President's Commiitte on Administrative Management (Washington, 1937) 39–40.

elected on a different basis from the House of Representatives and has much greater power to block legislation than that of the UK House of Lords, the legislature potentially – depending on the balance of the parties in the Senate – has more power over the executive than in the UK. On the other hand, party discipline is probably even stronger in Australia than in the UK, so that provided the government can command a majority in the Senate, it has even greater control of the legislature than governments in the UK. Because of this integration of the executive and the legislature, independence of the judiciary is at least as important in Australia as in the UK. But its significance is further enhanced by the fact that Australia is a federation. Isolation and independence of the federal judiciary from the federal executive is considered crucial not only for protecting the rights of the individual against the government but also for protecting the States against the Commonwealth. Much more than in either the UK or the US, in Australia separation of judicial power and independence of the judiciary are considered essential for maintenance of the 'rule of law', thus making explicit the link between these two ideas that was only implicit in Dicey's analysis of the English constitution.

This strict understanding of the role of the judiciary in the system of government has had several important consequences. For one thing, although the Constitution has not been interpreted to prevent judges of federal courts from undertaking tasks other than performing their functions as such, it has been read as limiting the range of activities in which judges may engage to those that are not 'inconsistent' with their role as members of the judiciary.[28] Secondly, it has led the High Court not only to insist on preserving the integrity of the judicial role but also to attempt to define that role in terms of a categorical or formalistic understanding of 'judicial function' and 'judicial power'. It is possible to identify at least five different juridical approaches to defining judicial power and functions.

— According to an historical approach, judicial functions are those traditionally performed by courts. Under this approach (in the Australian context, anyway), the relevant period for determining the historical functions of courts is the heyday of the common law before the exponential growth of legislative activity from the 19th century onwards. 'Courts', as in Montesquieu's model, are the English superior central courts.

— A second, related approach rests on a public/private distinction. The private is associated with disputes between citizens, with common law and (in federal systems, especially the US) with state law; the public is associated with disputes between citizen and government, with statute and (in federal

---

[28] See 2.3.3 n 158.

systems, especially the US) with federal law. Matters that fall on the private side of the line may not be allocated to non-judicial bodies.[29]

— A third, essentialist approach, defines judicial power in terms of what courts do:[30] they find facts, identify relevant law,[31] and apply law to facts in order to make a final and enforceable decision about (theoretically) pre-existing rights and duties.

These three approaches we might loosely describe as 'formalistic'.

— A fourth, functionalist, approach identifies the exclusive province of courts by reference to the values protected by separation of judicial power. The question whether conferral of a particular function on a non-judicial body is impermissible depends on whether conferral unacceptably infringes the protected values.
— According to a fifth, 'reviewability' approach the separation principle does not require that judicial functions should not be allocated to non-judicial bodies but only that if they are, the work of the non-judicial body should be subject to review by a judicial body.

There are traces of all five approaches in the jurisprudence of both the US Supreme Court and the Australian High Court. However, whereas the latter two approaches are now dominant in the US,[32] the former three (formalist) approaches are dominant in Australia. The result of the High Court's formalist approach is a large, complex and (arguably) internally inconsistent body of case law.[33] It has also produced a sharp distinction between judicial and non-judicial

---

[29] This approach is extremely odd because it allows non-judicial bodies, whose members may not enjoy the same protections as judges, to adjudicate only disputes between citizens and government. That said, two complexities should be noted. First, in terms of the public/private distinction, criminal prosecutions should probably be classified as public. However, trying criminal prosecutions is considered a core judicial function that cannot be conferred on tribunals – except, anomalously, military tribunals. Secondly, there is at least one case in which the High Court, on the basis of highly formalistic reasoning, has classified a power to resolve disputes between private parties as non-judicial: *A-G for the Commonwealth v Breckler* (1999) 197 CLR 83. For criticism see L Zines, *The High Court and the Constitution*, 5th edn (Sydney, The Federation Press, 2008) 245–46.

[30] ie, it defines a function in terms of a procedure.

[31] This may involve creatively interpreting or even making rules.

[32] Useful discussions include: PM Bator, 'The Constitution as Architecture: Legislative and Administrative Courts under Article III (1989–90) 65 *Indiana Law Review* 233; RH Fallon Jr, 'Of Legislative Courts, Administrative Agencies, and Article III' (1987–88) 101 *Harvard Kaw Review 915;* MH Redish, 'Legislative Courts, Administrative Agencies and the *Northern Pipeline* Decision' [1983] *Duke Law Journal* 197; RB Saphire and ME Solimine, 'Shoring up Article III: Legislative Court Doctrine in the Post *CTFC v Schor* Era' (1988) 68 *Boston University Law Review* 85; PL Strauss, 'The Place of Agencies in Government: Separation of Powers and the Fourth Branch' (1984) 84 *Columbia Law Review* 573; PL Strauss, 'Formal and Functional Approaches to Separation of Powers Questions – A Foolish Inconsistency?' (1986–87) 72 *Cornell Law Review* 488.

[33] For a general discussion see Zines, *The High Court and the Constitution*, ch 10.

power and an interpretation of the Constitution that prohibits the conferral of judicial power on bodies that are not courts and, conversely, the conferral of non-judicial power on courts.[34]

This distinctive interpretation of separation of powers has been read out of (or into) the architecture of the first three Chapters of the Australian Constitution concerning, respectively, the legislature, the executive and the judiciary. Because this basic arrangement is also found in the US Constitution, a version of the principles that judicial functions may not be conferred on non-judicial bodies and that non-judicial functions may not be conferred on judicial bodies is also part of US law. However, because the US Supreme Court has mainly followed the functional and reviewability approaches in developing the idea of separation of powers – and, in this sense, has taken a less rigid approach to allocation of functions between courts and other organs of government than the High Court[35] – US lawyers seem happy to accept that administrative tribunals perform essentially judicial functions[36] (although sometimes betraying unease by adding the prefix 'quasi'),[37] that administrative adjudicators are 'judges' (as opposed to tribunal 'members' in Australia), and that they perform no function that could not alternatively be allocated to courts established in accordance with Article III of the US Constitution. The main problem, as they see it, is how to prevent excessive or inappropriate Congressional allocation of judicial functions to judicial officers that are not Article III judges and to institutions that are not Article III courts.

The result of all this is that because the characteristic function of federal administrative tribunals in Australia – merits review – is understood to be non-judicial, merits review bodies are not and cannot be established as courts. Rather, they belong to a distinct genus of adjudicatory institution. However, merits review tribunals are not only thought of as performing a function that courts cannot; they are also commonly commended for having the sorts of pragmatic advantages over courts that have figured prominently in UK debates about tribunals – speed, cheapness, accessibility, informality and so on. As in the UK, however, in the latter part of the 20th century people started to question the extent to which tribunals realised these advantages in practice. As in the UK, too, there are continuing attempts to make courts more accessible and user-friendly. Partly to this end and partly in order to overcome limitations imposed on the use

---

[34] Although the Canadian Constitution does not entrench separation of powers, the Supreme Court of Canada has interpreted the Constitution to limit the power of provincial governments to confer on administrative tribunals certain powers traditionally exercised by superior courts: M Groves, 'Administrative Review of Judicial Action in the High Court of Australia' (2008) 33 *Queen's Law Journal* 327, 345 n 60, 349 n 79.

[35] Ironically, Australian judges and lawyers tend to think of the US version of separation of powers as more rigid than the Australian version, which it may be in respect of the relationship between the executive and the legislature but certainly not in relation to separation of judicial power.

[36] See 2.3.2 n 111.

[37] B Schwartz, 'Administrative Justice and its Place in the Legal Order' (1955) 30 *New York University Law Review* 1390, 1398.

of tribunals by the High Court's strict interpretation of separation of powers, in 1999 the federal Parliament created the Federal Magistrates Court one objective of which, according to the court's webpage, is 'to provide a simpler and more accessible alternative to litigation in the superior courts'.

Moreover, despite the constitutionally based distinction between tribunals and courts and between merits review and judicial review, merits review tribunals are plugged into the federal court system by appeals (for instance, from the AAT to the Federal Court on points of law) and judicial review. Merits review tribunals do not constitute a self-contained system of administrative adjudication; indeed, it would be impossible for the Parliament to create such a system because of the entrenched judicial review jurisdiction of the High Court under section 75(v) of the Australian Constitution.

We can summarise by saying that the main point of difference between the UK and US models of administrative adjudication on the one hand and the Australian model on the other is that in the former tribunals are understood to be essentially similar to courts both in nature and function whereas in the latter they are classified as being categorically different.

3.4 The French Model

In 1790 the French revolutionary assembly passed a law (still in force) one of the clauses of which provided that

> it shall be a criminal offence for the judges of the ordinary courts to interfere in any manner whatsoever with the operation of the administration, nor shall they call administrators to account before them in respect of the exercise of their official functions.[38]

The 'ordinary courts' referred to in this provision were the *Parlements*, regional courts

> which in the eighteenth century in particular (under Louis XV and Louis XVI) not only interfered to a considerable degree in the executive government but also impeded such reforms as the Monarch sought to introduce.[39]

In fact, however, the *Parlements* were much more than courts. They were, in effect, multi-functional agencies – they 'exercised administrative functions, issued regulatory decrees, and could veto royal legislation'.[40] Judgeships were bought and sold, and the *Parlements* were effectively controlled by the nobility, who used

---

[38] This translation comes from LN Brown and JS Bell, *French Administrative Law*, 5th edn (Oxford, Clarendon Press, 1998) 46.

[39] ibid 45.

[40] J Allison, *A Continental Distinction in the Common Law: A Historical and Comparative Perspective on English Public Law* (Oxford, Clarendon Press, 1996) 138–39.

them to protect their interests against the Monarch and the bourgeoisie. This no doubt encouraged the revolutionary government to relegate the courts to resolving disputes between citizens. The effect of the 1790 provision was not only to separate the courts from the executive and judicial power from executive power, but also to prevent the use of judicial power to supervise the exercise of executive power and resolve disputes between citizen and government. It left an institutional vacuum, which was filled in 1799 by the creation of the *Conseil d'Etat*, a 'post-Revolutionary analogue to the pre-Revoluntionary *Conseil du Roi*'.[41]

The *Conseil* was very heavily criticised in France in the early-to-mid the 19th century primarily on the ground of lack of independence. It was argued that the judicial work of the *Conseil* should either be transferred to the 'ordinary' courts[42] or that the *Conseil* should be replaced by a newly-created administrative court. Neither course was taken, but the criticisms were met by a transformation of the *Conseil* in a series of reforms that were complete by the end of the 19th century.[43] The *Conseil* now stands at the top of a three-tier hierarchy of 'courts', the other two tiers consisting of the regional *Cours Administratives d'Appel* and the *Tribunaux Administratifs*.[44] These courts are responsible for administrative adjudication in France. In addition, there is a relatively small number of bodies that exercise 'specialised jurisdiction' in areas such as immigration.

An assessment of the 19th-century reforms of the *Conseil* led Dicey to modify his initial extremely negative assessment of the French system of '*droit adminsitratif*', first in an article in the *Law Quarterly Review* in 1901[45] and then in the 6th edition of *An Introduction to the Study of the Law of the Constitution*, published in 1902. In the Preface to the 8th edition, published in 1914, Dicey was even prepared to concede that,

> It may require consideration whether some body of men who combined official experience with legal knowledge and who were entirely independent of the Government of the day, might not enforce official law with more effectiveness than any Division of the High Court.[46]

There is no doubt that Dicey found it very difficult to abandon cherished ideas, and his re-appraisal of the French system may be thought half-hearted and grudging. However, Dicey's real genius lay in his ability to identify basic constitutional issues; and in the passage from which the last quotation comes he raises the three matters that lay at the heart of his life-long suspicion of a closed system

---

[41] ibid 142.

[42] Such an argument was apparently still being made as late as the 1920s: EA Buttle, 'A Long Quest: The Search for Administrative Justice' (1958) 44 *American Bar Association Journal* 450, 453 n 27.

[43] Allison, *A Continental Distinction in the Common Law*, 143–46.

[44] M Weston, *An English Reader's Guide to the French Legal System* (New York, Berg, 1991) 86–97. For a recent brief account of the *Conseil* see J-M Sauvé, 'Judging the Administration in France: Changes Ahead?' [2008] *Public Law* 531.

[45] 'Droit Administratif in Modern French Law' (1901) 17 *Law Quarterly Review* 302.

[46] *An Introduction to the Study of the Law of the Constitution*, 8th edn (London, Macmillan and Co, 1914), xlviii.

of administrative courts: independence, expertise and the power of the political executive relative to the non-political judiciary.

Concerning the last of these, Dicey's view was that in France,

> a kind of authority attaches to the Government and to the whole body of officials in the service of the state … such as is hardly possessed by the servants of the Crown in England.[47]

Dicey was not (and is not) alone in this judgment. According to John Allison (quoting American administrative lawyer Bernard Schwartz and French administrative lawyer M Waline),

> As understood and enacted by the revolutionaries, the separation of powers was … one-sided: 'the judges were … prevented from administering, but the administrators were not prevented from judging'.[48]

It seems reasonable to conclude that the French system of administrative courts and adjudication establishes a significantly different balance of power than any of the other three systems we are concerned with.

The independence of adjudicators is partly a function of institutional arrangements concerned, for instance, with appointments, dismissal, remuneration and the extent to which adjudicators can be directed by the executive; and partly of much vaguer concepts of influence and attitude. Independence is difficult to define and measure with any confidence of accuracy. Even so, Allison summarises his careful and balanced consideration of the independence of the *Conseil d'Etat* in these words:

> it does seem to have acquired judicial independence only in the narrow sense of absence of direct interference by the active administration in the outcome of individual cases. Generally, it has conformed to dominant opinion.[49]

On the other hand, the *Conseil* is generally agreed to be a successful body, and this is attributed by Allison to the balance it has managed to strike between independence and 'expertise'.

It is important to distinguish between two senses in which this latter word may be used.[50] In one sense, it may refer to the fact that an adjudicator or adjudicatory body has a narrow or 'specialised' as opposed to a broad or 'general' jurisdiction. For instance, the Australian AAT has broad jurisdiction over a diverse range of government activities and programmes whereas the jurisdiction of the Social Security Appeals Tribunal (SSAT) is, by comparison, relatively narrow and specific. In this sense, the *Conseil* is a non-specialist body. In a different sense, 'expertise' may refer to non-legal knowledge and experience possessed by a decision-maker and, in particular, knowledge and experience of the workings of the executive

---

[47]   ibid xlv.
[48]   Allison, *A Continental Distinction in the Common Law*, 142.
[49]   ibid 148.
[50]   See further 4.1.1 and 4.3.1.

branch of government. It is this latter type of expertise that is characteristic of the *Conseil*. In addition to its adjudicatory functions, the *Conseil d'Etat* plays an important role in the legislative process and acts as general legal adviser to the government. The *Conseil* is divided into two main sections – the administrative and the adjudicatory. All its members are (very high-calibre) public servants with advanced training or significant experience in public administration, and most participate in all the various activities of the *Conseil*, 'the intention being that the different viewpoints of the two sides of the *Conseil* should be represented in all its activities'.[51] Only a small number are engaged solely in the work of the adjudicatory section – the *Section du Contentieux*. The *Section du Contentieux* operates in ten *sous-Sections*, but these are not strictly organised according to subject-matter.

There is obviously a significant sense in which expertise in the sense of knowledge and experience of the workings of executive government is incompatible – or at least in tension – with independence.

> At bottom the *Conseil d'Etat statuant au contentieux* ... remains part of the administrative machinery of the French state. ... This very fact has helped to make the judicial control which it exercises more readily acceptable to the official ... [who] knows his judges are fully aware of the special problems besetting public administration ... [and] are not strangers to the administrative process ... not amateurs throwing legalistic spanners into the administrative works.[52]

A similar, but arguably lesser, conflict or tension is built into the US system by virtue of the power of agencies to review decisions of ALJs and to manage their work in various ways. However, this tension is counterbalanced by the fact that ALJs are legally trained and appointed by a process of competition that focuses on legal skills. From this perspective, the most important characteristic of the French system of administrative adjudication is the location of the administrative courts/tribunals within the executive branch coupled with the nature of the qualifications and training of their members and the internal operation of the *Conseil*. One of the purposes of any system of administrative adjudication is to strike a balance between social interests and individual interests. The French system seems to have at least the potential to strike that balance more in favour of social than of individual interests, and to do so more than the UK, US and Australian systems. Whether it actually realises that potential would be an extremely difficult question to answer depending not only on facts about all four systems but also on contestable assessments of the facts. However, it was arguably this potential bias towards collective interests at the expense of individual interests on which Dicey's life-long suspicion of the French model was ultimately founded; and it is on the basis of a normative judgment about the desirable balance between social and individual interests that Dicey's approach deserves to be judged.

---

[51] Brown and Bell, *French Administrative Law*, 67.
[52] ibid 80–81.

3.5 Conclusion

The aim of this chapter has been roughly to sketch the structure of four different models of administrative adjudication. We might arrange these four models along a continuum with the UK model at one end and the French model at the other. In the UK model, both courts and tribunals engage in administrative adjudication. Not only are administrative tribunals subject to supervision by courts but also they are understood as belonging to the same genus of institutions as courts. Many administrative adjudicators in the UK system are trained lawyers. Like courts, tribunals are separated from the executive. In the French model, by contrast, administrative adjudication is the exclusive province of a set of 'public-law' institutions that are unsupervised by 'private-law' courts. The public-law adjudicative institutions are staffed by public administrators and they are understood to be part of the executive branch of government.

The US and Australian models sit somewhere between these two extremes. In the US, administrative adjudicators are structurally part of institutions of the executive branch; but within such institutions, adjudication and adjudicators are separated from other officials and activities of the agency. Administrative adjudication is understood as a species of judicial function, and administrative adjudicators are typically legally trained. Administrative adjudication is supervised both by the executive institutions within which adjudicators operate and also by courts. In contrast to the position in both the UK and the US models, in the Australian federal system, tribunals and their characteristic function are considered to be categorically different from courts and their characteristic function. However, administrative tribunals are supervised by courts, and the peak administrative tribunal – the AAT – has a strongly judicial ethos.

The detailed implications of these models are yet to be explored. In the chapters that follow the models will provide a basis upon which to build an analysis of various issues of institutional and constitutional design to which administrative adjudication gives rise.

4

Form

HAVING TRACED THE historical development of administrative adjudication and administrative tribunals in each of our comparator jurisdictions and sketched models of these phenomena based on those histories, we can now embark on a more general analysis of various features of administrative adjudication and tribunals. This chapter is concerned primarily with the nature and structure of tribunals and tribunal systems. Chapter 5 deals with the function of tribunals, focusing on the characteristic function of the Australian Administrative Appeals Tribunal – the mode of administrative adjudication called merits review – and its relationship to the other mode of administrative adjudication, judicial review. Chapters 2–5 lie, as it were, on a horizontal plane, emphasising constitutional structure and the design of governmental institutions. In Chapter 6 the orientation shifts, we might say, from the horizontal to the vertical, focusing on the relationship between administrative tribunals and 'tribunal users' through the lens of the increasingly ubiquitous concept of 'administrative justice'. Finally, in Chapter 7, the two orientations are combined in an examination of the place of administrative tribunals in the governmental and political system as a whole.

The structural issues considered in this Chapter are membership of tribunals, including appointments and composition; separation and independence; and the structure of the tribunal system. The discussion will be at the level of general principle rather than technical detail.

4.1 Membership, Appointments and Composition

4.1.1 Membership

4.1.1.1 Expertise and Specialisation

The paradigm administrative tribunal is a 'specialist' adjudicatory body. In this context, specialisation has two aspects. One – tribunal jurisdiction – is discussed in 4.3.1. The other – the subject of this section – is the membership of tribunals. Tribunal members can be divided into three categories: those appointed on the basis of legal qualifications; those appointed on the basis of qualifications in some branch of knowledge other than law (often referred to as 'experts'); and those appointed on some other basis (often referred to as 'lay' members)[1]. The use of the term 'expert' to refer to the second of these categories is misleading because members in the first category are also appointed for their expertise. The explanation for the traditional usage is that tribunals are understood to be legal institutions and in that context, lawyers speak without an accent (as it were) because law is the language in which the proceedings are conducted. It may be more fruitful to think about the various categories of membership in terms of perspectives rather than expertise or its lack. In this way of thinking, lay persons are eligible for membership of tribunals not because they (negatively) lack expertise but because they can (positively) bring to the proceedings a perspective that is valuable precisely because it is not that of an expert in law or some other relevant area of theory or practice. Research suggests that non-legal members of multi-member tribunals, and lay members in particular, may be marginalised in or frozen out of the decision-making process.[2] Thinking positively rather than negatively about their role might contribute to their greater integration into the work of tribunals.

One glaring omission from the list of categories of tribunal member is that of 'administrator'. Public administration is not thought of as an area of expertise for the purposes of the second category of membership. A common criticism of external reviewers of government decisions – although one perhaps more often directed at courts than at tribunals – is that they have insufficient knowledge of the bureaucracy and of the context, problems and practicalities of administrative decision-making. For admirers of the French system of administrative courts, one of the secrets of its success is that members of the *Conseil d'Etat*, in particular, have training in and experience of public administration.[3] It may seem surprising, therefore, that experts in public administration do not, as such, find a place on the tribunal bench. In Australia, the Kerr Committee suggested that 'an officer of the Commonwealth Department or authority responsible for administering the decision under review' should always be a member of the proposed general administrative review tribunal in order to 'ensure that particular knowledge of the area of administration which produced the decision under review would be available to the Tribunal'.[4] Unsurprisingly, the Bland Committee rejected this suggestion on the ground that it would create at least the appearance

---

[1] But this last term has fallen out of favour because 'it fails to properly convey the conscientious and professional attitude' that such people bring to their job: *Transforming Tribunals: Implementing Part 1 of the Tribunals, Courts and Enforcement Act 2007*, Consultation Paper CP 30/07, (London, Ministry of Justice, 2007) (hereafter '*Transforming Tribunals*') para 241.

[2] eg N Wikeley and R Young, 'The Marginalisation of Lay Members in Social Security Tribunals' (1992) 14 *Journal of Social Welfare and Family Law* 127.

[3] eg J Allison, *A Continental Distinction in the Common Law: A Historical and Comparative Perspective on English Public Law* (Oxford, Clarendon Press, 1996) 146–49; LN Brown and JS Bell, *French Administrative Law*, 5th edn (Oxford, Clarendon Press, 1998) 79–83.

[4] Report of the Commonwealth Administrative Review Committee, Parliamentary Paper No 144 of 1971, para 292.

of conflict of interest and lack of independence; but the Committee was 'attracted' to the idea that ex-bureaucrats might sit on administrative tribunals.[5] Another approach would be to provide tribunal members with training in public administration. At all events, the typical lack of expertise in public administration on the tribunal bench reinforces the identification of tribunals with the judicial branch of government.

The two aspects of specialisation – membership and jurisdiction – are obviously related. Consider, for instance, social security tribunals. The fact that such bodies specialise in reviewing social security benefit decisions may be thought a reason and a justification for including professionals such as doctors, social workers, psychiatrists and physiotherapists, in addition to lawyers, amongst those eligible for membership. Furthermore, members of such tribunals, on whatever basis they were appointed, are likely to gain more expertise in social security law and other relevant non-legal areas of theory and practice than would members of a tribunal that had jurisdiction to review various types of decisions including social security benefit decisions and who, as a result, reviewed fewer social security decisions than they would if the tribunal specialised in reviewing such decisions. Another suggested connection between membership and jurisdiction is that 'non-legal expertise' may be particularly relevant to the matters with which at least some tribunals deal.[6] However, the idea that non-legal expertise is more relevant to some areas of law than to others may be questioned. It is more plausible to think that the more specialised the tribunal's jurisdiction, the easier it is to identify areas of non-legal expertise that are likely to be relevant to a significant proportion of the tribunal's caseload and the more sense it makes to involve relevant experts in the decision-making process directly rather than indirectly as witnesses, for instance.

4.1.1.2 The US

Membership is a central feature of the models of administrative adjudication discussed in Chapter 3. In the US, ALJs, whose terms and conditions of service are regulated by the Administrative Procedure Act 1946 (APA), are appointed as the result of a competitive process run by the central personnel agency of the federal government (the OPM). The minimum qualifications to become an ALJ are that the applicant must be an attorney and have at least seven years of experience as a judge, a participant in the administrative review process or a practitioner before the ordinary courts.[7] The fact that ALJs are lawyers reinforces

---

[5] Final Report of the Committee on Administrative Discretions, Parliamentary Paper 316 of 1973, paras 148–52.

[6] eg G Richardson, 'Tribunals' in D Feldman (ed), *English Public Law* (Oxford, OUP, 2004) para 20.13.

[7] JS Lubbers, 'Federal Administrative Law Judges: A Focus on our Invisible Judiciary' (1981) 33 *Administrative Law Review* 109, 113.

identification of administrative adjudication as a judicial function and government agencies (by which ALJs are employed) – along with Article I courts – as non-Article III repositories of judicial power. ALJs are greatly outnumbered by 'another group that ... decides more cases, but does so with less prestige, compensation and job security'.[8] Immigration decisions form the largest category of decisions reviewed by this other group of so-called 'administrative judges' (AJs).[9] Another large category consists of veterans' benefits decisions. A significant proportion of AJs are non-lawyers. AJs are typically appointed directly by the agency whose decisions they review, and they do not enjoy the protections conferred by the APA on ALJs. At the same time as the status of ALJs was being raised (for instance, by the change of name from 'hearing examiner' – as they were originally called – to Administrative Law Judge), Congress was allowing increasing use of non-ALJ adjudicators by omitting to require that adjudications under new government programmes be held 'on the record' – the formula that triggers application of the APA and the requirement of a hearing before an ALJ.

4.1.1.3 The UK

In the US, perhaps the main locus for participation by non-lawyers in the administration of justice is the jury. By contrast, in the UK there is a long and strong tradition of participation of lay persons not only as triers of fact but also as adjudicators – notably in the guise of JPs.[10] It was for this reason, in 19th century England, that the decision not to use courts to adjudicate disputes arising out of the implementation of new statutory schemes and the consequent appointment of non-lawyers as administrative adjudicators 'did not cause alarm to the legal establishment'.[11] As in the case of JPs, property ownership was adopted as a qualification for membership of some tribunals (those dealing with taxation, for instance), while in other cases – notably railway tribunals – the emphasis was on non-legal expertise. On the other hand, members of statutory tribunals, like judges, were required to take an oath 'under which they bound themselves to act in a judicial manner';[12] and the risk of partisanship was put forward as a 'potent objection' to adjudication by non-legal experts.[13] A century

---

[8] PR Verkuil, 'Reflections Upon the Federal Administrative Judiciary' (1991–92) 39 *UCLA Law Review* 1341, 1345.

[9] The Supreme Court has held that Due Process Clause of the US Constitution does not require that reviews of administrative decisions be conducted by ALJs in accordance with the requirements of the APA: ibid 1348.

[10] Justices of the Peace were essentially local officials, and representing the local community is sometimes suggested as a function of non-legal members of tribunals. A recent English survey found that lay members were most prevalent in tax and valuation tribunals and that non-legal experts were most common in party-and-party employment tribunals and in social security tribunals: *Transforming Tribunals*, 75.

[11] C Stebbings *Legal Foundations of Tribunals in Nineteenth Century England* (Cambridge, CUP, 2006) 110. What immediately follows relies heavily on ch 3 of Stebbings' book.

[12] ibid 112.

[13] ibid 128.

later, the idea that non-judicial, administrative adjudicators should bring 'a judicial mind' to bear on their work was central to William Robson's vision of the ideal tribunal, despite his insistence on the distinctiveness of tribunals.[14] However they were staffed, administrative tribunals were from the start implicitly understood to be performing an essentially judicial task; and as we saw in 2.3.1, by the end of the 19th century this similarity of function was seen to have serious implications for the relationship between administrative adjudicators and the executive. Nor did the acceptance of non-legal membership mean that legal input into the adjudicative process was not considered necessary or valuable.[15] Some tribunals were required to have a legally qualified member, and in other cases the model (as in magistrates courts) was for legal advice to be provided to members by a legally qualified employed official.

In the 19th century, non-legal members were seen as having a significant contribution to make to administrative adjudication provided adequate legal input was available. In the first half of the 20th century debates about the identity of administrative adjudicators focused not on the issue of legal versus other kinds of expertise but on the role as adjudicators of elected members of the executive (and, by implication, of non-elected departmental officials acting on their behalf). Neither the Donoughmore Committee nor the Franks Committee addressed the former issue. With the increasing judicialisation of tribunals in the latter part of the century, the main questions being asked about non-legal members of tribunals were whether they had enough (of the right kind of) expertise and assuming they did, whether they were willing and able to inject that expertise into the decision-making process.[16] For instance, what role might non-legal members play in the resolution of cases resolved under the auspices of the tribunal but without a formal hearing (by ADR techniques)? It is sometimes argued (but also sometimes denied) that the presence of non-legal members helps to make tribunals more accessible and informal and increases public confidence in the system. However, such claims have not been subjected to

---

[14] WA Robson, *Justice and Administrative Law* (London, Macmillan and Co Ltd, 1928) ch 5.

[15] *Legal Foundations of Tribunals in Nineteenth Century England*, 128–30. It seems reasonable to assume that lawyers are more likely to make legally correct decisions than non-lawyers. However, this is a very difficult assumption to test, if only because it is hard to define legal correctness in an abstract, non-institutional way. Appeal rates may provide a surrogate: F Meredith, '"How Would You Know, You're Not a Lawyer": Decision-making in a Merit Review Tribunal' (2001) 10 *Journal of Judicial Administration* 149.

[16] Do they 'add value'? (*Transforming Tribunals*, para 230). The 'overriding principle' is that they should be used selectively and only when they can make a contribution that tribunal judges cannot: ibid paras 229, 231. In 1992, Baldwin, Wikeley and Young concluded that non-legal members of social security tribunals in Britain had been 'effectively sidelined by ... increased legalization': J Baldwin, N Wikeley and R Young, *Judging Social Security: The Adjudication of Claims for Benefit in Britain* (Oxford, Clarendon Press, 1992) 151.

rigorous investigation, and increasingly the benefit of simply 'being there' without making a distinctive and relevant personal contribution to decision-making has not been considered sufficient to justify non-legal membership.

The TCE Act creates a formal distinction between Judges and Members of the First-tier and Upper Tribunals. One of the aims of the new system is to 'encourage judicial career development'. The idea is that the grouping of specialised jurisdictions within the one (Lower-tier or Upper) Tribunal will give adjudicators the opportunity to acquire skills that are transferable from one jurisdiction to another, thus enabling them to deal with a wider variety of subject matter.[17] However, it seems likely that the most transferable skills will be legal and that non-legal members will have fewer opportunities for such career development than legal members (tribunal judges). The tradition of non-legal participation in adjudication remains much more robust in the criminal justice system (where magistrates, who need not be legally qualified, handle the vast majority of criminal cases) than in the area of administrative justice. The model for the tribunal is apparently the civil court and the civil justice system, which are dominated by lawyers.

4.1.1.4 Australia

Although the participation of non-lawyers as adjudicators in the criminal and civil justice systems is much less common in Australia than in the UK,[18] the general approach to their involvement in administrative adjudication is similar to that in the UK. Contrary to what might be expected, the separation of powers entrenched in the Australian Constitution does not prevent either the appointment of lawyers to tribunals or the appointment of non-lawyers to courts. In practice, judges of federal courts have legal qualifications, but requirements that they do so are statutory, not constitutional. Separation of powers has been interpreted as requiring that federal judges do not perform functions that are inconsistent with exercise of judicial power under Chapter III of the Constitution. However, membership of merits review tribunals has been held not to breach this requirement because 'independently of any instruction, advice or wish of the Executive Government … [t]he tribunal must give what it considers to be the correct or preferable decision'.[19] The President of the AAT must be a judge of the Federal Court,[20] and a significant proportion of members of the AAT are judges of Chapter III courts. A significant proportion of the non-judicial members of the AAT, and a significant proportion of the members of first-tier

---

[17] *Transforming Tribunals*, paras 160–65.

[18] On the history of Justices of the Peace in Australia see T Skyrme, *History of the Justices of the Peace, Vol III* (Chichester, Barry Rose, 1991) ch VII; and on the early history in New South Wales see D Neal, *The Rule of Law in a Penal Colony: Law and Power in Early New South Wales* (Cambridge, CUP, 1991) ch 5.

[19] *Drake v Minister for Immigration and Ethnic Affairs* (1979) 2 ALD 60; *Wilson v Minister for Aboriginal and Torres Strait Islander Affairs* (1996) 189 CLR 1, 18.

[20] AAT Act s 7(1).

merits review tribunals – such as the Migration Review Tribunal and the Social Security Appeals Tribunal – have legal qualifications or experience.

4.1.1.5 The Tasks of Non-court Administrative Adjudicators

In theory, at least, non-court administrative adjudicators perform two main tasks. Their most obvious job is to make a decision. Despite superficial differences between our three main comparator jurisdictions, it seems that in all of them, non-court administrative adjudicators, whether or not they are appointed on the basis of legal qualifications, are expected to 'act like lawyers' when they perform their decision-making function. Equally importantly, however, adjudicators contribute knowledge, information and normative points of view (which we might, purely for convenience, collectively call 'data') to the decision-making process. In adjudicatory contexts, three main sources of data are available: the parties to the proceedings, the adjudicator(s), and third parties in the guise either of witnesses called by the parties to the proceedings or persons solicited or allowed by the adjudicator to provide data. In the traditional adversarial model of adjudication, the parties to the proceedings and their witnesses are the main providers of data. Provision of data by *amici curiae*, 'assessors' and the like is exceptional, and strict rules of 'judicial notice' are designed to confine the contribution of the adjudicator more-or-less to the provision of legal data. In this model, which courts paradigmatically exemplify, the main task of the adjudicator is to make a decision, and the fact that the formal qualifications for being an adjudicator are typically legal can be understood as both a corollary and an explanation of the limited role of the adjudicator in contributing data to the decision-making process.

From this perspective, the significant difference, in terms of provision of data, between the traditional adversarial model of adjudication and the model exemplified by tribunals with expert and lay members lies in the sources of data for the adjudicatory decision-making process. Under the latter model adjudicators (especially non-legal experts and lay-persons) are allowed and, indeed, expected to contribute non-legal data to the decision-making process to a much greater extent than is allowed to legally-qualified adjudicators under the former model. One reason for allowing adjudicators to provide more data may be to increase the total amount of available data. A more likely and significant goal is to shift the burden of providing data from the parties and their witnesses to the adjudicator(s) and to relieve the adjudicator(s) of the need to outsource the provision of data to 'friends of the tribunal' and the like. Jurisdictional specialisation aids this shift by enabling the adjudicator(s) to acquire much more personal knowledge and information (both legal[21] and non-legal) relevant to the decision-making

---

[21] '[U]sers [of specialist tribunals] should not have to explain to the tribunal what the law is': *Gillies (AP) v Secretary of State for Work and Pensions (Scotland)* [2006] 1 WLR 781, [36] (Baroness Hale of Richmond).

process than would be possible if their work was more jurisdictionally varied. The implications for adjudicatory procedure and the cost of adjudication of this shift of responsibility for the provision of data have a more significant bearing on debates about the role of non-lawyers in administrative adjudication than does their decision-making function.

In the US, the UK and Australia the court is the quintessentially 'legal' institution and the judge is the quintessentially legal official. There is great cultural resistance to appointing non-lawyers to offices bearing the title 'judge' or 'justice' to serve on bodies called 'courts'.[22] In the early years of development of tribunals in 19th-century England the agencies in which administrative adjudication was embedded were not (thought of or called) courts and administrative adjudicators were not (thought of or called) 'judges'. This, no doubt, helped to overcome any cultural resistance to the involvement of non-lawyers in administrative adjudication. However, as tribunals have increasingly come to be understood as belonging to the same genus as courts, the role of non-lawyers has generally diminished and the rationale for their involvement has, in many areas, become less and less clear or agreed. Increasingly, non-lawyers are valued as administrative adjudicators only if they possess some specific and obviously relevant expertise other than law, or in areas where governments wish to minimise the involvement of lawyers and the promotion of legal values ('legalism'). This is true even in Australia where, unlike in the US and the UK, administrative tribunals, in theory at least, perform a significantly different task from courts: superficially at least, legal expertise might be thought less relevant to reviewing decisions on the merits than reviewing them for legality. However, despite the increasing dominance of lawyers in the tribunal system, non-legal members remain more acceptable in tribunals than in courts; and it is unlikely in the foreseeable future that tribunals will become as dominated by lawyers as courts are. Nevertheless, the position of non-lawyers in tribunals is now probably more precarious than it has been since the dawn of the modern tribunal system in the first half of the 19th century.

4.1.2 Appointment Processes

The significant issues relating to appointments are who appoints, by what procedures and on what terms and conditions?

4.1.2.1 Who Appoints and How?

The view that tribunals are essentially judicial bodies favours minimising the involvement in the appointment process of the agency responsible for making the

---

[22] In England, non-lawyers play a major role in the criminal justice system at the inferior 'court' level; but they are called 'magistrates' or 'Justices of the Peace', not 'judges', and they are not addressed as 'Judge' or 'Justice'.

decisions that the tribunal has jurisdiction to review. Conversely, the view that tribunals are essentially administrative bodies favours significant involvement by the agency in the appointment process. The latter view tends to be associated with a preference for jurisdictional specialisation and the idea that non-legal expertise has a greater role to play on the tribunal bench than on the court bench. This association reinforces the argument for agency involvement in appointments by suggesting that agencies are likely to be better than an external appointing body at identifying the people best suited for reviewing their decisions. Although the basic issues are the same, the precise contours of debates about the appropriate role of agencies in the appointment process differ according to whether administrative adjudicators are embedded within agencies (as in the US) or located in free-standing tribunals (as the UK and Australia). In particular, it is easier in the latter situation than in the former to argue that agencies should have no role at all in the appointments process.

As we have already noted, in the US ALJs are appointed as the result of a competitive process conducted by the federal general appointments agency (the OPM).[23] ALJs are employed by one or another federal agency. For any particular vacancy, the employing agency is presented with a ranked list of three candidates from which it may choose any one. Agencies may also hire ALJs 'laterally' from other agencies provided the ALJ has served at least one year with the original employing agency. AJs are appointed directly by employing agencies according to their own criteria and processes.

In England, it is necessary to distinguish between members of the traditional judiciary ('court Judges') who sit as members of tribunals, legally-qualified members of tribunals ('tribunal Judges') and non-legally-qualified members ('Members'). Court Judges can sit as Judges of the Upper Tribunal, and the Senior President of the Tribunals Service is a Lord Justice of Appeal (a judge of the Court of Appeal). Tribunal Judges and Members of the First-tier Tribunal, and Members of the Upper Tribunal, are appointed by the Lord Chancellor (a government minister). Tribunal Judges of the Upper Tribunal (like court Judges) are appointed by the Queen on the advice of the Lord Chancellor. The independent Judicial Appointments Commission (JAC) plays a central role in the appointment not only of court Judges but also of tribunal Judges and Members of the First-tier and Upper Tribunals.[24] The JAC runs competitive public selection processes according to published criteria and makes recommendations to the Lord Chancellor. The Lord Chancellor can reject a JAC recommendation, but must give reasons for doing so and cannot select an alternative. The statutory criteria for appointment are that selection must be solely on merit and that a person must not be appointed unless the JAC is satisfied that they are of good

---

[23] The basic criterion is 'merit', but there is a controversial veteran's preference.
[24] The role of the JAC in relation to non-judicial Members of tribunals is regulated by Constitutional Reform Act 2005 Sch 14.

character.[25] In performing its functions the JAC must have regard to the need to encourage diversity in the range of persons available for selection.[26] These appointment arrangements replace a system in which many members of tribunals (whether or not legally-qualified) were appointed by the Ministers of the various departments whose decisions they had power to review.

In Australia, members of federal tribunals are formally appointed by the Governor-General (the Queen's representative in Australia and the Australian Head of State) on the advice of the Executive Council (ie, the Government). In effect, appointments are made by the relevant departmental Minister; in the case of the AAT (which has jurisdiction to review decisions falling within the responsibility of many government departments and agencies), this is the Attorney-General. Although posts are commonly advertised, the appointment process is based primarily on informal and largely unregulated consultation within government and between departments and tribunals. In practice, the Australian system for appointment of both (court) judges and tribunal members resembles that in the UK before the creation of the JAC, taking place largely behind closed doors.

Despite the many significant differences between these three systems, in each tribunals are understood as performing functions for the proper execution of which 'independence' from the executive branch is considered essential. As a result, the basic issue in debates about appointments concerns the extent to which any particular process potentially identifies or associates the appointee with the executive to an unacceptable extent. The ideal is an open, public and transparent process based on the application of criteria that minimise the risk that appointees will be partial towards the agencies whose decisions they will be reviewing.[27] In France, by contrast, the *Conseil d'Etat* is fully identified with the executive. Its members are recruited either from the elite national institute for training public administrators (*l'Ecole Nationale d'Administration*) or from the administration itself. Ironically, in both Australia and the US there is a stronger emphasis on openness of procedure and 'merit'-based criteria in relation to tribunals than courts. In the US, for instance, many judges of state courts are popularly elected, and legislative confirmation requirements may give weight to criteria other than 'merit'. In Australia, the emphasis on openness and merit may reflect the fact that all judges are lawyers whereas a significant proportion of tribunal members are not, the underlying assumption being that a legal training provides some assurance of impartiality and independence of mind.

---

[25] Constitutional Reform Act 2005 s 63.

[26] ibid s 64.

[27] For a discussion in the Canadian context see L Sossin, 'The Uneasy Relationship Between Independence and Appointments in Canadian Administrative Law' in G Huscroft and M Taggart (eds), *Inside and Outside Canadian Administrative Law: Essays in Honour of David Mullan* (Toronto, University of Toronto Press, 2006) (arguing that the purpose of a body will 'drive the logic' of its appointments process and that '[t]he purpose of adjudicative tribunals suggests the logic of a credible, transparent and merit-based appointment system' (ibid 72).

4.1.2.2 Terms and Conditions of Service

The gold standard for the terms and conditions of judicial service and the 'independence of the judiciary' is that set by the Act of Settlement 1701, namely appointment for life or until a fixed retiring age, removal only at the behest of the legislature and only on very limited grounds of incapacity or misbehaviour, and immunity from salary reduction. However, unless such terms and conditions are constitutionally entrenched (as they are, for instance, at the federal level in Australia), legislatures have a certain leeway in defining the terms and conditions of judicial service subject only to some minimum concept of independence.[28] A *fortiori*, such leeway exists in defining the terms and conditions of service of non-court administrative adjudicators. Judicial members of tribunals who enjoy such terms and conditions by virtue of their appointment to the traditional judiciary will not necessarily enjoy them in relation to their tribunal appointment.

The terms and conditions of service of tribunal members vary greatly. In the US, for instance, ALJs are effectively appointed indefinitely[29] and can be removed only after a hearing and only 'for good cause' as established by an independent agency (the Merit Systems Protection Board (MSPB)).[30] In 1941 the Attorney-General's Committee on Administrative Procedure recommended that agencies should be allowed to make probationary appointments provisional on adequate performance;[31] and more recently, one commentator has expressed the opinion that this proposal merits serious consideration despite its potentially negative impact on independence.[32] The salary level at which an ALJ is appointed is determined by the OPM; maximum salaries and methods of increasing salaries are fixed by legislation. Reduction in salary can be challenged before the MSPB.

In England, members of tribunals are typically appointed for a fixed term of years. Under the provisions of the TCE Act, Tribunal Judges and Members may be removed from office by the Lord Chancellor with the concurrence of the Lord Chief Justice but only on the ground of inability or misbehaviour. Most non-legal members, and many legal members sit part-time and are paid fees rather than a salary.

---

[28] See eg, *North Australian Aboriginal Legal Aid Service Inc v Bradley* (2004) 218 CLR 146, [3], [5]. Note, too, that the traditional formula does not address salary levels or the procedure for fixing salaries: J Resnik, 'Independent Federal Judiciaries: Puzzling About Why and How to Value the Independence of Which Judges' (2008) 137(4) *Daedalus* 28, 40.

[29] By contrast, judges of some Art I courts are appointed for a terms of years.

[30] VG Rosenblum, 'Contexts and Contents of "For Good Cause" as a Criterion for Removal of Administrative Law Judges: Legal and Policy Factors' (1983–84) 6 *Western New England Law Review* 593. According to Rosenblum, 'good cause' is easier to establish than the equivalent standard for dismissal of Art III judges. See also M Asimow (ed), *A Guide to Federal Agency Adjudication* (Chicago, American Bar Association, 2003) 171–77.

[31] Final Report of the Attorney-General's Committee on Administrative Procedure (Washington, 1941) 48.

[32] DJ Gifford, 'Federal Administrative Law Judges: The Relevance of Past Choices to Future Prospects' (1997) 49 *Administrative Law Review* 1, 58.

All appointments to federal tribunals in Australia are for a relatively short, fixed term of years (three, five or seven) with the possibility of re-appointment. There is very little publicly available information about the re-appointment process, which is largely unregulated. Members of the AAT may be removed from office at the behest of Parliament for 'proved misbehaviour or incapacity' and must be dismissed for bankruptcy. The tenure of members of the main specialist tribunals is not as secure as that of members of the AAT. They may be removed from office by the Governor-General, without the involvement of Parliament, not only for misbehaviour or incapacity but also on grounds unrelated to competence, such as undisclosed conflicts of interest and unapproved absence from work. In general, salary levels for members of the various tribunals are determined by an independent remuneration tribunal.

In France – ironically – the tenure of members of the lower tiers of administrative courts is more secure than that of members of the *Conseil d'Etat*, who are protected in matters of promotion and discipline only to the same extent as other civil servants. The former 'cannot be transferred to a new post, without their consent, even by way of promotion'.[33] On the other hand – according to Brown and Bell – 'it is unthinkable that a member [of the *Conseil*] should be dismissed or otherwise disciplined by reason of political considerations.'[34] Furthermore, in practice, promotion is by seniority, and this 'principle of automatic promotion is regarded by members of the *Conseil* as the essential guarantee of their independence.'[35]

Reference to the issue of promotion flags an important systemic difference between the French (civil law) system and our other three (common law) comparator jurisdictions. In civil law jurisdictions judicial service, like civil service, is a career in its own right. By contrast, in common law systems, judicial service is most commonly the culmination of a career as a practising lawyer. This is as true of judicial service in inferior as in superior courts. Despite the common association between tribunals and courts, the inferior status of tribunals as adjudicatory institutions makes serving as a legal member on a tribunal unattractive as the culmination of a successful career in legal practice except, perhaps, in relation to a few very senior posts which, if not filled by members of the traditional judiciary, carry equivalent status. At the same time, except where administrative adjudicators enjoy (effective) security of tenure (as is the situation of ALJs in the US), tribunal membership does not provide a career either. In a speech delivered at the 2nd International Conference on Administrative Justice in 2001[36] the then-President of the AAT, Justice Deidre O'Connor, argued that it was becoming possible in Australia to have a 'de facto' career in administrative

---

[33] LN Brown and JS Bell, *French Administrative Law*, 5th edn (Oxford, Clarendon Press, 1998) 87.
[34] ibid 85.
[35] ibid.
[36] <http://www.aat.gov.au/SpeechesPapersAndResearch/speeches/oconnor/administrative.htm> accessed 1 May 2008.

adjudication by combining tribunal membership with stints in related institutions, such as government agencies and academia, which are part of the 'administrative justice world' very broadly conceived. However, such 'careers' are likely to be precarious and unattractive to high-flyers so long as tribunal appointments are made by government ministers for relatively short periods.

To the extent that tribunal appointees do not enjoy the gold-standard terms and conditions of the traditional judiciary, their independence is widely thought to be compromised. However, this opinion does not usually lead to the conclusion that tribunal appointments should adhere to the gold standard. Rather it is said that the independence of tribunal appointees can be protected in other ways that can make up for the deficit produced by departure from the gold standard. This probably partly explains the emphasis on appointment processes and criteria noted in the last section.

4.1.3 Composition

How are tribunals constituted for the hearing of individual cases? The basic choice is between single-member and multi-member panels. Appellate courts are typically constituted by more than one judge and first-instance courts by a single judge. At the appellate level, the use of multi-member courts can be understood as a technique for resolving substantive disagreement by the procedural device of majority voting.[37] Amongst first-instance courts, magistrates courts in England are a major exception to the general pattern, reflecting, no doubt, the fact that legal qualifications are not necessary for appointment as a JP (legal advice being provided by a legally qualified clerk to the justices). The underlying assumption may be that non-lawyers are more prone than lawyers to 'idiosyncrasy and bias',[38] against which members of a multi-member body can check each other.

The association between composition and membership is also found in the tribunal world. While second-tier tribunals commonly sit in multi-member panels, practice is more varied in first-tier tribunals, which may sit in panels of one or three and less often in panels of two or even four. Commonly, administrative adjudicators who sit alone are legally qualified – ALJs in the US system are the paradigm example. However, in some contexts, particularly immigration (in Australia and the US, at least, although not in the UK), suspicion of lawyers and antipathy to legal values is reflected in greater use of single non-lawyer adjudicators. Non-lawyers also sit alone in tax tribunals in the UK. In Australia, there has been a trend over the years to make increasing use of non-lawyer single

---

[37] P Cane, 'Taking Disagreement Seriously: Courts, Legislatures and the Reform of Tort Law' (2005) 25 *Oxford Journal of Legal Studies* 393.

[38] J Fulbrook, *Administrative Justice and the Unemployed* (London, Mansell, 1978) 208.

adjudicators across the tribunal sector.[39] Multi-member panels – at first-tier level, anyway – typically contain at least one non-lawyer. Like the choice between whether to have non-legal tribunal members at all, the choice between single and multi-member panels at the first-tier level is essentially a choice about how non-legal knowledge, information and points of view will be injected into the decision-making process: will the tribunal rely primarily on the parties and witnesses or will it rely significantly on its own resources?

In Australia, the ARC's view in 1995 was that multi-member panels should be the norm in first-tier tribunals because any additional cost would be outweighed by increased quality and acceptability of decisions.[40] Not only are two (or three) heads better than one, but multi-membership also promotes desirable pluralism of perspective.[41] It has been argued that the use of multi-member panels is particularly appropriate 'where there is only one tier of external review or where the decision will have a profound impact on the applicant's life'.[42] In the AAT, the President has always had considerable discretion in constituting the Tribunal for individual cases, and that flexibility was increased by various amendments to the AAT Act in 2005. Factors to be taken into account in making decisions about composition include the complexity, and the public and financial importance of the matters in issue, and 'the degree to which it is desirable for any or all of the persons who are to constitute the Tribunal to have knowledge, expertise or experience in relation to the matters' in issue.[43] In the UK the Senior President of Tribunals has wide discretion to determine the composition of the various chambers of the new tribunals subject to statutory default rules that the Upper Tribunal will be constituted by a single adjudicator and that when a tribunal is constituted by a single adjudicator, that person will be a Tribunal Judge, not a Tribunal Member.[44]

In principle, the basic pattern found in the court system of first-instance adjudication by a single adjudicator and appellate adjudication by a multi-member panel seems reasonable. The more tribunals become identified, along with courts, as essentially legal institutions, the more likely it is that this pattern will be replicated in the tribunal sector. Increasingly, general arguments for the

---

[39] The migration tribunals are typically constituted by a single member, as is the AAT. The SSAT, by contrast, typically sits in multi-member panels.

[40] The abortive Administrative Review Tribunal Bill 2000 (cl 69(2)) established a presumption against the use of multi-member panels. This provision was seen as particularly problematic given the absence from the Bill of any requirement of or reference to legal qualifications for membership and even Presidency of the Tribunal.

[41] Administrative Review Council, *Better Decisions: Review of Commonwealth Merits Review Tribunals*, Report No 39 (Canberra, Australian Government Publishing Service, 1995) paras 3.47– 3.58.

[42] J Disney, 'Reforming the Administrative Review System: For Better of For Worse? For Richer or For Poorer? in J McMillan (ed), *The AAT: Twenty Years Forward* (Canberra, Australian Institute of Administrative Law, 1998) 338.

[43] AAT Act s 23B.

[44] The First Tier Tribunal and Upper Tribunal (Composition of Tribunal) Order 2008.

use of non-lawyers on tribunals have fallen out of favour to be replaced by much more jurisdictionally-specific justifications based on a clear and demonstrable need for non-legal expertise or a rejection of legal values. In addition, the issue of whether non-legal knowledge, information and points of view are best provided by including non-lawyers on the tribunal bench or in other ways has become a matter of some debate. In future we might expect the role of non-lawyers in administrative adjudication to be discussed and decided not at the level of the tribunal system as a whole but at the level of particular categories of decisions. Ironically, this may result in greater willingness to allow non-lawyers to sit alone at the first-tier level. One possible development is that the basic first-tier/single adjudicator, second-tier/multi-member panel will be common to courts and tribunals, the difference lying in the identity of first-tier adjudicators. We might expect appellate panels in both tribunals and courts to be increasingly dominated by lawyers; and while first-instance adjudication in courts will likely continue to be the province of lawyers, first-tier adjudication in tribunals may be divided between lawyers and non-lawyers according to categories of decisions under review. Whatever happens, the role of non-lawyers in administrative adjudication will continue to be a matter for debate and disagreement for the foreseeable future.

4.2 Separation and Independence

In the previous section we considered the relationship between processes, criteria, and terms and conditions of appointment and the 'independence' of individual tribunal members. Independence in this sense may be understood as a function of institutional design that promotes, but is not synonymous with, 'impartiality', which is a characteristic of reasoning processes or a frame of mind. Also relevant to independence is the relationship between adjudicatory institutions and other organs of government.

Because concepts of separation and independence were developed in relation to the traditional court judiciary, we should begin this section with a discussion of independence of 'the judiciary' in this sense. A close association between independence of the judiciary and separation of powers can be traced back at least to Blackstone's domestication of Montesquieu for an English audience in the late 18th century.[45] However, the connection is not straightforward. As traditionally understood, separation of powers has both institutional and functional elements. Perhaps the most basic requirement of institutional separation of the executive and the judiciary is that officials should be prohibited from serving in both branches simultaneously. The English office of Lord Chancellor is

---

[45] See 2.2 n 31.

frequently said to breach this requirement; but by the end of the 20th century the breach was largely technical, Lord Chancellors very rarely sitting in the Appellate Committee of the House of Lords. Far from representing executive involvement in the administration of justice, the office had come to be seen as a bulwark against government interference with the judiciary. Independence was understood to demand that the judiciary should not have to protect and defend itself against improper external criticism, particularly by government ministers, and that it should have a champion and guardian in the highest echelons of government. In other words, the office of Lord Chancellor had come to be seen not as a danger to judicial independence but its guarantor.[46] In Australia, where there is no equivalent to the office of Lord Chancellor, there have been acrimonious debates at the federal level about whether protection of the judiciary is one of the Attorney-General's functions. Given that separation of judicial power is more deeply entrenched in Australian federal law than in English law, the support of judges and lawyers for such a role indicates that they see it not only as compatible with but also essential for an independent judiciary.

Avoidance of shared membership is primarily concerned with preventing an appearance of executive influence or control over the decision of individual cases. This is considered important in general, but particularly where the government is directly affected or has a special interest. Other aspects of the relationship between the executive and the legislature on the one hand and the judiciary on the other, such as the management and funding of courts and the location of court buildings, relate to the independence and the appearance of independence of courts and judges in a more general or systemic way. There can obviously be no mechanical formula for determining when the potential for influence and control inherent in the relationship between the executive and the legislature on the one side and the courts on the other is so great as to pose an unacceptable threat to the independence of thought and action of judges and courts. No single aspect of the relationship is critical on its own, and the way the various aspects are handled may vary significantly as between systems in all of which the judiciary is perceived to be (sufficiently) independent.

The implications of the functional aspect of separation of powers for judicial independence are at least equally complex. At its most severe, functional separation requires that no particular function be performed by more than one type of institution. As was argued in Chapter 1, adjudication is one mode of the activity of identifying relevant general norms and applying them to individual cases. This is the core activity of courts; but it is also one of the core activities of the

---

[46]   The Constitutional Reform Act 2005 stripped the office of Lord Chancellor of the judicial role and transferred the headship of the judiciary to the Lord Chief Justice. However, s 1 of the Act cryptically announces that it does not 'adversely affect … the Lord Chancellor's existing role in relation to' the 'constitutional principle of the rule of law'. For an argument (in the US context) that attacks on the judiciary are based on a view that 'courts and the judges who sit on the bench are part of ordinary politics' see SB Burbank, 'Judicial Independence, Judicial Accountability and Interbranch Relations' (2008) 137(4) *Daedalus* 16.

executive. When courts engage in administrative adjudication they review decisions of the executive and they do so by engaging in essentially the same activity as the primary executive decision-maker. From this perspective, there is no separation of powers – 'checks and balances' is not a version of separation of powers but its negation. This helps to explain the French system of administrative courts: separation requires that primary executive decision-making and review of primary decisions be performed by one and the same branch of government because they are essentially the same function. The implication is that adjudicating disputes between citizen and citizen ('civil adjudication') is a different function and, therefore, properly allocated to a different institution – the 'ordinary' courts. Ironically, this implication is echoed in the distinction drawn in both US law and Australian law between adjudication of disputes about 'private rights ' and adjudication of disputes about 'public rights'. Adjudication of disputes of the former type is considered to be a core judicial function normally to be undertaken only by courts whereas adjudication of disputes of the latter type can appropriately be allocated to non-judicial 'administrative' adjudicators. This approach sits uneasily with the commitment, implicit in the promotion of the independence of administrative adjudicators, to minimising executive involvement in cases by which the government is directly affected or in which it has some special interest.

On the other hand, it was also argued in Chapter 1 that 'adjudication' is a significantly different mode of applying general norms to individual cases than 'implementation' in that it favours resolving conflicts between individual and social interests in favour of the former whereas implementation favours resolving such conflicts in favour of the latter. From this perspective, the functional aspect of separation of powers would require that adjudication and implementation respectively be undertaken by different types of institution. This may help to explain why Hewart and Robson, for instance, were so opposed to allowing ministers to review decisions made in the first instance by other officials of the executive branch. In the French system, implementation and adjudication are allocated to the same branch of government because they are considered to be essentially similar, whereas in the UK and Australian systems they are allocated to different types of institutions because they are considered to be different in an important respect. However, it may be difficult to determine the practical significance of this institutional difference. It is by no means clear whether or not the French system protects individual interests any less well than the UK system; and even if it does protect them less well, it must be a matter of judgment whether the balance struck by the UK system is preferable to that struck by the French.

The position in the US system is different again. There – as was argued in 3.2 – ideas of institutional balance play a more important part than judicial independence in establishing explaining the place of courts in the governmental structure. More than in the UK or Australia, courts in the US are seen as being part of the governmental and political process, not as standing outside it; and as noted earlier in this section, there is an important sense in which 'checks and balances' is the negation of separation of powers. In a system of checks and balances neither institutional nor functional separation are seen as crucial. The fundamental principle is that the power of each component in the system should be subject to limitation and constraint by some other component. Interdependence is what matters, not independence. This helps to explain both popular election and legislative vetting of judges in the US – practices that are commonly thought, in the UK and Australia, to pose significant potential threats to judicial independence.

So much for courts. What about administrative tribunals? We will consider the position in the UK first, then the US and finally Australia. Before doing that, it is worth making a general point about the relationship between separation and independence on the one hand and specialisation (4.3.1) on the other: specialist tribunals have closer links with the agencies whose decisions they review than do general tribunals. This is necessarily true of embedded adjudication; but it is also contingently true of free-standing tribunals, as the history of tribunals in the UK in the last 100 years clearly demonstrates. In Australia, for instance, the links between the immigration tribunals and the Social Security Appeals Tribunal on the one side and the relevant agency on the other are closer in various respects – management, funding, support personnel and so on – than the links between the AAT and the various agencies whose decisions it reviews.[47] A general tribunal is likely to be more separate from primary decision-making agencies, and therefore to appear more independent, than a specialist tribunal.

4.2.1 The UK

Significantly, the word 'independence' does not appear in the index of Chantal Stebbings' authoritative study of tribunals in 19th-century England. In her account, it was not until the end of the century, when tribunals came to be seen as essentially similar to courts, that the issue of 'independence in dispute-resolution' began to figure in debates about tribunals.[48] In the 1920s and 1930s the likes of Hewart and Robson were primarily concerned that administrative adjudication should not be in the hands of ministers or civil servants. Robson's discussion of independence focuses on the tenure and salary protections enjoyed by the traditional court judiciary and their 'psychological effects' on the 'mental processes which are involved in making a decision'.[49] In his eyes, the critical characteristic of judges was that they were not '"employed" in the sense that a

---

[47] R Bacon, 'Are the Babies Being Thrown Out with the Bathwater? Retaining the Benefits of Specialist Tribunals within the ART' in C Finn (ed), *Administrative Law for the New Millenium* (Canberra, Australian Institute of Administrative Law, 2000) 150, 156–61.

[48] Stebbings *Legal Foundations of Tribunals in Nineteenth Century England*, 329.

[49] WA Robson, *Justice and Administrative Law* (London, Macmillan and Co, 1928) 43–50.

civil servant is employed.'[50] The Donoughmore Committee recommended that in exceptional cases, judicial functions might be conferred on a 'Ministerial Tribunal' appointed by the Minister but 'independent of him in the exercise of their functions';[51] an 'independent person' being one who is not 'an officer ... of the Department concerned'.[52] Beyond this, no thought seems to have been given to the relationship between tribunals and the executive. The Franks Committee's focus was on tribunal procedure, and this explains why its classic trio of values includes 'impartiality' rather than independence, the latter (in contrast to the former) being primarily a structural rather than a process-related concept (and a frame of mind). Nevertheless, the Committee did discuss the appointment process for tribunal members, recommending that responsibility for appointment of tribunal chairs should rest with Lord Chancellor and for appointing tribunal members with the proposed Council on Tribunals.[53]

It was not until the end of the 20th century that concern about tribunal independence took centre stage. The Leggatt Review of Tribunals devoted a whole chapter of its Report to the issue, declaring in the first sentence that, 'A clear majority of those who responded to our Consultation Paper thought that tribunals generally, or particular tribunals, were not perceived as independent'.[54] In addition to appointment processes, concerns revolved around the role of government departments in providing administrative support and funding to tribunals responsible for reviewing decisions made by officials of the department. Significantly, the Review linked independence with institutional separation:

> We have concluded that the only way in which users can be satisfied that tribunals are truly independent is by developing clear separation between the ministers and other authorities whose policies are tested by tribunals, and the minister who appoints and supports them.[55]

The Review's general approach was that in terms of independence, tribunals should be equated to courts. The Franks Committee sought to (re-)make tribunal procedure in the image of court procedure under the banner of openness, fairness and impartiality. The Leggatt Review sought to construct a tribunal system in the image of the court system under the banner of independence, coherence and 'user-friendliness' (aka 'accessibility'). Thus, Leggatt proposed the establishment of a new non-departmental agency – the Tribunals Service – to manage the tribunal system just as the already-existing Courts Service managed

---

[50] ibid 44. 'Without independence ... tribunals offer nothing more than ... a review process within the agency that made the original decision': G Fleming, '"The Proof of the Pudding is in the Eating": Questions about the Independence of Administrative Tribunals' (1999) 7 *Australian Journal of Administrative Law* 33, 34.

[51] Report of the Committee on Ministers' Powers 1932 (Cmd 4060) 116.

[52] ibid 109.

[53] Report of the Committee on Administrative Tribunals and Enquiries 1957 (Cmnd 218) paras 45–54.

[54] *Tribunals for Users: One System, One Service* (London, TSO, 2001) para 2.2.

[55] ibid para 2.23.

the bulk of the court system. It also recommended that the appointment process for members of tribunals should be the same as that for judges. Just as importantly, a fragmented collection of adjudicatory bodies identified with particular government programmes and agencies were to be amalgamated into a two-tier general tribunal integrated with the court system and more clearly identified than ever with the judicial branch of government. Symbolic of these various changes is the extension from the court judiciary to the tribunal judiciary (and tribunal members) of the guarantee of independence enshrined in the Constitutional Reform Act 2005.[56]

4.2.2 Australia

In Australia, it seems clear that independence was not uppermost in the minds of the members of the Kerr Committee. Although some have seen judicial presidency of the AAT as significant for its independence,[57] the Committee's expressed reasons for recommending that the President of its proposed tribunal be a judge were that it would raise the status of the institution and the acceptability of its decisions, and that 'the judge could rule on all questions of law'.[58] Moreover, it recommended that tribunal panels should include an officer of the agency whose decision was under review![59] Dissenting from the view of the Franks Committee, the Kerr Committee did not think 'complete independence' to be necessary.[60] In *Better Decisions*, the ARC asserted the importance of tribunal independence, but thought that this did not require tribunal members to enjoy the tenure and salary protections accorded to judges.[61] It proposed the establishment of a new tribunal that would operate in several specialist divisions and one general division; and it did not baulk at the involvement of the relevant portfolio minister in appointment of members to specialist divisions.[62] The ARC considered performance monitoring inappropriate in relation to 'review outcomes – in terms of set-aside or variation rates' but not in relation to 'such matters as timeliness of decisions and written reasons, the process employed in dealing with cases, and quality of

[56] Article 6 of the European Convention on Human Rights lurks in the background: *Tribunals for Users*, paras 2.11–2.17; C Harlow, 'The ECHR and Administrative Justice' in M Partington (ed), *The Leggatt Review of Tribunals: Academic Seminar Papers* (Bristol, Faculty of Law, University of Bristol, 2001) 43–46; G Richardson, 'Tribunals' in D Feldman (ed), *English Public Law* (Oxford, OUP, 2004) para 20.20.

[57] Including the ARC in *Better Decisions*, para 4.19. However, it recommended only that the President of its proposed Administrative Review Tribunal be required to have legal qualifications: ibid para 8.32.

[58] Kerr Committee Report, para 293.

[59] ibid para 292.

[60] ibid para 321.

[61] *Better Decisions*, para 4.6, 4.54–4.66.

[62] ibid paras 448–52, 8.33. The ARC argued that any threat to independence involved in such an arrangement would be counterbalanced by its proposals for a more public and structured appointment process.

reasoning'. But it rejected the idea of performance pay.[63] Furthermore, in spite of a strong emphasis in *Better Decisions* on enhancing the capacity of tribunals to improve the quality of primary decision-making (see further 5.5 below), the ARC, unlike some commentators,[64] stopped short of proposing that tribunals should engage extra-curially with agencies as a way of promoting quality in primary decision-making.[65]

Overall, the ARC's approach to independence was informed by the idea that tribunals are different from and perform a different function than courts, and that they should not be equated with courts in respect of their independence. By contrast, the UK approach is to treat tribunals and courts alike in this respect. In Australia, on the other hand, the independence of members of the AAT is better protected than that of members of the specialist federal merits review tribunals; for instance, the former can be appointed for a longer period than the latter. Institutionally, too, the AAT operates at a greater distance from the executive than specialist tribunals.[66] For instance, it has its own constitutive legislation (the AAT Act) whereas the constitutive legislation of the specialist tribunals is embedded within subject specific legislation. The AAT Act contains many details of a kind commonly found in legislation dealing with courts and largely missing from the constitutive provisions of the specialist tribunals. The AAT falls within the Attorney-General's portfolio whereas the specialist tribunals fall within the portfolio of the minister responsible for the relevant policy area. The AAT is treated as an independent statutory authority for funding, administrative and staffing purposes. The specialist tribunals, by contrast, are more-or-less closely integrated into the structure and operations of the relevant department.

---

[63] *Better Decisions*, paras 4.74–4.83

[64] G Fleming, 'Administrative Review and the "Normative" Goal – Is Anybody Out There?' (2000) 28 *Federal Law Review* 61, 81–82.

[65] The AAT meets regularly with 'regular users and other stakeholders' but apparently only to discuss administrative matters: Administrative Review Tribunal, *Annual Report 2006–07*, 39. In the UK the Social Security Act 1998 imposed on the President of the (Social Security) Appeal Tribunals a duty to make an annual report, based on the cases coming before tribunals, on standards of primary decision-making. The jurisdiction of the Appeal Tribunals has been transferred to the Upper Tribunal, and the Senior President of Tribunals has no such reporting obligation. The President's Reports have been based on statistical analyses of relatively large numbers of cases. In his final report (*Report by the President of Appeal Tribunals on the Standard of Decision-Making by the Secretary of State, 2007–08* (The Tribunals Service, 2008) the President says that 'there is little evidence of significant change over time in standards of administrative decision making, as gauged by cases coming before tribunals' (2); and reports that the most common reason why tribunals overturn primary decisions is because the tribunal was given additional evidence that was not available to the decision-maker. The President expresses scepticism about the value of statistical analysis, and considers feedback based on individual cases to be more likely to bring about improvement in decision-making (paras 1.9 and 1.18).

[66] Here I have relied heavily on R Bacon, *Amalgamating Tribunals: A Recipe for Optimal Reform*, University of Sydney PhD Thesis, 2004, 54–70. For an account of some very crude political interference with the Refugee Review Tribunal see SH Legomsky, 'Refugees, Administrative Tribunals and Real Independence: Dangers Ahead for Australia' (1998) 76 *Washington University Law Quarterly* 243.

At least so far as administrative adjudication is concerned, protecting the independence of tribunal members less well than that of court judges is a very odd approach. Our attitude to *judicial* independence shows that independence of adjudicators from the executive is important even where all the directly interested and specially affected parties are citizens. It is even more important where one of those parties is the executive. What is the basis of this strange approach to the independence of non-judicial administrative adjudicators? One possible ground is the idea that reviewing of decisions is part of the process of implementing rules rather than a different and separate process. If reviewers are expected to resolve conflicts between individual and social interests in favour of the latter, it might seem to follow that they should have no more independence from policy-makers than do rule-implementers. However, if review is understood in this way, it is unclear why it should ever be conducted externally rather than internally. Externality puts distance between the reviewer and the implementer precisely in order to give the reviewer the freedom to focus on the individual and to prefer the individual's interests to relevant social interests where this seems 'fair' or 'just'. If creating this possibility is thought inappropriate, there seems little reason to add a layer of external review on top of however many layers of internal review are thought justifiable or necessary.

Another possible explanation for the approach of protecting the independence of tribunal members less well than that of (court) judges is that tribunal members as a group (excluding judicial members) are generally considered to be of lower calibre than judges, excellence being defined in terms of legal skills and experience. A corollary would be that tribunal members, unlike judges, could appropriately be subject to removal for incompetence. However, surely no-one believes that all judges at all levels of the judicial hierarchy are (equally) competent, and it remains unclear why this pragmatic justification for lower protection should be adequate in relation to tribunal members but not judges. Putting the point another way, why should tribunals be thought of as non-courts rather than as inferior courts? The answer that Australian law gives to this question is that tribunals perform a categorically different function than courts – namely merits review. But what is the connection between this and independence? In *Better Decisions* the ARC answered the question by saying that the needs of users of tribunals change over time; and because tribunals can review decisions on the merits and not merely for legality, such changing needs argue against tenure for tribunal members in a way that they do not argue against tenure for judges: tribunal independence should not prevent tribunals responding to the changing needs of their users.[67] While the logic of the argument is clear enough, it rests on an unanalysed and untested assumption that 'law' is less time-sensitive than are 'merits'.

---

[67] ibid paras 4.55–4.56.

4.2.3 The US

In the UK context, it is worth noting that in the move from procedure (Franks) to structure (Leggatt), embedded adjudication through public inquiries dropped off the agenda. In a system in which the prime significance of separation of powers lies in the independence of adjudicators of disputes between citizen and government, embedded adjudication looks at least anomalous. By contrast, in a system of checks and balances, embedded adjudication may be thought acceptable provided the relationship between decision-maker and adjudicator is suitably calibrated. As we saw in 3.2, the primary decision model of adjudication in the context of regulation (regulatory policy-making through case-by-case adjudication) dominated debates about administrative adjudication in the 1930s and 1940s. Of great concern was the combination within agencies of powers of investigation and enforcement on the one hand and adjudication on the other. The scheme – of internal separation of adjudicators from other agency staff, strict limits on 'ex parte contact', tenure and salary protection for hearing examiners (later ALJs) and the ceding to them of initial decision-making authority – put in place by the Administrative Procedure Act 1946 (APA) addressed such concern. This scheme was a compromise between the President, who sought maximum control by agencies over adjudication, and those who favoured the hiving off of the adjudicatory function from agencies into a separate, independent administrative court. As might be expected, the APA scheme fell significantly short of the aspirations of contemporary English reformers, such as Hewart and Robson, in that there was effectively a right of appeal from a hearing examiner to the head of the agency (analogous to an appeal to the minister in the English context), designed to enable the agency to maintain ultimate control over policy-making. Since the enactment of the APA there have been numerous proposals for the creation of an independent administrative adjudication agency, but such a significant change in the balance of power between adjudicators and agency heads has never garnered sufficient political support to become a reality.

Control of adjudication by agency heads through the mechanism of hearing appeals in individual cases became less attractive with the shift in the 1960s and 1970s from policy-making through case-by-case adjudication to policy-making through rule-making, especially in high-volume areas such as social security. However, agency heads retain ultimate control of policy-making. In some agencies, attempts have been made to exercise such control partly through the creation of second-tier adjudicatory bodies,[68] but – in the Social Security Administration in particular – also through monitoring the performance of individual adjudicators.[69] Performance monitoring, as such, need not unduly

[68] In very high-volume jurisdictions even this is may be an impractical way of making general policy.
[69] See eg, DJ Gifford, 'Federal Administrative Law Judges: The Relevance of Past Choices to Future Directions' (1997) 49 *Administrative Law Review* 1, 52–55; CH Koch, 'Administrative Presiding

de-stabilise the relationship between the agency and its adjudicators. After all, even the judicial gold standard of independence allows monitoring of the probity and the physical and mental capacities of judges. Ultimately, the technical question, so far as individual ALJs are concerned, is what constitutes 'good cause' (under the APA) for suspension, reduction in grade or salary, or removal.[70] The critical issue in the present context is whether or not this concept could extend to deciding cases inconsistently with agency policy. It seems not.[71] Nevertheless, it may be that in practice a more potent threat to the stability of the relationship between agency and adjudicator than the power of the agency to control policy would be willingness on the part of adjudicators to take a very active a part in the policy-formation process. Maintaining a suitable balance between decision-maker and adjudicator is as much a political as a legal matter, as dependent on conventions as on enforceable rules. This helps to explain why '[t]rench warfare between administrative law judges and policy makers at the Social Security Administration … continued unabated'[72] despite several attempts at resolution in the courts.

4.3 Structure and Systematisation

This section has two parts dealing respectively with specialisation and amalgamation, and supervision and accountability.

4.3.1 Jurisdictional Specialisation

As we noted in 4.1.1.1, specialisation has two aspects: membership and jurisdiction. This section is concerned with jurisdictional specialisation. The idea of jurisdictional specialisation is underpinned by some concept of a universe of legal issues consisting of all the types of matter[73] that could in principle be considered by bodies of a particular type – courts or tribunals, for instance. A court or tribunal of specialised jurisdiction is one with power to consider a

---

Officials Today (1994) 46 *Administrative Law Review* 271; JS Lubbers, 'Federal Administrative Law Judges: A Focus on our Invisible Judiciary' (1981) 33 *Administrative Law* 109, 125–26; JL Mashaw, RA Merrill and PM Shane, *Administrative Law: The American Public Law System*, 5th edn (St Paul, Minn: Thomson West, 2003, 441–51; PR Verkuil, 'Reflections upon the Federal Administrative Judiciary' (1991–92) 39 *UCLA Law Review* 1341, 1354–58; JS Wolfe, 'Are You Willing to Make the Commitment in Writing? The APA, ALJs and the SSA' (2002) 55 *Oklahoma Law Review* 203. For a brief discussion in the Australian context see Fleming, n 50 above, 43–47.

[70] Rosenblum, n 30 above.

[71] ibid 642.

[72] Mashaw, Merrill and Shane, n 69 above, 449.

[73] The word 'matter' has a technical meaning in Australian constitutional law. Here I am using it in a non-technical and deliberately vague sense.

relatively small class of legal matters. The universe of legal issues may be divided up in various ways. For instance, a particular court or tribunal may have jurisdiction to consider only legal matters that arise in a particular geographical area. Our prime concern here is with categorisation of legal issues in conceptual terms – criminal law versus civil law, public law versus private law, and so on; and in 'functional' terms – family law, immigration law, housing law and so on. But we are also concerned with a very different classification of legal matters on the basis of types of 'jurisdiction': original, supervisory and appellate. The fewer the categories of legal matter (however classified) over which a court or tribunal has power, the more specialised it is; and conversely, the more categories of legal matter over which a court or tribunal has power, the more 'generalist' it is. Specialism and generalism are matters of degree. In these terms, for instance, the AAT is relatively generalist: not only does it have power to review decisions made in many areas of government activity, but it also exercises a mix of original (or 'first-tier') and appellate (or 'second tier') jurisdiction.

From the very earliest days of the common law there have been courts located at various points on the specialist/generalist spectrum. By contrast, administrative tribunals have traditionally been created to exercise relatively narrow, specialised jurisdiction, typically defined in functional terms. The classic administrative tribunal is an adjudicatory body established to review primary decisions made in implementation of specific statutory government programmes and policies in areas such as social welfare, immigration and economic regulation. The term 'specialist', applied to a tribunal, normally means that the body in question has power in relation to only one government programme or area of activity; and this is the sense in which it will normally be used in this section.

The issue of amalgamation is closely – indeed inextricably – related to that of specialisation because the effect of amalgamation is to produce a body the jurisdiction of which is broader (and in that sense less specialised) than that of the various institutional elements of the resultant body.

The remainder of this section is in two parts – the first descriptive and the second analytical.

4.3.1.1 Patterns of Specialisation

This sub-section deals first with the situation in Australia and then with the position in our two main comparator jurisdictions – the UK and the US.

(i)   Australia

The Kerr Committee's vision for the new administrative law included the creation of a general tribunal to review administrative decisions on the merits. However, the Committee also contemplated that existing specialist tribunals might continue to exist and that new specialist tribunals might be created in 'special circumstances'.[74] The Bland Committee, which was appointed in the wake of the Kerr Committee to 'examine existing administrative discretions ... and to advise on those in respect of which a review on the merits should be provided',[75] proposed the creation of three new tribunals: a Valuation and Compensation Tribunal, a Medical Appeals Tribunal and a general Administrative Appeals Tribunal. Despite expressing concern about the continuing proliferation of tribunals, the Bland Committee did not propose that existing specialist tribunals be integrated into the proposed general tribunal or that new specialist tribunals should not be created; but it did recommend a presumption in favour of integration of existing specialist tribunals and against creation of new specialist tribunals.[76]

One of the statutory functions conferred on the ARC was to 'make recommendations to the Minister as to the desirability of administrative decisions that are the subject of review by tribunals other than the Administrative Appeals Tribunal being made the subject of review by the Administrative Appeals Tribunal'.[77] In the course of the 1980s the ARC – applying the presumption recommended by the Bland Committee[78] – examined a number of high-volume merits review tribunals and in some cases (such as those of the Income Tax Boards of Review and the Commonwealth Employees' Compensation Tribunal) recommended integration into the AAT. In other cases (notably social security[79] and veterans' benefits) it recommended a two-tier system, the AAT constituting the second tier.[80] The latter course was considered appropriate for high-volume jurisdictions, the first-tier tribunal providing 'economical, expeditious and informal review' and the second dealing with a small number of cases in greater depth and developing general principles of decision-making.

In the area of immigration,[81] the AAT was initially given power to review criminal deportation decisions and, later (in 1992), certain decisions to refuse or cancel visas. However, most external reviews of immigration decisions are undertaken by two specialist tribunals, the Migration Review Tribunal (MRT) –

---

[74] eg Kerr Committee Report, para 280.

[75] Final Report of the Committee on Administrative Discretions (Canberra, Australian Government Publishing Service, 1973) (Bland Committee Report) para 1.

[76] Bland Committee Report, paras 187–88.

[77] Administrative Appeals Tribunal Act 1975 s 51(1)(f).

[78] *Sixth Annual Report 1981–82*, para 102. The ARC supported the presumption by noting four features of the AAT: flexible constitution, high calibre of members, advantageous procedures and its ability to develop clear and uniform decision-making guidelines: *Twelfth Annual Report 1987–88*, para 229. See also *Thirteenth Annual Report 1988–89*.

[79] According to Jack Richardson, the decision to confer second-tier review jurisdiction over social security decisions to the AAT 'established the principle that the AAT should be a general administrative appeals tribunal': Address by Professor Jack Richardson AO in Administrative Review Council, *Record of the 25th Anniversary Proceedings*, 67.

[80] Administrative Review Council, *Review of Commonwealth Merits Review Tribunals: Discussion Paper* (1994) paras 2.51–2.57. In relation to most types of reviewable decisions, the AAT operates as a first-tier reviewer.

[81] *Review of Commonwealth Merits Review Tribunals: Discussion Paper*, paras 2.58–2.63.

originally established as the Immigration Review Tribunal in 1989 – and the Refugee Review Tribunal (RRT), which was set up in 1993. The MRT and the RRT are administratively integrated and there is no appeal from these tribunals to the AAT, although the MRT/RRT can refer to the AAT cases raising important issues of general significance.[82] In its 1988 Annual Report the ARC was critical of this arrangement on the ground that it was 'the first significant example of fragmentation of the integrated review system' with the AAT at its centre.[83]

The ARC returned to the issue of the structure of the tribunal system in its 1995 *Better Decisions* report. In that report the ARC – '[running] with the tide of government pressure to amalgamate all the tribunals into the one mega-tribunal'[84] – recommended the creation of a new two-tier tribunal. The first tier would consist of six specialist divisions and a general division. The general division would exercise any review jurisdiction that did not conveniently fall within the jurisdiction of one of the specialist divisions. The expressed aims of this re-organisation – which never materialised – were to retain

the positive attributes of the individual merits review tribunals, but ... also ... [achieve] greater perceived and actual independence, improvements in agency decision making, and improved accessibility and economic efficiencies.[85]

The recommendations in the *Better Decisions* report focused on the specialist tribunals in the areas of social security, veterans' benefits and immigration.[86] It is not clear precisely how many specialist federal merits review tribunals there are; but it seems safe to say that there is only a handful in addition to those dealt with in *Better Decisions* (the Australian Competition Tribunal being one). Thus, despite its somewhat fragmented state, the situation in Australia at the federal level is very different from that found in the UK in 2001 when there were some 70 administrative tribunals[87] established in 'an almost entirely haphazard way'.[88]

The AAT currently operates in six divisions: General Administrative, Medical Appeals, Security Appeals, Taxation Appeals, Valuation and Compensation, and Veterans' Appeals. It exercises second-tier jurisdiction in the areas of social security and veterans' benefits and first-tier jurisdiction in a wide variety of areas. However, most of the AAT's first-tier caseload consists of taxation and workers' compensation cases, and its second-tier jurisdiction accounts for about 40 per cent of its total caseload. The main first-tier specialist merits review tribunals are the Social Security Appeals Tribunal; the immigration tribunals – the MRT

---

[82] As at 22 April 2008, this power had apparently been exercised only once: *Re SRPP and Minister for Immigration and Multicultural Affairs* (2000) 62 ALD 758.

[83] *Thirteenth Annual Report 1988–89*, paras 8–11. See also *Sixteenth Annual Report 1991–92*, para 207.

[84] D Pearce in Administrative Review Council, *Record of the 25th Anniversay Proceedings* (Canberra, 2002) 36.

[85] *Better Decisions*, para 8.6. For more details of the ARC proposals see 2.3.3.

[86] *Better Decisions*, para 1.20.

[87] *Tribunals for Users*, 5.

[88] ibid 15.

and the RRT; and the Veterans' Review Board. It should be noted that while the AAT conducts first-tier external review in some areas and second-tier review in others, the AAT itself is a single-tier body which lacks an internal appeal structure. In this respect, arrangements in Australia are very different from the new tribunal system in the UK.

(ii) The UK

As we saw in 2.3.1, debates about tribunals in Britain in the 20th century were significantly influenced by Dicey's opposition to the French system of administrative 'courts'. These bodies are specialised in the conceptual sense that they deal only with matters of public law; but generalist in the functional sense that they have jurisdiction in relation to a very wide range of government activities and in the sense that they can entertain not only (what a common lawyer would call) applications for judicial review, but also claims for damages. In functional terms, they can be contrasted with the so-called 'specialised jurisdictions' mentioned in 3.4.

Dicey's objections to the French system were based partly on his extreme dislike of the distinction between public law and private law and its institutional embodiment in the court structure. William Robson was the leading advocate of the creation in England of a system analogous to the French; but as we have seen, both the Donoughmore Committee and the Franks Committee rejected his proposals. The Donoughmore Committee did so on two grounds: one was that under the proposed arrangements, the existing courts would be deprived of both supervisory and appellate jurisdiction over decisions of the administrative courts; and the other was that such a system would have involved transfer to an administrative court of certain decision-making powers currently exercisable by a minister, thus removing the possibility of scrutiny by Parliament and public opinion.[89] These objections reflected the Committee's basic strategy of favouring allocation of adjudicative functions either to courts or to ministers, and allocating them to tribunals only as a last resort and in exceptional cases.

The Franks Committee did not fully share the Donoughmore Committee's suspicion of tribunals, preferring them to ministers, if not to courts, as administrative adjudicators. Nevertheless, despite expressing 'much sympathy' for the idea of a 'general administrative appeal tribunal' that would exercise a mix of first-instance and appellate jurisdiction in relation to administrative decisions, it rejected the proposal for three reasons.[90] First, the Committee thought that creating a right of appeal from a more specialised to a less specialised body would

---

[89] Report of the Committee on Ministers' Powers 1932 (Cmd 4060) 110. Robson himself argued that avoidance of Parliamentary scrutiny was one motivation for establishing tribunals: WA Robson, 'Administrative Justice and Injustice: A Commentary on the Franks Report' [1958] *PL* 12, 15.

[90] Report of the Committee on Administrative Tribunals and Enquiries, 1957 (Cmnd 218) paras 120–23.

undermine the expertise and experience for which tribunals were valued. Secondly, no good case had been made for departing from the traditional principle that inferior adjudicatory bodies should be subject to control of the superior courts 'in matters of jurisdict[i]on'. Thirdly, the proposal would lead to the creation of 'two systems of law ... with all the evils attendant on this dichotomy'.

Like that of the Donoughmore Committee, the approach of the Franks Committee to this issue may have been based on some misunderstanding of Robson's position – a result, perhaps, of imprecision and a certain lack of clarity in Robson's proposals. As we saw in 2.3.1, Robson did not contemplate that the administrative tribunal system that he proposed would be completely immune from judicial control. As he said in his commentary on the Franks Committee report,

> proceedings of administrative tribunals should be liable to be reviewed and their decisions quashed by courts if it can be shown that the members of the tribunal did not hear the case with an open mind or had prejudged the issue; or that they had exercised their powers to promote unauthorised purposes; or had been influenced by improper motives of [*sic*] extraneous considerations.[91]

On the other hand, Robson opposed what he called 'a general right of appeal to the courts on points of law'. His opposition was based on the expense, complexity and formality of court proceedings and the courts' 'lack of expert knowledge'.[92]

For its part, the Franks Committee recommended that there should normally be 'a general appeal on fact, law and merits' from first instance tribunals to an appellate tribunal[93] as well as a right of appeal to a court on points of law.[94] On appeal, the Committee said, the court could (in effect, at least) make a substitute decision. In the end, it seems, the respective positions of Robson and the Committee were not far apart. Both apparently favoured a two-tier system of administrative tribunals operating in parallel with, but ultimately subject to limited control by, the superior courts. They may have held different views about how much control the courts should exercise over tribunals, but that is unclear.

However, there does appear to be one respect in which the Franks Committee's vision was significantly different from Robson's: whereas Robson argued for a single general administrative appeals tribunal, the Committee apparently favoured specialist review tribunals exercising jurisdiction at appellate level in the same area as the first instance decision-makers whose decisions they had power to review. This approach is consistent with the Committee's concern that establishment of a single appeal tribunal would undermine the values of experience and expertise. The emphasis placed by the Committee on expertise also motivated its rejection of a proposal for creation of an Administrative Division of the

---

[91] Robson, n 89 above, 18.
[92] ibid 18–19.
[93] 1957 (Cmnd 218) paras 105–06.
[94] ibid para 107, in addition to the possibility of judicial review to 'challenge the jurisdiction of a tribunal' (ibid para 114).

High Court.[95] The Committee apparently believed that limiting judicial control over tribunals to matters of 'law' overcame the objection to giving a generalist court power to review decisions of a specialist tribunal. At all events, the Franks Committee left unresolved the issues of proliferation of tribunals and rationalisation of appeals.

As we have seen (2.3.1), the TCE Act creates a two-tier tribunal structure consisting of a First-tier Tribunal and an Upper Tribunal, with a right of appeal to the Court of Appeal (in England) on a point of law. The Review of Tribunals by Sir Andrew Leggatt – whose report, *Tribunals for Users: One System, One Service*, led to the enactment of the TCE Act – took the view that both the first-tier tribunal and the appellate tribunal should operate in such a way as to preserve the specialisation-based expertise of the existing system. The aim of the proposed structural changes was to make tribunals more user-friendly, accessible, and administratively coherent and efficient, without encroaching on the traditional system of specialisation in administrative adjudication. To this end, it was proposed that the first-tier tribunal would operate in functionally specialised divisions into which existing tribunals would be grouped; for each tribunal there would be 'a corresponding appellate tribunal' and these, too, would be grouped into divisions.[96] The Review was particularly concerned to ensure that the creation of the appellate tribunal would not lead to any loss of expertise in its membership,[97] despite the fact that appeals from a first-tier tribunal to an appellate tribunal were to be on points of law only and that the appellate tribunal was to have no power to make a substitute decision.[98]

Under the TCE Act, appeals to the Upper Tribunal are limited to points of law, but the Upper Tribunal may set aside, and either remit or remake, a decision of the First-tier tribunal (TCE Act section 12). The functions of existing administrative tribunals are transferred to either the First-tier Tribunal or the Upper Tribunal.[99] Typically, first-instance reviews of primary decisions take place in the First-tier Tribunal, although the Upper Tribunal has some first-instance jurisdiction in complex cases and cases raising issues of general significance in relation to which it is considered appropriate that an appeal should lie directly to the Court of Appeal rather than another tribunal. The First-tier Tribunal is very large, consisting of some 190 judges and 3,600 members handling around 300,000 cases a year across a great range of subject matter.

---

[95] ibid paras 124–25.

[96] *Tribunals for Users*, 7. This was essentially Robson's approach in his submission to the Franks Committee: Committee on Administrative Tribunals and Enquiries, Minutes of Evidence (London, HMSO, 1956) 482–512. Grouping of tribunals can be distinguished (although only in degree) from integration: grouping preserves the identity of individual tribunals to an extent that integration does not.

[97] ibid paras 6.10–11.

[98] ibid para 6.12–6.13.

[99] At the time of writing, the new tribunal structure is in a state of flux, and it will take some time for it to become fully operational. The following account should be treated as indicative only.

The First-tier Tribunal operates in Chambers into which pre-existing tribunal jurisdictions are grouped. At June 2009, there were four Chambers: Health, Education and Social Care; Social Entitlement; War Pensions and Armed Forces Compensation; and Tax. A General Regulatory Chamber follows later in 2009 and an Asylum and Immigration Chamber in 2010. It is recognised that there may be significant differences between the functions and procedures of the various jurisdictions grouped together within a Chamber, and that in some jurisdictions it is desirable to retain regional diversity and identity. In the short-term, the anticipated benefits of amalgamation are primarily financial and organisational. At first, it is expected that members will only hear cases in the jurisdictions in which they sat prior to amalgamation; but in the longer term, that some may sit in more than one jurisdiction. In other words, the Chamber structure is designed to reduce the degree of jurisdictional specialisation in the operation of tribunals.[100]

As at June 2009, the Upper Tribunal had three Chambers: Administrative Appeals; Finance and Tax; and Lands. An Asylum and Immigration Chamber follows in 2010. In general, the jurisdiction of the Upper Tribunal is the result of transfer to it of jurisdiction formerly exercised either by a second-tier tribunal or the High Court. Historically, decisions of many first-instance tribunals were not subject to appeal to a higher tribunal, and many were not subject to any appeal at all. Moreover, very few cases moved out of the tribunal system into the court system. One avowed reason for establishing the Upper Tribunal is to provide for tribunals the sort of appellate guidance that the higher appeal courts provide in the court system. This partly explains why – contrary to the approach of the Leggatt Review – there will be fewer chambers in the Upper Tribunal than in the First-tier Tribunal, and why the Upper Tribunal is constituted as a superior court of record. Some indication of the intended relationship between the Upper Tribunal and the High Court may be gleaned from the statement that the Upper Tribunal's judicial review jurisdiction should be limited to cases raising no 'constitutional issues'.[101] The Upper Tribunal is being groomed, it seems, as a sort of junior Court of Appeal – essentially a law-making body but lacking the clout to take on the government in the most tricky and controversial cases.

We saw earlier that in its *Better Decisions* report, the ARC recommended the creation of a two-tier ART. It saw this as a way of preserving the expertise-related benefits of the existing system while at the same time enhancing tribunal independence, improving accessibility and economic efficiencies, and – perhaps most importantly – promoting improvements in agency decision making (the

---

[100] In terms of the distinction between grouping and integration (n 96 above) we may say that the changes are intended in the short term to group tribunals but in the longer term to achieve a lesser or greater degree of integration. They are also, presumably, intended to significantly slow down or halt the creation of new specialist jurisdictions. In the White Paper *Transforming Public Services: Complaints, Redress and Tribunals* (London, HMSO, 2004) the distinction between grouping and integration is put in terms of one between a federal and a unified jurisdictional structure: paras 6.4, 6.37.

[101] *Transforming Tribunals*, para 213.

so-called 'normative function' of merits review). With this last objective in mind, the ARC proposed that although the appellate level of the ART would conduct full merits review (covering law, fact and policy), access to the appellate level would be limited to cases of 'manifest error' by the lower tribunal or cases raising issues of general significance.[102] The ARC seems to have thought that such issues might be of relevance to the making not only of decisions of the type under review but also of decisions of other types or even to administrative decision-making generally. To this extent, the ARC apparently contemplated that the appellate level of the ART would be less specialised than the lower level and that the ART might, as a result, realise in one body the benefits of both specialisation and generalism. By contrast, the Leggatt Review of Tribunals had a narrower vision of the role of the upper level of its tribunal, limiting it to questions of law (as opposed to full appeal on the merits) and seeking to preserve in its operation the specialist jurisdictional focus of the lower-tier tribunal that made the decision under review.

Structurally, the system being established under the TCE Act seems closer to that proposed by the ARC than to that contemplated by the Leggatt Review. However, the driving motivation of the ARC proposals was enhancement of the normative effect of tribunal review on primary administrative decision-making whereas the main goal of the new UK system seems to be the development of a set of principles of administrative law applicable across a wide range of government decision-making. Although, at bottom, the difference may be one of emphasis, it is nevertheless significant. By reason of adopting as its overarching rationale the making of correct and preferable decisions in individual cases, the Australian concept of merits review distinguishes tribunals from courts. In contrast, by casting the Upper Tribunal in the role of a traditional law-maker, the UK system aligns tribunals with courts. Both approaches inject a significant element of generalism into the tribunal system, but to different ends.

(iii)   The US

Administrative adjudicators who are embedded within specialised administrative agencies are necessarily specialised. The choice between specialism and generalism only arises once adjudication is taken out of agencies and put into free-standing tribunals. In the UK the shift from embedded to free-standing administrative adjudication began in the late 19th century and (except in the area of land-use planning, where is still exists) proceeded apace in the 20th. It was not until the 21st century, however, that the opportunity for generalism, presented by this shift, was exploited. In Australia, tribunals did not start to develop until after

---

[102]   *Better Decisions*, paras 8.42–8.53.

the shift had taken place, and the model adopted was that of the free-standing tribunal. This may partly explain why generalism was introduced earlier in Australia than in the UK.

In the US, administrative adjudication developed in the 19th century in the embedded pattern. The pressures that led to the shift from embedded to free-standing tribunals in the UK resulted in the US in internal separation within agencies. However, the APA scheme was adopted against the background of proposals made throughout the 1930s for the removal of adjudicatory powers from agencies and the creation of an independent administrative court. Such proposals were abandoned in the late 1930s in favour of internal re-configuration of agencies. Proposals for an administrative court or a central corps of administrative adjudicators have been frequently made since the passage of the APA. Such proposals tend to be supported not in the name of generalism versus specialism[103] but primarily for the sake of further increasing the professional status of administrative adjudicators[104] and their independence from control by the heads of agencies, especially in relation to policy-making.[105] Other arguments in support refer to enhanced administrative efficiency and 'facilitation of uniformity in administrative procedures and in productivity norms'.[106] Against is the argument that it would be undesirable to combine in the one institution the two quite different modes of administrative adjudication, the one being part of the primary decision-making process in the regulatory context and the other involving review of primary decisions (especially in the social security context). The UK analogy would be the integration of the land-use planning system (in which hearings by inspectors constitute one stage of the decision-making process) into the First-tier and Upper Tribunal structure focused on review of primary decisions.

The failure of proposals for a single, centralised adjudicative body at the federal level can be contrasted with the position at the state level where by 2000, according to Michael Asimow, about half the states had 'stripped at least some of their agencies of their captive judges, moving the judges into a separate agency.'[107]

---

[103] An exception is JJ Simeone, 'The Function, Flexibility and Future of United States Judges of the Executive Department' (1992) 44 *Administrative Law Review* 159, 174–76.

[104] Simeone, for instance, argues that administrative adjudicators should be recognised as being functionally equivalent to Art III judges and should be called 'United States Judges of the Executive Branch': ibid 176–77.

[105] eg, DJ Gifford, 'Federal Administrative Law Judges: The Relevance of Past Choices to Future Directions' (1997) 49 *Administrative Law Review* 1, 38–42, 58–59.

[106] JS Lubbers, 'Federal Administrative Law Judges: A Focus on our Invisible Judiciary' (1981) 33 *Administrative Law* 109, 124. See also B Schwartz, 'Adjudication and the Administrative Procedure Act' (1996) 32 *Tulsa Law Review* 203, 217.

[107] M Asimow, 'The Administrative Judiciary: ALJ's in Historical Perspective' (2000) 20 *Journal of the National Association of Administrative Law Judges* 157, 164.

Asimow predicted that 'the vast majority of the states will … have central panels in the next twenty years'; and in his opinion, '[u]ltimately the federal government will have to fall into line.'[108]

4.3.1.2 The Theory of Specialisation and Amalgamation

How might we make theoretical sense of legal debates about the relative merits of specialisation and generalism? One approach is that of Stephen Legomsky,[109] who understands specialisation in terms of 'expertise'. In turn, he defines 'expertise' in terms of non-legal skills and asks when the case for expert adjudication is strongest. Unsurprisingly, he concludes that expertise is likely to be more valuable for addressing issues of fact than for addressing issues of law, and most valuable for making what he calls 'discretionary judgments' that involve making 'policy choices'. Nevertheless, says Legomsky, expertise can be valuable in interpreting 'complex legislation' contextually.[110] It follows that expertise will be most valuable at lower levels of a decision-making hierarchy where issues of law, fact and policy will typically all be relevant, and least needed at the highest levels where typically, the only relevant issues are legal. Legomsky argues that expertise is likely to promote consistency 'within the specialty area'.[111] However, he also thinks that consistency is least important in deciding issues of fact and policy – that is, precisely those issues for which, in Legomsky's view, expertise is most valuable.[112] He also argues that specialisation can promote efficiency in adjudication because specialists do not need to be informed about 'the basic aspects of the specialised area'.[113] On the other hand, Legomsky says, the most negative effect of specialisation is 'loss of the generalist perspective'.[114]

Concerning jurisdictional specialisation, Legomsky's preference is for what he calls 'multi-specialty units' – adjudicatory bodies that have jurisdiction over 'two or more … related subjects'.[115] He believes that under the right conditions such bodies can realise 'all the benefits of legal generalism' with only 'marginal sacrifice of specific expertise'.[116] Multi-specialty administrative tribunals facilitate the development of general principles in a way that takes account of the details of

---

[108] ibid. There is also an ongoing debated about whether judicial review of administrative adjudications should be undertaken (1) by trial or appellate courts; and (2) by generalist of specialist courts. See eg, DP Currie and FI Goodman, 'Judicial Review of Federal Administrative Action: Quest for the Optimum Forum' (1975) 75 *Columbia Law Review* 1; PR Verkuil and JS Lubbers, 'Alternative Approaches to Judicial Review of Social Security Disability Cases' (2003) 55 *Administrative Law Review* 731.

[109] SH Legomsky, *Specialized Justice: Courts, Administrative Tribunals and a Cross-National Theory of Specialization* (Oxford, Clarendon Press, 1990). See also HH Bruff, 'Specialized Courts in Administrative Law' (1991) 43 *Administrative Law Review* 329.

[110] Legomsky, ibid 11–12, 24–25.

[111] ibid 15.

[112] ibid 14.

[113] ibid 17.

[114] ibid 15.

[115] ibid 34.

[116] ibid 40.

particular statutory schemes. England's new First-tier and Upper Tribunals would seem, at least superficially, to approach Legomsky's ideal. The First-tier Tribunal brings together bodies dealing with a diverse range of subject matter and organises groups of tribunals dealing with cognate subject matter into Chambers. The Upper Tribunal is organised along the same lines except that there are fewer Chambers and the expectation seems to be that non-lawyers will play a lesser role in the Upper Tribunal than in the First-tier Tribunal. This is consistent with Legomsky's account because the Upper Tribunal deals only with questions of law, and expertise is supposedly less valuable for addressing such questions.

There are several problems with Legomsky's approach. One is lack of recognition of the largely conclusory nature of the distinctions between law, fact and policy.[117] Another is tautology: non-legal expertise (Legomsky tells us) is valuable for addressing non-legal issues. A third, related to the second, is the exclusion of the practice of law as a form of expertise. Law, like other forms of expertise, provides a lens through which the world can be viewed. Different lenses privilege different values – bureaucratic, technological, therapeutic, legal, and so on – and bring different aspects of complex situations into focus.[118] Once the lens has been chosen, the aspects of the situation that will be emphasised and the values that will be brought to bear on dealing with the situation will have been set. The critical decision is the choice of lens. Describing an issue as one of law involves a choice of lens, and having chosen the lens it makes no sense to ask which of the available lenses will give the best fix on the issue. Similarly, expertise of any particular type will increase 'efficiency' only if the values and criteria associated with that type of expertise are considered appropriate; but if they are, it necessarily follows that expertise of that type will increase 'efficiency'.

I would argue that 'generalism' should be understood not as a counterpoint to 'specialisation' but as involving the privileging of one form of specialism, namely legal expertise, and one set of values, namely legal values. It is clear from this perspective why it is important to distinguish between expertise and jurisdictional specialisation. It is a matter of choice whether members of tribunals with relatively narrow jurisdiction will be lawyers or non-lawyers; and the choice turns on what are considered to be the appropriate decision-making values and criteria. In the US, for instance, ALJs work for specialised agencies but have legal

---

[117] P Cane, 'Merits Review and Judicial Review: The AAT as Trojan Horse' (2000) 28 *Federal Law Review* 214, 220.

[118] JL Mashaw, *Bureaucratic Justice: Managing Social Security Disability Claims* (New Haven, Yale University Press, 1983) is a classic exposition of this point. I do not mean to imply that the distinctions between these various sets of values are sharp or impermeable, nor that the various sets of values *necessarily* conflict with one a other in their application to specific situations. The differences between the various sets of values may be ones of emphasis and degree. So understood, legal values may be thought of as emphasizing procedural propriety and protection of individual rights. This point, however, does not undermine the argument in the text that jurisdictional generalism will tend to promote legalisation.

qualifications and experience. On the other hand, although it is also a matter of choice whether members of tribunals with relatively broad jurisdiction will be lawyers or non-lawyers, we might hypothesise that replacement of a larger number of tribunals with relatively narrow jurisdiction by one or a small number of tribunals with relatively broad jurisdiction will favour one set of decision-making values and criteria. Because tribunals are understood to be essentially legal institutions, we might also hypothesise that legal values and criteria will come to dominate and that non-legal values and criteria will be used less and less. It is misleading to conceptualise the shift from narrow to broad jurisdiction in terms of a shift from specialisation to generalism. It is more accurately understood as a shift from value pluralism to legalism, or simply as legalisation.

If my argument so far is correct, grouping of specialised jurisdictions within a single tribunal may be understood not in terms of 'reaping the benefits of both specialisation and generalism' but rather as an attempt to prevent total legalisation of administrative adjudication and to leave room for application of non-legal values and criteria. In practice, this end may be promoted either by allowing non-lawyers to sit alone or by including at least one non-lawyer on a multi-member panel. Arrangements of the latter type create the possibility of conflict and competition between the values and decisional criteria associated with the various types of expertise (legal and non-legal) represented on the panel. How is such conflict and competition to be managed?

Administrative tribunals are legal bodies in the sense that the ultimate question to be decided arises within a framework of legal rules and principles. If the legal framework within which the decision falls to be made is highly directive, it may obviate competition between various sets of values and decisional criteria either by specifying the precise role that non-legal criteria are to play in the decision[119] or by effectively excluding non-legal criteria from consideration and relegating non-legal experts to the role of information providers.[120] On the other hand, if the legal framework provides the tribunal with more or less freedom to choose decisional criteria, conflict and competition may occur. In that situation, especially where the tribunal panel is chaired by a lawyer, we may hypothesise that legal values and criteria will have a competitive advantage over non-legal values, and that increased de facto or de jure legalisation will result.

According to Rachel Bacon, 'amalgamation' of specialist tribunals is attractive to governments for three main reasons: to reduce operating costs, solve the 'problem' of proliferation of tribunals, and increase government control over specialist tribunals that 'are perceived to act in a manner ... contrary to

---

[119] For instance, rules about discharge from institutions for the mentally ill may refer to medical criteria: G Richardson and D Machin, 'Judicial Review and Tribunal Decision Making: A Study of the Mental Health Review Tribunal' [2000] *Public Law* 494, 500–01.

[120] Of course, where a non-lawyer sits alone, that person cannot be relegated to the role of an information-provider. In that case, the balance between legal and non-legal values and criteria is likely to be more-or-less dictated by the criteria applied by any relevant review or appeal body.

government interests'.[121] She poses two questions: first, whether an amalgamated tribunal is more effective than a number of specialised tribunals at 'delivering administrative justice'; and secondly, how to amalgamate in such a way as to maximise the potential benefits.[122]

Bacon focuses on the second question,[123] but in doing so apparently assumes that the goal of amalgamation is not more effective delivery of administrative justice but what I earlier referred to as 'integration'.[124] Integration involves more than simply bringing a number of specialised jurisdictions under the one roof and may include developing common procedural rules and flexible deployment of adjudicators across jurisdictions, for instance. Bacon concludes – on the basis of an empirical study of two Australian 'super tribunals' into which were amalgamated tribunals that adjudicated civil disputes on the one hand and administrative tribunals on the other[125] – that the success of amalgamation in achieving integration of specialised jurisdictions depends on four main factors: a firm legislative foundation that is perceived to be neither 'regressive' nor 'impractical';[126] strong and continuing political commitment to integration; a *modus operandi* and organisation that foster cohesiveness and innovation in order 'to counteract the tendency of former specialist bodies to continue operation just as they did before';[127] and leadership and personnel committed to and capable of creating a cohesive and unified institutional culture. It is unclear to what extent integration is the goal of the recent UK reforms and only time will tell to what extent they will produce an integrated system of administrative adjudication.

In conclusion, we might observe that specialisation is commonly cited as one of the advantages that tribunals have over courts. In 19th-century England, jurisdictional specialisation and the embeddedness of administrative adjudication in multi-functional agencies went hand-in-hand (as they still do in the US), and it may be that jurisdictional specialisation makes less sense in a system of free-standing administrative tribunals.[128] However, by the time the shift from embedded adjudication to free-standing tribunals had occurred in the UK, jurisdictional specialisation had become such an entrenched feature of the

---

[121] R Bacon, 'A Study in Tribunal Amalgamation: The Importance of a Principled Approach' (2005) 12 *Journal of Social Security Law* 81, 88.

[122] ibid 82.

[123] Bacon discusses the concept of 'effectiveness' at ibid 89–91 but not specifically in relation to 'administrative justice'. The latter concept is discussed in some detail in ch 6 below.

[124] See nn 96 and 100 above. Of course, in theory integration may improve administrative justice, but Bacon does not discuss the relationship between the two concepts. In a separate discussion of the proposed Administrative Review Tribunal, into which existing specialist tribunals were to be amalgamated, she gives more weight to preserving distinctive features of the amalgamated tribunals: n 47 above, esp 169–75.

[125] The New South Wales Administrative Decisions Tribunal and the Victorian Civil and Administrative Tribunal. The latter is considered to have been more successful than the former.

[126] 'A Study in Tribunal Amalgamation', 95.

[127] ibid 100.

[128] And also perhaps in relation to adjudication as a mode of reviewing decisions as opposed to adjudication as a mode of policy-making (primary decision-making).

administrative adjudication system that the positive rhetoric of specialisation remained – and remains – powerful. The most obvious advantage of jurisdictional specialisation is the opportunity it provides for decision-makers, from whatever background and with whatever expertise, to acquire a depth of knowledge of a particular government programme that would not otherwise be possible. Its obvious disadvantage is that it may make it more difficult for decision-makers to discern differences, similarities and connections between the programme under scrutiny and other government programmes. The proposition that the advantage outweighs the disadvantage is typically supported by assertion rather than argument. If it is true, why are there not more specialist courts? Is there any reason to think that specialisation is more advantageous in relation to the sorts of areas in which tribunals operate than those in which courts operate?

So far as membership is concerned, the argument in this section suggests that non-legal expertise is an advantage only if it has already been decided that decisions should be made according to non-legal rather than legal criteria and values. The paradigm member of a court is legally trained not because this is 'advantageous' but because it is the job of courts to make decisions according to legal values and criteria. To the extent that tribunals are understood to be legal institutions essentially similar to and performing an essentially similar function as courts, it is arguable that non-legal expertise will not add value to their operation. To the extent that non-legal values and criteria are relevant to decision-making, the real question is not whether non-legal expertise should be available but whether it should be provided by a decision-maker or by a third party (such as a witness). From this perspective, the advantage, if any, of tribunals over courts must reside in the fact that in tribunals, non-legal expertise is more often provided by the decision-maker than it is in courts. Once again, however, the proposition that on balance, the benefits of provision of expertise by the decision-maker rather than by a third party outweigh its costs is typically supported by assertion than argument. If it is true, why are non-legal experts not appointed to courts and why do courts rely as much as they do on expert witnesses?

4.3.2 Supervision and Accountability

In constitutional terms, there is a significant relationship between supervision and accountability ('supervision' for short) on the one hand and separation and independence on the other. Although it seems simplistic to say that 'judicial independence is merely the other side of the coin from judicial accountability',[129] certain modes of supervision may significantly threaten independence. For instance, while an obligation to give public reasons for decisions poses no threat

---

[129] Burbank, n 46 above, 17.

to independence properly understood, an obligation that courts and tribunals justify individual decisions to the legislature or the executive certainly would.

We may distinguish between 'hierarchical' and 'external' supervision. The former refers to supervision of an inferior by a superior within an institutional hierarchy; examples are supervision of trial courts by appeal courts and, in our immediate context, of a first-tier tribunal by a second-tier tribunal. By contrast, the latter refers to supervision of a body belonging to one institutional hierarchy by a body belonging to a different institutional hierarchy: supervision of a tribunal by a court, for instance. According to the French way of thinking, external supervision is inconsistent with separation and independence, but hierarchical supervision is not. The distinction between hierarchical and external supervision cannot be mechanically applied because the allocation of particular institutions to particular hierarchies may depend on contestable value judgments: for instance, should administrative tribunals be allocated to the executive or to the judicial institutional hierarchy? Or should they be considered to constitute a hierarchy in their own right? Nevertheless, the distinction is useful if only because it underpins the distinction between the 'pure' and 'checks and balances' approaches to separation of powers.

4.3.2.1 Hierarchical Supervision

All of our comparator jurisdictions supply examples of hierarchical supervision of a first-tier tribunal by a second-tier tribunal: for instance, in Australia, the Administrative Appeals Tribunal hears appeals from the Social Security Appeals Tribunal and the Veterans' Review Board; in the UK the Upper Tribunal hears appeals from the First-tier Tribunal; in the US the Board of Immigration Appeals hears appeals from decisions of Immigration Judges;[130] and in France *Cours Administratives d'Appel* hear appeals from *Tribunaux Administratifs*. On the other hand, this form of hierarchical supervision is not universal. In Australia, for instance, the Migration Review Tribunal and the Refugee Review Tribunal are not

---

[130] SH Legomsky, 'Forum Choice for the Review of Agency Adjudication: A Study of the Immigration Process' (1985–86) 71 *Iowa Law Review* 1297. Immigration adjudication at both levels is conducted by the Executive Office for Immigration Review within the Department of Justice, not within the United States Citizenship and Immigration Services (USCIS – formerly the Immigration and Naturalization Service (INS) and now part of the Department of Homeland Security). Recall the distinction between the primary decision-making model and the review model of administrative adjudication (3.2). This distinction gives rise to another between two models of hierarchical supervision which Freedman calls 'administrative' and 'judicial' respectively: JO Freedman, 'Review Boards in the Administrative Process' (1968–69) 117 *University of Pennsylvania Law Review* 546, 558–59. In these terms, our concern is with the model of supervision that corresponds to the review model of adjudication: the merits review and legality review models (identified in the next paragraph) are models of this species of hierarchical supervision. The APA regulates hierarchical supervision of decisions of ALJs by agencies, but does not regulate hierarchical supervision of decisions of ALJs by intermediate bodies such as the Board of Immigration Appeals or review by the agency of decisions of such intermediate bodies. Technically, the supervisory body exercises the agency's power of review as a delegate. However, similar issues of 'independence' arise in relation to such intermediate bodies as in relation to adjudication by ALJs: Freedman, ibid 568–70.

subject to the hierarchical supervision of the AAT, but they are subject to external supervision by courts (by way of judicial review).

There are two basic idealised models of hierarchical review of tribunal decisions. In one model the function of the appellate tribunal is to reconsider all aspects of the decision of the first-tier tribunal, typically on the basis of relevant material available at the time of the appeal. The powers of the appellate tribunal will normally include making a decision in substitution for that of the first-tier tribunal. In terms of the concepts to be analysed in Chapter 5, we may call this the 'merits review' model of supervision. Review by the AAT of decisions of the SSAT, for instance, exemplifies this model. In a second model, the scope of review is more limited, typically being confined to questions of law; review will normally be based on the material available to the lower tribunal and the appellate tribunal may have no or only limited power to make a substitute decision. Review by the UK Upper Tribunal of decisions of the First-tier Tribunal exemplifies this model, which we may refer to as 'legality review'. In this model, the appellate tribunal has two main functions: to correct errors made by the lower tribunal and to develop the law. Legality review is a non-court analogue of judicial review.

Two-tier systems of tribunal review of primary administrative decision-making in which second-tier review follows the merits review model tend to be found in high-volume jurisdictions such as social security and immigration.[131] In relation to most types of decisions that fall within its jurisdiction, the AAT performs first-tier review and there is no provision for second-tier review. Tax and worker's compensation are the only areas of the AAT's first-tier jurisdiction that are high volume. By contrast with the Australian situation, subject to certain exceptions, there is a general right of appeal from the UK First-tier Tribunal to the Upper Tribunal.[132] This right of appeal is analogous to that provided from decisions of the AAT to the Federal Court. This difference perhaps reflects the greater judicialisation of the UK system as compared with the Australian system.[133]

---

[131] In Australia, as already noted, there is no appeal from first-tier immigration tribunals to the AAT. Matters can be referred by the immigration tribunals to the AAT, but the power has been exercised only once. Moreover, there is no requirement for referral and so this process should not be understood as a mode of supervision.

[132] The ARC adopted a cross between the two models in its proposals for an Administrative Review Tribunal to replace the Administrative Appeals Tribunal: review panels would have conducted review according to the merits review model, but access to review would have been limited to cases of error of law or involving an issue of general principle: *Better Decisions*, paras 8.42–8.63.

[133] Attempts have been made to develop principles for the design of review systems based on values such as accuracy, efficiency, acceptability and consistency: see, eg, Legomsky, n 130 above and Freedman, n 130 above. Cass concluded that it was effectively impossible to test empirically whether such principles promoted their underpinning values: RA Cass, 'Allocation of Authority Within Bureaucracies: Empirical Evidence and Normative Analysis' (1986) 66 *Boston University Law Review* 1.

4.3.2.2 External Supervision

We may usefully distinguish four modes of external supervision, which we might for convenience respectively call judicial, political, bureaucratic and public.

(i) Judicial Supervision

Judicial supervision is supervision by a court and may take the form of either judicial review or an appeal. Typically, however, appeals from tribunals to courts are limited to questions of law. They are, as a result, functionally equivalent to judicial review which is, in theory at least, review for legality. Appeals from the AAT to the Federal Court under section 44 of the AAT Act provide a good example.[134] Appealable errors include misinterpretation of legislation, procedural unfairness, and failure to take account of a relevant consideration or taking account of an irrelevant consideration. A factual error may constitute an error of law, but only if it is egregious. The Federal Court has a general power to 'make such order as it thinks appropriate by reason of its decision' including the powers to affirm or set aside the decision and remit it to the AAT for reconsideration; but it has no express power to substitute its own decision for that of the AAT.[135] This has been interpreted as creating a presumption in favour of remitting for reconsideration rather than making a substitute decision. In general, appeals are conducted on the basis of the material available to the AAT. However, since 2005 the Federal Court has had limited power to make findings of fact and, for that purpose, the power to receive further evidence.

The AAT is also amenable to judicial review. The scope of judicial review is one of the most obscure and complex aspects of Australian federal administrative law;[136] but it is at least possible that judicial review of an AAT decisions might be available in circumstances where an appeal to the Federal Court would not. If an appeal were available, this would probably rule out an application for judicial review.[137]

---

[134] See generally D Pearce, *Administrative Appeals Tribunal*, 2nd edn (Australia, LexisNexis Butterworths, 2007) ch 10. It is 'axiomatic' that in hearing an 'appeal' under s 44 the Federal Court is exercising original, not appellate, jurisdiction: *Minister for Immigration and Ethnic Affairs v Gungor* (1982) 4 ALD 575, 584 (Sheppard J). 'The task of the court on an appeal under s 44(1) is essentially to undertake judicial review of the tribunal's decision': *BTR plc v Westinghouse Brake & Signal Co (Aust) Ltd* (1992) 26 ALD 1, 7 (Lockhart and Hill JJ). However, there may be exceptional cases in which the court must effectively review a decision of the tribunal on its merits: *Wong v Minister for Immigration and Multicultural and Indigenous Affairs* (2007) 93 ALD 61.

[135] By contrast, on appeal (on a point of law) from the UK Upper Tribunal the appeal court (in England, the Court of Appeal), the court has power either to remit or remake the decision (Tribunals, Courts and Enforcement Act 2007 s 14 (2); and if it decides to remake the decision, it 'may make any decision which the Upper Tribunal could make if the Upper Tribunal were remaking the decision' (s 14(4)(a)), and for that purpose may 'make such findings of fact as it considers appropriate' (s 14(4)(b)).

[136] See generally P Cane and L McDonald, *Principles of Administrative Law: Legal Regulation of Governance* (Melbourne, OUP, 2008) ch 3.

[137] eg *Szajntop v Gerber* (1992) 28 ALD 187.

In England there is a right of appeal (subject to certain exceptions) on a point of law from the Upper Tribunal to the Court of Appeal. The First-tier and Upper Tribunals are both, in principle, amenable to judicial review, although the scope for such review is likely to be very limited given that there is a general right of appeal from the First-tier Tribunal to the Upper Tribunal and from the Upper Tribunal to the Court of Appeal.

In the US, one result of the embedded nature of administrative adjudication is that it is the decision of the agency that is amenable to judicial review rather than that of the ALJ as such. This can cause problems in cases when the agency rejects a finding of fact by an ALJ, especially in cases where the agency uses adjudication as part of the policy-making process. How much weight should the court give to the findings of the ALJ when the agency's different view of the facts is explicable in terms of furthering its policy objectives? The Supreme Court's pronouncements on this issue are inconclusive.[138]

A significant difference between US judicial review law on the one hand, and English and Australian judicial review law on the other, relates to review for misinterpretation of legislation. In very broad terms US law requires greater judicial deference to interpretations by administrative decision-makers (including adjudicators) of the legislation it is responsible for administering[139] than does English and Australian law. In English law, the basic position is that the court has the final word on matters of law, including legislative interpretation. In Australia, a distinction is drawn between inferior courts and administrative tribunals. The basic rule in relation to tribunals is that the court has the final word on all matters of law, including legislative interpretation.[140] By contrast, when it comes to reviewing other aspects of the reasoning of administrative decision-makers, US courts are inclined to take a less deferential approach than English and Australian courts, especially in relation to rule-making by regulatory agencies.[141] For our purposes – concerned as we are with administrative review of the implementation of rules – the former difference is likely to be more significant than the latter.

Judicial review is an invention of judges whereas appeals are statutory. This means that rights of appeal exist only if they are expressly provided for, whereas judicial review will be available (within its judicially or statutorily defined

---

[138] Mashaw, Merrill and Shane, *Administrative Law*, 431–33; PL Strauss, *Administrative Justice in the United States*, 2nd edn (Durham, NC, Carolina Academic Press, 2002) 343–48. See also 3.2, n 18 and text; 5.7.2, nn 237–40 and text.

[139] This approach is tailored to interpretations by specialist administrative bodies of the legislation underpinning the programme each administers. It could not easily be applied to a tribunal with wide jurisdiction across government programmes. See generally Strauss, n 138 above, 360–75.

[140] *Craig v South Australia* (1995) 184 CLR 163. The basis of the distinction between inferior courts and tribunals is that whereas the former are 'constituted by persons with either formal legal qualifications or practical legal training', the latter may be 'constituted, wholly or partly, by persons without legal qualifications or legal training' (176–77).

[141] See generally Strauss, n 138 above, 375–86.

scope)[142] subject to any (valid) statutory provision to the contrary – known variously as an 'ouster' or 'privative' or 'preclusion' clause. Under English law, the power of the legislature to oust judicial review is limited to some extent by European Union law and the European Convention on Human Rights. Furthermore, since the late 1960s courts have adopted a general principle tht ouster clauses should be interpreted strictly against the government. In Australian federal law the power of the legislature to oust judicial review is limited by the 'entrenched minimum provision of judicial review' guaranteed by section 75(v) of the Constitution, which confers on the High Court jurisdiction over applications for prohibition, mandamus and an injunction against officers of the Commonwealth.[143] Section 75(v) has this effect even in cases that raise no constitutional issue. The US Constitution contains no equivalent to section 75(v), and it is unclear to what extent Congress can preclude judicial review[144] of administrative decisions in cases raising no constitutional issue.[145]

The fundamental argument of principle (as opposed to constitutional or statutory interpretation) against preclusion of review rests on a rule-of-law understanding of separation of powers according to which ultimate authority to ensure that administrative decision-makers, tribunals and inferior courts observe limits on their powers is allocated to the highest courts – in England, the historic central superior courts and in Australia and the US, constitutional courts. This understanding of separation of powers, which places the highest 'ordinary courts' at the apex of the legal system marks the fundamental structural difference between the French system of administrative adjudication on the one hand and the UK, US and Australian systems on the other. It explains why the Kerr Committee said that introduction of a system of administrative courts, analogous to the French, at the federal level in Australia would require a constitutional amendment.[146] It is a corollary of the rule-of-law interpretation of separation of powers that the courts with the ultimate authority to enforce the law against other branches of government must be as independent as possible from those branches. It is imperative that judges who bear ultimate responsibility for enforcing legal limitations on governmental power enjoy the gold standard of

---

[142] Judicial review is regulated, for instance, by the Australian Administrative Decisions (Judicial Review) Act 1977 and the US Administrative Procedure Act 1946 but is part of the common-law background against which the statutes operate.

[143] This term includes members of tribunals and judges of Ch III courts (except the High Court). The High Court can also entertain applications for judicial review under s 75(iii) of the Constitution. To the extent that s 75(iii) confers wider judicial review jurisdiction than s 75(v), it may increase the guaranteed minimum of judicial review. See generally Cane and McDonald, *Principles of Administrative Law*, 200–07.

[144] In the US context, this means review by an Art III (constitutional) court as opposed to an Art I (legislative) court. In relation to embedded first-instance administrative adjudication, review by an Art I court could provide a half-way house between Art III judicial review and hierarchical supervision by an embedded second-tier review body.

[145] RE Levy and SA Shapiro, 'Government Benefits and the Rule of Law: Toward a Standards-Based Theory of Judicial Review' (2006) 58 *Administrative Law Review* 499.

[146] Kerr Committee Report, para 222.

security. From this perspective, far from being an infringement of the independence of administrative adjudicators (as the French see it), judicial review is its guarantor, allowing courts to protect administrative adjudicators from improper interference by the political executive. The only basis on which it can be acceptable to protect the independence of administrative tribunals less well than that of traditional courts is that those courts, enjoying the greatest independence, are available as the ultimate enforcers of the law against the political executive.

(ii) Political Supervision

A second mode of external supervision is political. The core example of political supervision of administrative adjudication is provision for appeals to and reviews by members of the political executive – ministers and heads of agencies.[147] In England, elimination of the involvement of ministers in administrative adjudication at the review level was central to the campaign waged by Robson from the 1920s onwards in England for the creation of a system of administrative courts, and the general principle is now firmly established that appeals from first-tier administrative adjudicators should lie to a second-tier tribunal or to a court.

By contrast, political supervision is a fundamental feature of the US system of embedded administrative adjudication. As we have seen, although under the APA ALJs exercise first-instance decision-making power, their decisions are subject to review by or appeal to the agency itself. The prime purpose of this arrangement is to enable the agency to retain ultimate control over policy-making. The threat thus posed to the independence of adjudicators is mitigated by internal separation of functions. We have also noted that this mode of control, even if mediated through an appellate adjudicatory body, is inefficient in high-volume areas of administration. Two main alternative strategies are available: policy-making through rules and monitoring of the performance of individual adjudicators. The former strategy transforms adjudicators from participants in what Cass calls 'comprehensive' policy-making to being (like courts) 'incremental' policy-makers.[148] Because of the generality of rules, it poses no threat to the independence of adjudicators in deciding individual cases. Performance monitoring may not interfere with such 'decisional' independence either; but it does potentially weaken the tenure and salary protections accorded to adjudicators. The threat to decisional independence increases as monitoring extends beyond propriety and capacity to competence, and exponentially when it is used as a disguised surrogate for rule-making or review of individual decisions.

---

[147] Formal political supervision of this variety must, of course, be distinguished from negligent and deliberate failure by the executive to comply with tribunal decisions and orders. It should also be distinguished from a statutory power not to comply with a tribunal decision: eg, Freedom of Information Act 2000 (UK) s 53.

[148] See n 133 above.

(iii) Bureaucratic Supervision

A third mode of external supervision is bureaucratic. This mode of supervision, like the political version, is undertaken by politicians, but it may take place in a context where the supervisor does not have power to review individual decisions of adjudicators – ie, where adjudicatory institutions are free-standing rather than embedded. It may involve the establishment of performance and process standards for individual adjudicators or for a tribunal as an institution. In the latter case, failure to achieve prescribed standards may adversely affect the provision of funding and other resources. The obvious danger here is that performance monitoring may (appear to) be used as a way of influencing policy and affecting outcomes without the need to have recourse to publicly observable and politically accountable modes of policy-making. This danger is greatest where the management and funding of individual tribunals is the responsibility of the agency whose decisions they monitor. The danger may be less where tribunals as a group are managed and funded by a ministry of justice, especially if the task is delegated to an independent management agency such as the Tribunals Service in the UK. Another way of reducing the danger without compromising legitimate management goals might be to replace political actors as the setters and monitors of performance and process standards with an independent bureaucratic agency such as an auditor or ombudsman, perhaps backed up by a committee of the legislature.

This may be a suitable place to make brief mention of a phenomenon found in all our comparator jurisdictions. In England, the Council on Tribunals was established on the recommendation of the Franks Committee to keep the constitution and working of tribunals under continuous review'.[149] The Australian Administrative Review Council (ARC), established by Part V of the Administrative Appeals Tribunal Act 1975 was given a wider remit covering the 'administrative law system' more generally. The successor to the Council on Tribunals – the Administrative Justice and Tribunals Council (AJTC) – is modelled on the ARC, its task being to keep the 'administrative justice system' as a whole under review. The Administrative Conference of the United States (ACUS) started operation in 1968, its main function being to study administrative processes with a view to recommending to Congress and agencies improvements to the administrative process.

---

[149] Report of the Committee on Administrative Tribunals and Enquiries, 1957 (Cmnd 218) para 43. See generally RE Wraith and PG Hutchesson, *Administrative Tribunals* (London, George Allen & Unwin, 1973) ch 8; DGT Williams, 'The Council on Tribunals: The First 25 Years' [1984] PL 73; O Lomas, 'The 25th Annual Report of the Council on Tribunals – An Opportunity Sadly Missed' (1985) 48 *Modern Law* Review 694; DJ Galligan, *Due Process and Fair Procedures: A Study of Administrative Procedures* (Oxford, Clarendon Press, 1996) 299–302; C Harlow and R Rawlings, *Law and Administration*, 2nd edn (London, Butterworths, 1997) 467–71; HWR Wade and CF Forsyth, *Administrative Law*, 9th edn (Oxford, OUP, 2004) 924–26.

Because all of these bodies are purely advisory, their significance and impact is difficult to assess.[150] In an ideal world, such agencies would identify weaknesses in existing arrangements and make proposals for improvement that were accepted and given effect by governments and legislatures. However, the general consensus seems to be that the Council on Tribunals, lacking resources and political support, achieved little (except, perhaps, in the area of tribunal procedure). The hope is that the AJTC will play a more active role. However, if this confidence is based on the experience of the ARC, it seems misplaced. In its early years in the 1980s the ARC did important work in relation to the jurisdiction of the AAT (6.3); but its major 1995 report on the structure of the merits review system – *Better Decisions* – was largely fruitless (2.3.3), and by 1997 a parliamentary committee asked to examine the role and function of the ARC produced a lacklustre assessment of its achievements and a lukewarm recommendation for its continued existence.[151] Its output now consists largely of quasi-academic surveys and bland 'best practice' guides. By contrast, despite lacking the power to impose its recommendations on agencies, ACUS is said to have had considerable influence and success in areas such as ADR and rulemaking. The Conference also published guides including a *Manual for Administrative Law Judges*. Its success might help to explain why the Conference's funding was terminated by Congress in 1995.[152]

It is perhaps not inevitable either that advisory bodies will be unadventurous or that outspokenness will attract disapproval or even provoke abolition. Nevertheless, experience suggests that such bodies are unlikely, at least in the longer term, to contribute significantly to the supervision of administrative justice institutions.

(iv) Public Supervision

A fourth mode of external supervision is public. This may be based on the publication of annual reports and other information. Fundamental to accountability to tribunal users is the giving of reasons for decisions. The AAT, for instance, is required to give reasons for its decisions either orally or in writing and must provide each party to the proceedings with a copy. The wider public is

---

[150] A point made explicitly in a *Report on the Role and Function of the Administrative Review Council* by the Legal and Constitutional Affairs Committee of the Australian Senate in 1997, paras 1.22–1.34.

[151] See previous note.

[152] For other explanations see TM Fine, 'A Legislative Analysis of the Demise of the Administrative Conference of the United States' (1998) 30 *Arizona State Law Journal* 19. On 25 February 2009 the US House of Representatives voted start-up funds of $1.5 million for the re-establishment of ACUS. On ACUS more generally see Strauss, n 138 above, 291; Schwartz and Wade, *Legal Control of Government*, ch 7; and in its first five years see JL Mashaw, 'Reforming the Bureaucracy: The Administrative Conference Technique' (1974) 26 *Administrative Law Review* 261; GO Robinson, 'The Administrative Conference and Administrative Law Scholarship (1974) 29 *Administrative Law Review* 269; WW Gardner, 'A Review of the Work of the Administrative Conference' (1974) 26 *Administrative Law Review* 281.

served by the reporting of the AAT's reasons for decision in cases that are of more general significance. Reporting of decisions underpins the AAT's normative function (5.5) and promotes consistency in its decision-making – a value that has always been considered central to its operations even though the AAT cannot 'make law' and its decisions are not technically 'binding' (5.3.2.2 (iii), Error of Law). As in the case of courts, public reporting of decisions establishes lines of communication between the tribunal and important audiences such as policy-makers, legal practitioners and academic lawyers, and facilitates public discussion and assessment of the performance of tribunals as adjudicators and rule-makers.

Tribunal users may have access to a mechanism for dealing with complaints about tribunal administration or (as in the case of the Office for Judicial Complaints in the UK) the conduct of tribunal judges and members that are unrelated to the management of or decision in a particular case.

4.4 Conclusion

The matters dealt with in this chapter constitute the bread and butter of a large slice of the literature on tribunals. The discussion has shown the value of paying attention to historical and constitutional context in accounting for the institutional framework of administrative adjudication. In the next chapter we move, as it were, from form to substance.

5

Function

5.1 Introduction

S O FAR WE have been concerned primarily with the institutional characteristics of administrative tribunals. In this chapter the focus of attention shifts to what administrative tribunals do. This is a topic on which (outside Australia, anyway) there is surprisingly little literature. Several explanations suggest themselves. First, in the UK and the US the general assumption seems to be that tribunals do essentially the same thing as courts and that analyses of what courts do can be applied more-or-less unmodified to tribunals. Secondly, relatively few tribunal decisions are publicly reported, thus depriving observers of the basic raw materials on which to build analyses of what tribunals do. The internet has considerably increased the accessibility of tribunal decisions, but we await systematic analysis of what the available material tells us about the nature of tribunal adjudication. A third possible explanation is based on the specialised jurisdiction of the typical tribunal. Despite the fact that tribunals are generally assumed to do the same thing as courts, in performing their functions individual administrative tribunals are generally understood to be part of the machinery for running a specific government programme of regulation or welfare provision (for instance) rather than as exercising one of the three governmental 'powers' in terms of which ideas of separation of institutions and functions are commonly elaborated and, more generally, in terms of which theoretical discussions of constitutions and governmental structures are commonly conducted.

In all these respects, the Australian Administrative Appeals Tribunal (AAT) provides a counterpoint. First, because of the interpretation of constitutional separation of powers adopted by the High Court of Australia, the AAT and other analogous federal tribunals are understood to perform a categorically different function from that of courts – a function, moreover, that could not be conferred on a court. Secondly, major decisions of the AAT are reported in several series of law reports (as well as being available on the internet), and the decision-writing style adopted by the AAT is modelled on that of superior courts. Such reporting of elaborately and traditionally reasoned decisions enables the AAT to contribute to the development not only of the substantive law in the various areas of its jurisdiction but also of theoretical accounts and understandings of its characteristic function – merits review. Thirdly, the AAT has power to review decisions made under statutory provisions dealing with such a diverse range of government activities that it is not thought of specifically as part of the machinery of any of the many government programmes within its jurisdiction. For these reasons, the AAT provides the prime focus of this chapter. The concern is not with the AAT's contributions to the substantive law of social security, veterans' benefits, taxation and so on but rather its understanding and elaboration of the concept of 'merits review'.

However, before tackling that topic it will be useful to say a little more about the way governmental functions are categorised.

5.2 Categorising Governance Functions: the Legacy of Montesquieu

Certainly since the late 18th century issues about the design of constitutions and the institutions of government have been conducted primarily in terms of a three-fold division of 'functions' or 'powers'. The concepts of legislative, executive and judicial functions are extremely abstract. Their abstraction partly explains why it has been found very difficult to provide robust accounts of the distinctive nature of the various functions and of the differences between them. It also explains why the prefix 'quasi' is sometimes added particularly to the terms 'legislative' and 'judicial': the prefix typically indicates that the speaker senses a distinction between the real thing and the imitation, but cannot pinpoint it with confidence.

Vile argues that this highly abstract way of thinking about governmental activity was preceded by an approach cast in terms of what he calls governmental 'tasks', such as taxation, defence, welfare provision and so on.[1] This approach not only describes government activity more concretely, but also shifts from what we might call a 'process-related' scheme of classification[2] to what might be called a 'task-related' scheme. In this latter way of thinking, the abstract functions of government are modes of performing substantive governmental tasks. A different way of discussing governmental activities in more concrete terms would be to divide the categories of legislating, executing and judging into smaller elements such as investigation (or 'fact-finding'), prosecuting, ascertaining law, making coercive orders and so on.

Both of these alternative and more concrete methods of classification – the process-related and the task-related – are helpful in describing and accounting

[1] MJC Vile, *Constitutionalism and the Separation of Powers* (Oxford, Clarendon Press, 1967) 16–17.
[2] ibid 346–48.

for administrative tribunals and adjudication. The distinction between the two methods tracks that between tribunals of general jurisdiction and specialised tribunals. Although there are courts with task-specific jurisdiction, the paradigm court is a body of general jurisdiction in the sense that its core function is understood and typically described in process-related rather than task-related terms. By contrast, although there are tribunals of general jurisdiction – notably the AAT and now the UK's First-tier and Upper Tribunals – the paradigm administrative tribunal has task-specific jurisdiction. One of the reasons why the characteristic activity of the AAT is understood in process-related, not task-related, terms is that the AAT is a tribunal of general jurisdiction. Moreover, just as the work of specialist courts can be thought of in process-related terms (exercising judicial power) because they are understood to constitute a task-specific species of a genus that is defined in such terms, so in the Australian system the work of task-specific tribunals (such as the SSAT and the VRB) can be thought of in process-related terms ('merits review') because such tribunals constitute a species of a genus that is defined in such terms. One of the likely results of the creation of tribunals of general jurisdiction in the UK will be a greater tendency to think about and describe their work in process-related terms. So, for example, the jobs of the Upper Tribunal are described in terms of hearing appeals on points of law from the First-tier Tribunal and, in certain circumstances, undertaking 'judicial review'.

The distinction between abstract and more concrete process-related categorisations of governmental activity is also helpful in understanding administrative adjudication. For instance, the central concepts of 'review', 'merits review' and 'judicial review' are relatively concrete descriptions of modes of dealing with disputes between citizen and government. Even more concretely, the concepts of 'finding facts', 'ascertaining law' and 'applying law to facts' are elements of each of these modes of dispute-handling. By deploying these and other concepts, we can describe what administrative tribunals do, and the similarities and differences between what they do and what other governmental institutions do. Indeed, because of their greater concreteness and specificity, they are much more useful for describing and understanding what administrative tribunals and courts do than the much more abstract concepts of executing and judging.

On the other hand, of course, because of the continuing prominence of the three-fold abstract categorisation in constitutional thinking, use of more concrete categories – no matter how descriptively valuable they might be – creates problems because of uncertainty about the relationship between the abstract and the more concrete categories. These problems are at their most acute when separation of powers is understood, in a formalistic way, to associate each function primarily with a separate set of government organs, to require that all exercises of government power be classified as belonging to one or other of the three categories of power, and to require that all organs of government be classified as belonging to one or other of the three categories of institutions. This is the basic position in the Australian federal system, in which a dense thicket of case law about the meaning of the term 'judicial power' encases the federal Parliament in a straight-jacket that significantly limits its room for manoeuvre in creating adjudicatory institutions.

A different approach is to interpret separation of powers purposively rather than categorically and formalistically. Under such an approach, one reason for institutional multiplication and differentiation is to hinder undue concentration of power. From this perspective, it does not matter whether power is divided along process-related lines or task-related lines, so long as it is divided.[3] In the US, for instance, in process-related terms multi-functional agencies exercise concentrated power but only in a restricted area, defined in task related terms.[4] Conversely, Article III courts in the US operate over a much wider area than such agencies but are more restricted in procedural terms. The generalist administrative tribunal has wide power in task-related terms but restricted power in process-related terms, while the specialist administrative tribunal is restricted in both process-related and task-related terms.

Another reason for institutional multiplication and differentiation is to create tensions within government so that 'autonomous centres of power' with 'differing values' will check and restrain each other.[5] This is the fundamental justification for independence of the judiciary; and in the case of the US multi-functional agencies, it explains the scheme established by the APA under which the agency plays only a limited part in hiring and firing ALJs. It also underpins the distinction between implementation and adjudication (1.2.2). These two activities are similar in process-related terms (they both involve finding facts, ascertaining law[6] and applying law to facts), and adjudication is necessarily coincident in task-related terms with implementation (for instance, social security claims officers and social security tribunals operate in the same area of government activity). However, implementation and adjudication are in tension and can be mutually restraining because they promote different values in the sense that their rationale is to strike respectively different balances between social and individual interests. For this reason, they need to be allocated to different institutions. In the US system, the desirability of institutional balance explains the respective roles of the executive and the legislature in the making of legislation, the institution of judicial review of legislation and the role of the legislature in the appointment of judges.

Such a system of checks and balances obviously requires institutional separation but also a certain sharing of functions. Short of simply preventing an activity, supervising, controlling and restraining its performance necessarily involves a degree of participation in the activity. This creates a risk that the

---

[3] TD Rakoff, 'The Shape of the Law in the American Administrative State' (1992) 11 *Tel Aviv University Studies in Law* 9, 21–22.
[4] ibid.
[5] ibid 16.
[6] Both hard and soft.

supervisor will become too involved in the activity. The danger in this is not that the supervisor of the activity will become its performer – not for instance, that the adjudicator will take over as implementer – but that the values of the supervisor will come to dominate performance, thus breaking the tension between supervision and performance. There are various ways of preventing this from happening. One is to rely on the self-restraint of the supervisor. For instance, Australian courts and tribunals tend to exercise their supervisory powers over the executive in a relatively deferential way. Another technique is to impose some external restraint on the supervisor in the form, for instance, of statutory provisions limiting the incidence, scope or grounds of supervision. A third strategy is to embed the supervisor within the entity responsible for performing the activity. The APA scheme in the US is one version of this last strategy, and the system of administrative courts in France is another.

Whereas division and differentiation of functions on a task-related basis is primarily important as a way of preventing concentration of power, division and separation of functions on a process-related basis is also important as a way of avoiding conflicts of interest. This explains why, in US multi-functional agencies, officials who perform investigative and prosecuting functions may participate in formal hearings only as witnesses or counsel and why ALJs must not be subject to the supervision or control of such officials or consult with them off the record.

In practice, the categorical and purposive approaches to separation of powers tend to co-exist. For instance, although the categorical approach explains the creation of the AAT, a purposive approach informs the widely accepted argument (examined in more detail in 5.4) that the existence of the AAT as a merits review tribunal requires and justifies restraint on the part of courts in developing the grounds of judicial review. It is also manifest in the restraint of the AAT (examined in more detail in 5.3.2.2) in its approach to reviewing general policies developed by the executive as opposed to reviewing the application of such policies to individual cases. Implicit in such arguments for self-restraint is a view about the proper end of external review in the constitutional scheme, to which categorisation of institutions and functions is only a means. There is a certain irony in the fact that a system in which great weight is given to the categorical approach to separation of powers should have generated a subtle and complex purposive account of the respective roles of tribunals and courts that cuts across the traditional categories of institutions and functions. It is to that account we now turn.

5.3 Merits Review

5.3.1 Merits Review is a Mode of Review

The first important point to make about merits review is the absolutely obvious – indeed definitional – one that, like judicial review, it is a mode of reviewing decisions. The purpose of reviewing a decision is to decide whether that decision should be affirmed, varied or set aside and, possibly, replaced by a substitute decision. Merits review tribunals such as the AAT have no power to award compensation for loss or damage resulting from the making and execution of decisions. In Australian law, as in the law of the US and the UK, the basic rule is that the remedy of damages is not available for breaches of public law rules as such but only for private law wrongs, notably torts and breaches of contract. A breach of public law may constitute a private law wrong; but unless it does, or unless there is some statutory or constitutional basis for the award of damages, breaches of public law cannot attract compensation. Furthermore, in Australian federal law, adjudicating claims for damages in contract and tort is classified as a judicial function that cannot be conferred on a non-judicial body such as a merits review tribunal.

In this light it is noteworthy that a large proportion of the caseload of the AAT is concerned with decisions about the award of monetary benefits of three main types – workers' compensation benefits, social security benefits and veterans' benefits. In *Re Reserve Bank of Australia and Comcare*[7] a Deputy President of the AAT expressed the opinion that 'determinations of the Tribunal in [workers'] compensation matters' involve the exercise of judicial power because they 'impose liability or affect rights'. An argument that review of workers' compensation decisions by the AAT involves exercise of judicial power could be rested on an analogy between an action in tort and a claim for workers' compensation: liability to pay workers' compensation is, in effect, a form of strict employers' liability. It can be contrasted with a claim for social security benefits under a 'no-fault' workplace injuries scheme such as was introduced in the UK after the Second World War. The critical difference between a workers' compensation scheme and a no-fault workplace injuries scheme is that under the latter, unlike the former, claims are made against a fund, not against an individual. On this basis, it would seem safe to say that the AAT does not exercise judicial power when it reviews social security benefit decisions – or when it reviews decisions (not) to award veterans' benefits, which may be understood as a form of work-related social security payments. On the other hand, an argument that the AAT does not exercise judicial power in its compensation jurisdiction might be based on the fact that primary decisions about entitlement to benefits under the

---

[7] (1989) 17 ALD 682.

Commonwealth workers' compensation scheme are made by an administrative process. In this respect, the Commonwealth scheme differs from the classic workers' compensation scheme, which is administered in much the same way as the tort system – that is, by or against the background of civil claims in the courts.

If, indeed, the AAT does exercise judicial power when it reviews workers' compensation decisions, it is acting unconstitutionally – a situation that would clearly demonstrate the disutility of using the concept of judicial power to regulate the legislature's choice between conferring jurisdiction on a court and creating a tribunal.

5.3.2 The Substantive Element of Merits Review

Merits review, as exemplified in the work of the AAT, can be said to have three elements, which we might loosely call the substantive, the procedural and the remedial respectively. The substantive element is encapsulated in the idea that the task of the AAT is to ensure that the 'correct or preferable' decision is made; the procedural element is colloquially captured in the idea that the AAT 'stands in the shoes of the primary decision-maker'; and the remedial element relates to the powers of the AAT when it reviews a decision. This section deals with the substantive element and the following two sections will deal respectively with the procedural element and the remedial element.

5.3.2.1 The 'Correct or Preferable' Formula

As we have seen, the Kerr Committee's starting point in its 1971 Report was that 'traditional supervision by the courts of the administrative process must be supplemented by provision for review … on the merits of administrative decisions'.[8] In so doing, it introduced into Australian law a concept that had not hitherto been explicitly formulated. The Committee went on to contrast merits review with review limited to the question of whether the decision was made 'according to law'.[9] However, it said little else directly about the new concept, instead approaching the topic obliquely from the perspective of constitutional law.

The important constitutional question facing the Kerr Committee was whether merits review, thus understood, was a judicial function (or a function incidental to a judicial function) that could be entrusted to a court; or whether, on the contrary, it was a non-judicial function that could only be entrusted to a

---

[8] Report of the Commonwealth Administrative Review Committee (Kerr Committee Report), Parliamentary Paper No 144 of 1971, para 5.
[9] ibid para 11.

(non-judicial) tribunal.[10] After expressing the view that the distinction between 'judicial and administrative functions' was 'artificial rather than functional' and 'productive of considerable practical problems',[11] the Committee proceeded to make two points. One was that 'the exercise of judicial power is generally associated with a tribunal which possesses the authority to enforce its own decisions'.[12] This matter will be considered in 5.3.4. The second point was that '[i]t is essential to the exercise of judicial power that the controversy concerns a justiciable issue, that is an issue which may be resolved by the application of legal standards and principles'.[13] Discretionary decision making, the Committee said, can be judicial, but only if the grounds on which the discretion is to be exercised are 'defined or definable, ascertained or ascertainable, involving the application of prescribed standards'.[14] Courts, the Committee said,

> cannot be entrusted with the unrestricted review of discretions which are not judicial; nor can courts be called upon to review administrative decisions on any basis which requires the ultimate decision to be given by reference to policy or non-legal considerations.[15]

Then, most crucially, the committee asserted that

> the vast majority of administrative decisions involve the exercise of a discretion by reference to criteria which do not give rise to a justiciable issue. It follows that for constitutional reasons there can be no review by a court on the merits of these decisions unless those criteria are changed appropriately so as to raise justiciable issues.[16]

Reduced to its core, the Committee's argument is that because the vast majority of administrative decisions involve the exercise of discretion on non-justiciable grounds, reviewing the merits of such decisions is a non-judicial function.

On the assumption that by 'administrative decisions' the Committee meant decisions made in the course of implementing statutory provisions, the proposition that the vast majority of administrative decisions involve the exercise of discretion on non-justiciable grounds seems highly questionable.[17] In fact, the vast majority of decisions made in exercise of statutory powers are made by the application of more-or-less detailed and more-or-less formal principles and rules

---

[10] There was, in theory, a third possibility, namely that merits review was an 'innominate' or 'hybrid' function that could be entrusted to either a judicial or a non-judicial body. Such a function takes its colour from body in which the function is invested: if entrusted to a non-judicial body the function is non-judicial; and if entrusted to a judicial body, it is judicial. The concept of an innominate function was first enunciated by Isaacs J in *Federal Commissioner of Taxation v Munro* (1926) 38 CLR 153, 175–77.

[11] Kerr Report, para 62.

[12] ibid para 64.

[13] ibid para 65.

[14] ibid para 66.

[15] ibid para 67.

[16] ibid para 68.

[17] A point made extra-judicially as early as 1980 by Brennan J: FG Brennan, 'Comment: The Anatomy of an Administrative Decision' (1980) 9 *Sydney Law Review* 1, 2.

no different from those regularly applied by courts. It is only in relation to the very highest levels of policy-making that the Committee's view seems at all valid. Decisions that are made on no definable or ascertainable ground or according to no definable or ascertainable standard must represent a very small proportion of decisions made in exercise of statutory powers.

More to the point, perhaps, it is far from clear that such decisions would suitably be reviewed by a tribunal any more than by a court. A curious, unstated assumption underlying this aspect of the Committee's approach is that it would be appropriate for an external, independent review body such as the AAT to review the merits of non-justiciable decisions in the sense in which the Committee used that term. As we will see (5.3.2.1 (ii)), the AAT has taken a very cautious approach to reviewing the criteria on which statutory decisions are made (as opposed to the application of the criteria in individual cases). Such caution seems to be consistent with the Kerr Committee's discussion of the powers of its proposed tribunal. For instance, it recommended that the tribunal should have power to substitute its decision for that of the original decision-maker, but not 'when it is shown that the ... decision is properly based on government policy'.[18] (In this context, 'policy' can be understood to mean the (non-statutory) criteria on which statutory decisions are based.) The Committee contemplated that government policy would be 'explained to the Tribunal by written or oral evidence'. It did not anticipate that the tribunal would have power to act inconsistently with government policy but proposed, instead, that the tribunal should be given the power to 'transmit to the appropriate Minister an *opinion* ... that although the decision ... was properly based on government policy', that policy had operated 'in an oppressive, discriminatory or otherwise unjust manner'.[19] Ironically, then, although the Kerr Committee took the view that a non-judicial tribunal was needed to review the merits of statutory decision-making because such review would typically raise non-justiciable issues, it understood the role of the tribunal in a way that would effectively prevent it from resolving non-justiciable issues.

The committee, appointed in the wake of the Kerr Committee to consider which classes of statutory decisions should be subject to review by the proposed tribunal (the 'Bland Committee'), also expressed the opinion that the proposed tribunal 'should not be entitled to question the government policy grounds on which a decision is based or a decision to the extent that it gives effect to policy'.[20] Indeed, it went further and, disagreeing with the Kerr Committee, recommended that the tribunal should not be empowered to express negative opinions about government policy.[21] Whereas the Kerr Committee seems to have conceived of

---

[18] ibid para 297(ii).

[19] ibid. Emphasis added.

[20] Final Report of Committee on Administrative Discretions ('Bland Committee Report'), Parliamentary Paper No 316 of 1973, para 183.

[21] ibid para 172(g)(iii).

the proposed tribunal as a sort of court-substitute and to have based the case for restraint in reviewing the merits of policy on that conception,[22] the Bland Committee apparently thought that the tribunal should not question policy for precisely the same reason that unelected government officials are expected not to question policy, namely that their basic responsibility is to follow decision-making criteria laid down by others, not to establish such criteria. In the Bland Committee's scheme, the proposed tribunal would be an integral part of the process of implementing statutes whereas in the Kerr Committee's picture the role of the tribunal would be to supervise the implementation of statutes.

The lack of systematic analysis of the concept of merits review in these two foundational documents is reflected in the provisions of the legislation that established the AAT – the Administrative Appeals Tribunal Act 1975 (AAT Act). According to section 43 of the AAT Act, in reviewing decisions the AAT 'may exercise all the powers and discretions that are conferred by any relevant enactment on the person who made the decision'; it may affirm or vary the decision, or set it aside and either make a substitute decision or remit the matter to the original decision-maker for reconsideration; and a varied or substitute decision is deemed to be a decision of the original decision-maker with effect (unless the Tribunal otherwise orders) from the date on which the original decision took effect.[23] However, the AAT Act does not contain any indication of the criteria according to which the AAT should exercise its powers.

It might be thought to follow from the fact that the AAT 'stands in the shoes of the decision-maker'[24] – as it is colloquially put – that the job of the AAT should be understood in precisely the same way as that of the original decision-maker. However, as argued in 1.2.2, while the AAT can vary decisions and make substitute decisions, it is not an original decision-maker but a reviewer of decisions. The distinction between making and reviewing decisions, it was there argued, can be understood in terms of the distinction between rule-implementation and adjudication of disputes about rule-implementation. Because the focus of these two activities is crucially different in the sense that they involve striking the balance between individual and social interests in different ways, it is necessary to specify some criterion according to which the adjudicator is to exercise its power to review decisions. The formula that the AAT stands in the shoes of the decision-maker specifies the 'powers and discretions'

---

[22] See, eg, its discussion of the proposal that the president of the tribunal be a Chapter III judge (Kerr Committee Report, para 293) and the contrasting discussion of the Bland Committee: Bland Committee Report, paras 136 and 171.

[23] These provisions are similar to those used in relation to the Taxation Board of Review in the amended legislation that the High Court upheld in *Federal Commissioner of Taxation v Munro* (1926) 38 CLR 153; affirmed by the Privy Council in *Shell Co of Australia Ltd v Federal Commissioner of Taxation* (1930) 44 CLR 530 (2.3.3 above). On this basis the Board can be identified in retrospect as the first merits review tribunal in the modern sense.

[24] '[I]n reviewing a decision the Tribunal is to be considered as being in the shoes of the person whose decision is in question': *Minister for Immigration and Ethnic Affairs v Pochi* (1980) 4 ALD 139, 143 (Smithers J).

available to the AAT but it does not specify the criterion according to which those powers and discretions should be exercised. It is that criterion which constitutes the substantive element of merits review.

The first general statement of the nature of the AAT's function was made by the Federal Court of Australia in an appeal from a decision of the AAT affirming a deportation decision made by the Minister for Immigration and Ethnic Affairs.[25] Bowen CJ and Deane J said that the AAT

> is not restricted to considerations relevant to a judicial determination of whether a discretionary power ... has been validly exercised ... it is not ordinarily part of the function of a court ... to determine what decision should be made in exercise of an administrative discretion in a given case ... It is the function which has been entrusted to the Tribunal. The question for the determination of the AAT is ... whether the decision which the decision-maker made was the correct or preferable one.[26]

'Correct' in this formula is taken to refer to situations in which the AAT considers that there is only one acceptable decision; and 'preferable' refers to situations where it considers that there is more than one acceptable decision. The 'correct or preferable' standard not only specifies what can trigger an exercise of the AAT's remedial powers – namely an application for review of a decision which the AAT considers not to be the correct or preferable one. It also specifies what the AAT should do once it has put on the primary decision-maker's shoes and what is the purpose of the AAT's remedial powers, namely to bring it about that the correct or preferable decision is made. If the AAT decides to vary a decision or make a substitute decision, it assumes responsibility for producing the correct or preferable outcome. If it decides to exercise its power to remit for reconsideration, it imposes responsibility on the primary decision-maker to produce the correct or preferable outcome.

The 'correct or preferable' formula is taken to encapsulate the substantive essence of merits review and to mark the substantive difference between review on the merits and review for legality.

5.3.2.2 The Basis of Merits Review

The 'correct or preferable' standard of merits review refers, in abstract terms, to norms of good decision-making departure from which triggers the remedial jurisdiction of the AAT and application of which underpins exercise by the AAT of its various remedial powers, and in particular the powers to vary a decision and to make a substitute decision. What are the norms of good decision-making by reference to which the question of whether a decision is 'correct or preferable'

---

[25] *Drake v Minister for Immigration and Ethnic Affairs ('Drake No 1')* (1979) 2 ALD 60; 24 ALR 577.

[26] (1979) 2 ALD 60, 68.

should be answered? In *Re Brian Lawlor Automotive and Collector of Customs* Brennan J (the first President of the AAT) said that[27]

> [a]lthough the Tribunal is, and a court is not, concerned with [the] merits of a reviewable decision which do not affect the validity of the decision, both are concerned to inquire whether the decision was made within the powers vested in the decision-maker. There is no dichotomy between the administrative standards upon which the Tribunal must insist and which by its decisions are made effective, and the principles of law which are applied by a court: administrative action which exceeds the power conferred is not only ineffective in point of law, but it constitutes unacceptable administrative conduct.

This statement suggests (perhaps surprisingly) that the norms of good decision-making that support judgments that decisions are correct or incorrect, preferable or not, are the same as those that support judgments that decisions are legal or illegal, valid or invalid. These latter norms can be conveniently sorted into three categories concerned respectively with the procedure followed by the decision-maker, the decision-maker's reasoning process and the decision itself. We will consider each of these categories in turn.

(i) Procedure

Breach of the rules of procedural fairness (or 'due process') (notably the requirements of a fair hearing and that the decision-maker should not be biased) and of statutory procedural requirements is, perhaps, the archetypal ground on which decisions can be held illegal or invalid. Procedural unfairness may also, of course, support a conclusion that a decision is not correct or preferable and that it ought to be set aside. However, the AAT's prime task is not to identify procedural defects and require the decision-maker to repair them, but rather to reach the correct or preferable decision, and to repair procedural defects if this is necessary to enable it to do that.[28] In this sense, procedural unfairness has no independent significance as a basis for merits review. Review of a decision by the AAT may 'cure' any procedural errors committed by the original decision-maker.[29] Of course, it will have this effect only if the AAT itself complies with the requirements of procedural fairness; and procedural unfairness on the part of the AAT may constitute a ground of appeal to the Federal Court[30] or provide a basis for seeking judicial review of the AAT's decision. The principles of procedural fairness provide a normative framework within which provisions of the AAT Act dealing with procedure – for instance, that the AAT is not bound by rules of

---

[27] (1978) 1 ALD 167, 177.

[28] Merits review is a process by which 'any errors or defects which have led to the making of a wrong decision may be set right': ibid. See also *Re Russell and Conservator of Flora and Fauna* (1996) 42 ALD 441, [15].

[29] *Re Brian Lawlor Automotive Pty Ltd and Collector of Customs* (1978) 1 ALD 167, 181.

[30] *Sullivan v Department of Transport* (1978) 1 ALD 383. 'The [procedural] duty of the tribunal can be likened to that of a court': *Fletcher v Federal Commissioner of Taxation* (1988) 16 ALD 280, 284.

evidence, and that it should operate with appropriate informality (see 6.5) – must be interpreted and put into effect. It is at this level that procedural fairness assumes independent significance in the merits review system.[31]

In principle, the AAT's power to remit a decision for reconsideration (see 5.3.4) could be exercised on the ground of procedural unfairness by giving directions or recommendations to the original decision-maker about procedure. But this would be appropriate only if, for some reason, the AAT concluded that remittal was necessary in order to produce the correct or preferable decision.[32]

(ii) Reasoning Process

Certain grounds on which a decision can be held to be illegal or invalid are concerned with whether the decision-maker had good reasons for the decision. The main grounds in this category are failure to take account of a relevant consideration, taking account of an irrelevant consideration, exercising a power for an improper purpose (that is, a purpose other than that for which it was conferred), and various forms of impermissible fettering of discretion (such as agreeing by contract not to exercise a power or to exercise it in a particular way) and transferring of discretion (such as unlawful delegation of power). Just as procedural defects may result in a decision that is not the correct or preferable one, so may defects in the decision-maker's reasoning process – in other words, in the relationship between the decision and the reasoning on which it is based. Just as the prime function of the AAT in relation to procedural defects is to cure them by acting in a procedurally proper way, so its prime function[33] in relation to defects in the decision-maker's reasoning is to cure them by reconsidering the decision under review in accordance with norms of good decision-making[34] (which, in principle, are enforceable through judicial review of and appeals from decisions of the AAT).

---

[31] The relevant question, in judicial review or appeal proceedings, in relation to a decision of the AAT, is not whether the AAT reached the correct or preferable decision but whether it made a reviewable or appealable error (as the case may be). Procedural unfairness on the part of the AAT may constitute such an error. But unlike a court exercising judicial review jurisdiction, the Federal Court has power, on hearing an appeal from a decision of the AAT under AAT Act s 44, to make a substitute decision: see 4.3.2.2 nn 134 and 5 and adjacent text, and D Pearce, *Administrative Appeals Tribunal*, 2nd edn (Australia, LexisNexis Butterworths, 2007) 183–86. On the nature of appeals from the AAT to the Federal Court see n 43 below.

[32] *Commonwealth of Australia v Julian Beale* (1993) 30 ALD 68; *Re RC and Director-General of Social Services* (1981) 3 ALD 334, 342. The AAT's overriding obligation to provide fair, economical and quick reviews seems relevant to making the choice: see eg, *BTR plc v Westinghouse Brake & Signal Co (Aust) Ltd* (1992) 26 ALD 1, 16–17 (Lockhart and Hill JJ), 24–25 (Beaumont J).

[33] But if a decision is made by an official to whom the power to make the decision could have been but was not delegated (in breach of the rule against delegation), it appears that the AAT may simply set the decision aside regardless of its merits: eg, *Kinsey v Veterans' Review Board* (1992) 29 ALD 109.

[34] eg *Minister for Human Services and Health v Haddad* (1995) 38 ALD 204; *Re Queensland Mines Ltd and Export Development Grants Board* (1988) 7 ALD 357; *Bramwell v Repatriation Commission* (1998) 51 ALD 56; *Re Mika Engineering Holdings Pty Ltd and Commissioner of Taxation* (2007) 92

In this context, the fact that the AAT is a reviewer of decisions rather than a primary decision-maker (an adjudicator rather than an implementer) has given rise to some of the most difficult issues in the law of merits review. Probably the thorniest concerns the role of the AAT in reviewing government 'policy'. For a start, it should be observed that the word 'policy' bears at least three different senses in discussions of merits review. First, it may be used to refer to 'administrative' (ie, internal governmental) rules, principles or guidelines that lack the status of primary or secondary legislation.[35] Other terms used in this sense include 'quasi-legislation'[36] and 'soft law'.[37] Policies in this sense are non-statutory general criteria for the exercise of particular statutory decision-making powers. Important uses of soft law include enunciation of considerations to be taken into account in exercising discretionary power and facilitation of control by elected officials of decision-making by unelected officials. The basic principle of Australian law is that while the adoption of soft law norms is acceptable and even desirable, such norms must be applied flexibly, paying due regard to the interests of the individual(s) affected by the decision. Moreover, adoption of a policy may inhibit the decision-maker's freedom not to follow the policy, at least without giving the affected individual(s) a chance to argue in favour of its application, by creating a 'legitimate expectation' that the policy will be followed.[38]

Secondly, 'policy' may be used in contradistinction to 'law' on the one hand and 'fact' on the other: issues of policy may be distinguished both from issues of law and from issues of fact.[39] In this sense, 'policy' is roughly synonymous with 'purposes', 'goals' or 'objectives'. The Kerr Committee seems to have used the word in this sense when it said that 'the jurisdiction [of the proposed tribunal] would still be workable although matters of government policy may be involved'.[40]

ALD 688. One way in which this point is sometimes made is to say that the AAT's task is not to review the 'reasons for' the decision (ie, the factors on which the decision was based, or its 'rationality') but the decision itself: *Drake No 1* (1979) 2 ALD 60, 77–78 (Smithers J). See eg, *Re Tait and Secretary, Department of Family and Community Services* (2003) 74 ALD 247.

[35] 'Primary' legislation is legislation made by the legislative branch of government. 'Secondary' legislation is legislation made in exercise of a power to legislate delegated by the legislature to another body or official.

[36] eg, G Ganz, *Quasi-Legislation: Recent Developments in Secondary Legislation* (London, Sweet & Maxwell, 1987).

[37] eg R Baldwin, *Rules and Government* (Oxford, Clarendon Press, 1995) 226–30, 248–52.

[38] P Cane and L McDonald, *Principles of Administrative Law: Legal Regulation of Governance* (Melbourne, OUP, 2008) 156–58.

[39] However, it is well recognised that the distinction between law and fact is very difficult to draw analytically. The distinctions between law and policy, and fact and policy are also porous, allowing covert review of policy: P Cane, 'Merits Review and Judicial Review – The AAT as Trojan Horse' (2000) 28 *Federal Law Review* 213, 220.

[40] Kerr Committee Report, para 299. In *Australian Broadcasting Tribunal v Bond* (1990) 170 CLR 321, 341 Mason CJ used the term in this sense when he said that exposing 'all findings of fact, or the generality of them, to judicial review ... would bring in its train difficult questions concerning the extent to which courts should take account of policy considerations when reviewing the making of findings of fact and the drawing of inferences of fact'.

Thirdly, 'policy' may be used as a rough synonym for what, in US law, are referred to as 'political questions' – ie, matters unsuitable for judicial consideration.

In 5.3.2.1 we noted the view of the Kerr Committee that review of administrative decisions would very often raise policy issues in the third, 'political questions' sense; but also its opinion that the AAT should not have power to set aside a decision that was properly based on government 'policy' – here used, it seems, in the first, 'soft law' sense. We have also noted that the AAT Act says nothing about the substantive element of merits review and, therefore, nothing about the role of the AAT in relation to 'policy' in any of the three senses identified here. The foundational discussions of the matter are found in the decision of the Federal Court in *Drake (No1)*[41] and the subsequent decision of the AAT in *Drake (No 2)*.[42] The AAT affirmed a Ministerial decision to deport an alien, who had permanent resident status, on the ground that he had been convicted of a criminal offence. The applicant appealed to the Federal Court under section 44 of the AAT Act.[43] One of the grounds of appeal was that the AAT had given too much weight to a relevant 'policy statement' by the Minister. In the Federal Court, Bowen CJ and Deane J began their joint consideration of this ground of appeal by saying that the function of the AAT was 'administrative', not 'judicial'. That function, they said, was to 'adjudicate upon the merits of the decision' (on whether it was 'the correct or preferable one'); and in a case where the decision was 'lawfully made in pursuance of a permissible policy', the AAT's job was to adjudicate upon 'the propriety of the policy'.[44] A 'permissible' policy – ie, a statement of non-statutory decision-making criteria – is one that is not inconsistent with any relevant provision of primary or secondary legislation (or with the Constitution). Like the original decision-maker, the AAT is entitled to give weight to such policies; but it is not

> entitled to abdicate its function of determining whether the decision made was ... the correct or preferable one in favour of a function of merely determining whether the decision made conformed with whatever the relevant general government policy might be.[45]

---

[41] *Drake v Minister for Immigration and Ethnic Affairs* (1979) 2 ALD 60; 24 ALR 577; see also n 26 above.

[42] *Re Drake and Minister for Immigration and Ethnic Affairs* (1979) 2 ALD 634.

[43] s 44 confers a right of 'appeal' on a 'question of law'. However, it is 'axiomatic' that in hearing an 'appeal' under s 44 the Federal Court is exercising original, not appellate, jurisdiction: *Minister for Immigration and Ethnic Affairs v Gungor* (1982) 4 ALD 575, 584 (Sheppard J). See also Federal Court Act 1976 s 19(2). Another way of putting this is to say that an appeal under s 44 is functionally equivalent to judicial review (eg, *BTR plc v Westinghouse Brake & Signal Co (Aust) Ltd* (1992) 26 ALD 1, 7 (Lockhart and Hill JJ)). In the taxation cases discussed earlier (2.3.3), the fact that there was a right of appeal from the Taxation Board of Appeal to the High Court *in its appellate jurisdiction* was one the factors that contributed to the unconstitutionality of the original scheme for reviewing taxation decisions.

[44] (1979) 2 ALD 60, 68.

[45] ibid 70.

Bowen CJ and Deane J distinguished between the values of 'consistency' and 'justice in the individual case'.[46] The AAT (they said) should not, in the interests of consistency, affirm a decision merely on the ground that it resulted from the application of an 'unobjectionable'[47] policy without also being satisfied that application of the policy did justice in the individual case.

Smithers J. in a separate judgment, said that

> it is essential that a policy adopted by an administrator should be under review to the same extent as his evaluation of relevant matters and his general process of reasoning ... for the purpose of deciding whether, by the objective standard of good government it was the right decision to make ... in the best interests of Australia.[48]

After a close examination of the AAT's reasons for decision, Smithers J concluded that the AAT had not made an independent assessment of the propriety of the policy or of whether the Minister's decision to apply the policy had produced the correct decision; Bowen CJ and Deane J accepted that conclusion despite the arguably different emphasis in their description of the Tribunal's task.

The case was remitted to the AAT for rehearing. The matter came before the then-President of the AAT, Brennan J, who took a robust approach to expounding the implications of the decision of the Federal Court – an approach encouraged by the Federal Court's view that the role government policy should play in the decision of individual cases by the AAT was a matter for the AAT. The tone of Brennan J's complex judgment is set by an argument about the potential for, and the undesirability of, inconsistency – on matters about which reasonable minds could differ – between decisions of the executive and the Tribunal on the one hand, and between decisions of different members of the Tribunal on the other.

> Decisions made under a statutory power and reviewed by the Tribunal are but a proportion of the decisions made under that power, and it would be a regrettable anomaly if the decisions which were not reviewed revealed different standards and values from those made on review.[49]

This perceived danger of inconsistency laid the foundation for what may be thought of as the ratio decidendi of *Drake (No 2)*, namely that the AAT should 'apply' relevant lawful government policies (soft law) unless doing so would 'work an injustice in a particular case'.[50] Brennan J used the term 'apply' to mean 'not ... unquestioning adoption of [the policy], but rather an assumption that, in

---

[46]   ibid.
[47]   ibid.
[48]   ibid 80–82.
[49]   (1979) 2 ALD 634, 644–45. This statement nicely raises the issue of the relationship between administrators and adjudicators that formed the basis of the analysis of the US model of administrative adjudication in 3.2. It also illustrates the point made in 5.2 that self-restraint on the part of bodies charged with supervising the performance of statutory functions is one method of preventing the values of the supervisor from dominating the performance of the function.
[50]   (1979) 2 ALD 634, 645.

the absence of any reason to the contrary', the policy is 'appropriate to guide the decision in cases falling within its terms.'[51] This statement makes two points. First, just as the original decision-maker must take proper account of the details of the individual case in applying soft law, so must the AAT. In other words, the basic principle about the force of soft law stated earlier applies to the AAT as well as to primary decision-makers. Secondly, however, because the AAT is a 'curial' rather than an 'administrative' decision-maker,[52] its basic responsibility is to apply policy, not to make it. 'The detachment which is desirable for adjudication', Brennan J says, 'is not in sympathy with the purposiveness of policy formation ... administrative policy ... [of] wide significance ... is not conveniently formulated by this Tribunal.'[53] The powers of the AAT are wide enough to 'permit the sterilisation or amendment of policy'. Indeed, '[i]n point of law, the Tribunal is as free as the Minister to apply or not apply ... policy. The Tribunal's duty is to make the correct or preferable decision in each case ... and the Tribunal is at liberty to adopt whatever policy it chooses, or no policy at all, in fulfilling its statutory function'.[54] Nevertheless,

> there are substantial reasons which favour only cautious and sparing departures from Ministerial policy, particularly if parliament has ... approved that policy ... It would be manifestly imprudent for the Tribunal to override a ministerial policy and adopt a general administrative policy of its own'.[55]

Laying down 'broad policy ... is essentially a political function ... the very independence of the Tribunal demands that it be apolitical'.[56] Its primary task is achieving justice in the individual case.

In the words of John McMillan, 'The *Drake* litigation predictably sparked a debate that permeated appraisal of the Tribunal during the first decade of its adjudication.'[57] The debate was particularly vigorous in relation to the AAT's jurisdiction to review deportation decisions,[58] not only because the *Drake* cases concerned such a decision but also, and perhaps more significantly, because this is an area of relatively high 'political' sensitivity. The line between setting a decision aside because of the way policy was applied in the particular case and setting it aside because of some demerit in the policy itself is inevitably a fine one. The judges in *Drake (No 1)* expressly accepted that whether the AAT had given

---

[51] ibid 642. Based on this definition of 'apply' the ratio of *Drake No 2* could be stated without the qualification, which seems to be built into the definition.

[52] ibid 643. On one reading, this statement flatly contradicts that of Bowen CJ and Deane J in *Drake (No 1)* that the AAT's function is administrative, not judicial.

[53] ibid.

[54] ibid 642.

[55] ibid 644.

[56] ibid.

[57] J McMillan, 'Review of Government Policy by Administrative Tribunals' in *Commonwealth Tribunals: The Ambit of Review*, Law and Policy Papers No 9 (Canberra, Centre for International and Public Law, Australian National University, 1998) 31.

[58] J Sharpe, *The Administrative Appeals Tribunal and Policy Review* (Sydney, Law Book Company, 1986) 76–94, 105–06, 157–93.

undue weight to ministerial policy in that case was a matter that could be resolved only by careful – and arguably creative – interpretation of the tribunal's reasons for decision. In areas of political sensitivity, the setting aside of decisions is more likely to be interpreted by government as impermissible interference with policy-formation; and conversely, the tribunal is more likely to explain its decisions in ways that cannot easily be interpreted as involving questioning the merits of the relevant policy as opposed to its application in the particular case. In practice, however, saying that a policy is unsuitable to be applied in the case at hand (and, by implication in like cases) is essentially similar to saying that the policy lacks merit in a certain respect. Setting aside a decision on the ground that the criteria on which it was based produced injustice in the case at hand may not involve 'broad' policy-making, but it involves incremental policy-making.

The ambivalence in Brennan J's approach in *Drake (No 2)* might be interpreted as an attempt to find a middle way between supporters and opponents[59] of review of the merits of government policy by independent tribunals. However, writing extra-judicially in 1986, Brennan said that arming a tribunal 'with authority to apply whatever policy it thinks appropriate' may enable it to 'engage in a constructive dialogue' with government. He contrasted such a 'lively role in policy formation' with the approach appropriate for a court.[60] Despite the apparent tempering of formal activism with informal restraint in *Drake (No 2)*, Brennan is clearly amongst those who, for reasons that have never been clearly articulated, consider it desirable and appropriate for tribunals to take a more active role in the formulation of government policy (ie, non-statutory criteria for statutory decision-making) than either unelected officials responsible for implementing rules or courts in reviewing the implementation of rules. This is a role traditionally allocated to elected officials within the executive branch. Brennan's apparent support for such activism not only provoked debate in the period after *Drake (No 2)* was decided, but has been a cause of continuing controversy, as McMillan noted in 1998.[61]

Against this background, it may be helpful to attempt a more systematic exposition of the place of 'policy' in the concept of merits review. We may begin by observing that considerations relevant to the exercise of a statutory decision-making power may be (though rarely are) exhaustively and exclusively spelled out in the legislation (whether primary or secondary) that confers the power. In that case, both the decision-maker in making the decision, and a reviewer in affirming or varying the decision or in making a substitute decision, would be

---

[59] One of the most high-profile doubters was Justice Michael Kirby, 'Administrative Review: Beyond the Frontiers Marked "Policy – Lawyers Keep Out"' (1981) 12 *Federal Law Review* 121.

[60] Sir G Brennan, 'The Purpose and Scope of Judicial Review' in M Taggart (ed), *Judicial Review of Administrative Action in the 1980s: Problems and Prospects* (Auckland, OUP, 1986) 34.

[61] n 57 above, 25.

bound to take account of all and only the stated considerations. Typically, however, relevant considerations are not fully specified by legislation. In *Drake (No 1)* Bowen CJ and Deane J said that

> the consistent exercise of discretionary administrative power in the absence of legislative guidelines will, in itself, almost inevitably lead to the formulation of some general policy or rules relating to the exercise of the relevant power.[62]

In the absence of explicit legislative decision-making criteria, consistency may be facilitated by, and may demand, the formulation of policies by the primary decision-maker as part of the decision-making process. Is the same true of the AAT?

The answer to this question is clear: the demands of consistency apply to the AAT as much as to the decision-makers over whom it exercises jurisdiction. As Brennan J said in *Drake (No 2)*: 'Inconsistency is not merely inelegant: it ... [suggests] an arbitrariness which is incompatible with commonly accepted notions of justice'.[63] It follows that although the AAT is not 'bound' by its own previous decisions,[64] it should aim to be consistent in its decision-making; and consistency may often be most effectively realised by the formulation of general[65] norms (in the nature of policies)[66] to structure not only the AAT's own decision-making but also that of decision-makers subject to its jurisdiction.[67] However, just as when courts make law they do so 'incrementally' or 'interstitially', as an incidental by-product of resolving individual disputes, and not 'legislatively' as a parliament does, so the AAT has always shied away from laying down what Brennan J in *Drake (No 2)* called 'general' or 'broad' policy.[68] The Tribunal

---

[62] (1979) 2 ALD 60, 69. See also eg, *Re Aston and Secretary, Department of Primary Industry* (1985) 8 ALD 366, 375.

[63] (1979) 2 ALD 634, 639. Of course, consistency is not of unqualified value. There is no virtue in being consistently wrong or unjust: *Federal Commissioner of Taxation v Swift* (1989) 18 ALD 679, 692 (French J).

[64] Pearce, *Administrative Appeals Tribunal*, 200–02. See also *R v Moore, ex p Australian Telephone and Phonogram Officers' Association* (1980) 148 CLR 600, 612–14 (Gibbs CJ), 615 (Stephen J). Some decisions may carry more weight than others: *Re Littlejohn and Department of Social Security* (1989) 17 ALD 482, 486.

[65] *Leppington Pastoral Co Pty Ltd v Department of Administrative Services* (1990) 20 ALD 607; *Re Malincevski and Minister for Immigration, Local Government and Ethnic Affairs* (1991) 24 ALD 331. Such norms may be designed to give decision-makers guidance about the interpretation of statutory provisions, or about how to exercise statutory discretions, or about procedures to be followed.

[66] As we will see in 5.3.2.2(iii), the AAT cannot conclusively decide questions of law. It follows that any general norms it articulates will not have the force of norms made by courts that have the power to decide issues of law conclusively. See eg, *Minister for Immigration and Ethnic Affairs v Pochi* (1980) 4 ALD 139, 154–55 (Deane J).

[67] *Re Scott and Commissioner for Superannuation* (1986) 9 ALD 491, 499; but contrast *Re McGrath and Defence Force Retirement and Death Benefits Authority* (1986) 9 ALD 562, [15]. The substantive decision in *Re Scott* was set aside and remitted to the AAT in *Commissioner for Superannuation v Scott* (1987) 71 ALR 408.

[68] eg *Re Australian Metal Holdings Pty Ltd and Australian Securities Commission and Others* (1995) 37 ALD 131, 144. See also J Sharpe, *The Administrative Appeals Tribunal and Policy Review* (Sydney, Law Book Company, 1986) ch VI.

understands its prime function in terms of doing justice in individual cases, not establishing general norms of correct or sound decision-making.[69]

The crucial legal distinction between a provision of primary or secondary legislation (hard law) and a policy (soft law) is that the former is binding in a strict way that the latter is not.[70] Policies are considerations to be taken into account along with other relevant matters, not binding rules to be followed to the exclusion of other considerations.[71] Nevertheless, policies *are* relevant considerations that must be taken into account by decision-makers. A central question in the present context is whether policies made by government agencies and officials[72] have the same force in relation to decision-making by the AAT as they do in relation to primary decision-making. This question arises precisely because the AAT is a reviewer of decisions, not a primary decision-maker. Suppose that in a particular case, the AAT considers that a primary decision is not the correct or preferable one precisely because it applies or is consistent with some government policy? Can it vary the decision or make a substitute decision in a way that is inconsistent with the policy? In other words, may the AAT consider the *merits* of (lawful) government policy?[73]

The first point to make in answering this question is that if government policy conflicts with some legal rule (whether constitutional, statutory or common law)

---

[69] eg *Re Presmint Pty Ltd and Australian Fisheries Management Authority* (1995) 39 ALD 625. See also *Re John Holman & Co Pty Ltd and Minister for Primary Industry and Australian Apple and Pear Growers' Association* (1983) 5 ALN No 154 and *Re Rendevski & Sons and Australian Apple and Pear Corporation* (1987) 12 ALD 280. These latter two cases, while reaffirming the inappropriateness of 'general' policy-making by the AAT, nicely illustrate its capacity to provoke or influence the development of policy in the way contemplated by Brennan J, n 60 above. A case that has been interpreted as an example of inappropriate policy-making by the AAT is *Re Secretary, Department of Social Security and 'HH'* (1991) 23 ALD 58, on which see I Thompson and M Paterson, 'The Federal Administrative Appeals Tribunal and Policy Review: A Re-assessment of the Controversy (1991) 2 *Public Law Review* 243, 256–57.

[70] In theory, a statute might expressly provide that a decision-maker (including the AAT) is bound by some non-statutory policy, effectively turning it into delegated legislation. Such a provision would be objectionable if it allowed the normal procedural controls over the making of delegated legislation to be avoided. In practice, the distinction between policies and binding rules is not always clear or easy to apply even when a statutory provision purports to make 'policies' 'binding': R Creyke and J McMillan, *Control of Government Action: Text, Cases and Commentary* (Chatswood, NSW, LexisNexis Butterworths, 2005) 628–33. Part of the problem is that policies themselves may leave room for the exercise of discretion by the decision-maker. In such cases it is unclear what it means to say that the policy is 'binding' rather than merely a relevant consideration.

[71] *Drake (No 2)* (1979) 2 ALD 634, 642. In *Re Loh and Minister for Immigration, Local Government and Ethnic Affairs* (1990) 11 AAR 150, 159 Hartigan J (President of the AAT) went so far as to describe policy as 'part of the body of *factual* circumstances' relevant to arriving at the correct or preferable decision (emphasis added).

[72] As opposed to policy-like norms laid down by the AAT.

[73] Statute may expressly provide that it shall not do so: *Leppington Pastoral Co Pty Ltd v Department of Administrative Services* (1990) 20 ALD 607.

it is illegal, and the AAT[74] (as well as a primary decision-maker)[75] would be bound not to act in conformity with it.[76] Secondly, it is illegal for a primary administrative decision-maker to 'fetter' its discretion by treating a policy as if it were legally binding and exclusive of other considerations;[77] and it would also be illegal for the AAT to do this. However, this conclusion is consistent with saying that the AAT is under an obligation to take account of the policy and to apply it in appropriate circumstances. The crucial question is whether the AAT is entitled to refuse to apply a lawful policy, not because the policy would lead to injustice in the particular case but because it is not, in the AAT's opinion, a sound or wise policy?[78] A further related question is whether the AAT is entitled to enunciate a new policy, inconsistent with an existing policy, as the basis for varying a decision or making a substitute decision?

The answer to these questions is quite obviously, yes. To understand this conclusion we need to note that one of the grounds on which decisions can be held illegal by a court is so-called '*Wednesbury* unreasonableness'.[79] Amongst other things, this ground allows a court to quash a decision which is consistent with relevant legal rules and well-grounded in relevant facts but which the court considers to be based on an unreasonable policy – ie, a non-statutory decision-making criterion. Merits review, as its name implies, is more concerned than

---

[74] *Australian Fisheries Management Authority v PW Adams Pty Ltd* (1995) 39 ALD 481; *Bateman v Health Insurance Commission* (1998) 54 ALD 408. The AAT must determine whether a policy is lawful 'not in order to supervise the exercise by the [primary decision-maker] of his discretion, but in order to determine whether the policy is appropriate for application by the Tribunal in making its own decision on review': *Re Drake (No 2)* (1979) 2 ALD 634, 645 (Brennan J).

[75] *Green v Daniels* (1977) 13 ALR 1. See eg, *Re Lanham and Secretary, Department of Family and Community Services* (2002) 67 ALD 173. But suppose that a Minister gives an undertaking to Parliament that a statutory provision will be applied, contrary to its express terms, in such a way as to benefit some citizens: *Re Sharpe and Department of Social Security* (1988) 14 ALD 681, 693–94. See also *Re Witheford and Department of Foreign Affairs* (1983) 5 ALD 534.

[76] This is so whether the policy affects the citizen adversely or beneficially: *Re Dunning and Department of Social Security* (1986) 10 ALD 89; *Re Williams and the Director-General of Social Services* (1981) 4 ALD 300.

[77] eg *Re Goodson and Secretary, Department of Employment, Education, Training and Youth Affairs* (1996) 42 ALD 651, 655; *Re Grylls and Department of Immigration and Citizenship* (2007) 99 ALD 394. In one sense, the question of whether a relevant consideration has been ignored concerns the decision-maker's subjective reasoning processes, which may be very difficult to prove (for explicit recognition of the problem see *Drake (No 1)* (1979) 2 ALD 60). In practice, therefore, the question will typically be answered objectively in terms of whether, in the reviewer's judgment, the policy has been given too much weight.

[78] However, the sharp theoretical distinction between 'lawful' on the one hand and 'sound or wise' on the other is not so clear-cut in practice. For instance, the AAT might reject government policy on the basis that its application involves unlawfully taking into account a consideration which is not relevant on a proper interpretation of the statutory provision conferring the power to make the decision (see discussion in Sharpe, *The Administrative Appeals Tribunal and Policy Review*, ch VII). In this way the AAT can reject government policy, which it considers unsound or unwise, on the ground that it is illegal. The difficult question is whether the AAT may reject a policy, which it considers to be lawful, on the ground that it is unsound or unwise.

[79] Cane and McDonald, *Principles of Administrative Law*, 179–81. A decision is vulnerable on this basis if it is 'so unreasonable that no reasonable decision-maker could have made it'.

legality-based review with whether administrative decisions are 'correct or preferable' as opposed to 'legal'. It seems to follow that merits review must be at least as concerned as legality-based review with the soundness of policies. And since, unlike a court, the AAT can vary, and make substitute, decisions, it must have the power to act inconsistently with government policy. So the difficult question is not whether the AAT can act inconsistently with government policy, but when?

A distinction is drawn between policies according to the 'political level' at which they are formulated.[80] For instance, the AAT is less likely to be justified in departing from a policy adopted by Cabinet and approved by Parliament, or from a policy that is the result of wide consultation amongst relevant organisations and individuals, than from an internal departmental guideline developed by officials, perhaps in consultation with the Minister. In one case the AAT said, in relation to a policy developed 'at the highest level', that the policy should be applied (ie, treated as a relevant consideration) by the Tribunal unless 'evidence showed that it was entirely misconceived or proceeded on a wholly erroneous basis'.[81] This test seems similar to the judicial review standard of *Wednesbury* unreasonableness. There are various statements in the cases that relate to policies apparently developed at 'lower levels';[82] but they do not address the question of whether the relevant policy was sound or wise, but rather whether the decision-maker paid due attention to the facts of the individual case in deciding whether or not to apply the policy (regardless of its desirability)[83] – the question, in other words, of whether the decision-maker's discretion had been fettered by inflexible application of the policy. Indeed, in one case Deane J reasoned in this way despite describing the policy as 'draconian and, indeed, callous'.[84]

It would seem, therefore, that although the AAT is entitled to act inconsistently with government policy and, as a corollary, to make policy inconsistent with existing government policy, it is very reluctant to do so, and perhaps even more reluctant than courts to reject government policy as 'unreasonable'. In other words, it is extremely unwilling to engage in a policy 'dialogue' with the elected

---

[80] *Re Becker and Minister for Immigration and Ethnic Affairs* (1977) 1 ALD 158. See generally Pearce, *Administrative Appeals Tribunal*, 194–98; Sharpe, *The Administrative Appeals Tribunal and Policy Review*, ch IV (review of ministerial policy) and ch V (review of policy made by departments and statutory authorities).

[81] *Re Aston and Secretary, Department of Primary Industry* (1985) 8 ALD 366, 380.

[82] eg *Re Evans and Secretary, Department of Primary Industry* (1985) ALD 627; *Re Jetopay Pty Ltd and Australian Fisheries Management Authority* (1993) 32 ALD 209, 231–32; *Stoljarev v Australian Fisheries Management Authority* (1995) 39 ALD 517.

[83] It has been said (somewhat equivocally) that the principle that policy should only be applied 'when it is appropriate and acceptable ... does not involve the Tribunal in reviewing policy or deciding what policy a primary decision-maker should adopt', but rather affects the weight to be given to the policy: *Federal Commissioner of Taxation v Swift* (1989) 18 ALD 679, 692 (French J).

[84] *Nevistic v Minister for Immigration and Ethnic Affairs* (1981) 34 ALR 639, 647. But for an implication that the AAT might have ignored a departmental guideline in a decision-making manual if it had been 'unreasonable or unjust' see *Re Petry and Secretary, Department of Families, Community Services and Indigenous Affairs* (2006) 92 ALD 799, [38]. See also *Re McPhee and Repatriation Commission* (2007) 93 ALD 732, [22]: 'unobjectionable' internal departmental guidelines applied.

executive in the way contemplated by Brennan J in his 1986 extra-judicial statement.[85] Instead of addressing the merits of government policy, the AAT is more likely, if it can, to hold a policy of which it does not approve to be illegal on the basis of a proper interpretation of the empowering statute.[86] If it feels unable to do this, it will typically[87] go no further than deciding whether the decision-maker, in applying the policy, took proper account of the interests of the applicant or, on the contrary, gave excessive weight to the policy at the expense of the applicant's interests. Provided the AAT properly addresses that question, any decision it reaches about whether to affirm, vary or set aside the decision on policy-related grounds cannot be challenged in the Federal Court on the ground of error of law.[88]

What is the relationship between the rule that soft-law norms must be applied flexibly and the distinction between implementation and adjudication? It will be recalled (from 1.2.2) that whereas implementation of norms by primary decision-makers (as well as by internal reviewers) involves resolving conflicts between social and individual interests in favour of the former, adjudication by external reviewers involves resolving such conflicts in favour of the latter. How does this distinction apply to soft law, given that both implementers and adjudicators (external merits reviewers) are explicitly required to take account of individual interests in applying policies? Two points need to be made. First, the fact that the law does not explicitly instruct decision-makers to take account of individual circumstances when applying hard law does not mean that individual circumstances need not be taken into account. As argued in Chapter 1, the very process of regulating conduct and circumstances of individuals in order to further the objectives of general rules potentially creates tension and conflict between individual and social interests. This tension is mediated through the judgmental processes of finding facts, identifying norms and applying norms to facts, each of which typically leaves the decision-maker room for adjusting individual and social interests in various ways. Secondly, the explicit instruction to decision-makers in relation to policy is to take account of individual circumstances and to avoid individual injustice. That formula does not determine how much weight is to be given to individual interests relative to social interests; in other words, it does not determine the meaning of 'injustice to the individual'. In many cases, reasonable decision makers may disagree about how to resolve conflicts between social and individual interests even in cases where they are instructed to take account of individual circumstances and avoid injustice. In this

---

[85] See n 60 above.

[86] See n 78 above.

[87] But see *Re Fischer and Australian Fisheries Management Authority* (2002) 71 ALD 665 in which the AAT apparently held that the application of a policy caused injustice in the case before it, but also that the policy was flawed. The AAT considered that it lacked the necessary expertise and knowledge to frame an appropriate policy and remitted the case to the decision-maker.

[88] eg *Nevistic v Minister for Immigration and Ethnic Affairs* (1981) 34 ALR 639.

way, the law's demand that policy be applied flexibly leaves room for implementers and adjudicators respectively to reach different decisions in individual cases,
the former by giving more weight to social than to individual interests and the
latter by giving more weight to individual than to social interests.

In this regard, the distinction between hard and soft law is one of degree, not
kind: hard law typically leaves decision-makers with less leeway to take account of
individual circumstances than soft law, but both require a balance to be struck
between individual and social interests and both leave open the possibility of
reasonable differences of opinion between implementers and adjudicators about
how the balance should be struck in individual cases.

(iii) The Decision

Here we are concerned not with decision-making procedure or the decision-
maker's reasoning process but with the substance of the decision itself. The main
substantive grounds on which a decision can be held illegal or invalid are error of
law, error of fact and *Wednesbury* unreasonableness (which was mentioned in the
previous subsection).

Error of Law

The concept of merits review is built on a contrast between the 'legality' and the
'merits' of decisions made in implementation of rules. On this basis it might be
assumed that merits review is concerned with whether a decision is 'correct or
preferable' and *not* with whether it is legal.[89] So what is the role of a merits review
tribunals in relation to illegal decisions? Typically, of course, a decision-maker

---

[89] The New South Wales Land and Environment Court (LEC) is a superior court of record that
exercises both merits review and judicial review jurisdiction. For instance, in its judicial review
jurisdiction it can decide the validity of a condition imposed by the Court itself, in exercise of its
merits review jurisdiction, on an application for development consent: *North Sydney Municipal
Council v Hunglen Pty Ltd* (1992) 74 LGRA 313, 317. The Court is staffed by judges (who have the
same status as judges of the NSW Supreme Court) and lay 'Commissioners'. Most merits review
applications are heard by Commissioners; procedure is informal, rules of evidence do not apply, and
costs are normally not awarded (see *Gee v Port Stephens Council* (2003) 131 LGERA 325). All judicial
review applications are heard by a judge; procedure is more formal, rules of evidence apply and costs
are usually awarded. The distinction between whether a decision is 'good or bad' and whether it is
'lawful' pervades the description of the Court's two types of jurisdiction on its website: <http://www.
lawlink.nsw.gov.au/lawlink/lec/ll_lec.nsf/pages/LEC_jurisdictionfull> accessed 1 April 2009. See also
ML Pearlman, 'The Role and Operation of the Land and Environment Court' (1999) 58 *Law Society
Journal* 58, 60; N Pain, 'Environmental Decision-making Processes' (1996) 79 *Canberra Bulletin of
Public Administration* 73, 74–75; Z Lipman, 'The NSW Land and Environment Court: Reforms to the
Merit Review Process' (2004) 21 *Environmental and Planning Law Journal* 415, 416–17. However,
s 56A(1) of the Land and Environment Court Act 1979, by providing for an appeal to the Court from
a decision of a Commissioner 'on a question of law' in a merits review application, seems to
undermine any idea that there is a mutually exclusive distinction between legality and merits. In
practice, too, it seems that the distinction may be difficult to observe. In the words of a former Chief
Justice of the LEC, 'the distinction … is not as clear as some lawyers believe … [I]n many 'review'
challenges planning merits get freely canvassed': Cripps CJ, cited in A Stewart, 'Effects of the Land and
Environment Court' (1999) 16 *Environmental and Planning Law Journal* 482, 489.

who makes an illegal decision will have attempted ('purported') to decide legally. But if the decision is in fact illegal, no question of its merits – of whether it is 'correct or preferable' – will arise. So does a merits review tribunal such as the AAT have jurisdiction to review an illegal (purported) decision and to set it aside on the ground that it is contrary to law (regardless of its merits)?

Not surprisingly, this was one of the first legal issues about the role of the AAT that arose for consideration. The decision that the AAT does have such power[90] established that although merits review tribunals (unlike courts) can review administrative decisions 'on the merits', this is not all they can do.[91] In addition to the non-judicial power of reviewing decisions on their merits, merits review tribunals can also exercise what, in Australian constitutional law, is sometimes called an 'innominate function' – ie, a function that can be allocated either to a judicial or a non-judicial body and which (like a chameleon) assumes the character of the body to which it is allocated: judicial if allocated to a judicial body and non-judicial if allocated to a non-judicial body. One of these functions is to decide questions of law.[92] However, in Australian constitutional law doctrine, what a merits review tribunal cannot do (but a court can) is to decide questions of law 'conclusively': this is an exclusively judicial function.[93]

---

[90] *Re Brian Lawlor Automotive Pty Ltd and Collector of Customs (NSW)* (1978) 1 ALD 167; affirmed *Collector of Customs (NSW) v Brian Lawlor Automotive Pty Ltd* (1979) 2 ALD 1; reaffirmed *Secretary, Department of Social Security v Alvaro* (1994) 34 ALD 72. See also *Deputy Commissioner of Patents v Board of Control of Michigan Technological University* (1979) 2 ALD 711. For a different interpretation of *Lawlor* from that given in the text see *Re Radge and Commissioner of Taxation* (2007) 95 ALD 711, [22]–[25]. In *Re Brian Lawlor* (1978) 1 ALD 167, 178 Brennan J said that it would be 'manifestly inconvenient' if the Tribunal lacked power to review illegal decisions. But the problem is deeper than this because the sorts of errors that enliven the AAT's jurisdiction by leading to the making of decisions that are not 'correct or preferable' are essentially similar to those that cause decisions to be 'illegal' (or 'beyond jurisdiction') as this term is understood in judicial review law. In other words, decisions that are not correct or preferable on their merits will very often (also) be illegal. The type of error that is most likely to go only to the merits of a decision and not affect its legality is error of fact (see next subsection). In Australian law, errors of law 'within jurisdiction' do not render decisions illegal; but this category of error is recognised only in relation to inferior courts, not tribunals or executive decision-makers. Merits review tribunals have no jurisdiction over decision-making by inferior courts.

[91] 'The (il)legality of the decision under review does not go to the jurisdiction of the AAT. Its jurisdiction is derived from s 25 of the AAT Act and statutory provisions on which that section operates. Deciding whether a decision under review is illegal or not is part of the function of merits review tribunals': *Collector of Customs (NSW) v Brian Lawlor Automotive Pty Ltd* (1979) 2 ALD 1, 7 (Bowen CJ).

[92] Including questions about the proper interpretation of the provisions of the AAT Act conferring jurisdiction on the AAT: eg, *Re Adams and Tax Agents Board* (1976) 1 ALD 251. However, the prevailing view is that the AAT has no power to set aside a decision on the ground that the provision under which it was made was unconstitutional or invalid, and so must act on an assumption of validity: Pearce, *Administrative Appeals Tribunal*, 18–21. The issue of validity could be referred by the AAT to the Federal Court under s 45 of the AAT Act (*Re Lower and Comcare* (2003) 74 ALD 547, 556). In the UK, it has been held that the highest tribunal in the social security adjudication system has jurisdiction to decide the validity of delegated legislation both because of its expertise in social security law and in order to avoid 'cumbrous duplicity of proceedings': *Chief Adjudication Officer v Foster* [1993] AC 754. In Canada, the matter has been much litigated, particularly in the context of the Canadian Charter of Rights and Freedoms. In upholding the power of tribunals to

The precise meaning of 'conclusively' is a matter of some debate. It may be related to the distinction between appeal and judicial review.[94] According to this approach, a conclusive decision could be challenged only by way of an appeal, whereas a non-conclusive decision could be challenged by way of judicial review or in 'collateral proceedings' – for instance, proceedings to enforce the decision. However, in the Australian context this approach is hard to reconcile with the fact that the Federal Court – which can exercise the judicial power of deciding questions of law conclusively – is subject to judicial review under section 75(v) of the Australian Constitution.[95] So it may be that the distinction between a conclusive and a non-conclusive decision turns entirely on whether the decision can be challenged 'collaterally'.[96] Be that as it may, (non-conclusive) decisions of the AAT on points of law can be challenged either by way of an 'appeal' to the Federal Court[97] or by way of judicial review.[98] Whatever the theoretical or

decide constitutional issues the Supreme Court has rejected the argument that separation of powers dictates that courts and not tribunals can decide such issues, requiring only that tribunal decisions on constitutionality be subject to judicial review according to a non-deferential 'correctness' standard. However, it should be noted that the Canadian constitution lacks entrenched separation of powers The desirability of making rights widely and easily enforceable has been influential in Canada. In this respect, it should be observed that Australia lacks a constitutional bill of rights. In Canada there is debate about whether a legislative provision prohibiting a tribunal from deciding constitutional issues would itself be unconstitutional. For an account of the earlier Canadian cases see MC Crane, 'Administrative Tribunals, Charter Challenges, and the "Web of Institutional Relationships"' (1998) 61 *Saskatchewan Law Review* 495; and for more recent developments see JM Evans, 'Principle and Pragmatism: Administrative Agencies' Jurisdiction over Constitutional Issues' in G Huscroft and M Taggart, *Inside and Outside Canadian Administrative Law* (Toronto, University of Toronto Press, 2006). In the UK, s 2 of the Human Rights Act 1998 imposes on tribunals the same obligation to protect rights under the European Convention on Human Rights as it imposes on courts. In general, however, only courts, and not tribunals, have power to entertain claims and award remedies for breaches of Convention rights as such. The position in Canada in this respect is unclear: JM Evans, above, 405–06. Concerning the US see Note, 'The Authority of Administrative Agencies to Consider the Constitutionality of Statutes' (1976) 90 *Harvard LR* 1682.

[93] At least if the question of law relates 'to a controversy about existing rights and duties': L Zines, *The High Court and the Constitution*, 5th edn (Sydney, The Federation Press, 2008) 236. AAT Act s 31 (decision of AAT about whether a person's interests are affected by a reviewable decision is 'conclusive') must be interpreted accordingly: *Comptroller General of Customs v Members of Administrative Appeals Tribunal* (1994) 32 ALD 463.

[94] The distinction between conclusive and non-conclusive decisions is also related to, and may be a version of, an older distinction between 'void' and 'voidable' decisions; as to which see generally M Aronson, B Dyer and M Groves, *Judicial Review of Administrative Action* 4th edn (Sydney, Lawbook Co, 2009) ch 10.

[95] As a matter of English common law, 'superior courts of record' are not subject to judicial review. However, all 'officers of the Commonwealth' are amenable to the entrenched judicial review jurisdiction of the High Court under s 75(v), and this phrase includes judges of all federal courts except the High Court: *Federated Engine Drivers' and Firemen's Association of Australasia v The Colonial Sugar Refining Company* (1916) 22 CLR 103, 117 (Isaacs, Gavan Duffy and Rich JJ).

[96] Disconcertingly, however, the Federal Court has held that decisions of the AAT cannot be challenged collaterally: *Coffey v Secretary, Department of Social Security* (1999) 56 ALD 338, 347.

[97] But as we saw earlier (n 43 above) an appeal to the Federal Court from the AAT is functionally equivalent to judicial review.

[98] But perhaps only in exceptional circumstances: Pearce, *Administrative Appeals Tribunal*, 253–55.

practical significance of the distinction between conclusive and non-conclusive decisions, it relates to their effects and not to the nature of the decision-making process: when a merits review tribunal decides (or, more accurately, expresses an opinion about) a question of law it performs a juristic task exactly similar to that performed by a court in deciding a question of law.

Most errors of law are, in essence, the result of misinterpretation or misapplication by the decision-maker of a statutory provision or a non-statutory policy (soft law).[99] A decision may be illegal because, for instance, it fell outside the power the decision-maker was purporting to exercise, or because the particular decision-maker had no power to make the decision.[100]

In Australian judicial review law, questions of law are generally treated as having only one correct answer. On the other hand, it is widely acknowledged that there is often room for reasonable disagreement about the meaning of particular statutory provisions. In effect, therefore, the idea that questions of law have a single correct answer reduces to the proposition that the correct answer to a question of law is the answer preferred by the court with the final say about what the answer is to any particular question of law. The task of the AAT is to review decisions that are not 'correct or preferable' and to identify the decision that is correct or preferable. In theory, the AAT's task in relation to questions of law is to identify the 'correct' answer. But in cases where reasonable minds could differ about which interpretation is correct, the 'correct' answer may be equivalent to the 'preferable' answer. However, it is probably not open to the AAT explicitly to apply the 'preferable' standard when reviewing decisions on questions of law.[101]

In some cases – where, for instance, the decision-maker simply had no power to make the decision under review – the appropriate course of action for the AAT would be to set the decision aside and direct the decision-maker to take no action to give it effect.[102] In other cases,[103] the AAT may be able to correct the legal error

---

[99] For an example of error in interpreting a policy see *Minister for Immigration, Local Government and Ethnic Affairs v Gray* (1994) 33 ALD 13.

[100] eg *Re Baran and Department of Primary Industries and Energy* (1988) 18 ALD 379.

[101] US judicial review law not only acknowledges that questions of law may have more than one reasonable answer, but also requires the court to 'defer' to administrators' interpretations of relevant statutory provisions by holding such an interpretation to be erroneous only if it is 'unreasonable'. The 'correct or preferable' standard could accommodate such an approach. If adopted, it would make it more difficult for the AAT to depart from government policy on the ground of inconsistency with statute (see n 78 above).

[102] As in *Re Brian Lawlor Automotive Pty Ltd and Collector of Customs (NSW)* (1978) 1 ALD 167. It is noteworthy that the order made in this case (that the decision be set aside and that no further action be taken on it) does not fit neatly into any of the remedial categories in AAT Act s 43. See the explanation at (1978) 1 ALD 167, 176. See also *Re SLE Medical Pty Ltd and Industry Research and Development Board* (1985) 10 AAR 13; *SZGME v Minister for Immigration and Citizenship* (2007) 102 ALD 31, 38–42.

[103] For instance, where the decision-maker acts in bad faith: see *Re Mika Engineering Holdings Pty Ltd and Commissioner of Taxation* (2006) 92 ALD 688, 692–93.

by varying the decision, making a substitute decision or remitting the decision to the decision-maker with appropriate directions.

What is the effect on the role of the AAT of a change in the relevant statutory law between the date of the decision under review (T1) and the date of the tribunal's decision (T2)?[104] This is said to depend on whether the issue before the tribunal concerns 'accrued rights or liabilities' on the one hand, or 'present entitlements' on the other. If the issue concerns accrued rights or liabilities, the law normally applied will be that in force at T1. The law in force at T2 will apply only if the amending provision – whether beneficial or disadvantageous to the applicant – is expressed to operate retrospectively. If the issue concerns present entitlements, the law in force T2 will normally be applied, once again regardless of whether the change is beneficial or disadvantageous to the applicant. However, the distinction between accrued rights and liabilities on the one hand and present entitlements on the other is effectively conclusory and may be manipulable to produce the result the tribunal thinks 'fair'. For instance, if the tribunal considers the relevant statute to be 'beneficial' – as in the case, for instance, of veterans' benefits legislation – it may be inclined to apply the law most advantageous to the applicant – whether that be the law at T1 or the law at T2 – and justify the result in terms of the accrued rights/present entitlements distinction.

It certainly seems objectionable as a matter of general principle to apply disadvantageous statutory changes to the law in the absence of express words (or at the very least, an irresistibly strong implication) indicating retrospective operation. The basis for this suspect approach seems to be that the AAT 'stands in the shoes of the decision-maker', and that the decision-maker's obligation is to apply the law at the time the decision is made, not the law at some former time. However, in this context it is arguably unfair to ignore the fact that although the AAT has the power to make a substitute decision, it is nevertheless a reviewer of decisions, not an original decision-maker. It is true, as we will see in the next section, that the AAT normally bases its decision on the evidence available at T2, even if this includes evidence that was not available at T1. However, since only the affected citizen(s) can apply for merits review, it is very unlikely that this rule will work to the disadvantage of the applicant(s) (assuming no change in the relevant law since T1). By contrast, applying the law in force at T2 may result in a decision adverse to the applicant in circumstances where, if the law in force at T1 had been applied, the application for review would have been successful.

In a case where an application for review is successful on the basis of a subsequent change in the law, it would obviously be inaccurate to say that the original decision-maker made an 'error of law'. The task of the AAT is not (only) to identify errors but (also) to make decisions in accordance with relevant law.

---

[104] Pearce, *Administrative Appeals Tribunal*, 187–89.

Error of Fact

There are two varieties of factual error. One – taking account of an irrelevant fact or failing to take account of a relevant fact – is a form of reasoning-process error. Here we are concerned with factual errors that consist in making factual findings on the basis of inadequate evidence. In *Australian Broadcasting Tribunal v Bond*[105] Mason CJ said that normally error of fact of this sort, which is a function of weight given to available evidence, will not provide a ground of judicial review – ie, a basis for holding a decision to be illegal or invalid – partly because review of decisions about questions of fact has been committed to merits review tribunals such as the AAT.[106] It appears that the AAT can review any and every question of fact relevant to a reviewable decision. If it concludes that a relevant question of fact admits of only one acceptable answer, which is different from that given by the decision-maker, it can intervene on the basis that the decision was not 'correct'. If it concludes that the question of fact admits of more than one acceptable answer, and that the answer given by the decision-maker was not the best of the available options, it can intervene on the basis that the decision was not the 'preferable' one.

As a general rule (subject to statutory provision to the contrary), in determining the relevant facts the AAT is not limited to evidence that was available to the decision-maker.[107] The AAT normally conducts reviews on the basis of the relevant facts as they are at the date of the review; and it has various powers to enable it to gather fresh evidence relating to factual findings made by the decision-maker as well as evidence of changes in relevant factual circumstances.[108] In this respect, the AAT can exercise even more control over fact-finding than appellate courts, which normally do not have power to admit new evidence. As a result, the AAT will typically be in a position to correct errors of fact by varying the decision under review or making a substitute decision. Rarely would it seem be appropriate for the AAT to set aside a decision for error of fact and remit it to the decision-maker for reconsideration.

In cases where an application for review is successful on the basis of evidence that was not available to the original decision-maker, it is obviously inaccurate to say that the original decision-maker made an 'error' of fact. The role of the AAT is not (only) to correct errors of fact but (also) to make decisions that accord with the relevant facts.

It is in this area of factual review that we find the greatest and most practically significant difference between merits review and legality-based review. Not only

---

[105] (1990) 170 CLR 321.

[106] It should be observed, however, that this reasoning strictly applies only in relation to decisions the AAT has jurisdiction to review, which is only a subset of decisions that, in theory, fall within the judicial review jurisdiction of federal courts.

[107] *Shi v Migration Agents Registration Authority* (2008) 248 ALR 390. The general rule was originally established in *Re Greenham and Minister for Capital Territory* (1979) 2 ALD 137.

[108] However, in practice these powers are little used. See further 6.5.1.1.

does the AAT have much wider power to review decisions about questions of fact but also, in theory at least, the 'correct or preferable' standard of review allows the AAT to exercise more control over the fact-finding process than courts can by way of judicial review. Moreover, whereas decisions of the AAT are subject to appeal to the Federal Court on questions of law, they are not subject to appeal on questions of fact.[109] The only way of challenging a decision of the AAT on a question of fact is by way of judicial review[110] or (perhaps) in collateral proceedings.[111]

Weighing Relevant Considerations

The third main substantive ground on which an administrative decision can be held illegal or invalid is *Wednesbury* unreasonableness. In the earlier discussion of this ground of review we were mainly concerned with the question of whether the decision-maker, in reaching the decision, took account of matters that ought to have been ignored or vice versa. Here we are concerned with the respective weights the decision-maker assigned to the various matters (facts, policies, statutory purposes and so on) that were rightly taken into account; or, in other words, how the various relevant considerations were balanced against one another to produce and justify the final decision. In judicial review law, a court will quash a decision only if the balance struck by the decision-maker can be described as so unreasonable that no reasonable decision-maker could have considered the decision reasonable. The AAT's task in this respect is, by contrast, to reconsider the decision and to ask whether it is the correct or preferable one. Whereas courts have often said that it is not for them to quash a decision merely because they do not consider it to be the best of the available options, it is precisely the job of the AAT to decide which of the possible outcomes is, in its view, the correct or preferable one. The fact that some other outcome could be considered reasonable or even preferable is of no moment. Here, then, we seem to find another stark contrast between legality-based review and merits review. However, in practice much may depend on how willing particular reviewers are, in particular contexts, to interfere with administrative decision-making. This may be especially true of merits review: different tribunal members may reasonably disagree in particular cases about which decision is the correct or preferable one; and, in general or in particular contexts, some tribunal members may be more or

---

[109] However, although '[t]here is no error of law in simply making a wrong finding of fact' (*Waterford v Commonwealth* (1986) 71 ALR 673, 689 (Brennan J)), an error on a factual matter may constitute an error of law. See also *Federal Commissioner of Taxation v Brixius* (1987) 14 ALD 470.

[110] But an error on a factual matter will probably provide a ground of judicial review only if it can be categorised as an error of law.

[111] This suggests that the AAT cannot decide questions of fact conclusively any more than it can decide questions of law conclusively, at least in cases where the question arises in a dispute about existing rights and obligations. See generally Zines, *The High Court and the Constitution*, 222–47. On the other hand, the constitutionality of the limitation of appeals to questions of law has been unsuccessfully challenged: *AB v Federal Commissioner of Taxation* (1998) 157 ALR 510.

less willing than others to set aside or vary administrative decisions. But even in the context of judicial review, judges may reasonably disagree about whether particular decisions are *Wednesbury*-unreasonable or not.

Nevertheless in theory, the difference between saying that a decision is extremely unreasonable and saying that it is not the preferable one is clear enough; and it prompts us to ask why a body such as the AAT should be empowered to set aside an administrative decision merely on the ground that if it had been the original decision-maker, it would have struck a different balance between the various relevant considerations?[112] This question leads to another: suppose that in a series of similar cases, the AAT repeatedly decides that too much or too little weight was given to a particular relevant consideration.[113] Should the AAT have power, in this way, effectively to create new policies about the balance to be struck between various considerations relevant to a particular type of decision? As we have already seen, the AAT has generally been wary of departing from government policy; and a certain willingness to do so in relation to immigration decision-making in the early days of the AAT was, no doubt, one reason why specialist tribunals, more closely integrated into the relevant government department, were established in this area; and why the AAT now has very little power in immigration matters. Whatever the theory, caution in questioning and departing from government policy is, no doubt, an essential survival strategy for the AAT.

5.3.3 The Procedural Element of Merits Review

Section 43 of the AAT Act provides that 'for the purpose of reviewing a decision, the Tribunal 'may exercise all the powers and discretions that are conferred by any relevant enactment on the person who made the decision':[114] as it is often put, the AAT 'stands in the shoes' of the primary decision-maker.[115] Because the AAT

---

[112] It has been argued that in choosing the best decision from amongst various possible alternatives, the good bureaucratic decision-maker applies a sort of situation sense that goes beyond the relevant hard and soft law and encompasses matters such as 'the current political scene, the affairs of his or her department or agency, and what Treasury and Finance are saying': P Bailey, 'Is Administrative Review Possible Without Legalism?' (2001) 8 *Australian Journal of Administrative Law* 163, 171. Bailey thinks that this mindset – which he associates with an 'administrative' as opposed to a 'judicial' way of thinking – should not and need not be lost in the shift from internal to external review. However, so long as external review is understood as a form of adjudication as opposed to implementation, the loss seems inevitable and right.

[113] For an example see Sharpe, *The Administrative Appeals Tribunal and Policy Review*, 76–94, 168–75.

[114] In a case where the AAT is functioning as a second-tier reviewer, it may exercise only such of the powers of the original decision-maker as the first-tier reviewer could exercise: *Walker v Secretary, Department of Social Security* (1997) 48 ALD 512.

[115] *Minister for Immigration and Ethnic Affairs v Pochi* (1980) 4 ALD 139, 143 (Smithers J). But there are exceptions to this principle. For instance, under s 58(5) of the Freedom of Information Act the task of the AAT is to decide whether there were reasonable grounds for the issue of a ministerial certificate: *McKinnon v Secretary, Department of Treasury* (2006) 228 CLR 423.

only reviews decisions made by members of the executive branch of government and of other merits review tribunals, this provision expressly confers executive power on the AAT and establishes merits review as an exclusively non-judicial function. 'All' has been interpreted to mean 'all and only'.[116] Despite this alignment between the primary decision-maker and the AAT, the AAT is not a primary decision-maker. It is a reviewer of decisions made by others. The power of the AAT (we might say) is not to make a decision of the type under review but to make a ('meta'-) decision about the decision under review, which may or may not be a (meta-) decision to make a substitute decision (or to vary the decision). In doing so, it is generally not limited to considering the material available to or the reasons given by the original decision-maker.[117] Furthermore, the AAT is not restricted to exercising the power(s) that the original decision-maker purported to exercise, but may exercise any of the powers available to the decision-maker relevant to varying or remaking the decision.[118]

Technically, the most significant function of the idea that the AAT stands in the shoes of the decision-maker (as it were) is to supply the essential underpinning for the AAT's powers to vary a decision and to make a substitute decision (see 5.3.4 for more discussion of the AAT's remedial powers). When the AAT varies a decision or makes a substitute decision, the decision as varied or the substitute decision is deemed to be a decision of the primary decision-maker. By contrast, when the AAT affirms a decision,[119] or sets it aside and remits it for reconsideration,[120] it exercises power conferred by the AAT Act, not any power of the original decision-maker. In such cases, the AAT performs a function similar in nature to that performed by a court exercising judicial review jurisdiction: the characteristic judicial review remedy is (in the terms of the AAT Act) setting aside and remittal to the primary decision-maker.

Despite a beguiling appearance of simplicity, the idea that the AAT stands in the shoes of the decision-maker is complex and problematic. On the one hand, for instance, like primary executive decision-makers, the AAT cannot decide questions of law conclusively. On the other hand, it has been held, for instance, that the AAT must interpret relevant legislative provisions for itself and must not merely accept an interpretation contained in a statement by an agency made for

---

[116] See eg, *Re Callaghan and Defence Force Retirement Authority* (1978) 1 ALD 227.

[117] *Shi v Migration Agents Registration Authority* (2008) 248 ALR 390. Whether the AAT is limited to material available at the time the original decision was made or may take account of subsequent developments is a question of statutory interpretation, both of the AAT Act (which is silent on the matter) and the legislation under which the original decision was made. The legislation under which the original decision was made may also limit the grounds on which the decision can be reviewed: eg, *Re Radge and Commissioner of Taxation* [2007] 95 ALD 711.

[118] Pearce, *Administrative Appeals Tribunal*, 176–77.

[119] *Powell v Department of Immigration and Multicultural Affairs* (1998) 53 ALD 228.

[120] *Re Brian Lawlor Automotive Pty Ltd and Collector of Customs (NSW)* (1978) 1 ALD 167, 175.

the guidance of its decision-making officials.[121] We have also noted that the AAT may take account of changes in the law since the date of the decision under review.

Another obvious area of difficulty is review of policy by the AAT. The AAT has jurisdiction to review decisions made by various categories of decision-makers: Ministers, officials exercising 'independent' discretion, officials making decisions as delegates of a Minister and first-tier tribunals. Policy plays a different role in decision-making by each of these categories of decision-maker. It seems clear that administrative decision-makers who act as delegates of a government Minister are under a prima facie obligation (perhaps based on the constitutional principle of ministerial responsibility)[122] to 'apply' government policy (in the sense of 'apply' adopted by Brennan J in *Drake No 2).*[123] A decision-maker who exercises an 'independent discretion' may have more freedom to disregard policy.[124] The logic of the principle of individual ministerial responsibility is that a Minister who makes a reviewable decision is free to apply, modify or abandon existing policy subject to the doctrine of legitimate expectation.[125] First-tier merits review tribunals are, in theory, in the same position as the AAT as regards government policy. It might seem to follow that the role of the AAT in relation to policy would vary significantly according to the status of the official or body that made the decision under review. However, the existing merits-review jurisprudence does not support a clear differentiation between categories of decision-maker in relation to policy review. Indeed, in one respect, at least, the case law seems to point in a different direction. We saw earlier that in principle, at least, the AAT takes a more deferential approach to policy developed at a 'high political' level than to policy developed at lower levels of government. There is clearly a tension between this well-established principle and the idea that the AAT should approach policy in the same way as the primary decision-maker. Also, there is at

---

[121] *Port of Brisbane Corp v. Deputy Commissioner of Taxation* (2004) 81 ALD 549. But even here, restraint may be appropriate: *Re Petry and Secretary, Department of Families, Community Services and Indigenous Affairs* (2006) 92 ALD 779, [33]–[39].

[122] Which is reflected in s 64 of the Australian Constitution. See also Public Service Act 1999 s 10(1)(f): 'The APS Values are as follows ... the APS is responsive to the Government ... in implementing the Government's policies and programs'; and s11(1)(a): the Public Service 'Commissioner must issue directions ... for the purpose of ensuring that the APS incorporates and upholds the APS Values'.

[123] See n 51 above.

[124] See *R v Anderson, ex p Ipec-Air Pty Ltd* (1965) 113 CLR 177; *Ansett Transport Industries (Operations) Pty Ltd* (1977) 139 CLR 54; P O'Connor, 'Knowing When to Say "Yes Minister": Ministerial Control of Discretions Vested in Officials' (1998) 5 *Australian J of Administrative Law* 168.

[125] J M Sharpe, 'Acting Under Dictation and the Administrative Appeals Tribunals Policy-Review Powers – How Tight is the Fit?' (1985) 15 *Federal LR* 109. However, the principle of collective ministerial responsibility may require a Minister to apply policies formulated by Cabinet, especially if they have been considered and approved by Parliament. See also J Goldring, 'Responsible Government and the Administrative Appeals Tribunal' (1982–83) 13 *Federal Law Review* 90. Regarding the doctrine of legitimate expectation see Cane and McDonald, *Principles of Administrative Law*, 130–32, 139–41.

least an element of circularity in the idea that the AAT, when hearing appeals from first-tier merits review tribunals, should adopt the same attitude to policy as the First-tier tribunal.

Yet another area where the shoe pinches, as it were, is review of findings of fact. As we have noted, in reviewing a decision the AAT is not limited to considering the material that was available to or the reasons given by the primary decision-maker: merits review provides the applicant with an opportunity to present new evidence and arguments for a decision in their favour not considered by the primary decision maker. The AAT is typically able (and expected) to spend more time investigating the facts of the case than the primary decision-maker.[126] More fundamentally, because reviewing decisions is a mode of adjudication, the AAT's function is to focus on the individual and the individual's circumstances and interests to a greater extent than officials responsible for implementing rules. We might go further and say that constructing a convincing rationale for external merits review depends on identifying a distinctive contribution that the reviewer can make to the decision-making process and the primary decision-maker cannot. Applying the shoe metaphor too literally could deprive the reviewer of the capacity to make such a contribution.

On the other hand, what we might call 'the argument from inconsistency', which was central to the judgment of Brennan J in *Drake (No 2)*,[127] pulls in the opposite direction. According to that argument, because only a very small proportion of decisions that theoretically fall within its jurisdiction are ever reviewed by the AAT, it is desirable, in the interests of consistency, that the AAT should not adopt different decision-making criteria from those applied by the primary decision-maker. Taken to its logical conclusion, this argument would limit the AAT to correcting 'errors' in a very narrow sense and would call into question the value of or need for an external independent review mechanism as formal and elaborate as the AAT. In practice, consistency across cases must be balanced against 'justice' in the individual case.

We might conclude that although the alignment of the powers of the primary decision-maker and the AAT encapsulated in the shoe metaphor plays an important technical function in underpinning the remedial powers of the AAT and distinguishing administrative adjudication by the AAT from administrative adjudication by courts, it gives little independent guidance about when and how the AAT should exercise its various remedial powers. This is because although the AAT is technically not a court, its function is to provide an independent, external check on executive decision-making. In the words of the ARC,

---

[126] However, there may be cases in which the original decision-maker has investigatory powers that the AAT lacks. In such a case, if the AAT decides to set aside a decision, it may be appropriate for it to remit the matter to the original decision-maker rather than make a substitute decision: *Shi v Migration Agents Registration Authority* (2008) 248 ALR 390, [68] (Kirby J).

[127] See text around n 49 above.

[i]t is true that review tribunals exercise the same statutory powers and discretions as the original decision maker. However, they will often be asked to consider new or more detailed information. Tribunals also operate according to different time and resource pressures, and may use different decision-making processes. Review tribunals also bring to their task a different perspective than that of the original decision maker.[128]

The shoe metaphor may be apt to describe the function of an internal reviewer whose job is to do again what the primary decision-maker has already done; but when applied to external review it may cause 'misunderstanding ... between decision-makers ... and reviewers'[129] based on lack of appreciation of the significant differences between the respective roles of the former and the latter. It may also lead to exaggeration of the differences between the criteria applied respectively by courts and tribunals in reviewing executive decision-making.

5.3.4 The Remedial Element of Merits Review

Section 43 of the AAT Act provides that,

> for the purpose of reviewing a decision, the Tribunal ... shall make a decision in writing (a) affirming the decision under review; (b) varying the decision under review; or (c) setting aside the decision under review and (i) making a decision in substitution for the decision so set aside; or (ii) remitting the matter for reconsideration in accordance with any directions or recommendations of the Tribunal.

When the AAT varies a decision or makes a substitute decision, the AAT's decision is deemed to be a decision of the original decision-maker as from the date of coming into effect of the original decision (unless the AAT otherwise orders). Of these powers, those to vary a decision or make a substitute decision characterise merits review and distinguish it from the other principal mode of administrative adjudication, namely judicial review. Expressed in the terminology of the AAT Act, the characteristic judicial review remedy is setting aside accompanied by remittal for reconsideration. The powers to vary decisions and to make substitute decisions, as such, are not non-judicial powers. A court hearing an appeal from an inferior court will normally have these powers. However, the AAT's power to vary a decision of the executive or to make a decision in substitution for such a decision is a non-judicial power because, in theory, it involves the exercise of executive power. By contrast, when an appellate

---

[128] *Better Decisions: Review of Commonwealth Merits Review Tribunals*, ARC Report No 39 (Canberra, Australian Government Publishing Service, 1995) para 2.55.

[129] S Hamilton, 'The Future of Public Administration: The Future of Administrative Law' in R Creyke and J McMillan (eds), *The Kerr Vision of Australian Administrative Law – At the Twenty-Five Year Mark* (Canberra, Centre for International and Public Law, 1998) 118.

court varies the decision of an inferior court or makes a decision in substitution for such a decision it exercises judicial power.[130]

In principle, it would seem appropriate for the AAT to remit a decision for reconsideration only in cases where it concludes that the original decision-maker (guided by the AAT's directions or recommendations) is in a better position than the AAT to make the correct or preferable decision. As we noted earlier in the discussion of review of findings of fact, because of its extensive powers to investigate facts and admit new evidence, it would rarely seem appropriate for the AAT to set a decision aside for error of fact and remit it to the decision-maker. If the decision-maker fails to consider relevant issues, the AAT should normally deal with those issues itself rather than remit the matter so that the decision-maker can do so.[131] By contrast, if the Federal Court, on an appeal under section 44 of the AAT Act, sets aside a decision of the AAT for error of law related to fact-finding, the proper course is normally for it to remit the matter to the AAT for reconsideration.[132] This is partly because fresh evidence is rarely admissible in an appeal under section 44.[133] It should be noted, however, that since these principles were established, the Federal Court has been given limited power make findings of fact.[134]

In practice, the power to remit is only exceptionally exercised by the AAT – in 2004–5 in less than one per cent of cases in which the review was finalised by a decision of the AAT.[135] The AAT rarely explains its decision whether or not to remit. In one case, the AAT was reviewing an order banning a securities dealer from engaging in business. The AAT reduced the period of the ban and required the dealer to give a written undertaking to Commission. The matter was remitted to the Commission on the basis that only the Commission had authority to receive the undertaking.[136] By contrast, in another case involving review of a decision to revoke a licence, the AAT said that because setting aside the decision automatically reinstated the licence, remittal was inappropriate because no action by the decision-maker was needed to implement the AAT's decision.[137] In yet another case, the AAT apparently held that the application of a policy caused

---

[130] In retrospect, it is a striking feature of the Kerr Committee Report that in explaining why merits review was a non-judicial function that could not be conferred on a court, the Committee focused unconvincingly on its substantive aspect (merits review involves the consideration of non-justiciable issues) rather than on its procedural element (in reviewing decisions the AAT exercises the powers of the primary executive decision-maker or of a first-tier merits review tribunal which, in turn, exercises powers of the primary decision-maker) and its remedial element (the power to vary decisions of the executive and to make decisions in substitution for such decisions involves the exercise of executive power).

[131] *Re Queensland Mines Ltd and Export Development Grants Board* (1985) 7 ALD 357.

[132] *Harris v Director General of Social Security* (1985) 7 ALD 277, 284.

[133] *Committee of Direction of Fruit Marketing v Delegate of Australian Postal Commission* (1979) 2 ALD 561.

[134] AAT Act s 44(7).

[135] *AAT Annual Report 2004–05*, 134, Table 3.5 (more recent reports do not contain this statistic).

[136] See also *Australian Securities and Investments Commission v Donald* (2003) 77 ALD 449.

[137] *Re Marnotta Pty Ltd and Secretary, Department of Health and Ageing* (2004) 82 ALD 514.

injustice in the circumstances before it, but also that the policy was flawed. The AAT considered that it lacked the necessary expertise and knowledge to frame an appropriate policy and remitted the case to the decision-maker.[138]

In addition to this remedial power of remittal, section 42D of the AAT Act empowers the AAT to remit a decision for reconsideration 'at any stage of a proceeding for review of a decision'. On reconsideration, the decision-maker has power to affirm or vary the decision, or to set it aside and make a substitute decision. If the applicant is dissatisfied with the reconsidered decision, the application for review is treated as an application for review of the reconsidered decision which the applicant may proceed with or withdraw. As in the remedial context, this interlocutory power of remittal is exercised only exceptionally – for instance, if the decision-maker effectively failed to consider the matter to be decided.[139]

Because federal merits review tribunals are not courts, they cannot be given power to enforce their decisions,[140] this being a judicial function.[141] Moreover, the AAT Act establishes no mechanism for the enforcement of decisions of the AAT. Some decisions of merits review tribunals may be 'self-executing' – for example, a decision affirming the decision under review. If the decision is not self-executing, and the decision-maker fails to comply with the tribunal's order (for instance, to reconsider the decision), proceedings of some sort before a court would be necessary to secure enforcement of the decision.[142] Similarly, if the effect of the Tribunal's decision is (for instance) that the applicant owes a debt to the government (perhaps as a result of receiving pension payments to which they were not entitled), the decision-maker would need to bring proceedings in a court of law to recover the debt if the applicant refused to pay. It is clear that in such proceedings, it must be open to the enforcing court to 'review' the decision;[143] but it is unclear what such a review must entail. For instance, would it be necessary for the reviewer to have the same powers to review the AAT's findings

---

[138] *Re Fischer and Australian Fisheries Management Authority* (2002) 71 ALD 665.

[139] Pearce, *Administrative Appeals Tribunal*, 174–75.

[140] Or to 'issue process requiring execution': *Re Ward and Department of Industry and Commerce* (1983) 8 ALD 324. In theory, it is possible for the AAT to be given the power only to make recommendations to the decision-maker as opposed to the power to vary the decision or make a substitute decision. In one sense, therefore, despite being unenforceable, except in cases where the AAT's power is purely recommendatory, its decisions are 'binding'. See generally Pearce, *Administrative Appeals Tribunal*, 208–09.

[141] At least if the decision concerns existing rights and obligations: *Brandy v Human Rights and Equal Opportunity Commission* (1995) 183 CLR 245; Zines, *The High Court and the Constitution*, 247. See generally E Campbell and M Groves, 'Enforcement of Administrative Determinations' (2006) 13 *Australian Journal of Administrative Law* 121. The same principle applies to State tribunals when dealing with issues of federal law: *A-G v 2UE Sydney Pty Ltd* (2007) 97 ALD 426.

[142] Where the AAT makes a substitute decision, that decision will become the decision of the decision-maker. This does not, of course, guarantee that the decision-maker will implement it, but it does presumably make it more likely than if (as in the case of judicial review) the tribunal's only power were to order the decision-maker (not) to act.

[143] *Brandy*, n 141 above.

of fact as the AAT has to review findings of fact by the primary decision-maker? Note that it is not enough that there be the possibility of review – the decision must actually be reviewed before being enforced.[144]

5.4 Merits Review and Judicial Review

Merits review and judicial review are two modes of administrative adjudication. As we have noted, there are some fundamental and obvious differences between them. For instance, the characteristic judicial review remedy is to 'quash' the decision – set it aside, in the language of the AAT Act – and effectively (when appropriate) remit it for reconsideration, while the characteristic merits review remedy is to vary the decision or to set it aside and make a substitute decision. In dispensing the characteristic merits review remedy, the AAT exercises by proxy the powers available to the primary decision-maker, whereas in dispensing the characteristic judicial review remedy courts exercise inherent judicial power. Again, judicial review is typically based on the material available to and the reasons for decision given by the primary decision-maker, and on the law as it stood at the time the original decision was made.[145] By contrast, merits review can take account of material available at the time of review even if it was not available at the time the decision was made and of changes in the law since that time; and the merits reviewer's consideration of the decision is not limited to the powers exercised or the reasons given by the primary decisions maker. The job of the merits reviewer is to ensure that the correct or preferable decision is made, whether by affirming or varying the decision, or by setting it aside and remitting it to the decision-maker or making a substitute decision.[146] In the respects that I have dubbed 'procedural' and 'remedial', merits review and judicial review are categorically different modes of administrative adjudication.

In what I have dubbed the 'substantive' respect, however, the relationship between the two modes is rather more complex. In an important sense, there are no 'grounds' of merits review equivalent to the 'grounds' of judicial review. The task of the judicial reviewer is the negative one of determining whether the decision under review is defective in some sense – or, in other words, of policing limits on decision-making power. Because the function of the judicial reviewer is a negative one, the grounds of judicial review are expressed negatively – illegality,

---

[144] ibid. For a different interpretation of *Brandy* from that presented in the text see M Allars, 'Theory and Administrative Law: Law as Form and Theory as Substance' (1996) 7 *Canberra Bulletin of Public Administration* 20, 20–24.

[145] *Kavvadias v The Commonwealth Ombudsman (No 2)* (1984) 6 ALD 198, 206.

[146] Once an application for review has been made to the AAT, the primary decision-maker is *functus officio* so that the matter cannot be settled by an agreement between the primary decision-maker and the applicant that the decision-maker will make a substitute decision. A fresh decision can be made only by the AAT or with its formal approval (under s 42C of the AAT Act): *Re The International Fund for Animal Welfare (Aust) Pty Ltd and Minister for Environment and Heritage (No 2)* (2007) 93 ALD 625, [10].

procedural unfairness, unreasonableness and so on – even though they imply positive criteria of good decision-making which judicial review can be thought of as promoting – legality, procedural fairness, reasonableness and so on. By contrast, the task of the merits reviewer is the positive one of bringing it about that the correct or preferable decision is made, not to decide whether there are grounds for setting the decision aside.[147]

However, it is an implicit, necessary precondition of the exercise of the remedial powers of the AAT that it decide whether or not the decision under review is the correct or preferable one. It cannot avoid this (negative) step in the review process because its power to affirm the decision can be exercised only if it is the correct or preferable one, and its other powers can be exercised only if the decision is not the correct or preferable one. In other words, the merits reviewer has the dual task of negatively deciding whether the decision under review is the correct or preferable one and, if it is not, of positively bringing it about that the correct or preferable decision is made. Unsurprisingly, the criteria of good decision making that – in their negative form – are used to determine whether the AAT should affirm the decision on the one hand, or vary it or set it aside on the other, are the very same criteria that inform the AAT's own process of making the correct and preferable decision (if it decides to vary the decision or make a substitute decision) and which should guide the primary decision-maker's reconsideration of the decision (if the AAT decides to remit the decision).

Because the AAT – while not technically a court – is a 'court-substitute', cast in a judicial mould, the criteria of good decision-making which perform this dual function in merits review are essentially similar to those implied by the negatively framed grounds of judicial review – legality, procedural fairness, reasonableness and so on. So, for instance, the concept of 'maladministration' encapsulates in negative form certain criteria of good administration promoted by ombudsmen – such as timeliness and politeness – which neither courts nor merits review tribunals purport to promote. Both judicial review and merits review focus on decisions and decision-making and promote similar bureaucratic values associated with good decision-making.

Nevertheless, the distinction between the 'merits' of a decision and its 'legality' is said to be central to the concepts of merits review and judicial review. Whereas judicial review is said to be limited to issues of legality, merits review (by definition) 'goes to the merits'. Because the same foundational criteria of good decision-making are promoted by judicial review and merits review alike, the distinction between legality and merits can be, at most, one of degree, not one of kind. Indeed, we have seen that the AAT has the same power as a court to set aside a decision on the ground of illegality and in all contexts – judicial review,

---

[147] But where there is only one decision that could have been correctly made and the decision-maker has committed no procedural or reasoning-process error, in substantive terms the task of the merits reviewer and the judicial reviewer will be essentially the same: *Re Radge and Commissioner of Taxation* (2007) 95 ALD 711, [21].

merits review and appeals – the accepted approach is that questions of law have one correct answer. When the AAT decides that a particular decision is illegal it can, like a court, remit the decision for reconsideration or, unlike a court, vary the decision or make a substitute decision. We have also seen that although, in theory, the AAT apparently has the power to vary or set aside decisions on the ground that they are based on unacceptable policy – ie, to question the merits of government policy as opposed to its application in individual cases – in practice it is no more willing to do this than courts. Like courts, the AAT understands its role in relation to soft law to extend little further than ensuring that its application does not cause injustice in individual cases.

In practice, it seems that it is only in the area of supervising fact-finding by primary decision-makers that merits review intrudes to any significantly greater extent than judicial review into the bureaucratic process. In the Australian context, at least, one (albeit conclusory) way of putting this is to say that a fact-related error will provide grounds for judicial review only if it is serious enough to be classified as an 'error of law' whereas a merits reviewer may be justified in varying a decision or making a substitute decision on the basis of an error of fact that is not serious enough to be so classified.

Ironically, it is in this area, perhaps, that the Kerr Committee's argument that merits review is a non-judicial function has least purchase. The difference between the approach of the AAT to questions of fact and the much less intrusive approach of courts exercising judicial review jurisdiction is not best explained by saying that extensive and intensive review of questions of fact involves the consideration of non-justiciable issues. Courts are just as unwilling to review fact-finding by inferior courts as by administrators. This is not because questions of fact raise non-justiciable issues but because only certain aspects of the trial process are replicated at the review or appellate level (unless the review or appeal is in effect a *de novo* re-hearing) and because of the need to ration scarce judicial resources. Concerning the first of these reasons, judicial review and appellate courts are typically less well-equipped than primary fact-finders to resolve disputed issues of fact because judicial review and appeals are typically con-ducted on the basis of a factual record generated at the primary decision-making level rather than on a fresh examination of the issues. By contrast, the AAT in particular and merits review tribunals generally are normally considered to be better equipped than primary fact-finders in terms of powers, time and resources to resolve disputed questions of fact.

Concerning review of fact-finding by organs and officials of the executive branch of government, judicial restraint can also be based on some concept of separation of powers. The argument might go something like this: even if it is appropriate for superior courts intrusively to review fact-finding by inferior courts, it is not appropriate for courts to review fact-finding by the executive in an equally intrusive way. Although the concept of non-justiciability may also be understood as grounded in ideas of separation of powers, its reference to the nature of the issues at stake in review of fact-finding makes it less salient in this context than an argument such as this about constitutional and institutional division of labour.

Viewed in this way, the prime function of merits review can be understood as being to provide a forum for the further and better investigation of the circumstances of the individual(s) affected by the decisions being reviewed. This understanding is consistent with the main thrust of the AAT's approach to policy, namely that it is rarely appropriate for a merits reviewer to go beyond scrutinising the application of policy to the particular case with a view to avoiding injustice in that case. Furthermore, it supports the argument that whether making provision for external merits review of a decision is appropriate depends on whether it is desirable to inject into the decision-making process the enhanced consideration of individual circumstances that external merits review affords (see further 6.3).

In 2000 I propounded the heretical thesis that the substantive distinction between merits review and judicial review – in other words, the distinction between legality and merits – was considerably less significant than commonly assumed.[148] The foregoing analysis supports that thesis. I also argued more speculatively that if the AAT had not been established, the law of judicial review would have developed to cover the ground now covered by merits review. There are several ways of supporting this conclusion. One is to observe that in *Australian Broadcasting Tribunal v Bond*[149] Mason CJ cited the existence and powers of the AAT as a reason why courts could and should take a relatively restrained approach to reviewing fact-finding by executive agencies and officials. Another is to observe that in England, where the distinction between merits review and judicial review has not been clearly articulated and where that between courts and tribunals lacks the constitutional significance it has in Australia, the law of judicial review has developed in the direction of more intrusive review of fact-finding – a development that has been rejected by Australian courts.[150] Nevertheless, it is unlikely, even in England, that judicial review of executive fact-finding – or, indeed, fact-related judicial appeals from decisions of the executive – will ever be as extensive and intrusive as merits review understood in the Australian sense, which allows for *de novo* rehearing of any and every relevant question of fact against the 'correct or preferable' standard.

---

[148] 'Merits Review and Judicial Review: The AAT as Trojan Horse' (2000) 28 *Federal Law Review* 213.

[149] (1990) 170 CLR 321, 341.

[150] Cane and McDonald, *Principles of Administrative Law*, 155–56, 173 n 285. To Australian eyes, other developments in the English law of judicial review – such as the doctrines of proportionality (ibid 184–85) and substantive legitimate expectations (ibid 141) – also involve intrusion on the merits. The former is a response to EC and European administrative law and to the European Convention on Human Rights.

A lynchpin of the Kerr Committee Report was the proposition that the existing law of judicial review did not provide citizens with adequate opportunities to challenge decisions 'on the merits'. As the law of merits review has developed, the term 'the merits' in this argument has come to be understood as referring primarily to the fact-finding aspect of decision-making. The Kerr Committee erroneously thought that intrusive review of fact-finding would involve consideration of non-justiciable issues; and, for that reason, it concluded that the merits review jurisdiction had to be conferred on a tribunal, not a court. By contrast, it gave relatively little thought to the question of whether the proposed Tribunal would be a suitable body to conduct intrusive review of fact-finding in the nature of a *de novo* appeal. Certainly, the AAT has been given adequate powers to conduct *de novo* appeals; and because full-time members of the AAT are predominantly judges and other legally qualified persons, it does not lack expertise in legal techniques of fact-finding. However, the Committee also cast the proposed tribunal in an essentially judicial mould, external to and independent of the executive; and that orientation was greatly reinforced by the decisions and influence of the first President of the AAT, Sir Gerard Brennan. If the AAT is understood as a court-substitute, it might be thought to fall foul of the argument (considered earlier) for restraint in reviewing fact-finding based on separation of powers and institutional division of labour. From this perspective, some model of embedded review of fact-finding, exemplified, perhaps, by the MRT and RRT[151] in Australia, might be thought constitutionally more appropriate.

---

[151] These two tribunals review visa and visa-related decisions. Although the MRT and the RRT are intended to provide 'independent' review, they are not external to the Department of Immigration and Citizenship in the way that the AAT operates externally to the various departments and organizations whose decisions it reviews. Members of the tribunals are treated as public servants. The relationship between the tribunals and the Department of Immigration and Citizenship is regulated by a Memorandum of Understanding, which provides, for instance, that the Principal Member of the Tribunals must report three times a year to the Minister. The Department provides the Tribunals with the Statement of Expectations, and the Tribunals reply with a Statement of Intent. In 2007 the Tribunals were the subject of a report by the Auditor-General (Parliament Audit Report No 44 of 2006–07: *Management of Tribunal Operations – Migration Review Tribunal and Refugee Review Tribunal*). The language of the Tribunals' Annual Report is business-like. For instance, 'To be successful the Tribunals must be resilient yet flexible and prepared to adapt our work practices to meet ongoing challenges in our decision-making environment. We have developed an efficient and effective Membership and staff workforce and organisational structure' (*2006–07 Annual Report*, 102). The primary decision-maker is not a party to proceedings before the Tribunals, which play a much more active role in fact-finding than the AAT. The Tribunals have a Research and Information Section which provides Members with relevant 'country and general information', and Members have access to governmental sources of country information. There is no appeal from the Tribunals to the AAT and there are statutory restrictions on judicial review of their decisions. Compared with the AAT, the MRT and RRT are much closer to being a form of internal review. 'The immigration tribunals provide very telling examples of review systems kept on a tight rein by their Ministers and pressured to serve the interests of government': K Cronin, 'Dispute Resolution in Administrative Law' in J McMillan (ed) *Administrative Law under the Coalition Government* (Canberra, Australian Institute of Administrative Law, 1997) 78.

More radically, we might question whether it is an appropriate use of resources to provide for extensive, external, *de novo* review of executive fact-finding. Fact-finding by inferior judicial officers is rarely subject to such scrutiny whether they are legally trained or not. Australian courts have given a great deal of attention to the appropriate scope of judicial review of executive fact-finding. Much less attention has been given to the appropriate scope of non-judicial, external review of executive fact-finding.

In the Australian system, merits review tribunals are second-class administrative adjudicators compared with courts exercising judicial review jurisdiction. There are various marks of such inferiority. As we have seen, merits review tribunals cannot decide questions of law conclusively. Only courts can do that. There is also uncertainty about whether they can decide questions of fact conclusively. As we have also seen, the AAT cannot enforce its decisions or make enforceable decisions; and its decisions cannot be enforced unless they are actually reviewed by a court. It is questionable whether the respects in which the AAT differs from a Chapter III court are sufficient to justify such technical limitations on its powers and distrust of its decisions. While the unenforceability of decisions of the AAT is of no great practical significance,[152] perhaps the centrality of the AAT (and of merits review tribunals more generally) in the federal administrative justice system justifies a reassessment of the relationship between courts and tribunals and between merits review and judicial review.

Whatever we can say about the 1970s when the merits review system was being established, it no longer seems satisfactory or even realistic to think of merits review as accessory to judicial review and of tribunals as inferior to courts. By reason of its breadth and depth, it can be argued that merits review is a more significant mechanism than judicial review for holding government accountable. In this light, it seems odd that the job of merits review should (and constitutionally must) be entrusted to bodies – tribunals – that have lower legal (and social) status than the courts that conduct judicial review. In theory, the inferiority of merits review tribunals is based on constitutional separation of powers. In practice, however perhaps the most significant ground of the relationship of inferiority and superiority between federal tribunals and courts is that the (non-constitutional) qualifications for appointment as a judge focus on legal expertise.[153] At the same time, however, even courts recognise that legal expertise

---

[152] Because (1) most applications are resolved without a formal hearing, (2) some of its decisions may be self-executing, and (3) the government can normally be expected to comply with AAT decisions.

[153] The subordination of tribunals to courts underpins the decision in *Craig v South Australia* (1995) 184 CLR 163, where the High Court distinguished between 'inferior courts ... constituted by persons with either formal legal qualifications or practical legal training' and 'tribunals . . . constituted, wholly or partly, by persons without legal qualifications or legal training' (176–77). For a particularly disparaging comment on the capacities of tribunal members who lack legal training see *NAIS v Minister for Immigration and Multicultural and Indigenous Affairs* (2005) 228 CLR 470, [91]–[92] (Kirby J). The tribunal in question in this case was the RRT. Ironically, about two-thirds of the members of the RRT listed in its 2004–05 Annual Report were trained, or practised, as lawyers, or

is not the only, or perhaps even the most useful, qualification for those whose job is holding government formally to account.

In this light, systemic subordination of tribunals to courts looks rather like a restrictive trade practice on the part of lawyers! The 20th century witnessed exponential growth in the 'sub-judicial' sector of the administrative-justice system. Perhaps it is time seriously and comprehensively to think through the implications of this development for the structure of that system and the relationship between its various parts. This issue will be addressed in Chapter 7.

5.5 The 'Normative Function' of Merits Review and the AAT

The AAT was the most radically innovative element of the set of institutional arrangements envisaged by the Kerr Committee. The other main elements of the vision were statutory restatement of the law of judicial review, establishment of a new federal court to exercise judicial review jurisdiction, and creation of the office of Commonwealth Ombudsman. The Committee's vision focused on strengthening the accountability of the executive branch of government. Yet from the start, debate about the AAT was as much about improving the quality of administrative decision-making as about accountability and the resolution of disputes. The AAT, it was said, should be understood as having a 'normative', forward-looking function, of promoting good decision-making in general, in addition to its backward-looking function of ensuring that the correct or preferable decision was made in individual cases.

Judicial review was not commonly understood in this way.[154] Two explanations of this difference suggest themselves. First, merits review is concerned with all aspects of the decision under review whereas judicial review is limited to its 'legality'. Secondly, whereas judicial review is negatively oriented towards identification by the court of bad decision-making, the prime, positive function of the AAT (and of other merits review tribunals) is to ensure that the 'correct or preferable' decision is made. In so doing, perhaps, the AAT was expected to lead by example.

This expectation may have been based on the idea that the AAT would stand in the shoes of the decision-maker – that the AAT would perform essentially the

---

both. For some Australian evidence against the traditional assumption of the need for legal expertise to produce high-quality adjudicative decision-making see F Meredith, '"How Would You Know You're Not a Lawyer: Decision Making in a Merit Review Tribunal' (2001) 10 *Journal of Judicial Administration* 149. See more generally 4.1.

[154] For an exception see GDS Taylor, 'May Judicial Review Become a Backwater?' in M Taggart (ed), *Judicial Review of Administrative Action in the 1980s: Problems and Prospects* (Auckland, OUP, 1986) 153, 153–54.

same function as the primary decision-maker, only better. However, we have seen that the role of the AAT differs in various significant ways from that of primary decision-makers. For one thing, the AAT is a reviewer, not a maker of decisions. It does not implement rules but rather adjudicates disputes arising out of the implementation of rules. When it affirms a decision or sets it aside and remits it for reconsideration, it does not stand in the shoes of the decision-maker but exercises powers analogous to those exercised by judicial-review courts. Like a judicial review court, the AAT can set a decision aside for illegality. In theory, at least, the AAT has greater power to modify or reject government policy than most executive decision-makers. Most importantly, perhaps, the main justification for the extensive and intensive review of bureaucratic fact-finding in which the AAT may engage must be that the AAT has resources, expertise and powers that primary decision-makers typically do not have. To the extent that the AAT performs functions different from those performed by decision-makers whose decisions it can review, and to the extent that it has different resources, expertise and powers than such primary decision-makers have, the case for expecting the AAT to be able to improve the quality of primary decision-making is weakened.[155] It is only to the extent that the AAT can show primary decision-makers how to do *their* job better with the resources at *their* disposal that we can reasonably expect it to have a significant normative impact. As the ARC has pointed out, because of various differences between primary decision-making and external merits review, it does not follow from the fact that a tribunal varies a primary decision or sets it aside that the decision was 'wrong' or 'unreasonable'. The primary decision-maker may have done the best job possible given the various constraints under which they were operating.[156]

The normative function is most commonly associated with the AAT in particular and less often with federal merits review tribunals in general, even though all such tribunals, in theory at least, perform an essentially similar function. There may be several explanations for this. One is that the main first-tier tribunals were not part of the Kerr Committee's vision and were brought into existence some time after the AAT was established. Another is that the AAT is the only second-tier external merits review tribunal. Thirdly, the AAT operates more like a court than any of the other federal merits review tribunals. Fourthly, decisions of the AAT resemble court judgments, and like court judgments, the most significant are reported. The law of merits review is largely to be found in

---

[155] In the literature on the normative function (see n 174 below) the contrary argument is much more common, namely that it is because the AAT has resources, expertise and powers that primary decision-makers lack that it can raise standards of decision-making. The underlying paradox is that although the AAT needs additional resources, expertise and powers to enable it to make better decisions than primary decision-makers can, the fact that they are needed is precisely the reason why primary decision-makers are unlikely to be able to emulate the AAT.

[156] *Better Decisions*, paras 2.62–2.63. Another persistent theme of the literature on the normative function is (put crudely) that primary decision-makers resent being told how to do their job by a much better resourced external reviewer.

the reported decisions of the AAT and, to a lesser extent, of the Federal Court. It is sometimes said[157] that the normative role of the AAT is severely compromised by the fact that the great majority of applications for review are resolved without a hearing and by the push for increased use of ADR techniques in tribunals. A possible response is that cases that can be resolved in this way are unlikely to have had much normative potential anyway. But this is an empirical issue about which we have no evidence. We might speculate, to the contrary, that agencies would be most likely to settle those cases with greatest normative potential in order to avoid the creation of an inconvenient precedent.

The normative function of merits review played a central role in the reasoning of the ARC in its 1995 *Better Decisions* Report. The ARC described the 'overall objective of the merits review system' as being 'to ensure that all administrative decisions are correct and preferable.'[158] The main way this objective is achieved is by review of individual decisions. However,

> some tribunal review decisions raise issues that have a broader significance and a potential long-term impact on Government administration. Advantage can be taken of the reasons for these decisions to improve the quality of future agency decision-making so as to benefit all Australians.[159]

In the opinion of the ARC, 'the merits review system had not been as successful as it could be in improving the quality and consistency of government decision making';[160] and the aim of enhancing its normative effect underpinned the ARC's major recommendation for structural change, namely the creation of a new two-tier general Administrative Review Tribunal (ART) into which the AAT and the existing first-tier specialist tribunals would be amalgamated. The ARC envisaged the second tier performing two functions. Its secondary function would be to review individual decisions of the first tier that involved 'manifest errors'. Its primary function would be to give particular attention to 'cases having normative effect – that is, cases involving 'an important issue or principle of general significance'.[161] The ARC recommended that access to second-tier review should be specifically limited to cases falling into either one of these two categories; but also – in order to maximise the chance that appropriate cases would reach the second tier – that cases which could be identified in advance as potentially having normative significance could be allocated initially to the second tier without first being considered by the first tier, or could be referred to the second tier by the first tier at any stage of the proceedings.[162]

---

[157] G Fleming, 'Administrative Review and the "Normative" Goal: Is Anybody Out There?' (2000) 28 *Federal Law Review* 61, 82–83.

[158] *Better Decisions*, viii,. Concerning the difference between 'correct *and* preferable' and 'correct *or* preferable' see *Better Decisions*, 16 n 31.

[159] *Better Decisions*, x, paras 2.4–2.11.

[160] *Better Decisions*, para 8.78; see also para 2.26.

[161] *Better Decisions*, paras 8.42–8.53.

[162] *Better Decisions*, paras 8.54–8.63.

The ARC's approach to the role of the second tier of the proposed ART neatly illustrates the tension between the concept of merits review and the attribution of a normative function to merits review tribunals. The ARC's proposed strategy for enhancing the normative effect was to establish a single, but two-tier, merits review tribunal and to allocate a different primary function to each of the tiers respectively. The prime task of the first tier would be the core merits review function of ensuring that correct or preferable decisions were made. By contrast, the prime function of the second tier would more closely approximate judicial review – ie, identification and correction of 'manifest errors' in decisions of the first tier, and the laying down of norms on matters of general significance. The ARC seems to have been subliminally aware of the tension: it felt it necessary to spell out explicitly that although, under its proposals, cases could go to the second tier only 'on specific grounds', the function of the second tier would be 'to conduct merits review of the entire decision: that is, to determine what is the correct and preferable decision'.[163]

If the ARC was right to conclude that the merits review system had not been very successful in improving the quality of primary decision-making,[164] this situation may be a product of the fact that the main task of a merits reviewer is not to instruct primary decision-makers about how to make correct and preferable decisions but rather to make such decisions and (as said earlier) in that way to lead by example. We may speculate that primary decision-makers are more likely to get clear messages, about how they should make decisions, from a court whose job is to identify some error or defect in the primary decision-making process or in the decision itself, than from a tribunal whose job is to make the correct or preferable decision and to explain why the decision it makes can be so described. Ironically, the fact that there are no 'grounds' of merits review in the sense that there are 'grounds' of judicial review might partly explain why a merits review system may be a relatively ineffective vehicle for improving the quality of primary decision-making.

A striking aspect of debates about the normative function of the AAT is the implicit assumption that establishing an accountability mechanism is a good way – perhaps even the best way – to improve the quality of administrative decision-making. This assumption reflects the dominance of lawyers and legal ways of thinking in the reform processes of the 1970s and the continuing lack of interaction between lawyers and public administrators. For instance, from a public administration perspective, adequate resources, good recruitment practices, careful training, effective personnel management and systematic performance-monitoring by agencies themselves (perhaps reinforced by an external inspection, audit and quality-assurance body) might be much more likely to produce significant improvements in the quality of decision-making than an

---

[163] *Better Decisions*, para 8.72.
[164] It is difficult to assess the validity of the conclusion, for which very little evidence or support was offered.

inevitably sporadic external review or appeal process.[165] Furthermore, of course, a citizen-initiated accountability system, however effective, deals with only one side of the matter, namely decisions adverse to the citizen – false negatives, we might say, and not false positives. From a public interest perspective, false positives may be as significant as false negatives.[166]

Of course, the relative efficacy of various techniques for improving the quality of primary decision-making is ultimately an empirical matter. There is no rigorous or systematic empirical research into the impact of merits review by the AAT on practices and standards of executive decision-making. There is a small but growing body of research, especially in the UK, about the impact of judicial review on bureaucratic decision-making. Even allowing for the differences between judicial review and merits review, the results are none too encouraging. For instance, on the basis of a study of the impact of judicial review on homelessness decision-making,[167] Simon Halliday suggests that the impact of administrative law is likely to be directly related to how much public decision-makers know about the law and its requirements. This hypothesis raises the issue of how knowledge of administrative law is communicated to and disseminated amongst decision-makers and agencies, a topic about which we know very little.[168] In *Better Decisions* one of the ARC's main concerns was to promote the normative goal of merits review. To this end it gave particular attention to the role of agencies in processing and disseminating relevant decisions of merits review tribunals and in training decision-makers.[169] One of the expressed aims of recent and ongoing major changes to the tribunal system in the UK is to give

---

[165] A classic exposition of this point of view is J Mashaw, *Bureaucratic Justice: Managing Social Security Disability Claims* (New Haven, Yale University Press, 1983). See also J Mashaw, 'The Management Side of Due Process' (1973–74) 59 *Cornell Law Review* 772. In the UK, the Social Security Act 1998 imposed on the President of [Social Security] Appeal Tribunals an obligation to report annually on standards of departmental decision-making. The Tribunals, Courts and Enforcement Act 2007 imposes no such duty on the Senior President of Tribunals. In the final *Report by the President of Appeals Tribunals on the Standards of Decision-Making by the Secretary of State 2007–08*, the gloomy conclusion is that 'there is little evidence of significant change over time in standards of decision-making as gauged by cases coming before tribunals' (2).

[166] D Volker, 'Just Do It: How the Public Service Made it Work' (2001) 8 *Australian Journal of Administrative Law* 203, 212–13.

[167] S Halliday, *Judicial Review and Compliance with Administrative Law* (Oxford, Hart Publishing, 2004).

[168] The project of which this book is the main fruit, as originally conceived, had an empirical element designed to explore mechanisms and methods by which information and knowledge about the AAT and its activities and jurisprudence are communicated to and within four Australian government agencies – The Australian Taxation Office, Centrelink, Comcare and the Department of Veterans' Affairs – that between them account for more than 80 percent of the caseload of the AAT. Such an investigation of agency procedures commended itself as a relatively manageable preliminary to a more theoretically and practically complex and difficult investigation of the impact of the AAT and its adjudicative activities on bureaucratic decision-making, The hope was that this preliminary empirical study would also make a contribution to understanding of the ways in which legal knowledge is (best) communicated to non-lawyers. Unfortunately, logistical difficulties led to the abandonment of the empirical element of the project.

[169] *Better Decisions*, paras 6.1–6.41.

tribunals a more active role – beyond merely resolving individual disputes and publishing reasons for decisions – in establishing lines of communication with agencies about primary decision-making processes.[170] The AAT regularly holds meetings with users and user groups, including agencies. Their aim is to provide assurance that the AAT is 'an approachable and transparent organisation that takes account of the needs of the people and organisations that use its services'. At such meetings 'changes to practice and procedure affecting parties' are explained and ' the Tribunal receives valuable feedback on the areas where we are performing well and areas where we might be able to make improvements'.[171] It is unclear whether the AAT uses these meetings to provide agencies with feedback about their decision-making performance.

The directness and, perhaps, the effectiveness of communication between tribunals and agencies is likely to be related to the closeness of the relationship between the tribunal and the agency. For this reason, methods such as these for promoting the normative goal may be in tension with the value of tribunal independence.[172]

Despite theoretical doubts about the realism of the expectation that the AAT could perform a normative function, the lack of systematic empirical data (as opposed to anecdotal commentary) and the absence even of explicit discussion or analysis of the concept of decision-making 'quality',[173] there is a widespread (but not universal) view that merits review and the AAT have had a beneficial effect on the quality of administrative decision-making. Three general themes recur in the literature.[174] One is that the very existence of the AAT and the very

---

[170]   White Paper, *Transforming Public Services: Complaints, Redress and Tribunals*, 2004 (Cm 6243) (London, HMSO, 2004) paras 6.32–6.34.

[171]   Administrative Appeals Tribunal, *Annual Report 2006–07*, 39.

[172]   See also 4.2.2, nn 64 and 65 and text.

[173]   The assumption must have been that quality should be understood in terms of the 'correct or preferable' formula. For some general discussion of the concept of quality see KJ de Graaf, JH Jans, AT Marseille and J de Ridder, *Quality of Decision-Making in Public Law: Studies in Administrative Decision-Making in the Netherlands* (Groningen, Europa Law Publishing, 2008), esp chs 1–4.

[174]   Contributions include AS Blunn, 'The Impact of the AAT on Social Security Administration' in J McMillan (ed), *The AAT – Twenty Years Forward: Passing a Milestone in Commonwealth Administrative Review* (Canberra, Australian Institute of Administrative Law, 1998) 99–107; R Creyke and J McMillan, 'Executive Perceptions of Administrative Law – An Empirical Study' (2002) 9 *Australian Journal of Administrative Law* 163; J Dwyer, 'The Impact of the AAT on Commonwealth Administration: A View from the Tribunal' in *The AAT – Twenty Years Forward*, 64–98; J Dwyer and G Woodard, 'Dreams of a Fair Administrative Law' in S Argument (ed), *Administrative Law and Public Administration: Happily Married or Living Apart Under the Same Roof?* (Canberra, Australian Institute of Administrative Law, 1994) 197–231; Fleming, n 152 above; D O'Brien, 'The Impact of Administrative Review on Commonwealth Public Administration' in M Harris and V Waye, *Australian Studies in Law: Administrative Law* (Sydney, The Federation Press, 1991) 101–19; P O'Neill, 'Can Review Bodies Lead to Better Decision-Making? – II' (1991) 66 *Canberra Bulletin of Public Administration* 123; T Rodgers and G Short, 'The Impact of Administrative Law: Immigration and the Immigration Review Tribunal – I' in J McMillan (ed), *Administrative Law: Does the Public Benefit?* (Canberra, Australian Institute of Administrative Law, 1992) 243–63; M Sassella, 'Administrative Law in the Welfare State: Impact on the Department of Social Security' (1989) 58 *Canberra Bulletin of Public Administration* 116; S Skehill, 'The Impact of the AAT on Commonwealth Administration: A View from the

possibility of merits review impressed upon managers in the public service the need to train decision-makers and to regulate and monitor decision-making processes.[175] A second theme concerns the positive impact of the requirement to give reasons for decisions, imposed on decision-makers by section 28 of the AAT Act. Thirdly, it is said that in some cases, at least, the AAT has improved decision-making by elaborating the meaning of statutory provisions that had not previously been 'authoritatively'[176] interpreted by an external reviewer – indicating, for instance, the considerations relevant to the exercise of a statutory discretion, or elucidating the requirements of a statutory procedural regime.

By the later 1980s – it is commonly said – the reforms of the 1970s had produced a sea-change in public administration, and the 'administrative law package' (as the various elements of the Kerr Committee's vision were collectively called) was counted a 'success'. By this time the 'new administrative law' (an alternative name for the Kerr vision) had been joined by the 'new public management', which put increased emphasis on financial efficiency and cost-cutting in government. Another important development of the 1980s was increasing use of internal merits review mechanisms[177] within government departments. Some started to question whether the AAT continued to represent value for money, given its supposed success in improving decision-making standards and its small case-load relative to the many millions of potentially reviewable decisions made every year.

The AAT is, of course, still with us, and the place of external merits review in the governmental system seems secure. It may be, however, that the AAT is seen as having a lesser role to play in transforming public administration and that it has settled into the sedate middle-age of a court-substitute – no longer a scourge for the public service but, like judicial review, a minor irritant.

5.6 Merits Review Outside the AAT

The concept of merits review is understood to describe the basic activity not only of the AAT but also of first-tier federal tribunals such as the Social Security

---

Administration' in *The AAT – Twenty Years* Forward, 56–63; P Stein, 'Can Review Bodies Lead to Metter Decision-Making? – I' (1991) 66 *Canberra Bulletin of Public* Administration 118; D Volker, 'The Effect of Administrative Law Reforms: Primary Level Decision-Making' (1989) 58 *Canberra Bulletin of Public Administration* 112; 'Just do it – How the Public Service Made it Work' (2001) 8 *Australian Journal of Administrative Law* 203.

[175] This impact was contemplated by the Kerr Committee: Kerr Committee Report, para 374.
[176] Remember that the AAT cannot decide questions of law conclusively; but in practice its interpretations of statutory provisions are typically treated as authoritative.
[177] Discussed in ch 7 of this book.

Appeals Tribunal and the Refugee Review Tribunal.[178] However, the concept has spread beyond the federal tribunal system. For instance, reconsideration of decisions by primary decision-makers and internal review of decisions by an official other than the primary decision-maker are often said to be modes of merits review. However, although reconsideration by the primary decision-maker and internal review, like review by independent external tribunals, involve *de novo* consideration of the case, because they are internal to the bureaucracy they are essentially modes of implementation, not adjudication.

State tribunals external to the bureaucracy such as the Victorian Civil and Administrative Appeals Tribunal, and State courts such as the New South Wales Land and Environment Court have the power to review public decisions (see 1.2.3) on the merits. In such contexts, merits review is understood essentially as it has been developed in the jurisprudence of the Federal Court and the AAT. For instance, in the New South Wales legislation establishing the Administrative Decisions Tribunal (ADT)[179] – the Administrative Decisions Tribunal Act 1997 (NSW) ('ADT Act') – it is expressly provided that the function of the ADT is to 'decide what the correct or preferable decision is';[180] and the Western Australian legislation establishing the State Administrative Tribunal (SAT)[181] – the State Administrative Tribunal Act 2004 (WA) ('SAT Act') – provides that review by the SAT is not confined to matters that were before the decision-maker but may involve the consideration of new material whether or not it existed at the time the decision was made'.[182] These provisions give statutory expression to basic principles of merits review established at federal level by the Federal Court and the AAT.

However, in the State context, there is at least one important respect in which the original concept may have been modified. Statutory attempts have been made to clarify the role of merits review tribunals in relation to government policy. Section 64 of the ADT Act, section 28 of the SAT Act and section 57 of the

---

[178] It may not follow that the concept will apply in the same way in all contexts. For instance, although the AAT is cautious in its approach to government policy, it has legal power to ignore, amend, or act inconsistently with, it if it thinks this is necessary to making the correct or preferable decision. It may be that the basic legal obligation (as well, not doubt, as the standard practice) of the closely-held immigration tribunals is to apply government policy unless doing so would cause injustice in the individual case.

[179] The main functions of the ADT are to review administrative decisions of New South Wales government agencies, to resolve discrimination and retail lease disputes, and to exercise disciplinary and regulatory functions over a range of professional and occupational groups. It operates in six divisions and an appeal panel.

[180] ADT Act s 63.

[181] The SAT deals with a broad range of administrative, commercial and personal matters including human rights, vocational regulation, commercial and civil disputes, and development and resources issues. The SAT is the primary forum for review of decisions made by central and local government agencies and officials in Western Australia.

[182] SAT Act s 27.

Victorian Civil and Administrative Tribunal Act 1998 ('VCAT Act')[183] provide, in effect, that the relevant minister may certify that at the time the decision under review was made, there was a 'statement of policy' (SAT and VCAT Acts) or a 'Government policy' (ADT Act) that applied to decisions of that kind. If the Minister so certifies, the Tribunal 'must give effect to' (ADT Act) or 'must have regard to' (SAT Act) or 'must apply' (VCAT Act) the statement of policy: (1) except to the extent that it is unlawful (all three Acts) or it 'produces an unjust decision in the circumstances of the case' (ADT Act); (2) if satisfied that the statement was published in the Gazette and applied to decisions of the relevant type (SAT Act), or that the applicant was aware of or could reasonably be expected to have been aware of the statement, or the statement had been published in the Government Gazette (VCAT Act); and (3) the decision-maker states to the Tribunal that it 'relied on' the statement in making the decision (VCAT Act) or 'had regard to' the statement in making the decision (SAT Act). The ADT Act further provides that the Tribunal 'may have regard to 'any other policy applied by the decision maker except to the extent that it is unlawful or produces an unjust decision in the circumstances of the case'.

Neither the VCAT Act nor the SAT Act contains a definition of 'policy'. The Administrative Appeals Tribunal of Victoria (a predecessor of the VCAT) has held that an instruction about how to interpret a statutory provision that is unambiguous on its face and has been the subject of a judicial decision, cannot qualify as a statement of policy.[184] The ADT Act defines 'Government policy' as a 'policy adopted by' the Cabinet, the Premier[185] or any other Minister 'that is to be applied in the exercise of discretionary powers by administrators'. All the provisions apply only to the subset of policies that satisfy the relevant certification and publicity conditions. Nevertheless, the ADT Act expressly allows the ADT to have regard to other policies; and neither the SAT Act nor the VCAT Act purports to be a code and neither would prevent the Tribunal giving weight to policies that do not fall within its provisions.

The SAT Act provides that the policy to which the Tribunal must have regard is the policy 'as in effect at the time of the review'. By contrast, the policy to which the ADT must give effect is that 'in force at the time the reviewable decision was made'. Earlier (in 5.3.2.2 (iii), Error of Law), we examined how the AAT deals with changes in the law between the date of the original decision and the date of the AAT's decision. There it was argued that it is unfair and contrary to basic principle for the AAT to give effect to a change in the law, adverse to the

---

[183] Which established the Victorian Civil and Administrative Tribunal by amalgamating 15 boards and tribunals. It resolves about 90,000 cases a year and has civil and human rights jurisdiction in addition to its administrative review functions.

[184] *Re Unthank and Estate Agents Board* (unreported, 18 Nov 1985). As we noted earlier (n 121 above) the Federal Court has held that the AAT has an obligation to interpret legislation for itself and that it must not accept an agency's statement about how the legislation should be interpreted: *Port of Brisbane Corp v Deputy Commissioner of Taxation* (2004) 81 ALD 549.

[185] ie the chief minister.

applicant, unless that change is expressed to operate retrospectively. The same argument could be made in relation to changes in soft law.[186] Although the provision in the SAT might be read as generally endowing policies that fall within the Act with retrospective effect, it can be argued that the provision should not be interpreted as requiring the SAT to have regard to policy made after the date the relevant decision was made that adversely affects the applicant for review.

None of the Acts defines the critical phrase 'have regard to' (SAT Act), 'give effect to' (ADT Act) or 'apply' (VCAT Act) respectively. A basic question is whether any of the statutes prevents the Tribunal from varying or setting aside a decision that conforms with a policy that satisfies the specified certification and publicity requirements *even though* application of the policy by the decision-maker caused injustice to the applicant. The ADT Act expressly distinguishes between policies that satisfy the requirements and policies that do not.[187] The Tribunal *must* give effect to policies in the former category and *may* give effect to policies in the latter category; but in either case, it may only give effect to a policy if doing so will not cause injustice in the individual case. Neither the SAT Act nor the VCAT Act says anything about injustice in individual cases. The interpretation of these latter provisions most consistent with *Drake (No 2)* would be that the Tribunal remains free to vary a decision or make a substitute decision if application of the policy has caused injustice to the applicant – in other words, that the provisions, in this respect, impliedly restate the position advocated by Brennan J. Indeed, it seems reasonable to interpret the word 'apply' in the VCAT Act as having the meaning given to it by Brennan J in *Drake (No 2)*, namely 'not ... unquestioning adoption of [the policy], but rather an assumption that, in the absence of any reason to the contrary', the policy is 'appropriate to guide the decision in cases falling within its terms.'[188]

Another important question is whether the provisions would prevent the Tribunal varying a decision or making a substitute decision on the ground that the policy itself was in some strong sense 'unreasonable'. Even if they do not prevent the Tribunal acting to undo individual injustice caused by application of

---

[186] In *Rokobatini v Minister for Immigration and Multicultural Affairs* (1999) 57 ALD 257 it was held (as argued by the appellant) that the AAT had made an error of law in failing to take account of a 'direction' (a policy statement made binding by statute) issued between the date of the challenged decision and the AAT's decision.

[187] However, this distinction may be more important in theory than in practice. In *Searl v D-G, NSW Fisheries* [2000] NSWADT 53, [84], Skinner PM called the distinction ' a fine one' and continued that although the policy in question had been made by an unelected public official, it had been 'carefully struck after wide consultation with stakeholders ... I would have to be persuaded by powerful and cogent considerations if I were not to give effect to the policy of the Government where the same has been clearly ascertained'. In *Picton v Minister for Fisheries* [2002] NSWADT 47, [21] the ADT apparently considered itself bound to give effect to a policy even though it did not meet the certification requirement 'because there was no dispute that such a policy formed part of the 1996 Licensing Policy of NSW Fisheries'. See also *Oliver and Thomson v Minister for Fisheries* [2002] NSWADT 28, [25]; *Reed v Minister for Fisheries* [2003] NSWADT 44, [16]. But contrast *Ireland v Minister for Fisheries* [2001] NSWADT 198, [68]–[69]

[188] (1979) 2 ALD 634, 642.

a policy, they might prevent it rejecting a policy on the ground that it is, in some more general sense, lacking in merit. This seems a possible interpretation. However, as noted earlier (5.3.2.2 (ii)), the line between saying that application of a policy caused injustice in a particular case and saying that the policy lacks merit is a fine one, if only because the latter statement seems to imply the former. A tribunal is likely to adopt the former reasoning unless it wants to provoke the government into changing the policy rather than merely to reverse its application to the case before it.

It may be that the intention of the provisions dealing with policy in the SAT Act and the VCAT Act was to change significantly the law governing the role of the Tribunals in relation to government policy developed by the AAT in *Drake (No 2)* and subsequent cases. However, the terms of the provisions do not clearly embody such an intention and it seems unlikely that it will be realised in practice. So far as concerns the provision in the ADT Act, the specific reference to 'injustice in the circumstances of the case' seems to embody the general approach enunciated by Brennan J in *Drake (No 2)*. There is, however, one factor favouring a different interpretation. Under section 77(iii) of the Australian Constitution the federal Parliament may confer federal judicial power on state courts. In this context, it has been held that the ADT is not a state court;[189] and one of the reasons given for this conclusion was that 'the Tribunal is required to give effect to government policy'.[190] On the other hand, since the Tribunal is only required to give effect to lawful policies if doing so would not cause injustice in the circumstances of the case, it is hard to see how this obligation is significantly different from that contemplated by Brennan J.

5.7 The Nature of Tribunal Review in Comparator Jurisdictions

5.7.1 The UK

Because the Australian Constitution has been interpreted to require a categorical distinction between merits review and judicial review and because the AAT is a free-standing tribunal of general jurisdiction which, in many respects, operates in a judicial way, Australian law has developed and articulated a much richer and more complex understanding of the function of administrative tribunals than the law of either of our main comparator jurisdictions – the US and the UK.

---

[189] *Trust Company of Australia Ltd v Skiwing Pty Ltd* (2006) 66 NSWLR 185. See generally G Hill, 'State Administrative Tribunals and the Constitutional Definition of a "Court"' (2006) 13 *Australian Journal of Administrative Law* 103.
[190] (2006) 66 NSWLR 198, [27].

As we have seen, the changes in the UK involve the transfer of existing tribunal jurisdictions to the new tribunals rather than a general conferral of jurisdiction on those tribunals such as characterised the creation of the AAT. The Tribunals, Courts and Enforcement Act 2007 ('TCE Act') says nothing in general about the functions of the First-tier Tribunal when making (as opposed to reviewing its own) decisions. However, the Act does contain an important provision about the powers of the Upper Tribunal when hearing appeals from the First-tier Tribunal. Appeals to the Upper Tribunal are limited to points of law. Under section 12 of the TCE Act, if the Upper Tribunal sets aside a decision of the First-tier Tribunal it must either remit the decision for reconsideration or remake the decision.[191] In remaking a decision, the Upper Tribunal may 'make any decision the First-tier Tribunal could make if the First-tier Tribunal were remaking the decision and ... make such findings of fact as it considers appropriate'. This section contains an amalgam of ideas. The provision that the Upper Tribunal may make any decision that the First-tier Tribunal could have made casts it procedurally[192] in the role of a merits reviewer. On the other hand, in providing that the Upper Tribunal may make findings of fact, the section seems to cast it in a role analogous to that of an appeal court – as does the provision that appeals to the Upper Tribunal are limited to points of law.

The reference to the First-tier Tribunal remaking a decision presumably alludes to section 9 of the TCE Act, which gives the First-tier Tribunal power to review its own decisions (once only) either on its own motion or on the application of a person who has a right to appeal the decision to the Upper Tribunal.[193] When it reviews a decision, the First-tier Tribunal may correct accidental errors in the decision or in a record of the decision, amend the reasons given for the decision or set the decision aside. If it takes the last course it must either re-decide 'the matter concerned' or refer it to the Upper Tribunal (which must re-decide the matter, and in doing so can make any decision the First-tier Tribunal could make if it were re-deciding the matter).[194] In re-deciding the matter, the First-tier Tribunal may make such findings of fact as it considers appropriate. These provisions about review contain the same amalgam of ideas as the provision about appeals to the Upper Tribunal. On the one hand, they cast the tribunal reviewing its own decision (and the Upper Tribunal in dealing with a reference) procedurally in the role of a merits reviewer. On the other hand, instead of

---

[191]   Formally, the Upper Tribunal has no power to vary the decision of the First-tier Tribunal.

[192]   Remember the distinction drawn earlier between the substantive, procedural and remedial elements of merits review.

[193]   TCE Act s 10 gives the Upper Tribunal a similar power. The Australian law in this area is complex and relatively undeveloped: Pearce, *Administrative Appeals Tribunal*, 204–08, 214–17; G Downes, 'Finality of Administrative Decisions', available on the Administrative Appeals Tribunal's website at <http://www.aat.gov.au/SpeechesPapersAndResearch/speeches/downes/HartiganLectureNovember2005.htm> accessed 21 April 2008.

[194]   The First-tier Tribunal cannot vary the decision. Obviously, the power of the Upper Tribunal to make any decision the First-tier Tribunal could make cannot include a power to refer the matter to the Upper Tribunal.

providing that on review (or reference) the decision may be remade, the Act provides that 'the matter' may be re-decided; and it refers to the role of the reviewer in relation to facts as being to make findings of fact.

It remains to be seen how these various provisions will be interpreted and understood. On their face, however, they appear to embody a rather different concept of the role and function of administrative tribunals from that encapsulated in the Australian concept of merits review. The nature of the role of the Upper Tribunal is further complicated by the fact that in addition to entertaining appeals from decisions of the First-tier Tribunal, it will also have some first-instance jurisdiction in complex cases and cases raising issues of general significance, as well as limited judicial review jurisdiction. Experience of the operations of the New South Wales Land and Environment Court, which exercises both merits review and judicial review jurisdiction, suggests that there may be a risk of 'cross-infection' between the Upper Tribunal's various roles, or at least a danger of confusion.[195]

In order to gain a deeper understanding of the function of tribunals in the UK system it is necessary to look at the legislation relevant to particular jurisdictions transferred to the new tribunals. Here we will briefly examine the role of social security and immigration tribunals. For simplicity and convenience the discussion is cast in terms appropriate to the period before transfer of the jurisdiction of the relevant tribunals to the new (First-tier and Upper) Tribunals.

Appeals to social security appeal tribunals are governed by section 12 of the Social Security Act 1998. This provision says almost nothing about the powers of the tribunal. However, the leading decision of the Social Security and Child Support Commissioners (SSCSCs) (the highest tribunal in the social security adjudication system)[196] establishes that an appeal to a social security appeal tribunal is by way of a complete rehearing of issues of fact and law.[197] The 'appeal tribunal is designed to be a superior fact finding body'.[198] Its basic task is to make what it considers to be the correct decision, and in doing so it 'may make any decision which the officer below could have made'.[199] The 'appeal tribunal's jurisdiction is not limited to affirming [the decision under appeal] or alternatively setting aside the decision' and remitting it to the decision-maker.[200] The

---

[195] See n 89 above.

[196] See generally T Buck, D Bonner and R Sainsbury, *Making Social Security Law: The Role and Work of the Social Security and Child Support Commissioners* (Aldershot, Ashgate, 2005).

[197] SSCSC Case R(IB) 2/04. See also SSCSC R(IS) 17/04, [26].

[198] ibid [14].

[199] ibid [24]. It follows, as it does under Australian merits review law (5.3.2.2 (i)) that procedural errors by the decision-maker will normally be of no practical significance because the appeal tribunal can cure defects of procedure: SSCSC Case R(H) 3/04.

[200] ibid [15]. By contrast, under s 120 of the Enterprise Act 2002 (UK) the Competition Appeal Tribunal, in hearing appeals from decisions of the Office of Fair Trading, the Secretary of State or the Competition Commission, may only quash the whole or part of a decision and refer the matter back to the original decision-maker. In deciding appeals, the Tribunal is to 'apply the same principles as would be applied by a court on an application for judicial review'.

tribunal 'in effect stands in the shoes of the decision-maker'.[201] Moreover, its jurisdiction is 'inquisitorial or investigatory' in the sense that it may consider issues relevant to making the correct decision even if they are not raised by the parties to the appeal.[202] Unlike an Australian merits review tribunal, however, a social security appeal tribunal may not 'take into account circumstances not obtaining at the time when the decision appealed against was made'.[203] This means that if the claimant's relevant circumstances change pending the hearing of the appeal, they are well-advised to make a new claim for benefit or apply for the decision appealed from to be 'superseded' by the decision-maker (under section 10 of the 1998 Act).

It has also been held (in the context of recovery of overpayment of housing benefit) that because a social security appeal tribunal is a 'purely judicial body', it cannot entertain appeals against exercises of discretion that involve consideration of 'non-justiciable' issues. Any appeal against such a discretionary decision is limited to 'points of law' understood in terms of the grounds of judicial review.[204] It will be recalled (see 5.3.2.1) that the main ground on which the Kerr Committee considered merits review to be a non-judicial function was that it would typically involve the consideration of non-justiciable issues. However, we have also seen (5.3.2.2 (ii) and (iii), Weighing Relevant Considerations) that in practice, the AAT takes a very cautious approach to reviewing the exercise of discretion. Nevertheless, in principle the distinction between justiciable and non-justiciable issues does not mark the boundary of the AAT's competence. Indeed, to the contrary, there is no technical bar to the AAT considering non-justiciable issues in the course of reviewing decisions. The substantive essence of merits review, in the Australian sense, is precisely that it extends beyond law and legality.

An appeal lies from a decision of an appeal tribunal to an SSCSC on a point of law. On appeal, if the decision is set aside, the Commissioner may make fresh or further findings of fact and make a substitute decision or, alternatively, refer the case back to the tribunal with directions for its determination.[205] Decisions of the SSCSCs on matters of law are binding on appeal tribunals and on primary decision-makers. This reflects the fact that tribunals in the UK are understood to be exercising judicial power.[206] By contrast, binding precedent has no place in the Australian merits review system not only because merits review tribunals – at the

---

[201] Case R(H) 3/04, [25].

[202] ibid [31]–[32].

[203] Social Security Act 1998 (UK), s 12(8)(b).

[204] SSCSC Cases R(H) 3/04 and R(H) 6/06.

[205] Social Security Act 1998 (UK) s 14(8). For an example of a case in which the SSCSCs refused to make findings of fact and referred the matter back see SSCSC Case R(IS) 17/04.

[206] On the concept of precedent as it applies to tribunals generally see T Buck, 'Precedent in Tribunals and the Development of Principles' (2006) 25 *Civil Justice Quarterly* 458; H Genn, 'Tribunal Review of Administrative Decision-Making' in G Richardson and H Genn (eds), *Administrative Law and Government Action* (Oxford, Clarendon Press, 1994, 259–60).

federal level, at least – cannot conclusively decide questions of law (this being a judicial function), but also because it is considered to be inconsistent with the basic task of such a tribunal – namely to bring it about that the correct or preferable decision is made in the individual case before the tribunal.[207]

Clearly, the idea that one of the functions of a second-tier tribunal is to make and develop law by creating binding precedents informs official understandings of the role of the Upper Tribunal. For instance, the Leggatt Review of Tribunals 'envisaged that it would be the function of the new appellate tribunal "to develop, by its general expertise and the selective identification of binding precedents, a coherent approach to the law"'.[208] According to the First Senior President of Tribunals, 'This provides an unprecedented opportunity to work towards a more coherent and distinctive system of tribunal justice, drawing together the strands of the principles developed for various jurisdictions'.[209] An effective system of precedent depends on the reporting of relevant decisions.[210] 'Reporting' is not the same as publication. Even before the days of the Internet, many decisions of both courts and tribunals, although publicly available, were 'unreported' and lacked the status and degree of bindingness accorded to reported decisions. With the advent of the Internet and the proliferation of published decisions, it has become pragmatically even more necessary to develop explicit criteria and methods for nominating certain published decisions as have binding status. It is certainly ironical that although decisions of the AAT lack the formal (if not the effective) status of precedents, since it started operation a selection of its decisions have been published in two series of hard-copy law reports (the Administrative Appeal Reports (AAR) and the Administrative Law Decisions (ALD)).

The understanding of the role of the SSCSCs as being judicial is also reflected in the fact that they 'often' set aside decisions because they are based on flawed reasoning and substitute a decision to the same effect but based on sound reasoning.[211] By contrast, in Australian merits-review law a sharp distinction is drawn between the decision and supporting reasoning. The task of the merits reviewer relates only to the decision. The remedial powers of the reviewer are not engaged by flawed reasoning unless it has led to the making of an incorrect decision.

---

[207] This may be the basis on which it was held, in *Merchandise Transport Ltd v British Transport Commission* [1962] 2 QB 173, that the tribunal was not bound by its own previous decisions (see P Cane, *Administrative Law*, 4th edn (Oxford, OUP, 2004) 388–89).

[208] R Carnwath, 'Tribunal Justice – A New Start' [2009] *Public Law* 48, 56.

[209] ibid.

[210] For a thorough discussion of the availability of decisions of the SSCSCs see Buck, Bonner and Sainsbury, n 196 above, ch 5.

[211] D Bonner (ed), *Social Security Legislation 2007, Volume III: Administration, Adjudication and the European Dimension* (London, Sweet & Maxwell, 2007) 245, 247. This practice raises important an difficult issues, and its legitimacy may be open to question in the light of the decision in *Office of Communications v Floe Telecom Ltd* [2009] EWCA Civ 47.

Under section 82 of the Nationality, Immigration and Asylum Act 2002 (UK),[212] 'where an immigration decision is made in respect of a person he may appeal to' the Asylum and Immigration Tribunal (AIT), which is a First-tier reviewer staffed by 'Immigration Judges'. As its name indicates, the AIT deals with both asylum and other immigration matters. The grounds of appeal are set out in section 84 of the 2002 Act. They fall into three categories: (a) inconsistency with the Immigration Rules;[213] (b) inconsistency with domestic or EC law; and (c) incompatibility with rights under the European Convention on Human Rights (ECHR). The AIT's powers are to 'dismiss' or 'allow' the appeal. The grounds on which an appeal can be allowed are (1) that the decision was not in accordance with the law (including the immigration rules) and (2) that a discretion exercised in making the decision should have been exercised differently. In addition to the ECHR, domestic and EC law, and the Immigration Rules, immigration decision-making is also regulated by extra-statutory 'policies' under which immigrants may be allowed to enter the UK even if not entitled to do so by any of the first three categories of provision. By statute, the AIT has no power to review an exercise of discretion under a policy if the decision in question is in accordance with the Rules. In other words, discretionary application, non-application or misapplication of an extra-statutory policy is not a ground of appeal, although such conduct may be relevant in deciding whether some other ground of appeal (such as unlawfulness or incompatibility with a Convention right) has been made out.[214]

It follows from this rule about review of discretions exercised outside the Immigration Rules that the basis on which the AIT may allow appeals on the basis of application, non-application or misapplication of departmental policies is the same as that on which a court, conducting a judicial review, may quash a decision for a policy-related reason, namely, that application or non-application of the policy, or the way the policy was applied was inconsistent with some legal rule or principle. Unlike the AAT, the AIT may not – even in theory – consider the merits of the policy. Only if a policy is in 'absolute terms' that leave the decision-maker with no discretion or where, 'on the facts of the case there is no proper opportunity, by application of the policy, to make a decision unfavourable to the claimant',[215] can the AIT allow an appeal on the ground of non-application or misapplication of the policy (and in such circumstances, the basis of the AIT's decision would be unlawfulness).

---

[212] As amended by the Asylum and Immigration (Treatment of Claimants, etc) Act 2004. It was originally planned that the AIT would operate as a separate pillar of the tribunal system and that its jurisdiction would not be transferred to the First-tier Tribunal. However, at the time of writing it seems likely that transfer will take place sometime in 2009.

[213] The Immigration Rules are a form of soft law, although not as soft as departmental 'policies'.

[214] *AG and others (policies; executive discretions; Tribunal's powers) Kosovo* [2007] UKAIT 00082, [44].

[215] ibid [48].

The task of the AIT when deciding appeals alleging incompatibility with Article 8 of the ECHR was considered by the House of Lords in *Huang v Secretary of State for the Home Department*.[216] That task, the House said, was not

> a secondary, reviewing, function dependent on establishing that the primary decision-maker misdirected himself or acted irrationally or was guilty of procedural impropriety. The appellate immigration authority must decide for itself whether the impugned decision is lawful and, if not, but only if not, reverse it.[217]

The House went on to contrast the role of the appellate immigration authority (for present purposes, the AIT) with that of a court reviewing a decision on the ground of incompatibility with Art 8 of the ECHR. Such review requires the court (like the AIT when deciding an appeal on this ground) to determine the legality of a decision by applying a test of proportionality, as opposed to the less intrusive test of *Wednesbury* unreasonableness. The House quoted a statement to the effect that although more intrusive than the unreasonableness test, the proportionality test does not require the court to engage in 'merits review'.[218] This was interpreted to mean that in applying the proportionality test, the court does not act as a 'primary decision-maker' with the task of deciding what decision ought to have been made; rather it reviews the decision of another decision-maker. By contrast, in exercising its appellate function the AIT does not review the decision of another decision-maker but rather decides 'whether or not [the decision] is unlawful ... on the basis of up to date facts'.[219] Moreover, like the AAT, the AIT is 'much better placed [than the primary decision-maker] to investigate the facts'.[220]

The role of the AIT is to decide, on the basis of a full reconsideration of the facts,[221] whether either of the grounds on which an appeal can be allowed has been established. Although the AIT's power is to 'allow' or 'dismiss' the appeal, in practical terms the effect of allowing an appeal will typically be substitution of a decision in favour of the appellant. However, the AIT may remit the matter for reconsideration by the primary decision-maker. As noted, appeals to the AIT on the ground of incompatibility with Article 8 of the ECHR (unlike, it seems, applications for judicial review on this ground) are decided on the basis of the facts as they are at the time of the appeal. Asylum appeals are also decided on this basis. By contrast, immigration (as opposed to asylum) appeals are generally dealt with on the basis of the facts as they were at the time of the decision

---

[216] [2007] 2 AC 167.

[217] ibid [11].

[218] For an early explicit recognition in the UK of the distinction between review for legality and merits review see Committee of the JUSTICE-All Souls Review of Administrative Law in the United Kingdom, *Administrative Justice: Some Necessary Reforms* (Oxford, Clarendon Press, 1988) 211–12.

[219] ibid [13].

[220] ibid [15].

[221] eg *AA v Entry Clearance Officer (Nigeria)* [2004] UKIAT 00019, [5].

appealed against.[222] In this respect, an appeal to the AIT is, in some cases, functionally equivalent to judicial review and in others to merits review as understood in the Australian system.

Like the SSCSCs, the AIT nominates certain decisions on issues of law as having a binding status. In asylum cases the AIT has also developed a practice of issuing 'country guidance'.[223] The purpose of such guidance is to promote consistency and efficiency in decision-making by the AIT. It is formulated by senior judges of the tribunal in the context of a particular appeal that raises issues common to a significant number of cases coming before the tribunal and as a by-product of deciding the appeal. Country guidance purports to provide authoritative factual information, relevant to deciding asylum appeals, about conditions in a particular country. Although country guidance has been described as 'factual precedent',[224] it is better understood – as the word 'guidance' implies – as establishing relevant considerations to be taken into account by Immigration Judges in deciding individual asylum appeals. In the words of one commentator, 'country guidance is to be treated as authoritative until fresh evidence demonstrates a change in country conditions; authoritative, though flexible, guidance, but not binding precedent'.[225] An AIT Practice Direction has 'made clear ... that unreasoned failure ... to follow clearly applicable country guidance might amount to a reviewable error of law'.[226]

The phenomenon of factual guidance (which, it seems, is not limited to the asylum context, and apparently has the approval of both the higher judiciary and the government) has very significant implications for understanding the role of tribunals – especially second-tier tribunals. In Australia (and Canada)[227] country information is provided to tribunals either by the executive or by research units within a tribunal itself. By contrast, the AIT has no information-gathering resources of its own and is dependent on the parties to a 'country guidance appeal' to provide relevant information. Moreover, as in the normal asylum appeal, the burden of proof in relation to such information rests on the appellant.[228] In Australia country information is treated as an input to the tribunal decision-making process lacking any authoritative status. In the UK, by contrast, country guidance constitutes an authoritative (though not strictly binding) output of the process. Acceptance that tribunals (unlike courts) may appropriately make authoritative general statements of fact (as opposed to law) is apparently based on the assumption that tribunals have relevant 'expertise' (that courts lack). This assumption may also encourage the view that in supervising

---

[222] *R v Immigration Appeal Tribunal, ex p Rajendrakumar* [1996] Imm AR 97.

[223] R Thomas, 'Consistency in Asylum Adjudication: Country Guidance and the Asylum Process in the United Kingdom' (2008) 20 *International Journal of Refugee Law* 489.

[224] *S v Secretary of State for the Home Department* [2002] INLR 416, 435 (Laws LJ).

[225] Thomas n 223 above, 520.

[226] Carnwath n 208 above, 60.

[227] Thomas n 223 above, 500 n 31.

[228] ibid 508.

tribunals, courts should show heightened deference by interpreting the concept of an appealable 'error of law' very narrowly.[229] Taken to an extreme, this approach could turn tribunals into a de facto system of administrative courts, effectively immune from control by the 'ordinary' courts. Less radically, it casts tribunals as something like 'super courts' which, by virtue of their jurisdictional specialisation and adjudicatory expertise, deserve norm-setting powers that the traditional courts have never claimed and have, in some contexts, expressly disavowed. Either way, the concept of factual guidance suggests a very different understanding of the role of tribunals from that prevalent in Australia (for instance).

A party to an appeal to the AIT may apply to a court (in England, the High Court), on the ground that the AIT made an error of law, for an order requiring the AIT to reconsider its decision.[230] A party may appeal from the reconsidered decision to a court (in England, the Court of Appeal) on a point of law.[231] On that appeal, the court may (inter alia) affirm the decision, make any decision the AIT could have made or remit the case to the AIT. In substantive terms, such an appeal is functionally equivalent to judicial review and in remedial terms, functionally equivalent to merits review in the Australian sense of those terms.

This brief consideration of the respective functions of social security and immigration tribunals shows that UK law embodies a significantly less clear, uniform and developed understanding of the role of tribunals than that found in Australian law. It remains to be seen what effect the creation and operation of the First-tier and Upper Tribunals will have on the juridical concept of administrative adjudication. For instance, it is unclear whether and how the practice of giving factual guidance will prove to be reconcilable with the limitation of appeals to the Upper Tribunal to points of law, especially if courts interpret the concept of 'law' narrowly in order to maximise the freedom of 'expert' tribunals from judicial control.

5.7.2 The US

In the US literature, discussion of the role of administrative law judges (ALJs) (and, by analogy, of other non-judicial administrative adjudicators) typically focuses on the relationship between ALJs and agencies (ie, agency heads) rather than that between ALJs and primary decision-makers. Put differently, the nature of administrative adjudication is understood primarily in terms of the role of agencies in reviewing decisions of ALJs[232] rather than in terms of the role of ALJs in making or reviewing primary decisions. In the model of administrative

---

[229] See eg, Carnwath, n 208 above, 56–64.
[230] Nationality, Immigration and Asylum Act 2002 s 103A. But 'decision' for these purposes does not include 'procedural, ancillary or preliminary decisions'.
[231] ibid s 103B.
[232] And of courts in reviewing decisions of agencies.

adjudication that underlies the provisions of the Administrative Procedure Act 1946 (APA), the characteristic function of the ALJ is to develop a factual record on the basis of which the agency can decide relevant issues of law and policy. It is true that unless 'the agency requires … the entire record to be certified to it for decision', the ALJ has power to make an initial decision; but the agency has power to review that decision *de novo* either on its own motion or in response to an appeal.[233] As we have seen (3.2), the APA model of administrative adjudication focuses on regulatory decision-making – licensing, enforcement and so on – rather than on decision-making about entitlement to state benefits. In this APA model, administrative adjudication is understood as the fact-finding stage of a single, integrated decision-making process; by contrast, in what I have called the 'review' model (as opposed to the 'primary decision' model) of administrative adjudication, it is understood in terms of review of a decision made by a primary decision-maker. Our concern in this book is with the review model of administrative adjudication. Indeed, the primary decision model is not a version of administrative *adjudication* in the sense in which the word is used in this book, which refers to review rather than implementation (1.2.2).

Although there is little explicit discussion of the matter in the US literature, it seems clear that in the review model of administrative adjudication, the role of the adjudicator is to undertake a *de novo* review of the primary decision and to decide whether the original decision should be affirmed, varied or set aside and replaced by a substitute decision. That role is elaborated primarily in terms of developing a factual record, and the characteristic of *de novo* review (as opposed to an appeal) is that the record 'remains open' until the reviewer completes the review process. In Australian terms, *de novo* review is undertaken on the basis of material available to the reviewer at the time of the reviewer's decision, not on the more limited basis of material available at some earlier time. Under the APA, if and when an agency reviews a decision by an ALJ, the agency 'has all the powers which it would have in making the initial decision except as it may limit the issues on notice or by rule.'[234] In other words, agency review is merits review in the procedural sense (5.3.3). In the APA model, the main purpose of agency review is to enable the agency to exercise control over 'policy' by having the last word (subject to judicial review) on issues of statutory interpretation and the development, application and interpretation of extra-statutory decision-making norms. In crude terms, the APA establishes a division of labour between ALJs and agencies, the former being responsible for fact-finding and the latter for law and 'policy'.

However, the respects in which this last statement is too 'crude' are significant. First, although the prime responsibility of ALJs is for fact-finding, the power to make an initial decision which, in the absence of review, stands as the decision of

---

[233] APA s 557(b).
[234] ibid. In the APA model, the power of initial decision resides in the agency, and ALJs make initial decisions as delegates of the agency.

the agency, necessarily imports the power (and the duty) to decide relevant issues of law and 'policy'. However, just as Australian merits reviewers cannot conclusively decide questions of law, so (it is said) the principle of stare decisis does not apply to decisions of ALJs. In other words, decisions by ALJs on issues of law do not create precedents that are in any sense binding on ALJs. In this respect, the most that can be said of ALJs (as of Australian merits review tribunals) is that they have a legal obligation of consistency in decision-making both in relation to their own earlier decisions and in relation to decisions of other ALJs (and of their agency when reviewing decisions by ALJs). Regarding 'policy' – in the sense of extra-statutory norms – the role of the ALJ is defined by the fact that although ALJs are understood as performing essentially judicial tasks, they are embedded within agencies and their decisions are ultimately subject to *de novo* review by the agency. This underpins the proposition that the function of ALJs is to apply and give effect to extra-statutory policies developed by the agency. Whereas the AAT (at least in theory) has power to question and to act inconsistently with government policy, ALJs are understood to have no such power.

The APA model assumed that any particular agency would undertake a relatively small number of adjudications, and that it would be practicable for agencies to control the 'policy' element of initial decisions by reviewing individual decisions by ALJs. However, the enormous increase since the 1950s of administrative adjudication in areas such as immigration and social security made it impractical for agencies in this way to police compliance by adjudicators with agency policy. The large volume of adjudications in such areas also made it impractical for agencies to control policy through an internal mechanism for review of ALJ decisions by a second-tier reviewer (such as the Appeals Council in the social security context). An alternative strategy was to make rules that legally bound ALJs and to establish extra-statutory norms to guide their decision-making. In the 1970s and early 1980s the social security administration utilised various other management techniques (such as performance monitoring), but these were eventually abandoned in the face of opposition from ALJs.

In this area of policy review we find a fundamental difference – in principle anyway – between administrative adjudication in the US and merits review by the AAT in Australia. Although the AAT is technically part of the executive branch, its ethos is essentially judicial. The institutional separation of the AAT from the agencies whose decisions it reviews and its status as an 'external' reviewer provide the foundation for this ethos of 'independence'. Ironically, however, the judicial ethos of the AAT explains not only why it technically has the power to question government policy but also why, in practice, it is very unwilling to do so. Nevertheless, there is a significant contrast between the AAT and the specialist merits review tribunals in the areas of social security and immigration (for instance). The latter – and especially the immigration tribunals – although technically 'external' reviewers of agency decisions, understand their role primarily in terms of the just and consistent implementation of agency policy in individual cases. In this respect, there is a closer analogy between the specialist

Australian tribunals and US administrative adjudicators than between the latter and the AAT. The role of US adjudicators as implementers of agency policy is reinforced by their embedded location within agencies. Although ALJs are understood to be exercising an essentially judicial function, their administrative ethos distinguishes them not only from Article III (constitutional) courts but also from Article 1 (legislative) courts.[235]

Fact-finding is central to the APA model of administrative adjudication, and the concept of a 'hearing on the record' provides the trigger for the application of the APA to administrative adjudication – the APA applies only if some other statute requires a hearing on the record.[236] The prime function of the ALJ under the review model of administrative adjudication is to develop the record of the decision under review by an inquisitorial fact-finding process. So long as the record remains open to development the administrative decision-making process continues. In principle, when and if an agency reviews a decision of an ALJ it can develop the record in the same way as the ALJ can. However, in practice, agency review is typically undertaken on the basis of the record developed by the ALJ; and factual issues at this stage normally concern inferences to be drawn from the facts rather than the primary facts themselves. Whether administrative adjudication is undertaken by an ALJ or by the agency itself, the decision is technically that of the agency; and when a court reviews a decision of an administrative adjudicator, technically it reviews a decision of an agency regardless of who actually made the decision.

A problem may arise where an agency reaches a different factual conclusion than that reached by an ALJ.[237] Although the power to decide factual issues ultimately resides in the agency, the main function of the ALJ is to find the

---

[235] CH Koch, 'Policymaking by the Administrative Judiciary' (2005) 56 *Alabama Law Review* 693; JE Moliterno, 'The Administrative Judiciary's Independence Myth' (2006) 27 *Journal of the National Association of the Administrative Law Judiciary* 53; A Scalia, 'The ALJ Fiasco – A Reprise' (1979–80) 47 *University of Chicago Law Review* 58, 61–62.

[236] The APA (ss 554, 556 and 557) lays down a set of trial-type procedures for hearings on the record. Administrative adjudication to which the APA does not apply is generically known as 'informal adjudication'. However, 'adjudication' in this phrase has a much wider meaning than that adopted in this book, covering primary decision-making as well as review. Informal adjudication affecting 'liberty' and 'property' interests is subject to constitutional due process requirements that typically fall short of those applicable to a hearing on the record under the APA. The APA requires a hearing before the decision in question is made, whereas due process may be satisfied by a post-decision hearing (by way of review of the decision). See generally PL Strauss, *Administrative Justice in the United States*, 2nd edn (Durham, NC, Carolina Academic Press, 2002) 199–218. For suggestions that the APA should be amended to extend to informal adjudication see M Asimow, 'The Spreading Umbrella: Extending the APA's Adjudication Provisions to All Evidentiary Hearings Required by Statute' (2004) 56 *Administrative LR* 1003; RJ Krotoszynski, Jr, 'Taming the Tail that Wags the Dog: Ex Post and Ex Ante Constraints on Informal Adjudication' (2004) 56 *Administrative Law Review* 1057. For an argument to the opposite effect see GJ Edles, 'An APA-Default Presumption for Administrative Hearings: Some Thoughts on "Ossifying" the Adjudication Process' (2003) 55 *Administrative Law Review* 787.

[237] In high-volume areas, an intermediate review body may be established, the decisions of which, like those of ALJs, are technically decisions of the agency. Factual disagreements between an ALJ and an internal review body may give rise to the same problem

facts.[238] Under the APA, the relevant test to be applied by a court in judicially reviewing a decision of an agency is whether the decision is supported by 'substantial evidence' taking into account 'the whole record' of the hearing.[239] The ALJ's decision will, of course, be part of the record. As a result, in practice the formal freedom of an agency to reject findings of fact by an ALJ is – to some undefined extent – constrained by the requirement that the ALJ's decision be given some weight. Moreover, to the extent that the disagreement between the agency and the ALJ relates to factual inferences rather than primary facts, the ability of the agency to develop policy by resolving the disagreement in a particular way may be limited. Although the formal task of ALJs in relation to agency policy is implementation, the limited freedom of agencies to disagree with ALJs about the proper inferences to be drawn from agreed facts may confer on ALJs a degree of de facto power to develop policy without interference from their agencies.[240]

As in the case of administrative adjudication in the US, fact-finding lies at the heart of the Australian concept of merits review. Like ALJs, the AAT and other merits review tribunals have the power to develop the record – in other words, merits review is based on material available at the time of review whether or not it was available to the original decision-maker. In the Australian system, merits review of a decision of a first-tier merits review tribunals by a second-tier tribunal extends to findings of fact by the first-tier tribunal; but findings of fact by merits review tribunals cannot be reviewed by the decision-making agency. The power of US agencies to review factual decisions by ALJs marks a significant difference between administrative adjudication as understood in the US and the Australian concept of merits review.

5.7.3 France

Although this book does not attempt a systematic analysis of the French system of administrative adjudication, some discussion of the French understanding of that concept is illuminating. In order to understand the position under the French model it is necessary to say a little more than was said in 3.4 about the

---

[238] SG Breyer, RB Stewart, CR Sunstein and A Vermeule, *Administrative Law and Regulatory Policy: Problems, Text and Cases*, 6th edn (New York, Aspen Publishers, 2006) 214–15; JL Mashaw, RA Merrill and PM Shane, *Administrative Law: The American Public Law System, Cases and Materials*, 5th edn (St Paul, MN, Thomson West, 2003) 830–38.

[239] Fact-finding in cases of 'informal adjudication' not falling within the APA is reviewed under an 'arbitrary and capricious' standard: *Citizens to Preserve Overton Park, Inc v Volpe* (1971) 401 US 402; PL Strauss, *Administrative Justice in the United States*, 2nd edn (Durham, NC, Carolina Academic Press, 2002) 348–49.

[240] I am grateful to Jerry Mashaw for discussion on this point. See also 3.2, n 18; 4.3.2.2 (i), n 138 and text.

institutional structure of the French system of administrative adjudication.[241] At the top of the French system sits the *Conseil d'Etat*, and below it the *Cours Administratives d'Appel* and the *Tribunaux Administrative*. In French law, such bodies (which are loosely referred to in English as 'administrative' – as opposed to 'ordinary' – 'courts') exercise '*juridiction*'; and they are characterised by the fact that the principle of *res judicata* applies to their decisions. In addition, however, there are bodies – called 'commissions' – that perform specialised administrative adjudication in areas such as immigration. Commissions are somewhat analogous to specialist tribunals in the UK and Australian systems. However, in the French system, commissions operate in relatively fewer subject areas than do tribunals in the UK or Australian systems, being supplementary to the system of general administrative courts. For instance, administrative review in the areas of taxation and civil service employment is conducted in France by administrative courts, not by commissions. Commissions are understood to be administrative bodies that stand in the shoes of the original decision-maker and that review the merits ('*l'opportunité*') of the original decision. The principle of *res judicata* does not apply to the decisions of commissions, which can be challenged by way of judicial review in an administrative court. When an administrative court reviews a decision of a commission (by way of a *recours de cassation*) it may not consider 'the merits of a decision'. Generally, it may 'only quash for procedural error or illegality (which may extend ... to a mistake of fact) and refer the case back for reconsideration'.[242]

Administrative courts in France exercise two types of judicial review jurisdiction in relation to administrative decisions (other than decisions of commissions): full jurisdiction ('*plein juridiction*') and '*recours pour exces de pouvoir*'. *Plein juridiction* is exercised in areas such as taxation and civil service employment, and in cases in which claims for damages are made against the administration. In such cases, the court typically has the power to make a substitute decision, and compared with the *recours pour exces de pouvoir*, the grounds of review in *plein juridiction* allow closer and more intrusive scrutiny of both the legal and factual aspects of the decision under review.

The *recours pour exces de pouvoir* is based on the principle of legality, and the typical remedy is setting aside of the decision and referral back to the original decision-maker. However, the principle of legality is much broader than the equivalent concept in English and Australian law. It requires that decisions not only comply with provisions of primary and secondary legislation and of

---

[241] This section is heavily dependent on and derivative of LN Brown and JS Bell, *French Administrative Law*, 5th edn (Oxford, Clarendon Press, 1998). I have also benefited from face-to-face discussion with John Bell. See further J Bell, 'The Expansion of Judicial Review over Discretionary Powers in France' [1986] *Public Law* 99.

[242] LN Brown and JS Bell, *French Administrative Law*, 5th edn (Oxford, Clarendon Press, 1998) 60. In exceptional cases, the *Conseil* may make a substitute decision. See also ibid 251–52. Appeals to the *Conseil* from the *Cours Administratives d'Appel* are also by way of *cassation*.

judge-made law but also with certain unwritten *principes generaux du droit*.[243] Some of these principles reflect and protect fundamental rights such as personal liberty, freedom of expression, equality before the law and so on. Others require the decision-maker to act impartially, to follow fair procedures and to give reasons. Impartiality, non-retroactivity, protection of legitimate expectations and proportionality are also recognised as *principes généraux*. So understood, the principle of legality potentially intrudes far further into the merits of decisions than does its common-law counterpart. The concept of illegality is elaborated in various grounds of review: *l'inexistence* (which is made out when 'the illegality is so gross and flagrant as to amount to the administration acting completely outside its jurisdiction');[244] *incompetence* (made out when 'an official acts completely without authority');[245] *vice de forme* (procedural unfairness); *violation de la loi* (concerned with whether the substance of the decision 'conforms with the legal conditions set upon administrative action in the particular case (including ... *les principes generaux du droit*))';[246] and *detournement de pouvoir* (made out when the decision-maker acted for an improper purpose understood in terms of the decision-maker's 'motives' as opposed to statutory language).[247]

All of these grounds of review are available in *cassation* proceedings relating to a decision of a commission, except the last – 'presumably because the French cannot imagine persons charged with a judicial [ie, adjudicative] function offending in this respect'.[248]

So far as policy is concerned, '[t]he administrative courts will not interfere with administrative policy – a term which (significantly) is untranslatable into French, the nearest equivalent being, *l'opportunité* ('the merits').'[249] On the other hand, in general the courts exercise extensive control both over the fact-finding process (to ensure that the decision was based on correct facts) and over the legal classification of facts (mixed questions of fact and law). In some types of case, a decision involving legal classification of facts will be annulled only for *erreur manifeste d'appréciation des fauts* – where the decision 'is found to be wholly unreasonable or grossly disproportionate to the facts'.[250] But in many types of case, the standard of review is considerably more favourable to the applicant for review. To this extent, the *Conseil* is understood to concern itself with *l'opportunité*.

In French administrative law, it seems, the closest counterpart to merits review tribunals in the Australian sense are the commissions. Despite the fact that

---

[243] LN Brown and JS Bell, *French Administrative Law*, 5th edn (Oxford, Clarendon Press, 1998) 216–39.
[244] ibid 241.
[245] ibid 242.
[246] ibid 244–45.
[247] ibid 245–50.
[248] ibid 251.
[249] ibid 253.
[250] ibid 258.

French administrative courts are technically part of the executive, not the judiciary, the mode of administrative adjudication they perform is more similar to common-law judicial review than to merits review. On the other hand, *plein juridiction* (in cases not involving claims for damages) is similar in both remedial and substantive respects to merits review as understood in Australia. Moreover, just as English courts have expanded the grounds of judicial review to cover matters that, in Australian law, would be classified as going to the merits, so the French concept of illegality, as elaborated and applied by the *Conseil d'Etat* and other administrative courts, potentially makes significant incursions into the merits. This might suggest that the most significant distinction between administrative adjudication across jurisdictions relates not so much to its substantive grounds and intensity as to the distribution of performance of the various modes of administrative adjudication across institutions within jurisdictions. There may also be significant inter-jurisdictional differences concerning the areas of government activity that are amenable to legality review and merits review respectively.

5.8 Conclusion

The main aim of this chapter has been to explain and analyse the concept of merits review as it has been developed primarily by the AAT and the Federal Court of Australia. It can be seen that merits review is a distinctive form of administrative adjudication, significantly different in various ways from judicial review. It can also be seen that the concept of merits review is informed by the institutional arrangements for administrative adjudication. The interaction between structure and function becomes even clearer when merits review is compared and contrasted with concepts of administrative adjudication that are more-or-less implicit in the practices of administrative adjudication found in comparator jurisdictions. The development of an explicit and distinctive jurisprudence of non-judicial administrative adjudication is, perhaps, the greatest contribution that Australian public lawyers have made to our understanding of the institutions and functions of government.

6

Purpose

S O FAR IN this book our main concern has been with the design and functions of administrative tribunals. The discussion – we might say – has lain on the horizontal plane of the institutional and functional relationships between tribunals and other organs of government. Chapters 3 and 4 focused on what administrative tribunals look like. Chapter 5 analysed what they do. In this Chapter the focus shifts – as it were – from the horizontal to the vertical, from the place of tribunals in the architecture of government to the interaction between tribunals and the citizens who (potentially and actually) use them – 'tribunal users' as they are now commonly called. The question considered in this chapter is what tribunals are for. With increasing frequency the purpose of administrative tribunals (and other administrative adjudicators) is abstractly described in terms of 'administrative justice'. Administrative tribunals are understood to be part of the 'administrative justice system' which, as its name implies, is in the business of doing (administrative) justice.

For the avoidance of misunderstanding, it is important to stress at the outset that the prime concern here is to analyse what administrative tribunals are meant to do and to examine various aspects of how they go about doing it. More particularly, the chapter examines what is meant by 'administrative justice' and how the *modus operandi* of tribunals relates to that concept. The chapter has little to say about how successful or unsuccessful administrative tribunals are at promoting the goal of administrative justice. This is an empirical question, and there is little available evidence relevant to answering it. Leaving aside the general difficulty and expense of empirical research about the social impact of law and legal institutions, part of the problem is that the concept of administrative justice is abstract and contested. The hope is that this chapter may make some contribution to its clarification – an essential precondition of robust empirical research.

6.1 What is Administrative Justice?

Because of its ubiquity and rhetorical force, the concept of administrative justice requires careful analysis. We may begin by observing that in this context as in many others, the word 'justice' is often used ambiguously: sometimes descriptively – as in the phrases 'the administrative (or 'criminal' or 'civil') justice system' and 'the administration of justice'; and at other times prescriptively – as in the term 'natural justice' (referring to the two basic principles of procedural fairness – that a decision maker should be unbiased and that the person affected by a decision should be allowed to participate in the decision-making process). Descriptive uses of the term are consistent with both justice and injustice in the prescriptive sense: for instance, the 'administrative justice system' may produce unjust as well as just outcomes. We need to be alert to the risk that descriptive applications of the word may misappropriate its positive evaluative connotations.

Despite its vagueness and high level of abstraction, in recent years the language of administrative justice has gained wide currency, especially in the UK. A very broad, descriptive understanding of the concept is contained in the TCE Act in the context of a statement of the functions of the AJTC, the successor to the Council on Tribunals. The Act defines the 'administrative justice system' as

> the overall system by which decisions of an administrative or executive nature are made in relation to particular persons, including – (a) the procedures for making such decisions, (b) the law under which such decisions are made, and (c) the systems for resolving disputes and airing grievances in relation to such decisions.[1]

In this definition, administrative justice encompasses substantive rules and norms, decision-making procedures, and institutions. Emphasising the institutional aspect, a 2007 UK government consultation paper describes administrative justice as covering 'the initial decision-makers, those who reconsider decisions, Ombudsmen and other independent complaints handlers, the tribunals and the courts, and how the system which they produce as a result of their individual roles functions'.[2]

According to the same document, '[a]dministrative justice is now broadly recognised as a separate part of the justice system in its own right.'[3] Justice (it declares),

> can be usefully sub-divided: criminal, civil, administrative, family, employment, housing and so on. There is room for debate about how many "justice systems" there are, the precise boundaries between them, and the extent to which they overlap. But the essential point is that justice, within each of these systems, is provided not just by courts but by a range of interlocking institutions and mechanisms.[4]

Such accounts do not, of course, appear out of nowhere, and they are rich in ideological content. In part, they are a reaction to the largely uncoordinated

---

[1] TCE Act Sch 7, cl 13

[2] *Transforming Tribunals: Implementing Part 1 of the Tribunals, Courts and Enforcement Act 2007*, Consultation Paper CP 30/07 (London, Ministry of Justice, 2007), [12].

[3] ibid [11].

[4] ibid [115].

growth, in the past 40 years or so, of a plethora of institutions that are all in one way or another concerned with holding government accountable;[5] and they underpin and serve to justify a programme of building these various types of institution into some sort of 'system' designed to promote efficacy, efficiency and accessibility. The plausible empirical assumption is that confusion caused by the large number and variety of grievance-handling institutions and avenues presents many people with a significant barrier to access, thus hindering effective resolution of citizens' genuine grievances against government.[6] In this account of administrative justice, a normatively just system is one in which the barriers to access to administrative justice institutions are as few and low as possible.

A second explanation for deployment of the concept of administrative justice is encapsulated in the phrase 'proportionate dispute resolution' (PDR), an idea that played a significant role in a 2004 White Paper devoted primarily to the UK Government's plans for tribunal reform.[7] At the core of this concept 'is the idea that policies and services must be tailored to the particular needs of people in different contexts, moving away from the limited flexibility of existing ... systems'.[8] PDR may perhaps be seen as the successor to ADR (alternative dispute resolution). Originally (in the common-law world, at least), the concept of ADR referred to dispute-resolution methods other than adversarial adjudication in a traditional court. In this frame of reference, administrative tribunals could themselves be understood as being ADR mechanisms.[9] However, in Britain (as we have seen) tribunals have been transformed into a species of court. In the case of both courts and tribunals, debates about ADR have come to focus on methods (such as 'early neutral evaluation',[10] mediation and negotiation) by which disputes can be dealt with more informally, efficiently, flexibly and quickly.[11] In terms of ADR, tribunals have been transformed from being part of the solution to being part of the problem. PDR can be understood as an attempt to replace ADR-type thinking – in terms of a paradigm mode of dispute resolution

---

[5] For a careful analytical account of accountability as a modern political phenomenon and legal idea see R Mulgan, *Holding Power to Account: Accountability in Modern Democracies* (Houndsmills, Palgrave Macmillan, 2003).

[6] For a useful review of relevant empirical work see M Adler and J Gulland, *Tribunal Users' Experiences, Perceptions and Expectations: A Literature Review* (London, Council on Tribunals, 2003). As the authors point out, 'most research is based on those who are *not* deterred by barriers that can prevent users from accessing the tribunal system and [this] makes it difficult to gauge the full extent of potential barriers' (ibid 24).

[7] *Transforming Public Services: Complaints, Redress and Tribunals* (London, HMSO, 2004).

[8] ibid para 2.4.

[9] However, it is important to remember that especially in the 1920s and 1930s in Britain, tribunals were promoted primarily as alternatives to ministerial, not judicial, administrative adjudication. The prime concern of the likes of Lord Hewart and William Robson was the rapid growth of secretive and unregulated ministerial and departmental adjudication.

[10] M Adler, 'Tribunal Reform: Proportionate Dispute Resolution and the Pursuit of Administrative Justice' (2006) 69 *Modern Law Review* 958, 976–77.

[11] See eg, T Buck, *Administrative Justice and Alternative Dispute Resolution: the Australian Experience*, DCA Research Series 8/05 (London, Department for Constitutional Affairs, 2005).

supplemented by a range of alternatives – with a scheme in which institutions and modes of dispute-resolution are organised in a sort of sequence from the least formal to the most formal and from the simplest to the most complex. The resulting PDR system would ideally be approached through a single gateway. Entrants would be provided with maps of the system and, possibly, some sort of triage facility.[12] The aim would be to find the most suitable method of resolution for each individual dispute without any threshold presumption in favour of one method or another – 'horses for courses' as the saying goes. Theoretically, the concept of PDR is highly complex, and its practical implementation is likely to present enormous challenges.[13] Be that as it may, its promotion implies that a just system of administrative justice is one in which each particular dispute is resolved by the most appropriate of a set of available dispute-resolution mechanisms.

A third strand in recent thinking about administrative justice focuses on primary decision-making. The basic idea is that *administrative* justice is concerned not only with promoting accountability, and fair and efficient dispute-resolution, but also with the quality of primary, bureaucratic decisions; and that administrative *justice* is more likely to be promoted within bureaucracies than by recourse to external accountability and review mechanisms.[14] In the words of the 2004 White Paper, the objective is to ensure

> that the framework of law defining people's rights and responsibilities is as fair, simple and clear as possible, and that State agencies, administering systems like tax and benefits, make better decisions and give clearer explanations.[15]

So understood, the project of improving the quality of administrative decision-making goes beyond not only the Australian idea that accountability institutions may perform a normative function (5.5),[16] but also what Mashaw calls 'the management side of due process' – the idea that *ex ante* recruitment practices, training programmes, management techniques and internal monitoring are at least as important as *ex post* external scrutiny of individual decisions in raising

---

[12] See eg, Law Commission, *Housing: Proportionate Dispute Resolution* (Law Com No 309 Cm 7377, 2008) Pt 3. The Law Commission's concept of 'triage plus' encompasses '(1) Signposting: initial diagnosis and referral. (2) Intelligence-gathering and oversight. (3) Feedback.' (ibid para 3.14).

[13] For an exploration of the concept of 'proportionality' and the complexities of matching disputes with modes of dispute-resolution see Adler, n 10 above. See also M Adler, 'The Idea of Proportionality in Dispute Resolution' (2008) 30 *Journal of Social Welfare and Family Law* 309.

[14] 'Indeed, the total volume of injustice is likely to be much greater among those who accept initial decisions than among those who complain or appeal. For this reason alone, thoroughness and procedural fairness are much more important in primary adjudication than they are in appellate processes.': T Ison, 'Administrative Justice: Is It Such a Good Idea?' in M Harris and M Partington (eds), *Administrative Justice in the 21st Century* (Oxford, Hart Publishing, 1999) 23.

[15] *Transforming Public Services*, para 2.3.

[16] '[W]e are entitled to expect that where things have gone wrong the system will learn from the problem and will do better in the future': ibid para 1.5. See also N Wikeley, 'Decision-Making and the New Tribunals' (2006) 13 *Journal of Social Security Law* 86, 88–92.

and maintaining bureaucratic decision-making standards.[17] According to the White Paper's approach, administrative justice apparently encompasses the concept of public law as well.

However unrealistically grandiose this vision may be, it is of value in shifting our attention from institutional and systemic to procedural and substantive aspects of 'justice'. To quote the 2004 White Paper again:

> Each of us has the right to expect that State institutions will make the right decisions about our individual circumstances…[The] job [of public decision-makers] is to get … decisions … right. The job of those who organise and lead departments and agencies is to establish, maintain and constantly improve the systems which will enable the individual decision-makers to get the decisions right … This is the sphere of administrative justice.[18]

According to this account, to be treated justly is to be treated in accordance with applicable norms (bracketing, in this context, the question of whether the applicable norms are 'as fair, simple and clear as possible'). In this passage, the word 'right' should not be read as implying that administrative justice is concerned only with 'legality'. To be just, a decision must be 'right' not only as a matter of law but also on its 'merits'. Nor should we read the word 'right' to imply that every dispute has a uniquely acceptable resolution. It would be better to substitute for 'right' something like 'correct or preferable'. However, even with these qualifications, we must remember that (in principle, at least) those involved in implementation on the one hand, and adjudication on the other, bring different perspectives to bear on the decision-making process, the former favouring social interests and the latter individual interests (1.2.2). A substantive account of administrative justice must make allowance for such institutional differences. In this sense, the substantive and institutional aspects of administrative justice are inextricably linked.

Perhaps the most influential academic discussion of substantive justice in the context of administrative decision-making is that of Jerry Mashaw in his path-breaking book *Bureaucratic Justice*.[19] Mashaw uses the term 'justice' in the phrase 'bureaucratic justice' to mean 'those qualities of a decision process that provide arguments for the acceptability of its decisions'.[20] According to Mashaw, a decision-making process is just if it produces decisions that can be accepted as 'legitimate'. Put differently, Mashaw is concerned with what makes decisions 'right' (in the terms of the 2004 White Paper) or 'correct or preferable' (in terms of Australian merits review law). In answer to such questions, Mashaw offers three 'structures of justificatory argument' or 'models of justice', which he calls

---

[17] J Mashaw, 'The Management Side of Due Process' (1973–74) 59 *Cornell Law Review* 772.

[18] *Transforming Public Services*, paras 1.3–1.6.

[19] JL Mashaw, *Bureaucratic Justice: Managing Social Security Disability Claims* (New Haven and London, Yale University Press, 1983).

[20] *Bureaucratic Justice*, 24–25.

respectively 'bureaucratic rationality', 'professional treatment' and 'moral judgment'. In understanding these models it is important to note that Mashaw's study is concerned with the administration of social security disability benefits. 'Professional treatment' refers particularly to the medical elements of disability-benefit decision-making. It involves dealing with individuals not according to applicable norms but according to their needs, in order to promote their well-being (as defined by professional standards) rather than to give effect to their entitlements. By contrast, both bureaucratic rationality and moral judgement involve the application of relevant norms to individual cases. At some risk of distorting Mashaw's analysis, we can understand the distinction between bureaucratic rationality and moral judgment roughly in terms of the distinction between implementation and adjudication. Both require a balance to be struck between the social objectives of rules and the interests of individuals, but with different emphases: in cases of conflict between social objectives and individual interests, bureaucratic rationality favours social objectives whereas moral judgment favours the interests of the individual.

Mashaw's normative conclusion is that as a mode of primary decision-making, bureaucratic rationality is a more 'promising form of administrative justice' than moral judgment because it 'permits effective pursuit of collective ends without inordinately sacrificing individualistic or democratic ideals'.[21] In assessing this conclusion, it is important to emphasise that Mashaw evaluates these approaches as models for primary decision-making, and he sees them as being in competition with one another in the bureaucratic process.[22] His main concern with moral judgment is not as a method of reviewing decisions made in implementation of norms but as a technique for generating norms and applying them to individual cases.[23] This focus is understandable given the history of administrative adjudication in the US (see 2.3.2 and 3.2); but it makes Mashaw's argument and conclusion less relevant to the focus of this book, which is not on policy making or primary decision-making but on (external) review of these activities. Our concern is not with alternative modes of primary decision-making but with the relationship and interaction between implementation and adjudication in a system where the former is the accepted mode of primary decision-making (and internal review), and the latter is the accepted mode of (external) review. Even so, Mashaw's conclusion is not without implications for the role of administrative tribunals as defined in this book. For instance, a normative preference for implementation as the dominant mode of decision-making would suggest that tribunals should, in general, take a deferential attitude to decisions of primary

---

[21] ibid 222. Mashaw marginalises professional treatment on the basis that it does not compete with the other two models , having been relegated to an 'evidentiary role' within the bureaucratic process. He also thinks that adjudication within the disability programme has lost 'much of its "moral judgment" flavour': ibid 45–46.

[22] JL Mashaw, 'Conflict and Compromise Among Models of Administrative Justice' [1981] *Duke Law Journal* 181.

[23] eg *Bureaucratic Justice*, 33.

decision-makers; and, in particular (for instance), that they should generally apply government policy even at the expense of some unfairness to the individual. It might also suggest that tribunals should take some account of efficiency considerations when imposing procedural constraints on primary decision-makers. Within this framework, implementation and adjudication may be understood not as competing modes of justice but as elements of a complex, multi-layered concept of administrative justice.

The ultimate concern of administrative justice is the acceptability and legitimacy of decisions by government agencies affecting individual citizens, and of primary decision-making processes and institutions more generally. Administrative adjudication by courts and tribunals may make a contribution to the realisation of this ultimate goal by providing facilities for the resolution of disputes and grievances about primary decision-making. Affirmation of a decision by an adjudicator may make it more acceptable to the adversely affected citizen(s). In cases where a decision is varied or a substitute decision is made by an adjudicator, provided the adjudicator's decision is itself found acceptable it may contribute to maintaining or increasing the acceptability of the decision-making process generally, including primary decision-making processes. This conclusion shows the significance of attribution to adjudicators of a normative function of improving the quality of primary decision-making. To the extent that the function of adjudication is understood in negative terms of correcting errors, it will be apt to undermine the legitimacy of primary decision-making processes in proportion to the frequency with which adjudicators vary primary decisions or make (or provoke the making of) substitute decisions. Attributing a positive normative function to administrative adjudicators may be understood as a strategy for lessening this corrosive effect.[24]

Michael Adler has built on Mashaw's approach by identifying three other models of administrative justice in addition to those discussed by Mashaw.[25] These he calls the 'managerial', 'consumerist' and 'market' models. It is not clear that these are all models of 'justice' in Mashaw's sense of criteria of decisional legitimacy. Managerialism, in the sense of a concern with the efficiency of bureaucratic organisations, may certainly have implications for the making of decisions about individuals; but it does not obviously provide a criterion for judging their acceptability. For instance, if a decision-maker is required to 'increase productivity' by dealing with more cases than formerly in a given period of time or with given resources, this may impair the decision-maker's ability to

---

[24] Incidentally, this analysis also suggests why a normative function is less often attributed to judicial review, the focus of which is on correcting errors.

[25] M Adler, 'Fairness in Context' (2006) 33 *Journal of Law and Society* 615. For a quite different approach see S Halliday and C Scott, 'A Cultural Analysis of Administrative Justice' in M Adler (ed), *Administrative Justice in Context* (Oxford, Hart Publishing, 2009).

make correct and preferable decisions. This would make managerialism a possible *cause* of injustice rather than a *criterion* of justice.[26] On the other hand, to the extent that managerialism is concerned with efficiency and timeliness, it may contribute to the legitimacy of the decision-making system as a whole and in that way indirectly contribute to the legitimacy of individual decisions. As Mashaw puts it,[27] legitimacy depends on striking an acceptable balance between accuracy and cost-effectiveness; and this, for him, is the essence of bureaucratic rationality.

Adler associates consumerism with provision of opportunities for citizen participation in decision-making and redress for individual grievances. Mashaw might consider participation not to be an independent criterion of legitimacy but an aspect of his moral judgment model: good procedure is certainly an aspect of justice but only one aspect. Any complete model of justice in decision-making will have both substantive and procedural elements. The provision of redress cannot be a criterion of acceptability because it assumes that the affected person (rightly) considers the decision unacceptable.

The market model, by contrast, does yield both a procedure – competition for available resources, and a decision-making criterion – the allocation of resources to their highest-value use. There may be areas in which allocation of resources by government on a competitive basis is considered acceptable and even desirable. For instance, government procurement of goods and services is, to a significant extent, conducted on market principles; and telecommunications licences may be distributed on the basis of competition. Furthermore, it is clear that acceptance of the market model as providing a suitable criterion for the making of primary decisions in a particular area may have a significant impact on what is considered an acceptable role for reviewers of government decisions and on the criteria of legitimacy of their decisions. For instance, courts have traditionally been quite unwilling to review decisions by government agencies to enter or not to enter contracts for the procurement of goods and services, and decisions made in exercise of powers conferred by such contracts. In other words, in this area courts have been less willing than in other areas of government decision-making to resolve conflicts, between individual and social interests, in favour of individual interests. So far as tribunals are concerned, their jurisdiction is typically defined in terms of particular types of decisions; and they are unlikely to be given jurisdiction to review government decisions made on market principles. The

---

[26] This conclusion is supported by Adler's account of research into the computerisation of social security decision-making (ibid 632–34). To the extent that computerisation is driven by a desire to reduce the cost of decision-making, it can be seen as a product of managerialism. But its effect on the acceptability of decisions will depend not on the motive for its introduction but on criteria such as accuracy (bureaucratic rationality) and capacity to take account of individual circumstances (moral judgment).

[27] *Bureaucratic Justice*, 25.

growing use in recent decades of contract as a technique of governance[28] has increased the role of the market model in government decision-making. Indeed, contractual ideas have even had an impact in the areas of social security and social welfare.[29]

Despite the reservations I have expressed about the relevance of Mashaw's approach to present concerns, his understanding of administrative justice in terms of the acceptability and legitimacy of government decisions about individuals provides a good starting point for analysis. In order to prevent administrative justice becoming justice *tout court*, it is necessary to bracket the questions of the acceptability and legitimacy of the basic regime of norms on which individual decisions are based. For instance, it is better not to treat the acceptability of the tax regime or the social security system as a matter of administrative justice. This is not to say that rule-making raises no issues of administrative justice. For instance, executive rule-making may be subject to external review on procedural and even substantive grounds by courts and tribunals. Nor does it mean that individual decision-making, whether by way of implementation or adjudication, may not involve rule-making. Ascertaining the appropriate rule(s) to be applied in individual cases may require creative interpretation of norms and even filling of gaps in the applicable normative regime. Nor does it mean that the acceptability of the basic normative framework of decision-making is irrelevant to understanding administrative justice. For instance, a plausible explanation for the establishment of at least some tribunals may be a desire to relieve ministers of responsibility for deciding individual cases that arise out of the implementation of controversial statutory programmes and to reduce opportunities for political scrutiny of such decisions. Nevertheless, however unclear it may be at the margins, the distinction between what we might call 'social justice' on the one hand and administrative justice on the other is sufficiently clear at its core to justify its application even if only for pragmatic reasons.

Our concern, unlike Mashaw's, is primarily with administrative justice in the review context, not the primary decision-making context. In the review context, the dominant model of administrative justice is what Mashaw calls 'moral judgment' and what Adler calls 'legality'. There are two modes of administrative adjudication – judicial review and merits review. Our prime concern is with the latter – ie, with administrative justice *in tribunals*. Some of the criteria of acceptability for decisions in these two modes were discussed in Chapter 4 in the context of institutional design – on the horizontal plane, we might say. Obviously, however, the substantive element of judicial review ('legality') and merits review ('correct or preferable') will also figure prominently in the analysis of

---

[28] P Cane and L McDonald, *Principles of Administrative Law: Legal Regulation of Governance* (Melbourne, OUP, 2008) 306–10; M Taggart, 'The Nature and Functions of the State' in P Cane and M Tushnet (eds), *The Oxford Handbook of Legal Studies* (Oxford, OUP, 2003).

[29] See eg, P Vincent-Jones, *The New Public Contracting: Regulation, Responsiveness and Relationality* (Oxford, OUP, 2006) ch 9.

administrative justice because it is by reviewing primary decisions according to criteria of legality and on their merits that courts and tribunals make their contribution to the acceptability and legitimacy of primary governmental decision-making. Similarly, the issues of institutional structure discussed in Chapter 4 have a vertical as well as a horizontal dimension. For instance, independence of administrative adjudicators from primary decision-makers contributes to the legitimacy of adjudicators' decisions and, in that way, contributes to the acceptability of individual primary decisions (when these are affirmed by the adjudicator) and primary decision-making processes more generally. In short, institutional design is a significant aspect of administrative justice.

In this chapter we will examine various issues that are related more directly to the (vertical) interaction between tribunals and tribunal users, and to the acceptability and legitimacy of individual decisions by administrative tribunals and, more generally, of administrative adjudication by tribunals.

6.2 A Formula for Administrative Justice in Tribunals?

Section 2A of the Australian Administrative Appeals Tribunal Act 1975 ('AAT Act') provides that '[i]n carrying out its functions, the Tribunal must pursue the objective of providing a mechanism of review that is fair, just, economical, informal and quick'.[30] This has become a standard formula which, we might say, offers an aspirational account of administrative justice in Australian merits review tribunals. It establishes two types of criteria of success, which we might dub 'legal' (the first two) and 'managerial' (the last three).

Even as an aspiration, the formula is problematic. The difficulty is not that the two sets of criteria are potentially in conflict and that satisfaction of one may compromise or jeopardies satisfaction of the other.[31] Justice and fairness are not priceless and in many situations are not worth seeking regardless of cost. The real problem is that the formula does not even provide a framework for thinking about how to resolve such conflicts. So, for instance, while degrees of satisfaction of the managerial criteria (cost and speed, anyway) may be quantified reasonably easily, satisfaction of the legal criteria is much more difficult to measure. Moreover, although justice and fairness are not literally priceless or invaluable, it is not unreasonable to think (contrary to what the formula might suggest) that they are worth more than their purely financial cost. Another concern is that setting managerial criteria in competition with legal criteria may encourage

---

[30] For present purposes we may assume that 'fair' refers to procedure and 'just' to outcomes.

[31] For a valiant attempt to minimise the tension see *Re The Australian Department of Families, Community Services and Indigenous Affairs* (2006) 92 ALD 179, [68] (Deputy President Forgie).

encourages proliferation of complex, multi-tier systems of review primarily for financial reasons and regardless of whether the additional tiers add value or only save money.[32]

Nevertheless, in addition to the substantive element of administrative justice, the formula does draw attention to two other important issues: tribunal procedure (6.5) and the resources of time and money available to and consumed by tribunals (6.6). The cost of applying to a tribunal is one of the basic aspects of 'access to justice'.[33] 'Access to justice' has been a catchcry and fundamental concern of policy-makers and socio-legal scholars for at least 40 years; and like 'administrative justice', it is a term used in various ways. In England, the Franks Committee considered 'accessibility' to be one of the advantages of tribunals over courts.[34] By contrast, in 1977, Tony Prosser propounded the highly influential thesis that certain social security tribunals were originally created not to make up for defects in courts but for financial and political reasons.[35] Extending Prosser's argument, Adler warns that 'the general point that tribunals have been preferred to the courts on political and cost grounds rather than because it is believed that they provide better access to justice is one that must be taken seriously'.[36]

In the late 1990s a major British study of 'what people do and think about going to law' more-or-less ignored tribunals;[37] but more recent research has found that 'members of the public revealed generally weak levels of understanding about avenues of redress for administrative grievances and limited awareness of tribunals'.[38] 'Poor information about systems of redress' was seen as a serious obstacle to access, as was 'the dominance of criminal justice in the public imagination' and lack of understanding of the difference between criminal courts and other legal institutions. A major concern of the Leggatt Review of Tribunals was that lack of a coherent institutional structure was impeding citizens' access to tribunals,[39] and one of the aims of Tribunals Service – a government agency created in 2006 to manage the tribunal system and the reforms instituted by the

---

[32] This point is discussed further in 7.3.

[33] Another is the ease with which tribunal proceedings may be commenced. For instance, applications to the AAT must be in writing and are not accepted by email.

[34] Report of the Committee on Administrative Tribunals and Enquiries, 1957 (Cmnd 218) para 38. Under s 2 of the Tribunals, Courts and Enforcement Act 2007 the Senior President of Tribunals 'must, in carrying out the functions of that office, have regard to (a) the need for tribunals to be accessible, (b) the need for proceedings before tribunals (i) to be fair, and (ii) to be handled quickly and efficiently'.

[35] T Prosser, 'Poverty, Ideology and Legality: Supplementary Benefit Appeal Tribunals and Their Predecessors' (1977) 4 *British Journal of Law and Society* 39.

[36] M Adler, 'Lay Tribunal Members and Administrative Justice' [1999] *Public Law*, 172, 173.

[37] H Genn, *Paths to Justice: What People Do and Think About Going to Law* (Oxford, Hart Publishing, 1999).

[38] H Genn and others, *Tribunals for Diverse Users*, DCA Research Series 1/06 (London, Department for Constitutional Affairs, 2006), i.

[39] Report of the Review of Tribunals by Sir Andrew Leggatt, *Tribunals for Users: One System, One Service* (London, TSO, 2001) ch 3.

TCE Act – is to make it easier for users to understand the process of seeking redress.[40]

Besides knowledge and resources, access is also, of course, affected by the legal regime governing matters such as the jurisdiction of tribunals and standing to make applications for review. It is to these that we now turn.

6.3 Jurisdiction

In 4.3.1 we examined the jurisdictional issue of specialisation versus generalism. This section is concerned more specifically with how the jurisdiction of administrative tribunals is determined and defined. The two matters are obviously related. Historically, the paradigm administrative tribunal was established to review decisions made in the course of implementing a discrete government programme established by and conducted under a statute. In this sense, the paradigm tribunal was a specialist adjudicator. The jurisdiction of such a tribunal could be defined in terms of decisions made in exercise of powers conferred on officials by provisions of the statute. When the AAT was established as a general appeal tribunal, the question inevitably arose of how its jurisdiction was to be defined. One possibility was to adopt the traditional technique, but instead of conferring jurisdiction on the AAT under only one statute, to give it power to review decisions made under a large number of statutes that established and governed the conduct of government programmes. A second was to define the AAT's jurisdiction without reference to particular statutes or particular statutory provisions.

The first option was adopted. Section 25 of the AAT's constitutive statute – the Administrative Appeals Tribunal Act 1975 ('AAT Act') – provides that 'an enactment may provide that applications may be made to the Tribunal … for review of decisions made in exercise of powers conferred by that enactment…[which] shall specify the person or persons to whose decisions the provision applies…[and] may be expressed to apply to all decisions of a person, or to a class of such decisions…' By contrast, the Administrative Decisions (Judicial Review) Act 1977 (ADJR Act), which creates a general statutory judicial review regime, defines the jurisdiction of the court in terms of decisions 'of an administrative character made, proposed to be made, or required to be made … under an enactment … by a Commonwealth authority or an officer of the Commonwealth'. This broad definition is subject to only a few exceptions cast in terms of particular statutes, a particular officer (the Governor-General), and certain classes of decisions. The basic definitional technique adopted in the ADJR Act reflects the common law which, at the time the ADJR Act was drafted, defined

---

[40] *Transforming Tribunals*, para 70.

the limits of judicial review basically in institutional terms: decisions made by government officials and agencies. The major jurisdictional differences between the ADJR Act regime of judicial review and the common law were that the former was confined to decisions 'of an administrative character'[41] (thus excluding judicial and, especially, 'legislative' decisions); and to decisions made in exercise of *statutory* powers (thus excluding non-statutory powers).

The effect of these contrasting approaches is that whereas the AAT has jurisdiction to review a decision only if a statute confers jurisdiction to make a decision of *that* sort,[42] the ADJR Act confers jurisdiction to review any decision made under any Commonwealth statute, subject to any express provision to the contrary. A possible explanation for this difference is that whereas the ADJR Act merely purported to codify the law relating to the courts' already-existing general power of judicial review, the merits review system was proposed in answer to the open question of how much more external review was needed in addition to that already provided by judicial review and the various tribunals in existence in the early 1970s. We might further speculate that because the Kerr Committee had to persuade the government of the need for more external review, it was seen as politically wise to give the Parliament as much power as possible over the expansion.

The distinction between the two techniques for defining jurisdiction to review has important ramifications for the impact of privatisation and outsourcing of the provision of public services on the availability of external review. The fundamental issue is whether decisions of non-governmental ('private') providers of services should be subject to review if decisions of that type, made by a governmental ('public') provider of that service, would be subject to review. So far as common law judicial review is concerned, a desire to prevent privatisation and outsourcing of the provision of services from disadvantaging service-recipients has led courts, particularly in the UK, to develop the concept of a 'public function'. Decisions made in the performance of such a function may be subject to judicial review regardless of whether made by a public or a private service provider. This development involves a shift from defining the scope of judicial review 'institutionally' (was the decision made by a public body or official?) to defining it 'functionally' (was the decision made in the performance of a public function?). Under the statutory judicial-review regime established by the ADJR Act, the relevant parameter of judicial review is whether the decision in

---

[41] P Cane and L McDonald, *Principles of Administrative Law: Legal Regulation of Governance* (Melbourne, OUP, 2008) 58–59.

[42] This requirement is interpreted strictly. See eg, *Re Radge and Commissioner of Taxation* (2007) 95 ALD 711; *Re Woods and Secretary, Department of Education, Science and Training* (2007) 94 ALD 265; and generally D Pearce, *Administrative Appeals Tribunal*, 2nd edn (Australia, LexisNexis Butterworths, 2007) 31.

question was made 'under an enactment'; and answering this question has given rise to some very difficult decisions,[43] as has answering the question whether particular functions are public or not.[44]

By contrast, such thorny issues are unlikely to arise where the technique chosen for defining the scope of review jurisdiction is that adopted in the AAT Act so that the power to review has to be expressly conferred rather than excluded by statute. Consider, for instance, *NEAT Domestic Trading Pty Ltd v AWB Ltd*.[45] Under a statutory provision, the Wheat Export Authority had power to consent to the export of wheat, but only with the written approval of a non-statutory corporation owned by wheat growers. Was a decision of the corporation, whether or not to give approval, made under the statutory provision? Such a question would be unlikely to arise in an application to the AAT because typically it could not convincingly be argued that a decision, such as that of the corporation whether or not to give approval, was reviewable by the AAT unless such a decision was expressed to be reviewable in a statutory provision.[46] Of course, this conclusion raises the underlying normative question of the appropriate scope of tribunal jurisdiction in an environment where functions formerly performed by government are privatised or contracted-out.

In other ways, the seemingly straightforward technique of defining the jurisdiction of the AAT in terms of classes of statutory decisions has raised some tricky issues. First, in the discussion of questions of law in 5.3.2.2 (iii) we saw that very soon after the AAT began operation, the question arose of whether it had jurisdiction over decisions that were illegal irrespective of their merits. The decision that it did established the principle that merits review tribunals have jurisdiction over 'purported' decisions – ie, decisions which, in theory, have no legal existence because they are treated as having been illegal from the moment they were made ('*ab initio*').

Secondly, whereas the AAT Act confers on the AAT jurisdiction to review 'decisions' on their merits, the ADJR Act confers on the court jurisdiction to judicially review not only decisions but also (in section 6) 'conduct' in which 'a person has engaged, is engaging, or proposes to engage for the purpose of making a decision'. The distinction between decisions and conduct played an important part in the reasoning, in the leading case of *Australian Broadcasting Tribunal v Bond*,[47] about the meaning of 'decision' under the ADJR Act. In *Bond*, the existence of section 6 was used to justify giving a narrower rather than a broader meaning to the word 'decision' on the basis that giving it a relatively narrow

---

[43] P Cane and L McDonald, *Principles of Administrative Law: Legal Regulation of Governance* (Melbourne, OUP, 2008) 65–68.

[44] For some discussion see ibid 307–10.

[45] (2003) 216 CLR 277 (3.4.5.2).

[46] *Re Qantas Airways Ltd and Deputy Commissioner of Taxation (Western Australia)* (1979) 2 ALD 291. See also Administrative Review Council, *The Contracting Out of Government Services*, Report No 42 (1998) ch 6.

[47] (1990) 170 CLR 321.

meaning (referring to something that is 'ultimate' or 'final' or 'determinative' or 'operative') was consistent with the limited nature of judicial review. The particular question at issue in *Bond* was whether certain findings of fact constituted 'decisions' for the purposes of the ADJR Act. Mason CJ held that 'in ordinary circumstances, a finding of fact ... will not constitute a ... decision' under the ADJR Act.[48] This was because in interpreting the ADJR Act, account had to be taken of the existence of the AAT and the merits review system: judicial review (as opposed to merits review) 'ordinarily does not extend to findings of fact as such'.[49]

Another argument used by Mason CJ in *Bond* in favour of a narrow interpretation of 'decision', was that a broad interpretation (allowing review of decisions that were not 'ultimate' or 'final' or 'determinative' or 'operative') would create the risk of 'fragmentation of the processes of administrative decision-making' and of adversely affecting 'the efficiency of the administrative process'.[50] The worry here is that allowing elements of the decision-making process other than the final 'decision' to be challenged by way of judicial review would allow the processes of administration to be interrupted and delayed for illegitimate purposes (whatever they might be).[51] Assuming there is a significant risk of such disruption, and that it is important to prevent it materialising, would the same reasoning count against giving a broad interpretation to 'decision' in the AAT Act? One commentator thinks not, on the ground that the 'AAT is part of the administrative process'.[52] But while the AAT is, in theory, part of the administration, in reality it provides an external check on the administrative process, and an application to the AAT might significantly disrupt the decision-making process.

At all events, an implication of the reasoning in *Bond* is that the word 'decision' has a wider meaning under the AAT Act than it has under the ADJR Act, and there are decisions and statements in cases before the AAT supporting a broader interpretation of the term 'decision' under the AAT Act than under the ADJR Act.[53] On the other hand, in various AAT decisions *Bond* has been used to justify refusal of merits review and a leading commentator has concluded that overall 'the impact of *Bond's* case ... is still unclear as far as AAT applications are concerned'.[54]

Much more significant than either of these rather technical matters is the general question of which classes of decisions should be subject to merits review.

---

[48] (1990) 170 CLR 321, 340.

[49] ibid 341. See further the discussion of error of fact in 5.3.2.2(iii).

[50] ibid 337.

[51] Note, too, that the ADJR Act definition of 'decision' (unlike that in the AAT Act) refers to decisions 'proposed to be made' as well as decisions 'made'.

[52] D Pearce, *Administrative Appeals Tribunal*, 2nd edn (Australia, LexisNexis Butterworths, 2007) 31.

[53] See D Pearce, *Administrative Appeals Tribunal*, 2nd edn (Australia, LexisNexis Butterworths, 2007) 28–31.

[54] ibid 30.

Because of the absence of a clear distinction between merits review and judicial review, this issue cannot be framed in these terms in relation to either the UK or the US. In the UK, the common view is that the development of tribunals in the 20th century was haphazard and unplanned, and to the extent that the choice between courts and tribunals was governed by criteria, they seem to have referred to the perceived contingent differences between the two types of body (speed, formality, expertise and so on) rather than to the subject matter of primary decision-making. In the US, the key debates have been about whether administrative adjudicators should be embedded within agencies or free-standing; and they have turned on the general relationship between implementers and adjudicators and the location of ultimate control over policy rather than on the particular subject matter of decision-making.

In considering the general question posed at the beginning of the preceding paragraph, it is important to recall that the Kerr Committee's recommendation for a general administrative appeals tribunal was justified on the basis that judicial review provided an inadequate avenue of redress for citizens who were dissatisfied with administrative decisions. Merits review was conceived as a supplement to judicial review, and the question inevitably arose of how extensive a supplement was required to provide adequate redress. Perhaps because the paradigm tribunal is a body with narrow jurisdiction, the Kerr Committee seems never to have entertained the possibility that merits review might be available co-extensively with judicial review. Instead it contemplated that it would 'be necessary to consider in detail ... each discretion and power of decision which might be subjected to review'.[55] Although the Committee had no doubt that many specific powers would be 'suitable for such treatment', it considered that '[t]he selection of them would require careful and detailed work'.[56]

In 1971 a Committee on Administrative Discretions was established under the Chairmanship of Sir Henry Bland 'to examine existing administrative discretions under Commonwealth Statutes and Regulations and to advise as to those in respect of which a review on the merits should be provided'.[57] Peter Bailey who, as the Deputy Secretary of the Department of the Prime Minister and Cabinet, was a member of the Bland Committee, describes how it

> met almost weekly over ... two years. During that time we reviewed and categorised ... tens of thousands of discretions. Each week we would be confronted with a pile of legislation perhaps two feet high ... Harry Bland forced us along at breakneck speed ... We had forms with columns prepared, and entered each discretion as reviewable or not reviewable, and the reason....The more than 250 discretions we considered should be made reviewable ... were contained in 75 Acts ... Of these, some 235 discretions in 56 Acts were subject to no review and we recommended that they should be. In addition

---

[55] Kerr Committee Report, para 301.
[56] ibid para 308.
[57] Final Report of the Committee on Administrative Discretions (the 'Bland Committee') (Canberra, Australian Government Publishing Service, 1973) ('Bland Committee Report') para 1.

we found 28 discretions in a further 19 Acts that provided for judicial review only. In 19 of those 28 provisions we considered that administrative tribunals review should be substituted or (in three cases) made an option.[58]

According to what general principles, if any, was this extraordinary exercise conducted?

The Committee interpreted the reference to 'administrative' discretions in its terms of reference as requiring a distinction to be drawn between matters of administration and matters of policy, only the former being eligible for subjection to merits review. General rule-making, it thought, is more likely than the application of rules to individual cases to 'fall in the policy area'.[59] Bailey says that the Committee was influenced by the approach of the Donoughmore Committee, and that what it was looking for were powers to make 'quasi-judicial' decisions.[60] Nevertheless, the Committee recommended that the exercise of administrative discretions under social security legislation should not be subject to review by a tribunal, apparently because it considered that more informal review processes were appropriate in this area. It anticipated the planned establishment of the office of ombudsman and also proposed improved internal review mechanisms.[61] More generally, the Committee declared, 'the Government's decision to legislate for an Ombudsman has enabled and justified a much more selective approach to the nomination of those administrative discretions in respect of which there should be some more formal external review process.'[62] Beyond these few indications, we know very little about how the Bland Committee approached its job.

The Kerr Committee proposed that one of the tasks of the Administrative Review Council (ARC) should be to 'carry on continuous research into discretionary powers with special reference to the desirability of subjecting their exercise to tribunal review'.[63] The Bland Committee concluded that the work it had done made it unnecessary to charge the ARC with this responsibility.[64] On this point the Kerr Committee's view prevailed, and one of the functions of the ARC under section 51 of the AAT Act is to advise the government about which classes of administrative decisions should be subject to review by a court, tribunal or other body. In the 1980s the ARC did significant work in this regard in areas such as social security and immigration. In 1999 it issued a document entitled *What Decisions Should be Subject to Merits Review?* The principles put forward are

---

[58] P Bailey, 'Is Administrative Review Possible Without Legalism?' (2001) 8 *Australian Journal of Administrative Law* 163, 165.

[59] Bland Committee Report, para 29. In reviewing decisions made in exercise of administrative discretions the Committee recommended that the tribunal should not be entitled to question government policy: ibid para 183.

[60] Bailey, n 56 above, 164.

[61] Bland Committee Report, paras 45–73.

[62] ibid para 109.

[63] Kerr Committee Report, para 283.

[64] Bland Committee Report, paras 207–08.

in no sense binding; and ultimately, the scope of merits review is a political issue.[65] It has been held by the High Court of Australia that section 75(v) of the Australian Constitution – which confers on the High Court jurisdiction 'in all matters in which a writ of Mandamus or prohibition or an injunction is sought against an office of the Commonwealth' – provides a guaranteed minimum of judicial review that cannot be excluded by Parliament.[66] However, there is no analogous constitutionally guaranteed minimum of merits review.

The ARC considers that there are only two classes of decisions that are, by their nature, unsuitable for merits review, namely 'legislation-like provisions of broad application' and 'decisions that follow automatically from the happening of a set of circumstances'.[67] In relation to decisions not in either of those categories, the ARC identifies 'factors that may justify excluding[68] merits review'. Such factors are further divided into three groups: factors lying in the nature of the decision, in the effect of the decision and in the costs of review. Factors of the first type the ARC associates with preliminary or procedural decisions, decisions to institute proceedings, decisions to allocate scarce resources between competing applicants, decisions relating to access to parliamentary or judicial records, policy decisions of high political content, decisions of a law enforcement nature and financial decisions with a significant public interest element. Factors of the second type it associates with decisions to delegate a power or to appoint a person to undertake a specified function, recommendations to ultimate decision-makers and decisions for which there is no appropriate remedy; and factors of the third type it associates with decisions involving extensive inquiry processes and decisions which have such a limited impact that the costs of review cannot be justified. It is not clear what distinction the ARC intends to draw by dealing separately with decisions by their nature unsuitable for review and decisions in the nature of which resides a factor that justifies excluding review. Perhaps the ARC thinks that decisions in the former category should never be subject to review whereas decisions in the latter category may sometimes be appropriately subject to review. If so, the ARC provides no guidance for deciding when decisions in the latter category would be appropriately subject to review.

It is also unclear what, if any, general principles, underpin the ARC's catalogue,[69] which constitutes a rather mixed bag. For instance, the reason why the

---

[65] This conclusion is perhaps supported by the view of one writer that, tested against the ARC principles, the current jurisdiction of the AAT is riddled with inconsistencies: V Thackeray, 'Inconsistencies in Commonwealth Merits Review' (2004) 40 *AIAL Forum* 54.

[66] *Plaintiff S157/2002 v Commonwealth* (2003) 211 CLR 467; P Cane and L McDonald, *Principles of Administrative Law: Legal Regulation of Governance* (Melbourne, OUP, 2008) 205–07.

[67] However, the law relating to review of decisions under so-called 'self-executing provisions' is complex: *Re Nelson and Repatriation Commission* (2007) 94 ALD 418

[68] More accurately, 'not providing for'.

[69] In its Report No 47, *The Scope of Judicial Review* (Canberra, Commonwealth of Australia, 2006) 37–53 the ARC similarly lists various factors that may justify excluding judicial review or limiting its operation. Surprisingly, perhaps, there is no analysis of the relationship between judicial review and merits review.

Council suggests that 'decisions to institute proceedings', should not be subject to review is that they are, in fact, not 'decisions'.[70] On the other hand, the suggestion that decisions 'of a high political content' should not be subject to merits review[71] seems to rest on some concept of 'non-justiciability' or unsuitability for external review. The ARC's position here reinforces the point that although the AAT is technically part of the executive, it is in reality an external, court-substitute reviewer of the executive. The principle that 'legislation-like decisions of broad application' are unsuitable for merits review perhaps echoes the provision, contained in the ADJR Act but absent from the AAT Act, that only decisions that are of an 'administrative character' are reviewable. The ARC's general statement is so broad and conclusory as to provide no real guidance at all: 'As a matter of principle, the Council believes that an administrative decision that will, or is likely to, affect the interests of a person should be subject to merits review'.[72]

There are at least three considerations that together might provide a foundation on which policy-makers could base the choice of whether or not particular classes of decisions should be subject to merits review (and tribunal review more generally). One consideration relates to the nature of the body that will undertake merits review. Where, for constitutional reasons, merits review jurisdiction must be conferred on a tribunal rather than a court (and, conversely, judicial review jurisdiction must be conferred on a court rather than a tribunal), alleged pragmatic advantages and disadvantages of tribunals and courts relative to each other may affect the decision whether to subject a particular class of decisions to merits review. By contrast, where there is no constitutional bar to conferring merits review jurisdiction on a court (or, conversely, judicial review jurisdiction on a tribunal), this consideration will be of less weight. Even so, unwillingness to devalue the status of courts and judges creates a preference for tribunals, especially in high-volume jurisdictions such as social security; and this status conversely creates a preference for restricting judicial review jurisdiction to courts rather than tribunals at least in cases involving high-profile, politically-charged challenges to executive decisions. In other words, institutional differences may be relevant regardless of whether or not the allocation of merits review jurisdiction to tribunals and judicial review jurisdiction to courts is constitutionally mandated.

The history of review of immigration decisions in Australia illustrates another way in which institutional differences may affect the incidence of merits review.

---

[70] Administrative Review Council, *What Decisions Should be Subject to Merits Review?* (Canberra, Commonwealth of Australia, 1999) 13.

[71] ibid 16–18.

[72] ibid 5. See similarly *The Scope of Judicial Review*, 37: 'the Council takes the pubic [*sic*] law values that underlie judicial review to be the rule of law, the safeguarding of individual rights, accountability, and consistency and certainty in the administration of legislation ... [these] are paramount values in Australian society and under the Australian Constitution. A strong justification is needed to reduce judicial review in such a way as to allow unlawful conduct to proceed without the availability of any remedy'.

Governments may be willing to allow merits review of immigration decisions even when they are not happy about such decisions being amenable to judicial review. Allowing merits review in the 'closely held' MRT and RRT has gone hand-in-hand with exclusion to the greatest possible extent of much more 'independent' judicial review of immigration decisions (and also, incidentally, with not providing for second-tier merits review of immigration decisions in the less closely held AAT).

A second consideration relates to the respective nature and functions of merits review and judicial review. The Kerr Committee's starting-point was that judicial review provides inadequate redress and needs to be supplemented by merits review – but only selectively. As we have seen, the main practical differences between merits review and judicial review are that the former allows much greater scrutiny of fact-finding and typically involves the making of a substitute decision. These differences must obviously be relevant to the decision whether to supplement judicial review with merits review. Judicial review may be thought appropriate and acceptable even when merits review is not.

A third consideration relates to the distinction between implementation and adjudication (1.2.2). This distinction, it will be recalled, rests on the difference between resolving disputes between social and individual interests in favour of the former on the one hand (implementation) and in favour of the latter on the other (adjudication). The idea is that whereas the basic function of administrative adjudication (both merits review and judicial review) is to ensure that administrative decision-makers duly respect individual interests, the prime function of implementation is to promote the social objectives of government programmes, albeit with respect for individual interests. Implementation focuses on the characteristics that individuals share with members of some relevant group rather than those that set them apart from other members of the group, which take centre stage in adjudication.[73] In 'high volume' decision-making contexts such as tax, immigration and social security, this principled difference between implementation and adjudication is reinforced by constraints of time and resources that limit the attention that can be paid to individual circumstances. As a result, it is to be expected that a certain proportion of primary decisions will be unfair because they take insufficient account of the personal situation of an affected individual. Adjudication provides a technique for identifying and redressing such injustice.

Viewed in this light, the two modes of administrative adjudication represent different ways of redressing individual injustice and injecting a greater element of individualisation into the decision-making process. Judicial review typically does this by identifying defects in the implementation process and requiring the process to be re-run, whereas merits review typically adds to the decision-making process an external decision-maker charged with paying greater attention than

---

[73] See also Bailey, n 58 above.

the primary decision-maker to the interests of the affected individual. This approach emphasises on the one hand the individualistic orientation of merits review relative to implementation, and on the other its role, relative to judicial review, as a supplement to rather than an intervention in the implementation process.

6.4 Standing

In relation to judicial review it is well recognised that standing rules both reflect and play a significant role in defining its function. Crudely put, narrow standing rules that require the applicant to have a personal interest in or be personally affected by the decision under review identify judicial review as a mechanism for ensuring that individual interests are properly taken into account by administrative decision-makers. By contrast, broad standing rules that allow representatives of groups or of the public to challenge administrative decisions by making applications for judicial review identify judicial review not only as a mechanism for protecting the interests of individuals but also as a way of contesting the social interests promoted by the decision under review. So far in this book judicial review has been identified as a mode of administrative adjudication. However, to the extent that judicial review may serve the latter function, this account must be qualified. Administrative adjudication is a technique that allows the balance struck by primary decision-makers between social and individual interests to be re-adjusted in favour of individual interests. By contrast, broad standing allows judicial review to be used to challenge the primary decision-maker's conception and definition of relevant social interests.

So understood, judicial review is not a mode of adjudication, but neither is it a mode of implementation. Whereas implementation is a technique for regulating individual circumstances in accordance with general norms, 'broad' judicial review is concerned with the nature and content of the relevant general norms. It contributes to the policy-making process by providing individuals and groups with an opportunity to participate (albeit indirectly) in the process of establishing relevant decision-making norms. This explains the sense in which it can be argued that broad standing rules turn judicial review into a surrogate political process, and why it is said that traditional judicial procedures and evidence-gathering methods, which were developed for use in adjudication, are inappropriate to broad judicial review. It also explains why the broadening of standing raises the issue of third-party intervention in judicial review proceedings: without the focus on individuals and their interests, it is difficult to justify limiting participation to the applicant for review. In Mashaw's terms, standing rules not only correlate with the function of judicial review but also affect the criteria for the acceptability of decisions of courts in judicial review proceedings.

In the UK in the course of the past 30 or 40 years standing rules have been broadened to the point where standing is rarely an issue in judicial review proceedings. In the UK it now seems accepted that it is appropriate for courts to engage in non-adjudicatory activities under the banner of judicial review. By contrast, in the US and Australia standing rules have not been equally relaxed and there is still debate about whether judicial review should be understood primarily as a mode of adjudication or whether it should be available as a forum for political contestation.

What are the implications of this analysis for merits review?[74] Under section 27 of the AAT Act, an application for review of a decision may be made by or on behalf of any person whose interests are affected by the decision. The term 'person' includes a Commonwealth agency. The phrase 'a person whose interests are affected by the decision' includes a corporation or an unincorporated association, provided the decision relates to a matter included in its objects or purposes, unless the association was formed, or the relevant matter was included in its object or purposes, only after the decision was made. The term 'interests' is understood broadly; but it is not enough for a person to have an interest in a decision – the interest must be affected by the decision.[75] However, if the effect is too slight or indirect, the person affected may lack standing. Concerning participation by parties other than the applicant, section 30 of the AAT Act[76] provides that the person who made the decision under review is a party to the proceedings in the AAT.[77] In addition, the Attorney-General may intervene (as a party) on behalf of the Commonwealth in any application before the AAT. Any other 'person whose interests are affected' may, with the consent of the AAT, become a party either to support[78] or oppose the decision under review. This last provision makes no express mention of unincorporated associations; but a member of such an association could be given consent to become a party on behalf of (all the members of) the association.[79]

On their face, these provisions seem to establish a regime of standing-cum-intervention rules lying at the broad rather than narrow end of the spectrum. However, the AAT Act was drafted against a background of a common law regime of narrow standing for judicial review, and the Federal Court has held that the basic, relatively narrow rule of standing established by the High Court of Australia in a case decided not long after the AAT Act was drafted[80] – namely that

---

[74] On standing in the AAT generally see D Pearce, *Administrative Appeals Tribunal*, 2nd edn (Australia, LexisNexis Butterworths, 2007) ch 4; and on intervention see ibid 64–71.

[75] *Re Gay Solidarity Group and Minister for Immigration and Ethnic Affairs* (1983) 5 ALD 289; *Re Rudd and Minister for Transport and Regional Services* (2001) 65 ALD 296.

[76] Which does not apply to proceedings in the Security Appeals Division of the AAT. Concerning standing for security appeals see AAT Act s 27AA.

[77] This contrasts with the position in the first-tier immigration tribunals in which the decision-maker is not a party.

[78] *Re Sew Eurodrive Pty Ltd and Collector of Customs* (1994) 35 ALD 790.

[79] *Arnold (on behalf of Australians for Animals) v State of Queensland* (1987) 13 ALD 195.

[80] *Australian Conservation Foundation Inc v Commonwealth* (1980) 146 CLR 493.

the applicant for judicial review must have a 'special interest' in the matter to which the application relates – applies equally to applications to the AAT for merits review.[81] On the other hand, the High Court has said that whether a person is affected by a decision made under a statutory provision has to be determined by reference to the statute, not by reference to common law concepts of standing.[82] It follows that whether a person is affected by a decision for the purposes of section 27 of the AAT Act has to be determined not by reference to the provisions of the AAT Act but by reference to the provisions of the statute under which the decision was made and which confers jurisdiction on the AAT. A person may in some sense be 'affected' by a decision but not have standing to apply to the AAT for merits review because the statute under which the decision was made is interpreted as not granting the right to apply for review.[83]

Views about the function of merits review will be relevant to this process of statutory interpretation. An understanding of merits review as a mode of adjudication would favour interpretations that define the class of affected persons relatively narrowly since such an approach would help to preserve the adjudicatory character of merits review. Interpretations that defined the class of affected persons broadly could be understood as contemplating a non-adjudicatory role for merits review. Because merits review is a statutory creation and merits review jurisdiction is conferred by reference to specific classes of decisions, the legislature can limit the role of merits review to adjudication in two ways: first, by making no provision for merits review of decisions that are unlikely to have a direct effect on particular individuals; and secondly, by drafting statutes containing provisions for merits review in such a way as to require or encourage interpretations that define the class of affected persons narrowly. By contrast, because judicial review is essentially a judicial creation and its scope is defined in abstract terms (such as 'decisions of an administrative nature made under an enactment' or decisions made by 'officers of the Commonwealth') it is less easy for legislatures to exclude its availability in relation to decisions that are unlikely to have a direct effect on particular individuals.

Concerning intervention by persons other than the applicant, the AAT Act provides for participation in merits review proceedings only by being made a party; and in general, only a 'person affected' may be made a party. There is no provision for individuals or groups to participate as 'friends of the tribunal' in the way that an individual or group may be allowed to participate in judicial review proceedings as an *amicus curiae*. In theory, the phrase 'person affected' is understood in the same way in this context as in the standing context.[84] However,

---

[81] *Allan v Development Allowance Authority* (1998) 51 ALD 208.

[82] *Allan v Transurban City Link Ltd* (2001) 208 CLR 167 (on appeal from *Allan v Development Allowance Authority*, previous note).

[83] eg *Brisbane Airport Corporation Ltd v Deputy President Wright (as a Presidential Member of the Administrative Appeals Tribunal)* (2002) 77 ALD 411.

[84] *Re C and Collector of Customs (NSW)* (1983) 5 ALN N222.

it is hard to say whether, in practice, the person-affected test has been applied more or less generously to persons seeking to become parties as compared with persons seeking to make an application for review. There are good practical reasons for limiting intervention rights: the more parties to an application, the more time-consuming and expensive the proceedings are likely to become for everyone involved and the more wide-ranging the issues raised.[85] However, in theory at least, such factors can be taken into account in the exercise of the Tribunal's discretion whether or not to grant an application to be made a party[86] rather than in determining whether a person is affected by the decision.

Like standing rules, intervention rules both reflect and play a part in defining the nature and function of merits review. In 5.3.2.2 (ii) we saw that in theory, the AAT has power to participate in the policy-making process by acting inconsistently with existing government policy and by making new policy. This might suggest that the AAT's functions are not limited to the adjudicatory task of protecting individual interests but extend to a concern with the general norms according to which individual decisions are made. Broad standing and intervention rules would be consistent with such an understanding of the AAT's role as an active participant in the policy-making process. The range of interests appropriately represented in that process is much wider than that appropriately represented in adjudication of disputes about the implementation of norms in individual cases. However, we have also seen that in practice, the AAT is very wary of questioning government policy. The relatively narrow regime of standing and intervention rules contained in the AAT Act is consistent with this latter approach, as would be a restrictive approach to the interpretation and application of the 'person affected' criterion of access. On the whole, an understanding of the nature and functions of merits review in terms of adjudication and the protection of individual interests seems consistent with both the terms of the AAT Act and the concept of merits review as developed and expounded in the case law of the AAT and the Federal Court.

In Australian law judicial review, like merits review, is understood in essentially adjudicatory terms. In English law, by contrast, standing and intervention rules are broader and judicial review is understood to extend to consideration of social interests as well as individual interests. Is there any reason to expect the width of access to tribunal review and judicial review respectively to be similar, as in Australia, or are there reasons why the basic access rules for the two modes of review might differ? This question is unlikely to present itself except in a system, such as the Australian, where a general concept of merits review exists alongside the general concept of judicial review. That is not the case in England, and it remains to be seen whether a distinct general jurisprudence of tribunal review

---

[85] See eg, *Re Control Investment Pty Ltd and Australian Broadcasting Tribunal (No 1)* (1980) 3 ALD 74, 80–81.

[86] See generally D Pearce, *Administrative Appeals Tribunal*, 2nd edn (Australia, LexisNexis Butterworths, 2007) 65–67.

will develop in the wake of the creation of the First-tier and Upper Tribunals. If it does, should we expect the rules governing access to tribunal review to be similar to those governing access to judicial review? The answer to this question may depend on the path of development of the role of tribunals in reviewing government policy. We might speculate that the more active that role, the more likely it is that access to tribunals will be governed by a regime of broad standing and intervention rules. If tribunal review is understood in essentially adjudicative terms, it is likely that access to tribunal review will be relatively narrow even if access to judicial review is broad.

6.5 Processes

Of the various traditionally touted and celebrated advantages of tribunals over courts, amongst the most tangible, and most immediately important to and observable by tribunal users are procedural informality and flexibility.[87] The benchmark of formality is, perhaps, the criminal trial, and the ideal of informality contemplates greater or lesser modification of or departure from various of its elements. Flexibility can be understood as an element of informality – an ability and willingness to modify or waive particular procedures when this seems appropriate or desirable in individual cases. Flexibility may also refer to ways of processing cases that are alternative to the tribunal's paradigm mode of proceeding. So, for instance, if the paradigm mode is the oral hearing, 'decision on the papers' or 'pre-hearing settlement' may provide alternatives. Tribunals may vary both in terms of their paradigm mode of proceeding and in terms of any alternatives they provide.

Debates about procedural (in)formality and flexibility assume a theory about the function(s) of decision-making procedures. Traditionally, procedures are said to promote both instrumental and non-instrumental values. Non-instrumentally, the role of procedure is understood in terms 'fairness', and respect for the 'dignity' and 'autonomy' of parties to the decision. The essence of procedural fairness (or 'due process')[88] is said to be embodied in the so-called 'rule against bias' (which promotes the value of impartiality in decision-making) and the 'fair hearing rule' (which requires disclosure to parties of information relevant to making the decision and an opportunity to 'put their case').[89] In short, the concept of procedural fairness is based on the values of impartiality and participation.

---

[87] There is a contrary view that procedural informality produces a form of inferior justice: H Genn, 'Tribunals and Informal Justice' (1993) 56 *Modern Law Review* 393, 397.

[88] Whether grounded in a constitution – as in the US and, perhaps, in Australia (F Wheeler, 'Due Process, Judicial Power and Chapter III in the New High Court' (2004) 32 *Federal Law Review* 206) – or in the common law.

[89] See AAT Act s 39.

Although the requirements of procedural fairness are sensitive to context ('flexible'),[90] they establish a minimum, irreducible set of obligations for all decision-makers including tribunals. From an instrumental perspective, procedure is related to the purpose of the decision-making process. For instance, the difference between the so-called 'inquisitorial' and 'adversarial' modes of decision-making is sometimes said to be that the goal of the former but not of the latter is to discover the 'real truth'.[91]

Instrumentally, the role of procedure is to promote decision-making that complies with the relevant substantive criteria for making decisions of the relevant type. The instrumental approach raises the issue – amongst others – of the relevance to procedure of the distinction between merits review and judicial review, explored in Chapter 5. In particular, what are the procedural implications of the objective of producing the 'correct or preferable decision' as opposed to that of assessing the 'legality' of the decision under review? The instrumental goal of procedure may be expressed in terms of 'accuracy' of decisions, 'accuracy' being understood in terms of proper application of relevant decision-making criteria (such as 'correct or preferable').[92]

In summary, we might say that the ideal procedure promotes impartiality, participation and accuracy. In Australia (as we have seen) these due process values are explicitly set in tension with 'managerial' values by a statutory formula that requires merits review tribunals to 'pursue the objective of providing a mechanism of review that is fair, just, economical, informal and quick'.[93] As the order of the words in this statement implies, informality is associated with economy and speed. However, whether or not this association is justified depends

---

[90] And so, for instance, can accommodate various models of the role of the adjudicator: see n 108 below.

[91] J Thibaut and L Walker, 'A Theory of Procedure' (1978) 66 *California Law Review* 541 argue that a procedure that gives the parties a high degree of control is suited to resolving 'conflicts of interest' and a procedure that gives a third party a high degree of control is suited to resolving 'cognitive conflicts'. This approach may help to explain why procedure of the latter type is strongly associated with judicial decision-making in civil law systems whereas procedure of the former type is strongly associated with judicial decision-making in common law systems. In civil law systems the role of courts is traditionally understood primarily in terms of applying a legal code to individual cases. So understood, the prime function of the court is to ascertain the facts of the case – in the terms used by Thibaut and Walker, to resolve cognitive conflicts. By contrast, in common law systems, courts are understood not only as law appliers but as law-makers. In the terms used by Thibaut and Walker, disputes relevant to what the law is (or should be) are conflicts of interest, not cognitive conflicts.

[92] 'Accuracy' is, however, a deeply problematic concept because the criteria of accuracy are abstract, requiring the exercise of judgment in their application to individual cases (see JL Mashaw, 'The Management Side of Due Process: Some Theoretical and Litigation Notes on the Assurance of Accuracy, Fairness and Timeliness in the Adjudication of Social Welfare Claims' (1973–74) 59 *Cornell Law Review* 772, 791–804). Ultimately, the test of accuracy will be authority: the correct or preferable decision is that which the decision-maker with the final say considers correct or preferable.

[93] eg AAT Act s 2A. On the relationship between (in)formality and accuracy see H Genn, 'Tribunals and Informal Justice' (1993) 56 *Modern Law Review* 393; H Genn, 'Tribunal Review of Administrative Decision-Making' in G Richardson and H Genn (eds), *Administrative Law and Government Action* (Oxford, Clarendon Press, 1994) 272–80.

on the meaning of 'informality'. For instance (as we will see later), tribunals may have powers that enable them to collect evidence independently of the parties, and such powers are sometimes understood as an aspect of 'informality' because they represent a departure from traditional court procedure. Informality in this sense may increase the length and total cost of proceedings relative to what they would be if the tribunal did not seek, by its own independent activities, to supplement the evidence provided by the parties.

In practice, the balance between due process and managerialism may vary from one tribunal to another. For instance, there is reason to believe that the AAT gives relatively less weight to managerial considerations in its *modus operandi* than do the specialist immigration tribunals. At all events, the High Court of Australia has said that the statutory formula is 'intended to be facultative, not restrictive', its purpose being to 'free tribunals, at least to some degree, from constraints otherwise applicable to courts, and regarded as inappropriate to tribunals'.[94] This interpretation makes it clear that even though merits review tribunals are not courts, they operate within a curial paradigm that limits their capacity to trade fairness and justice off against economy and speed.[95] In practice, the obligation to promote the managerial objectives has little more than rhetorical force in the absence of any meaningful attempt to compare the relative performance of tribunals with courts in relevant respects and to establish, monitor and enforce performance targets for tribunals. In this regard, the AAT is effectively a self-regulator, whereas the specialist immigration tribunals are subject to some departmental control; but meaningful measurement, of the relative performance of courts and tribunals on the one hand and of the AAT and specialist tribunals on the other, is lacking.

As a result debates about tribunal procedure tend to focus on the relationship between the three due process values on the one hand and (in)formality and flexibility on the other and largely to ignore the factors of speed and cost.[96] Because all of these concepts are vague and highly abstract, such debates are typically inconclusive. However, underlying them all are certain assumptions: first, that traditional court procedures are relatively formal and inflexible; secondly, that compared with courts, tribunals should follow procedures that are relatively informal and flexible; thirdly, that if certain conditions are satisfied, relatively informal and flexible procedures can promote impartiality, participation and accuracy at least as well as relatively formal and inflexible procedures, but can do so with greater speed and at less cost.

---

[94] *Minister for Immigration and Multicultural Affairs v Eshetu* (1999) 197 CLR 611, 628.

[95] See also AAT Act s 33 (1)(b): 'the proceeding shall be conducted with as little formality and technicality, and with as much expedition, as the requirements of this Act and of every other relevant enactment and a proper consideration of the matters before the Tribunal permit'.

[96] For instance, Genn, n 93 above, explores the relationship between (in)formality and accuracy ('justice').

None of these assumptions has been rigorously tested and none is self-evidently justified. Therefore, in the discussion that follows an attempt will be made to avoid vague abstractions and to think about tribunal processes more concretely first in relation to paradigm modes of decision-making and then in relation to alternatives.

6.5.1 The Paradigm Mode of Decision-Making

Perhaps the most that can be said in general about the paradigm mode of decision-making by tribunals is that it involves an official or a group of officials, on the application of a citizen (individual, group or corporation) affected in a certain way by a 'primary' decision, making a ('review') decision to affirm or vary the primary decision or to set it aside and either make a substitute decision or remit it to the primary decision-maker for reconsideration. In other words, non-judicial administrative adjudication is a tripartite process. Procedural norms regulate and specify the roles played in that process by the reviewer, the original decision-maker and the applicant. Although the roles of each of these participants are inter-related and cannot be understood in isolation from one another, for analytical purposes it will be useful to consider them in turn.

The fact that so little can be said in general about the process of administrative adjudication is reflected in debates about the desirability of 'general' codes of procedure. In one sense, of course, the rules of procedural fairness (no bias, fair hearing) constitute such a general code; but the debates we are concerned with focus on statutory and quasi-statutory regulation of procedure. They typically rest on an assumption that the paradigm tribunal has limited, subject-specific jurisdiction. The basic question is to what extent procedures should be tribunal-specific or, on the contrary, common to all, or a group of subject-specific, tribunals. There is a common opinion that general regulation of procedure should be light, leaving as many details as possible for local variation as between tribunals and even as between individual cases. The justification for this opinion is found in the diversity of subject matter dealt with by various tribunals (ranging, for instance, from social security benefits for the disabled to corporate taxation) and the diversity of applicants (ranging, for instance, from poor, ill-educated immigrants to multi-national businesses).[97] By contrast, the US APA establishes a quite detailed procedural code for administrative

---

[97] See eg, JA Farmer, 'A Model Code of Procedure for Administrative Tribunals – An Illusory Concept' (1970) 4 *New Zealand Universities Law Review* 105; M Taggart, 'The Rationalisation of Administrative Tribunals Procedure: The New Zealand Experience' in R Creyke (ed), *Administrative Tribunals: Taking Stock* (Canberra, Australian Institute of Administrative Law, 1992); M Allars, 'A General Tribunal Procedure Statute for New South Wales?' (1993) 4 *Public Law Review*, 19; Administrative Review Council Report No 39, *Better Decisions: Review of Commonwealth Merits Review Tribunals* (Canberra, Australian Government Publishing Service, 1995) 3.12–46.

adjudication that involves a hearing 'on the record'.[98] Such hearings represent a tiny proportion of adjudications (as contrasted with rule-making),[99] and a proposal to extend the code to cover all 'hearings' elicited fears of 'ossification' of adjudication.[100] In practice, the APA provisions are applied in some contexts where there is no requirement of a hearing on the record; but even so, the large majority of adjudications are not subject to the APA. Nevertheless, those to which they do apply cover a wide diversity of subject matter.

The choice between generality and specificity does not present itself in quite the same way in a system that has a general administrative tribunal (even if it also has some specialised tribunals) as in a system which lacks such a tribunal. However, to the extent that a general tribunal operates in subject-specific divisions, similar issues may arise. Although a certain amount of procedural variation as between subject-specific divisions may be thought desirable, it would be odd if the concept of generality did not find expression in a more-than-minimal degree of procedural uniformity across divisions. So, for instance, while the new UK Upper Tribunal will operate under a single set of procedural rules, each of the Chambers of the First-Tier Tribunal will operate under its own set of procedural rules which will, nevertheless, share certain elements with the procedural rules of the other Chambers. The logic of uniformity is perhaps particularly strong where a general tribunal is created by amalgamation of pre-existing disparate subject-specific tribunals.[101] Under the UK TCE Act 2007 a Tribunal Procedure Committee has been created responsible for drafting procedural rules and monitoring their operation. The aim is to create a procedural code analogous to the Civil Procedure Rules that regulate the procedure of the High Court and the county courts.

From the perspective of applicants, procedural specificity holds out the promise that any particular application will be dealt with in a way appropriate to its subject matter and the applicant's circumstances and resources. Since most applicants are single-shot, not repeat, players, and since government participation in tribunal proceedings is typically organised in a subject-specific way, it may be said that the advantages of specificity are likely to outweigh those of generality. On the other hand, it is sometimes suggested that procedural variety is confusing

---

[98] See generally M Asimow (ed), *A Guide to Federal Agency Adjudication* (Chicago, American Bar Association, 2003).

[99] On this distinction see 3.2.

[100] GJ Edles, 'An APA-Default Presumption for Administrative Hearings: Some Thoughts on "Ossifying" the Adjudication Process' (2003) 55 *Administrative Law Review* 787. In support of limited extension see M Asimow, 'The Spreading Umbrella: Extending the APA's Adjudication Provisions to All Evidentiary Hearings Required by Statute' (2004) 56 *Administrative LR* 1003. A 'hearing' in the relevant sense is a proceeding in which the decision-maker is limited to considering only evidence contained in the formal 'record'. Constitutional 'due process' may not require a hearing in this sense. On the requirements of due process see Asimow (ed), *Guide to Federal Agency Adjudication* ch 2.

[101] R Bacon, 'A Study in Tribunal Amalgamation: The Importance of a Principled Approach' (2005) 12 *Journal of Social Security Law* 81.

and makes tribunals more intimidating and less accessible. The relative force of such competing arguments is hard to assess.

Debates about tribunal procedure are often conducted within the framework of a distinction between 'inquisitorial' and 'adversarial' procedures. However, it is better to avoid these terms because they are imprecise and lack agreed meanings. Instead, I will discuss, in turn, the role played in tribunal processes by the reviewer, the applicant and the respondent (being, or representing, the primary decision-maker).

6.5.1.1 The Reviewer

At the end of the process, the reviewer's job is to make a decision.[102] As we saw in Chapter 5, the performance of this task is regulated in various ways. For instance, the rule against bias effectively regulates who may properly act as a reviewer;[103] the decision-maker must not take account of irrelevant considerations and must make a decision that is consistent with applicable legal rules. The making of the decision may be regulated in other ways, too. For instance, the decision may have to be in writing,[104] and the decision-maker may have to give (written) reasons for the decision.[105]

What is the role of the reviewer in the process leading to the making of the decision? To some extent, this is a function of the personal interaction between the reviewer and the applicant. What does the reviewer wear? Where does the reviewer sit relative to the applicant? What steps, if any, does the reviewer take to make the applicant feel comfortable and help the applicant understand and follow what is going on? Such matters of 'style' or 'atmosphere' are typically not regulated by specific procedural rules, although the principles of procedural fairness may impose limitations on how 'relaxed' an approach can be taken. They are one aspect of '(in)formality', and it is commonly said both that informality (which is, of course, a matter of degree) is more appropriate and desirable in tribunals than in courts and that it is more appropriate and desirable in some decision-making contexts (such as social security) than in others (such as corporate taxation). There is some tension between these two statements because courts may make decisions in some contexts where informality might seem appropriate and desirable, and tribunals may make decisions in areas where formality might seem appropriate and desirable. Nevertheless, in each of our comparator jurisdictions there seems to be a persistent tendency to divide

---

[102] Of course, the reviewer may also make decisions at earlier points in the process either about some aspect of the claim or about procedure.

[103] eg in *Gillies (AP) v Secretary of State for Work and Pensions (Scotland)* [2006] 1 WLR 781 the House of Lords held that it was permissible for a doctor who provided 'independent' medical reports to primary decision-makers to sit as a part-time member of a tribunal that reviewed primary decisions based on such reports (made by other doctors).

[104] eg Administrative Appeals Tribunal Act ('AAT Act'), s 43(1).

[105] eg AAT Act s 43(2). For an interesting discussion see D Dyzenhaus and M Taggart, 'Reasoned Decisions and Legal Theory' in DE Edlin (ed), *Common Law Theory* (Cambridge, CUP, 2007).

adjudicatory institutions into two categories – the relatively formal and the relatively informal; to keep the relatively formal category significantly smaller than the relatively informal; and to make the relatively informal category the primary forum for administrative adjudication while the relatively formal category provides the primary forum for non-administrative adjudication.[106]

The law has more to say about the role of the reviewer in the collection and presentation of evidence.[107] Here it is useful to distinguish between two different (stylised) models of the reviewer's role – the 'active' and the 'passive'.[108] In the passive model the reviewer plays no part in the collection of evidence. In the presentation of evidence the passive reviewer plays a management role (keeping order, for instance, and regulating the admission of evidence), but does not participate as a presenter. In the active model, by contrast, the reviewer may manage collection of evidence by the parties particularly in order to prevent wastage of time and resources. The active reviewer may go further and participate in collection by requiring parties to gather specified evidence or evidence on specified matters, or even by gathering evidence personally. In the presentation of evidence, the active reviewer may go beyond managing the presentation of evidence to assisting (or 'enabling') the parties (especially the applicant) to present evidence, or – especially where the evidence is presented in writing rather than orally – to marshalling evidence provided by the parties and – in the US terminology – 'developing the record'.

Dealing first with collection of evidence, it should be noted at the outset that rules determining the nature of the material on which the decision should be based – notably rules of evidence – are independent of the distinction between active and passive reviewing, which concerns the source of the material, not its nature. So, for instance, the common principle that tribunals are not 'bound' by the rules of evidence[109] applies regardless of whether and to what extent the

---

[106] This is not to say, of course, that bodies in the relatively informal category may not play a significant role in non-administrative adjudication. Employment tribunals in England and 'super tribunals' in the Australian states (that engage in both administrative and non-administrative adjudication) provide obvious examples.

[107] The distinction between collection and presentation is drawn for analytical convenience only.

[108] For a careful analysis of the relationship between 'procedural fairness' and passivity ('non-intervention') see M Allars, 'Neutrality, the Judicial Paradigm and Tribunal Procedure' (1991) 13 *Sydney Law Review* 377.

[109] eg AAT Act s 33(1)(c). The meaning of the phrase 'rules of evidence' in this principle is unclear: N Rees, 'Procedure and Evidence in "Court Substitute" Tribunals' (2006) 28 *Australian Bar Review* 41, 69–83. The principle restates the common law: J Fitzgerald, 'The Commonwealth Administrative Appeals Tribunal: Aspects of the System of Fact-Finding and Rules of Evidence' (1996) 79 *Canberra Bulletin of Public Administration* 127, 127–28. See also P Rowe, 'The Strict Rules of Evidence in Tribunals: Rhetoric Versus Reality' (1994) 1 *Journal of Social Security Law* 9. One explanation for at least some of the rules of evidence by which tribunals are not bound is that they were designed to regulate jury trials. Administrative tribunals are more analogous to civil courts than to criminal courts, and this explanation still has some force in the US where civil juries are still common (Asimow (ed), *Guide to Federal Agency Procedure*, 71; ME Mullins, 'Manual for Administrative Law Judges' (2004) 23 *Journal of the National Association of Administrative Law Judges* 1, 85). The widespread demise of civil juries in Australia and England by the mid-20th century perhaps explains

tribunal operates according to the active model or the passive model respectively. It is often said that the *purpose* of this principle is to render tribunal proceedings less 'formal' and 'flexible'. However, the standard understanding of the *effect* of the rule is that the tribunal may and should take account of and assign appropriate weight to all relevant evidence.[110] From this perspective, the rule can be explained as a corollary of the idea – made most explicit in the Australian concept of merits review – that the function of non-judicial administrative adjudication is to ensure that the 'correct or preferable decision' is made, not to identify errors in the primary decision(-making process). This also explains why the concept of onus of proof plays only a modified role[111] in relation to non-judicial administrative adjudication: the prime function of the reviewer is not to choose between the arguments of a proponent and an opponent of a decision but rather to decide what the correct or preferable decision would be.[112] This formulation leaves open the question of whether and to what extent the reviewer's decision ought to be made on the basis of the material provided by the parties or, by contrast, on the basis of material collected by the reviewer.[113]

---

why relieving tribunals of the obligation to follow rules of evidence is understood in terms of promoting informality rather than in terms of the difference between the typical juror and the typical tribunal member.

[110] eg *Rodriguez v Telstra Corporation Ltd* (2002) 66 ALD 579, [25]. Note, however, that certain exclusionary 'privileges', such as legal professional privilege and the privilege against self-incrimination, may continue to be available unless expressly excluded by the legislature: D Pearce, *Administrative Appeals Tribunal*, 2nd edn (Australia, LexisNexis Butterworths, 2007) 7.14–7.17. In *Valantine v Technical and Further Education Commission* (2007) 97 ALD 447 the New South Wales Court of Appeal justified the continued application of the privileges on the basis that the tribunal in question followed 'many of the procedures applicable to court hearings' ([37]) and acted in a 'quasi-judicial' way ([91]). The same can be said of the AAT: *Re Farnaby and Military Rehabilitation and Compensation Commission* (2007) 97 ALD 788. Regarding the US see Asimow (ed), *Guide to Federal Agency Adjudication*, 75.

[111] But a role, nevertheless: see generally *Minister for Immigration and Ethnic Affairs* (1980) 4 ALD 139; *McDonald v Director General of Social Security* (1984) 6 ALD 6. In a two-party situation where an official has to make a decision in implementation of a rule in an individual case after collecting evidence, the only question concerns the weight of various pieces of relevant evidence that have been collected. By contrast, in a three-party adjudication where the reviewer is presented with evidence from two independent sources, the concept of weight may not be enough to resolve all factual issues. A tie-breaker rule may also be needed. This is so whether or not the two information sources are understood to be in competition with one another. Even if the function of the reviewer is not to 'resolve a dispute', reviews are triggered by disputes and both the applicant and the respondent are entitled to present evidence independently of each other. See also D Pearce, *Administrative Appeals Tribunal*, 2nd edn (Australia, LexisNexis Butterworths, 2007) 7.40. The concept of onus of proof cannot be used to resolve issues on which evidence could be presented: Social Security and Child Support Commissioners Case R(IS) 17/04.

[112] D Pearce, *Administrative Appeals Tribunal*, 2nd edn (Australia, LexisNexis Butterworths, 2007) 7.37–7.41; *Kerr v Department for Social Development* [2004] 1 WLR 1372. However, the APA contains burden of proof rules (Asimow (ed), *Guide to Federal Agency Adjudication*, 67–70), reflecting the court-like model of procedure it embodies.

[113] Just as it leaves open the question of whether the reviewer's decision ought to be based only on the material available to the primary decision-maker or, by contrast, on material available to the tribunal. In other words, the concept of the 'correct or preferable decision' must be understood as being relative to a body of material the content of which that formula does not specify.

Tribunals are often – perhaps typically – given powers that allow them to play a more-or-less active role in the collection of evidence.[114] However, tribunals vary in their use of such powers. In Australia, for instance, the RRT obtains relevant 'country information' not only from its portfolio department (the Department of Immigration and Citizenship) but also through its own research staff.[115] On the whole, however, it seems that Australian merits review tribunals rarely obtain information other than from or through the applicant and the decision-maker. This may seem surprising because such powers may be explained as corollaries of the obligation of merits review tribunals to make the 'correct or preferable decision'.[116] On the other hand, tribunals that operate within a system, like the Australian, in which the default position for adjudicators is one of passivity, and in which active judging is understood primarily in terms of case-management and as a way of reducing delay and expense rather than as an intrinsic feature of the adjudicative process,[117] are unlikely to be willing, or to have the resources necessary, to call witnesses that the parties have not called or to collect documents that the parties have not produced.[118] In such an environment, the most that tribunals are likely to do is to invite, encourage or, perhaps, require, parties to provide additional evidence.[119]

---

[114] A useful survey of the procedures of major merits review tribunals in Australia is N Bedford and R Creyke, *Inquisitorial Processes in Australian Tribunals* (Melbourne, Australian Institute of Judicial Administration, 2006). For the US see ME Mullins, 'Manual for Administrative Law Judges' (2004) 23 *Journal of the National Association of Administrative Law Judges*, n 108 above, 6–7, 84. It is generally accepted that tribunal members should be freer than judges to draw on their own personal knowledge and experience and to 'take notice' of information not presented by the parties: JA Smillie, 'The Problem of "Official Notice": Reliance by Administrative Tribunals on the Personal Knowledge of Their Members' [1975] *Public Law* 64; H Katzen, 'Procedural Fairness and Specialist Members of the Administrative Appeals Tribunal' (1995) 2 *Australian Journal of Administrative Law* 169. Here it is useful to distinguish between legal and non-legal knowledge. Concerning legal knowledge, because the paradigm court is a generalist body, judges traditionally rely on the parties to provide legal information specific to their case. A suggested advantage of jurisdictional specialisation is that tribunal members will acquire greater knowledge of the relevant law and so need to rely less on the parties. This is said to reduce the need for (legal) representation and may be used to support or justify prohibition of (legal) representation: *Gillies (AP) v Secretary of State for Work and Pensions Scotland* [2006] 1 WLR 781, [36] (Baroness Hale of Richmond). Concerning non-legal knowledge, it makes obvious sense that members who are appointed to tribunals precisely on account of their non-legal expertise should be able to use it in the decision-making process. The difficult issue concerns the extent to which such knowledge should be contestable by the parties.

[115] Factual information obtained from third parties must be disclosed and the parties given an opportunity to make submissions about it: *Carlos v Minister for Immigration and Multicultural Affairs* (2001) 183 ALR 719.

[116] eg Allars, n 108 above, 407–10.

[117] As it is in France, where the institutional structure of the system for administrative adjudication is quite different from that in Australia, England or the US: G Osborne, 'Inquisitorial Procedure in the Administrative Appeals Tribunal – A Comparative Perspective' (1982–83) 13 *Federal Law Review* 150.

[118] J Dwyer, 'Overcoming the Adversarial Bias in Tribunal Procedures' (1991) 20 *Federal Law Review* 252; 'Fair Play the Inquisitorial Way: A Review of the Administrative Appeals Tribunal's Use of Inquisitorial Procedures' (1997) 5 *Australian Journal of Administrative Law* 5.

[119] eg *Re The International Fund for Animal Welfare (Aust) Pty Ltd and Minister for Environment and Heritage (No 2)* (2007) 93 ALD 625.

In a case where the AAT asked the department to conduct further investigation that failed to provide the necessary information, the tribunal was moved to say that its role was not 'to undertake investigative work to support the case of one party appearing before it. The tribunal's role is to make the correct or preferable decision on the material that is before it.'[120] The AAT interpreted the phrase 'the material that is before it' to mean 'the material the parties put before it', and it did not understand its responsibility to make the correct or preferable decision as requiring (or perhaps even authorising) it to collect evidence independently of the parties. As far as I have been able to ascertain, tribunals in the US and the UK are typically no more active in collecting evidence than Australian tribunals.

Turning now to the presentation of evidence, there is a widespread general expectation that tribunals will be more active in this respect than courts, except in cases where both parties are before the tribunal and have a legal or other specialist representative. In Australia, the obligation of a merits review tribunal to select the correct or preferable decision may be thought to provide some justification for such intervention in proceedings. In cases where no oral hearing is held, the reviewer will necessarily have to marshal and organise the evidence.[121] In cases where both the applicant and the primary decision-maker (respondent) appear before the tribunal at an oral hearing, intervention by the reviewer in the presentation of evidence is likely to be one-sided in favour of the applicant. In cases where an oral hearing is held but the primary decision-maker does not appear before the tribunal (as, for instance, in the Australian immigration tribunals and, commonly, in the UK in the areas of social security and immigration) or takes a passive stance,[122] the enabling role may put the reviewer effectively in total control of the proceedings, as appears to happen in the specialist immigration tribunals in Australia. This may promote efficient use of time and resources; but there is a risk that helping one of the parties and not the other, or helping one more than the other, may lead to a breach of the rule against bias by creating an appearance of partiality;[123] and that it may even lead to the making of a partisan decision. However, in *Richardson v Perales*[124] the US

---

[120] *Re Hanrahan and Repatriation Commission* (2008) 102 ALD 399, [22].

[121] The AAT can dispense with an oral hearing if satisfied that the application can be adequately dealt with in the absence of the parties and the parties consent to this course of action: AAT Act s 34J. For a general discussion of when oral hearings may (not) be appropriately dispensed with see G Richardson and H Genn, 'Tribunals in Transition: Resolution of Adjudication' [2007] *Public Law* 116, 125ff. See also Council on Tribunals Consultation Paper, *The Use and Value of Oral Hearings in the Administrative Justice System* (London, 2005), <http://www.council-on-tribunals.gov.uk/publications/619.htm> accessed 1 October 2008.

[122] N Wikeley and R Young, 'Presenting Officers in Social Security Tribunals: The Theory and Practice of the Curious *Amici*' (1991) 18 *Journal of Law and Society* 464.

[123] For instance, there may be a fine line between testing the applicant's evidence (acceptable) and cross-examining the applicant (unacceptable).

[124] (1971) 402 US 389; PR Verkuil, 'Reflections Upon the Federal Administrative Judiciary' (1991–92) 39 *UCLA Law Review* 1341, 1348–49.

Supreme Court held, for essentially pragmatic reasons,[125] that an arrangement in which the reviewer not only made the decision but also helped the applicant at the hearing and 'developed' the case of the absent decision-maker, did not breach statutory or constitutional procedural norms.

Acceptance that institutional arrangements involving a face-to-face meeting between an unrepresented applicant and the reviewer in the absence of the decision-maker are not, as such, procedurally unfair inevitably casts a heavy burden on reviewers to exercise their considerable powers in a fair way in individual cases. The lack of structural constraints built into the review process also puts a high premium on after-the-event review of administrative adjudication by an appellate tribunal or court. In Australia, however, there is no appeal from the specialist immigration tribunals to the AAT, and their decisions are subject to only limited judicial review. In such circumstances, cynics may wonder whether fairness has not been unduly sacrificed to considerations of 'efficiency' and political control of the review process. Suspicion may be fuelled by the relatively close relationship of dependency and control between the immigration tribunals and their portfolio department and the emphasis on managerial values in the tribunals' published literature.[126]

Willingness on the part of the tribunal to take an active part in the presentation of evidence may influence its approach to expert evidence. It has been said that expertise plays a 'particularly important part in matters before the [AAT]' because of its obligation to 'select' the correct or preferable decision.[127] The role of expert evidence in tribunal proceedings may depend to some extent on whether any members of the tribunal have been appointed on account of their expertise in the relevant area. Expertise on the bench may make the calling of expert evidence either wholly or partly unnecessary and in that way effectively transfer some of the cost of collecting and presenting evidence from the parties to the taxpayer. On the other hand, of course, the expertise of a tribunal member cannot be tested by cross-examination and so may not be an acceptable substitute for the testimony of an expert witness. In cases where expert evidence is tendered and admitted, expertise on the bench may improve the ability of the tribunal not only to assess the evidence but also to regulate the presentation of expert evidence and even to question the experts. In selected cases the AAT has arranged for 'concurrent' presentation of expert evidence in so-called 'hot tubs': instead of experts presenting evidence individually, a number of experts are brought together in one session at which areas of agreement and difference can be explored and developed by discussion and questioning between the experts

---

[125] JL Mashaw, 'The Management Side of Due Process: Some Theoretical and Litigation Notes on the Assurance of Accuracy, Fairness and Timeliness in the Adjudication of Social Welfare Claims' (1973–74) 59 *Cornell Law Review* 772, 787–89.

[126] See further 5.4, n 151.

[127] G Downes, 'Expert Witnesses in proceedings in the Administrative Appeals Tribunal' <http://www.aat.gov.au/SpeechesPapersAndResearch/speeches/downes/pdf/ExpertWitnessesMarch2006.pdf>, 2 accessed 14 August 2008.

themselves and at which the various experts can be cross-examined by the parties and questioned by the reviewer(s).[128] In a study of concurrent presentation of expert evidence a significant proportion of members of the AAT expressed the opinion that the practice improved the quality, assessability and presentation of expert evidence. Members also thought that in most cases the practice did not increase hearing length and in a reasonable proportion of cases saved time.[129]

6.5.1.2 The Respondent

The role of the primary decision-maker in the review process depends on the nature of the process and the decision-maker's status within it. The decision-maker will invariably be required to provide the tribunal with some information about the decision. Under the AAT Act (s 37(1AAA)), for instance, the decision-maker is required to lodge:

> (a) a statement setting out the findings on material questions of fact, referring to the evidence or other material on which those findings were based and giving the reasons for the decision; and

> (b) every other document or part of a document that is in the [decision-maker's] possession or under the [decision-maker's] control and is relevant to the review of the decision by the Tribunal.

The AAT has power to require the decision-maker to lodge further statements and documents if it considers those that were originally lodged provide it with inadequate assistance in selecting the correct or preferable decision.

In cases where the decision of the reviewer is made 'on the papers', this may be all the decision-maker is required to do. In cases where there is an oral hearing, the primary decision-maker's role will depend on whether or not they are entitled or required to appear at the hearing. In cases where the decision-maker appears at the hearing, their appropriate role may depend on how the task of the tribunal is understood. If its task is to identify the correct or preferable decision rather than to identify defects on the decision under review, the proper role of the primary decision-maker will be to assist the tribunal to make its decision rather than to support the decision and oppose the application. There is express provision to this effect in the AAT Act (s 33(1AA)). The obligation to assist the tribunal may also be based on a view that this function reflects, at the review level, the nature of the primary decision-making process.[130] However, if the distinction between implementation and adjudication drawn in this book (1.2.2)

---

[128] ibid 10–13. For an assessment of the process see G Edmond, 'Secrets of the "Hot Tub"; Expert Witnesses, Concurrent Evidence and Judge-led Law Reform in Australia' (2008) 27 *Civil Justice Quarterly* 51.

[129] Administrative Appeals Tribunal, *An Evaluation of the Use of Concurrent Evidence in the Administrative Appeals Tribunal* (November 2005): <http://www.aat.gov.au/SpeechesPapersAnd Research/Research/AATConcurrentEvidenceReportNovember2005.pdf> accessed 15 August 2008.

[130] G Downes, 'Government Agencies as Respondents in the Administrative Appeals Tribunal'. <http://www.aat.gov.au/SpeechesPapersAndResearch/speeches/downes/ GovernmentAgenciesJune2005.pdf>, 7 (accessed 8 Sept 2008).

is valid, this view seems doubtful. According to that distinction, whereas the role of the primary decision-maker in the implementation process in relation to conflicts between social and individual interests is to favour the former, the role of the tribunal in the review process is to favour the latter. In that light, the role of the decision-maker in the review process would be to explain and clarify the decision and its factual and legal basis. Because reviewing decisions is a different activity from making them in the first place, the role of the primary decision-maker in the review process must necessarily be different from their role in making the decision.

There is a view that tribunals can play a significant role in improving the standards of primary decision-making (the 'normative' function: 5.5) only if primary decision-makers appear or are represented before them when their decisions are being reviewed.[131] If this view is correct, it provides another reason for not relying too heavily on review as a mechanism for improving decision-making standards and paying much more attention to matters such as the training and supervision of primary decision-makers – what Mashaw calls 'the management side of due process'.[132]

6.5.1.3 The Applicant

If the decision-maker's role in the review process is to assist the reviewer, what is the applicant's? This question has been surprisingly little discussed. Once again, the answer may depend on how the role of the tribunal is understood. For instance, in appeals to the UK Asylum and Immigration Tribunal the appellant normally bears a burden of proof and is thereby cast in the role undermining the decision under appeal. On the one hand, it might seem to follow from the 'correct or preferable' formula that it would be no more the job of the applicant positively to oppose the decision under review than of the respondent to support it. On the other hand, since the applicant seeks from the reviewer is not the making of a primary decision in his favour but the variation or setting aside of a decision that has already been made, the applicant will have to give the reviewer some good reason to do the latter. Although it is the job of the reviewer to identify the correct or preferable decision rather than to decide whether the primary decision is or is not correct or preferable, the reviewer will have no reason or occasion to vary or set aside the primary decision unless it is, in some respect, not the correct or preferable one. At the start of the primary decision-making process there will be a more-or-less open choice between a decision either for or against the applicant. Indeed, procedural fairness requires the primary decision-maker to come to the process with an open mind. At the review stage, by contrast, the

---

[131] eg *Report by the President of Appeal Tribunals on the Standards of Decision-Making by the Secretary of State 2007–08* (UK Tribunals Service, 2008) 1.9–1.10. See also N Wikeley and R Young, 'The Administration of Benefits in Britain: Adjudication Officers and the Influence of Social Security Appeal Tribunals' [1992] *Public Law* 238.

[132] See n 124 above.

decision against the applicant will have, as it were, the advantage of the incumbent. Therefore, it is tactically necessary and so must be legally appropriate for the applicant to argue against that decision as strongly as possible.

Commonly, the best way of doing this will be either to propose a different view of the evidence than that taken by the primary decision-maker or to provide new evidence that was not available to the primary decision-maker. In some cases, the applicant may be able to argue that the decision was unlawful, or that it was arrived at by an improper process of reasoning. At all events, even if the tribunal's job is to identify the correct or preferable decision, the applicant's first task must be to convince the reviewer that the decision under review is not the correct or preferable one and should not be affirmed. This helps to explain why the main question addressed in discussion and analysis of the relationship between the applicant and the merits reviewer is not whether the former should assist the latter but whether and when the latter should assist the former. Having convinced the tribunal that the decision under review should not be affirmed, the applicant might then need to do more to 'assist' the tribunal to select the correct or preferable decision.[133]

6.5.2 Alternatives to the Paradigm Mode

In this section we are concerned with alternative methods of processing applications for review that are available within the institutional framework in which the paradigm mode operates – 'tribunal-annexed' alternatives, we might say. In Chapter 7 we will explore alternatives to tribunals for reviewing decisions and resolving disputes and complaints.

The first point to make is terminological: this topic is often discussed in terms of alternative 'dispute resolution', thus implying that the function of the paradigm procedural mode is to resolve disputes. To the extent that administrative tribunals are understood to perform an essentially similar function to that performed by courts, this may be the best way to frame the issue. By contrast, if the role of the tribunal is understood to be that of reviewing decisions rather than resolving disputes,[134] the better way of approaching this topic may not be in terms of alternative ways of dealing with the disagreement between the parties but in terms of alternative methods by which the tribunal can perform its function; and this is the way the matter is framed in the AAT Act. Once an application for review has been made, the AAT alone can bring the proceedings

---

[133] eg by providing 'evidence of a more positive nature to support the conclusion for which a party contends as being the correct conclusion': *Re Hanlon and Commissioner for Superannuation* (1979) 2 ALN N657.

[134] See eg, *VEAL v Minister for Immigration and Multicultural and Indigenous Affairs* (2005) 225 CLR 88, [26].

to an end.[135] For instance, if the applicant notifies the AAT in writing that the application is discontinued or withdrawn, 'the Tribunal is taken to have dismissed the application without proceeding to review the decision'.[136] If the parties reach agreement 'the Tribunal may, without holding a hearing of the proceedings, make a decision in accordance with' that agreement 'if it appears to it to be appropriate to do so' and provided 'the Tribunal is satisfied that a decision in the terms of the agreement or consistent with those terms would be within the powers of the Tribunal'.[137] The ultimate aim of the review process is to bring it about that the correct or preferable decision is made. The paradigm method for achieving this aim is a hearing by the tribunal, and alternatives to a hearing are (in principle, at least) alternative methods of achieving that aim.

Nevertheless, the AAT Act itself uses the terminology of 'alternative dispute resolution'. Moreover, the meaning of the phrase 'within the powers of the Tribunal' is unclear. It has been said that any decision giving effect to an agreement must be lawful and proper.[138] Further guidance may be found in cases concerning acceptance by the AAT of agreements between parties and concessions made in the course of hearings. In that context it has been held that the parties cannot by agreement give the AAT jurisdiction it is not given by statute,[139] and the AAT takes a cautious attitude towards agreements and concessions about issues of fact and, particularly, issues of law.[140] It has been suggested that the AAT might refuse to give effect to an agreement 'if it were thought that one party was being overborne by the other and was being induced to agree to an unreasonable or inappropriate decision'.[141] On the other hand, there would be no meaningful role for agreement as a way of terminating proceedings if the AAT had to be satisfied that any decision giving it effect would be 'correct or preferable'. In this light, the function of the AAT should perhaps be understood as being to bring it about that the correct or preferable decision is made subject to (an acceptable) agreement between the parties to different effect.

Independently of limitations on the scope for agreement between the parties implicit in the concept of merits review, it is commonly argued that there is less room for 'settling' at least some disputes between citizens and the government than there is for settling disputes between citizen and citizen.[142] Such arguments

---

[135] *Re The International Fund for Animal Welfare (Aust) Pty Ltd and Minister for Environment and Heritage (No 2)* (2007) 93 ALD 625, [10].

[136] AAT Act s 42A(1A), (1B).

[137] AAT Act s 34D(1)(d), (2) (agreement reached 'in the course of an alternative dispute resolution process'). Similar provisions apply to agreement reached 'at any stage of a proceeding for review of a decision' other than in the course of an ADR process (AAT Act s 42C).

[138] *Re Liu and Comcare* (2004) 79 ALD 119, [9].

[139] *Kuswardana v Minister for Immigration and Ethnic Affairs* (1981) 35 ALR 186.

[140] D Pearce, *Administrative Appeals Tribunal*, 2nd edn (Australia, LexisNexis Butterworths, 2007) 7.4.

[141] ibid 172.

[142] The discussion by Richardson and Genn (n 121 above, 133–40), although directed to the question of when an oral hearing is appropriate, can also be understood as addressing the question of

partly rest on a distinction between public law rights and private law rights: there is no principled reason why people should not be free to bargain over their private law rights, but it is less obviously appropriate for government to enter into agreements by which citizens bargain away their rights against the state. Moreover, in some cases, it is said, a disputed decision is either lawful or unlawful, correct or incorrect, and there is simply no space for a legally enforceable 'third way'. On the other hand, there may be cases – involving, for instance, allocation of scarce resources in which no individual has a legal entitlement to a share – in which there may be legitimate room for compromise. Commentators vary in their assessment of the relative strength of such arguments.[143]

The AAT Act defines 'alternative dispute resolution processes' to include conferencing, mediation, neutral evaluation, case appraisal and conciliation but not arbitration.[144] In the AAT, conferencing is by far the most commonly used of these procedures. At least one conference is held in most cases. Parties can be directed to take part in a conference (or other ADR procedure) and have an (unenforceable) obligation to do so 'in good faith'.[145] To some extent, conferences take the place of pleadings: they provide a forum in which the issues can be presented and discussed and at which any gaps in the evidence can be identified in anticipation of and preparation for a hearing. However, they also provide an opportunity to explore prospects for agreement and the potential suitability of other forms of ADR.[146] In fact, the vast majority of applications to the AAT are resolved by this method without a hearing. The relationship between conferences and hearings is regulated in various ways. Conferences are normally held in private

when settlement might be inappropriate. For a different view – according to which 'informal agreements in administrative contexts can be fair … [provided] the agreement is real and … voluntarily entered into' see Galligan, *Due Process and Fair Procedures*, 281–87. See also S Boyron, 'The Rise of Mediation in Administrative Law Disputes: Experiences from England, France and Germany' [2006] *Public Law* 320, 331–33.

[143] M Supperstone QC, D Stilitz and C Sheldon, 'ADR and Public Law' [2006] *Public Law* 299 conclude that 'none of the traditional objections to the use of ADR in public law disputes presents an insuperable or universal barrier to the use of mediation in suitable cases' (319). Boyron, n 142 above, is less sure, as is Adler n 10 above, 978, 984.

[144] Arbitration is excluded probably because, as traditionally understood, its result binds the parties. This would be inconsistent with the scheme of the AAT Act under which only a decision of the Tribunal (whether as the result of an agreement or not) is binding.

[145] AAT Act s 34(5).

[146] The conference is 'the primary method of case-management … [and] … also the primary method of alternative dispute resolution … [by] mostly intuitive, not structured mediation': G Downes, 'The Tribunal Dilemma: Rigorous Informality', <http://www.aat.gov.au/SpeechesPapersAndResearch/speeches/downes/pdf/WhitemoreLectureSeptember2008.pdf>, 8 accessed 1 October, 2008. It is unclear to what extent these are compatible goals: D Gill, 'Formality and Informality in the Administrative Appeals Tribunal' (1989) 58 *Canberra Bulletin of Public Administration* 133. For instance, it has been said that 'in the conference … the tribunal member or officer … may take a more directive role than does a mediator': Administrative Review Council, *Better Decisions: Review of Commonwealth Merits Review Tribunals*, (Report No 39, Canberra, Australian Government Publishing Service, 1995) 3.139. See also Boyron, n 142 above, 336: 'It is imperative that the option of mediation be investigated before' any informal meeting between the adjudicator and the parties to discuss the case.

whereas hearings are typically held in public. As a general rule, evidence of things said or done at a conference is inadmissible at a hearing of the application, and if the conference is conducted by a member of the AAT (as is common but not universal), that member may not hear the application if either party objects. The AAT also uses mediation[147] and conciliation, the latter being compulsory in the workers' compensation area.[148] 'Process models' for each form of ADR and guidelines for assessing their respective suitability have been developed.[149]

The AAT has a highly developed set and system of alternatives to oral hearings focusing on conferences. By contrast, in the specialist immigration and social security jurisdictions the oral hearing (normally attended only by the applicant) is the standard mode of procedure, and there is no provision for alternative modes. A possible explanation for the position in the AAT is that although an applicant can unilaterally withdraw or discontinue an application for review, once an application has been made it cannot be resolved by agreement between the parties without the making of a decision by the AAT in the terms of or consistent with the agreement. For this reason, the tribunal itself needs to be involved in the 'settlement' process. Another noteworthy feature of proceedings in the AAT is that the decision-maker is a party and typically participates in the process. By contrast, the decision-maker is not a party to proceedings in the specialist immigration tribunals, and although a party to proceedings in the specialist social security and veterans' benefits tribunals, rarely participates in the proceedings beyond providing required information about the decision and making written submissions. The relevance of this is that ADR procedures typically assume active participation by both parties with a view to their reaching agreement. Another possible explanation for the absence of ADR procedures in the specialist tribunals is that the issues at stake in the sorts of cases they deal with are not suitably resolved by agreement. As we have seen, however, the strength of this type of argument is contested. Moreover, it assumes that the purpose of ADR is to reach by agreement an outcome that the tribunal could not impose rather than to produce, without a formal hearing, an outcome that the tribunal could impose.

---

[147] 'a voluntary, confidential ... process in which a Tribunal Member or Conference Registrar assists the parties to isolate the issues in dispute, develop options and reach a mutually agreeable settlement'. It is unlikely to be used 'in applications which raise issues of public importance ... [or] in which the non-government party is unrepresented, or if the only issue in dispute involves the interpretation of the law.': D Humphreys, 'Alternative Dispute Resolution in the Administrative Appeals Tribunal (AAT) in the Light of Recent Amendments to the *Administrative Appeals Tribunal Act (1975)*': <http://www.aat.gov.au/SpeechesPapersAndResearch/speeches/humphreys/Alternative Dispute2005.htm>, 7 accessed 1 April 2009. See also W De Maria, 'Mediation and Adjudication: Friends or Foes at the Administrative Appeals Tribunal?' (1991) 20 *Federal Law Review* 287.

[148] In this jurisdiction conciliation is considered appropriate because applications are generally amenable to settlement and the majority of applicants are represented ('which can facilitate settlement'): Downes, n 146 above, 5.

[149] G Downes, 'Alternative Dispute Resolution at the AAT' (2008) 15 *Australian Journal of Administrative Law* 137.

In the US, ADR in administrative adjudication is regulated by the APA.[150] ADR techniques include 'conciliation, facilitation, mediation, factfinding, minitrials, arbitration, and use of ombuds'.[151] The inclusion of (binding) arbitration is noteworthy given its express exclusion in Australia. An agency (ie, in effect, the adjudicator) may use ADR only with the consent of the parties. The APA expressly lists various situations in which use of ADR may not be appropriate. These include circumstances in which an authoritative resolution is needed as a precedent, in which significant policy issues are involved, in which consistency is important, where non-parties are significantly affected and in which it is important to have a public record of proceedings. The APA also contains several provisions the aim of which is to encourage adjudicators to attempt to settle cases by bringing the parties together in informal conferences and encouraging them to use other ADR techniques.[152] Use of ADR is promoted by the Federal Interagency Alternative Dispute Resolution Working Group (FIADRWG), which assists agencies to design and monitor ADR programmes and to train personnel in the use of ADR techniques. Notably, however, a recent (April 2007) *Report for the President on the Use and Results of Alternative Dispute Resolution in the Executive Branch of the Federal Government* by the FIADRWG makes no mention of ADR as an adjunct to administrative adjudication in the review sense of that term. There appears to be very little publicly available information about the extent to which administrative adjudication by ALJs and AJs involves hearings and, by contrast, the proportion of cases that are resolved without a hearing.

By contrast with the position in Australia and the US, the use of ADR in the tribunal sector in the UK is unregulated by statute. A recent survey of 44 tribunals by the Administrative Justice and Tribunals Council found that relatively few use ADR techniques.[153] The majority (in particular, those with jurisdiction to review governmental decisions) thought that the use of ADR was not suitable for the kinds of matters they dealt with because of lack of room for negotiation. Some also cited legislative barriers (such as being required to issue a formal determination after a hearing), and others worried that introduction of a variety of ADR options would create uncertainty and jeopardise timely resolution of cases. On the other hand, the majority of tribunals reported that they used various 'case-management' techniques, such as conferencing and 'early neutral evaluation', that could themselves be understood as forms of ADR. Indeed, lack of precision in the use of the term 'ADR' casts doubt on its value as an organising concept. Lack of systematic empirical evidence, about the ways in which various tribunals process their case-load and about the costs and benefits

---

[150] 5 USC, ss 571–83. These provisions were first enacted in 1990.

[151] 5 USC s 571(3).

[152] 5 USC s 556(c)(6)-(8); Asimow (ed), *Guide to Federal Agency Adjudication*, 141–43. See also ME Mullins, 'Manual for Administrative Law Judges' (2004) 23 *Journal of the National Association of Administrative Law Judges*, n 109 above, 9–39.

[153] 'The Use of Proportionate Dispute Resolution in Tribunals' *Adjust Newsletter* (Administrative Justice and Tribunals Council, Feb 2008).

of different methods of doing so, exacerbates the problem and gives policy debates in this area a frustratingly diffuse and inconclusive character. Discussion of alternatives to the paradigm mode of procedure in federal merits review tribunals is somewhat more focused in Australia. This, I would argue, is partly because the juridically well-developed concept of merits review gives a clearer and more precise account of what tribunals do, making it easier to debate how they might best and most appropriately do it. In the UK, by contrast, the aspiration to promote ADR (and PDR) is little more than rhetoric, driven by unsubstantiated assumptions about its advantages in terms of economy and speed and its impact on the 'quality' of decision-making.

6.6 Resources

The proposition that administrative adjudication by tribunals consumes – and should consume – fewer resources than administrative adjudication by courts has always been central to thinking about administrative justice. Tribunals, it is repeatedly said, are quicker and cheaper than courts. However, this seemingly straightforward statement bristles with complexities and difficulties. So far as cost is concerned, it is necessary to distinguish between overall cost, personal cost to applicants and cost to the taxpayer. Various factors may affect the way the overall cost of administrative adjudication is distributed between applicants and the public purse. These include fees payable by applicants, the availability of public funding for advice and representation, rules about the awarding of costs to a successful applicant[154] and the role of the adjudicator in the adjudication process (in terms of drawing on their own personal knowledge and expertise, and taking an active part in the collection of evidence at taxpayer expense).

In relation to both cost and speed, meaningful relative statements about courts and tribunals would need to be based on a common standard of measurement – resources consumed per unit of adjudication, we might say. As far as I am aware, no such common standard has ever been developed or even suggested; and this may partly explain why there is no systematic empirical evidence about the relative 'efficiency' of courts and tribunals. A serious problem in constructing any such standard of measurement arises from the widespread view that there may be a trade-off between resources consumed and the quality of the product. A persistent theme in the literature on administrative adjudication – put crudely – is that tribunals necessarily provide a second-class product precisely because they consume fewer resources. However, the concept of 'quality' in this context is extremely difficult to define and its relationship to resources is effectively impossible to measure.

---

[154] See generally E Campbell and M Groves, 'Award of Costs in Administrative Proceedings' (2004) 11 *Australian Journal of Administrative Law* 121.

The aspect of resources that has received most attention is that of representation. The basic argument is that the various characteristics of tribunal process that distinguish it from court process – informality, evidentiary freedom, active adjudicating and so on – are partly designed to make it unnecessary for applicants to be represented and are effective to this end. As a result (it is said), these characteristics of tribunal procedure reduce its overall cost. On the common assumption that representation increases the length of proceedings, it may further be argued that these characteristics also reduce the time required to resolve applications. As in relation to the more general issues of speed and cost, such arguments have not been (and perhaps could not effectively or efficiently be) subjected to systematic empirical investigation. Such empirical research as has been done addresses the relationship between representation and the rate of success of claims (although the distinction between success and justified success (accuracy) is not always explicitly acknowledged). On the basis of English research conducted in the 1980s[155] the common wisdom has been that represented applicants as a group are more successful than unrepresented applicants. So, for instance, in 1995 the Australian Administrative Review Council expressed strong opposition to limitation or exclusion of the right to be represented and recommended against any prohibition of legal representation.[156] These were general recommendations applicable equally to proceedings to which the decision-maker is a party and proceedings in which the decision-maker does not an active take part.[157] While it is rare for representation to be prohibited, the practical question is financial. Lack of public funding for representation and absence of a power in the tribunal to award costs may make it difficult for many tribunal users to secure representation, especially by a lawyer. However, more recent research shows that in certain UK tribunals, at least, the disadvantage, in terms of success, associated with lack of representation is significantly less than that found by the earlier research.[158] This change is atttibuted to the fact that the tribunals in question adopt a more 'active, interventionist and enabling approach' than was the case when the earlier research was conducted. This conclusion may be stronger than the somewhat impressionistic and, in certain respects, equivocal evidence can justify. Nevertheless, the research provides some support for the basic argument stated at the beginning of the previous paragraph.

---

[155] H Genn and Y Genn, *The Effectiveness of Representation at Tribunals* (London, Lord Chancellor's Department, 1989). For some wariness see K Cronin, 'Dispute Resolution in Administrative Law in J McMillan (ed), *Administrative Law under the Coalition Government* (Canberra, Australian Institute of Administrative Law, 1997) 79.

[156] Administrative Review Council, *Better Decisions: Review of Commonwealth Merits Review Tribunals* (Canberra, Australian Government Publishing Service, 1995) 3.163–3.189.

[157] It is sometimes suggested that a good reason for excluding the decision-maker from hearings is to reduce the need for the applicant to be represented.

[158] 'M Adler, 'Tribunals Ain't What They Used to Be', http://www.ajtc.gov.uk/adjust/articles/AdlerTribunalsUsedToBe.pdf, accessed 4 May 2009.

6.7 Conclusion

In this chapter we have examined the concept of 'administrative justice' in the context of the interaction between tribunals and their users. A recurring theme of the analysis has been the extent to which tribunal processes and procedure can be understood as a variant or version of court processes and procedure, on the one hand, and to what extent they can be understood in terms of a distinctive function performed by tribunals, on the other. These two understandings reflect two explanations for and justifications of tribunals. One is that tribunals perform an essentially similar function to that of courts, only better – or worse, depending on the view taken of the relationship between the 'legal' values of fairness and justice on the one hand, and informality, flexibility, speed and economy on the other. The other explanation and justification for tribunals is that they perform an essentially different function from courts. These two perspectives respectively yield significantly different concepts of the administrative justice provided by tribunals and of its quality and desirability.

7

Landscape

7.1 The Accountability 'Sector'

ADMINISTRATIVE ADJUDICATION BY officials and bodies other than courts is a firmly established feature of constitutional arrangements in each of our main comparator jurisdictions: the US, the UK and Australia. Our focus in most of this book has been on the relationship between tribunals and courts, and in particular on the differences and similarities between them. The aim of this chapter is to consider briefly the place and role of tribunals in the wider landscape of mechanisms for handling citizens' grievances against government of which tribunals and courts are only two components.

The discussion in this chapter will be less applicable to the US than to the UK and Australia. One reason is that the concept of accountability (and the related concept of responsibility) around which the discussion is organised plays a much more central role in theorising about public law (both constitutional and administrative law) in the non-US common-law world than in the US. This is partly a function of the fact that in a US-style presidential system of government, unlike a Westminster-type system, the relationship between the legislature and the executive is not structured or understood in terms of the responsibility and accountability of the latter to the former. Another likely (and related) explanation is that the fundamental goal of controlling, limiting and restraining government is understood in the US primarily in terms of the relationships between the various organs of government ('separation of powers' and 'checks and balances'). In Westminster systems, by contrast, the central ideas – notably, rule of law and responsible government – are more concerned with the relationship between governors and governed (historically, Crown and subjects). In the US, it seems, the dominant image of a good governmental structure is that of a machine made up of various well balanced components, whereas in the UK and Australia the dominant image is that of a set of bilateral relationships of giving and receiving explanations and accounts.

These contrasts are nicely reflected in attitudes towards judicial independence. Recurring themes of a conference held in Philadelphia in 2001 and a subsequent collection of essays published in 2002[1] were that judicial independence is not a useful concept in its own right and that it is only a means to an end. The apotheosis of this way of thinking may be found in EL Rubin's recommendation that analysis of government in terms of concepts such as independence of the judiciary should be replaced by 'micro-analysis' in terms of institutional 'networks'. By contrast, in Westminster-type systems independence of the judiciary is typically understood as an essential protection for the rights of the citizen against the combined power of the legislature and the executive. Accountability is central to this way of thinking: the control exercised by the government over the legislature so weakens the accountability of the former to the latter that an additional avenue of accountability of the executive to an independent judiciary is considered essential to protect the rights and interests of the governed.[2]

The past 50 years have witnessed ever-growing demand for accountability of governors to the governed, especially for individual decisions and actions. This demand has been addressed in various ways. Through judicial review, the courts have taken an increasingly active role in reviewing public decision-making. In Australia, the establishment of the AAT and the invention of merits review significantly increased opportunities for external review of public decision-making; and in the UK the number of tribunals and the number of decisions reviewed by them continued to grow. Such developments were accompanied by creation of the office of ombudsman, thus expanding the options for external accountability from reviewing of decisions to handling of 'complaints', the latter extending beyond decisions to conduct more generally. As the workload of such external monitors increased, they were supplemented by 'internal' procedures for reviewing decisions and handling complaints, and use of such procedures was sometimes made a precondition of applying to an external review or complaint body. In recent years, too, the role of courts and tribunals has increasingly been understood as being to provide facilities not just for 'hearings' but also for ADR processes, such as conferences and mediation, designed to assist parties to resolve disputes without a hearing.

---

[1] SB Burbank and B Friedman (eds), *Judicial Independence at the Crossraads: An Interdisciplinary Approach* (Thousand Oaks, Sage Publications, 2002).

[2] Implicit here is a contrast between accountability and politics. Politics gets in the way of accountability. Executive control politicizes the legislature and weakens its ability to hold the government to account. From this perspective, independence serves to protect the judiciary from politicization and to increase its capacity for enforcing accountability. In the US, by contrast, courts are typically viewed as political actors and their role is analysed in terms of their relationships with other political actors. This explains why political scientists in the US are much more interested in courts than their counterparts in the UK and Australia. However, US political scientists show little interest in administrative adjudication, probably because administrative adjudicators are strongly identified with (to the point of being subsumed within) agencies and the executive branch. In addition to 'positive' political analysis of the behaviour of courts and judges, there have been some attempts to explain particular laws in political terms. See eg, McNollgast, 'The Political Origins of the Administrative Procedure Act' (1999) 15 *Journal of Law, Economics and Organization* 180; A Schwartz, 'Comment on "The Political Origins of the Administrative Procedure Act" by McNollgast', ibid 218; LR Cohen and ML Spitzer, 'Solving the *Chevron* Puzzle' (1994) 57 *Law and Contemporary Problems* 65.

40 years ago the Kerr Committee in Australia thought that there were too few opportunities and avenues for the citizen to challenge bureaucratic action. Now, a more common concern is that although there are various mechanisms, the typical citizen is ignorant of their existence or their respective functions, or about how to apply to them. Systematisation, rationalisation and triage are the new policy priorities for the administrative justice system, especially in the UK. So how might we understand the respective roles of and relationships between the various institutions and mechanisms that populate the crowded public accountability landscape? In particular, how should we explain the role of tribunals and their relationships with other accountability institutions? In what follows we will examine tribunals first in relation to ombudsmen, and secondly in relation to internal review procedures. We will then look briefly at the issues of alternative dispute resolution (ADR) and proportionate dispute resolution (PDR). Finally, we will return to the issue of the relationship between tribunals and courts.

It may be helpful to preface the discussion of these matters with a tabular representation of some salient features of various accountability institutions found in the UK, Australian and other Westminster-style common law systems.

Table: Ideal-types of Salient Accountability Mechanisms

(1) Institution	(2) Location	(3) Basis of application	(4) Scope of application	(5) Typical remedial outcome	(6) Paradigm procedural mode	(7) Accessibility to applicant
original decision-maker	internal	legality + merits	decisions	substitute decision	ex parte reconsideration	high
bureaucratic reviewer	internal	legality + merits	decisions	substitute decision	ex parte reconsideration	moderate
bureaucratic complaint-handler	internal	legality + merits + 'administrative practice'	decisions and other action	recommendation, incl for substitute decision or compensation	ex parte investigation	high
ombudsman	external	legality + merits + 'administrative practice'	decisions and other action	recommendation, incl for substitute decision or compensation	ex parte investigation	high
tribunal	'external'	legality + merits	decisions	substitute decision	tripartite or bipartite hearing	moderate
court	external	legality	decisions and other action	set aside and remit; compensation	tripartite hearing	low

Certain aspects of this table require some explanation. The first, and extremely important, point to make is that the table must not be read as descriptive but rather as presenting a set of theoretical ideal-types. The reality in any particular jurisdiction will diverge from the picture presented in the table in various ways and to various degrees. Secondly, the table is only concerned with mechanisms that can be activated by people affected by government decisions. It does not refer to quality assurance systems (monitored, for instance, by auditors and inspectors) that operate internally within agencies or externally to agencies as management tools.

In column (2), the scare-quotes around 'external' in the tribunal row indicate that tribunals vary in the extent to which they are integrated into or distant from the agencies whose decisions they review. The US situation would probably be better represented by 'internal' in scare-quotes.

In column (3), the phrase 'legality + merits' captures the idea that merits review (at least understood in Australia) is enhanced judicial review in the sense that its substantive basis covers but extends beyond legality. The phrase 'administrative practice' refers to the concept of 'maladministration', which is a common description of the basis on which an ombudsman can provide redress to the applicant. The phrase 'legality + merits + administrative practice' captures the idea that an ombudsman might recommend redress for an applicant if an agency has acted illegally, or contrary to the merits or good administrative practice. There may be rules designed to channel claims based on legality or merits away from an ombudsman and into a court or tribunal; but in principle, it must be open to an ombudsman to recommend redress where an agency has acted illegally or made a decision that is not correct or preferable, and not only where it has breached some norm of good administration.

Columns (4) and (5) are related in the sense that there is a correlation between 'other action' in column (4) and 'compensation' in column (5). Tribunals, internal bureaucratic reviewers and original decision-makers (when they reconsider their own decisions) have no power to award compensation but can only review decisions. By contrast, courts can both review decisions (in judicial review proceedings and appeals from tribunals) and award compensation (in tort or contract, for instance) in relation to 'other action'. Similarly, ombudsmen and internal complaint handlers are not limited to reviewing decisions and may be empowered to make recommendations not only, for instance, that the agency should make a new decision but also that compensation should be paid for some breach of good administrative practice. Implicit in the formulae used in column (5) is a criterion of enforceability. Ombudsmen and other complaint handlers typically have the power only to make unenforceable recommendations, while courts can coercively enforce their own orders. Typically tribunals can make decisions enforceable by a court but not by the tribunal itself.

The formulae used in column (6) must be interpreted in the light of the discussion of procedure in Chapter 6. In particular, 'hearing' should not be read to exclude the possibility that the officer conducting the hearing may have certain powers of investigation. The formulae do not refer to whether the relevant process is based on a closed record or whether, on the contrary, the record remains open until completion of the process. Courts generally review on the basis of a closed record, whereas a tribunal may have power to develop the record. Record development is central to complaint handling. It is hard to generalise about internal review processes. One respect in which this column obviously oversimplifies a complex reality is that it ignores ADR mechanisms that may be available in courts and tribunals.

'Accessibility' in column (7) is a shorthand for a collection of factors such as ease of applying, cost, speed, informality and so on that affect 'user-friendliness'.

If applicants had a free choice between alternatives, the various parameters covered by this table would require (and enable) an applicant to make a series of strategic decisions in order to identify which institution was best equipped to handle their grievance. In practice, of course, applicants may not have a free choice. For instance, a citizen aggrieved by a social security benefit decision may be required first to apply for reconsideration by the original decision-maker, and then for internal review. Again, even if an aggrieved citizen has, in principle, a choice between applying for judicial review by a court and merits review by a tribunal, in practice the only realistic option may be to apply first to a tribunal rather than directly to a court.

In this context, it may be helpful to deploy a distinction used earlier in comparing the role of tribunals in the UK model on the one hand, and in Australian model on the other: the in the UK model (as in the US model), tribunals are understood to perform essentially the same function as courts, even though their respective powers and procedures may be different. By contrast, in the Australia model, tribunals are understood to perform a categorically different function than courts despite certain similarities between the respective powers and procedures. As a result of this difference, the most salient explanation for the existence of tribunals in Australia is different from the most salient explanation for their existence in the UK.[3] The same idea can be applied to accountability institutions more generally. In order to understand the interrelationships between various institutions we need to know whether they are understood to be performing essentially similar or categorically different functions.

7.2 Tribunals and Ombudsmen

At first sight, it would appear that ombudsmen[4] perform a categorically different function than either courts or tribunals. For one thing, the characteristic task of

---

[3] See further 7.4.1.

[4] Our concern here is only with public-sector ombudsmen. There are also many ombudsman schemes in the private sector.

ombudsmen is described not as reviewing decisions but as handling (individuals') complaints. This is particularly significant in Australia where the jurisdiction of merits review tribunals is defined in terms of 'decisions' and where the statutory law of judicial review (embodied in the Administrative Decisions (Judicial Review) Act 1977) establishes a distinction between decisions and 'conduct' related to the making of decisions. The jurisdiction of ombudsmen to handle complaints is not limited to complaints about decisions.[5] Secondly, ombudsmen typically have power only to make unenforceable recommendations, whereas tribunals can make orders enforceable by a court, and courts can enforce their own orders.

Thirdly, the paradigm mode of procedure followed by ombudsmen in handling complaints is very different from that of either tribunals or courts. Ombudsmen typically 'investigate' in private; and they have extensive powers to compel the production of documents and unrestricted access to relevant files of the agency under investigation. In cases where no formal investigation is conducted, the ombudsman may operate as a sort of mediator or broker between the complainant and the agency to hammer out a solution acceptable to both. Whereas hearing the applicant's (and also, in many cases, the respondent's) case is central to the paradigm mode of procedure in both courts and tribunals, the complainant remains passive throughout an ombudsman's investigation except to the extent that the ombudsman chooses to involve the complainant in the investigation.[6]

Fourthly, the classic formulation of the basis on which an ombudsman can find a complaint to be justified is 'maladministration'. Maladministration covers conduct such as delay, rudeness, inefficiency and incompetence regardless of whether it could provide a basis for judicial review or tribunal review. Unlike courts and tribunals, the recommendatory powers of ombudsmen are not limited by a narrow concept of the rule of law but promote a broader goal of 'good administration'.

However, closer examination softens the contrast between ombudsmen on the one hand and courts and tribunals on the other. Most importantly, perhaps, although the concept of maladministration extends beyond both illegality and making a decision that is not the correct or preferable, it clearly includes both. If tribunal review is enhanced judicial review, 'ombudsmanry' is enhanced tribunal review – and doubly so, extending beyond decisions and beyond the merits of

---

[5] It is said that the distinction between handling complaints and reviewing decisions is difficult for the average person to understand, no doubt because many complainants want a different decision: House of Commons Public Administration Select Committee, *When Citizens Complain* (Fifth Report of 2007–08 Session, HC 409, 2008) 10. It is certainly not clear that it makes sense to allocate the two functions to different sets of institutions, especially since they are combined in courts.

[6] For a more detailed analysis of the procedure followed by Australian ombudsmen, particularly the Commonwealth Ombudsman, see P Cane and L McDonald, *Principles of Administrative Law: Legal Regulation of Governance* (Melbourne, OUP, 2008) 263–66.

decisions.[7] Ombudsmen typically have discretion to refuse to investigate in cases where it would be reasonable to expect the complainant to apply to a court or tribunal; but this discretion assumes that the ombudsman has power to make findings of maladministration on the same grounds on which courts and tribunals can exercise their review powers.

On the basis of such an analogy between the respective functions of ombudsmen, tribunals and courts in reviewing administrative decisions, the English Parliamentary and Health Service Ombudsman (PHSO) has argued that public service ombudsmen should be understood 'as an integral part of the administrative justice "scene" … in fact as a coherent "system of justice" in [their] own right.'[8] She observes that many complaints to ombudsmen concern 'justiciable events',[9] and that in dealing with such complaints ombudsmen perform an 'adjudicatory function'.[10] In this regard, she proposes, what distinguishes ombudsmen from courts and tribunals is not what they do but how they do it – namely by a basically ex parte investigatory process. The PHSO refers to a recent decision of the Administrative Court in which it was said that although different from that of a tribunal, such procedure 'provides a substantial degree of due process'.[11] She paints the ombudsman as a 'warm and supple … softer, gentler … naturally enticing' alternative to courts and tribunals, and a 'mature and legitimate stable companion of the other two thoroughbreds'.[12] The aim, according to the PHSO, should be to integrate 'the ombudsman system of justice more consciously and thoroughly than at present into the wider administrative justice system'.[13] However, she also argues that ombudsmen can add value to that system, for instance, by addressing systemic issues, monitoring compliance and actively promoting good administration in ways that courts and tribunals cannot do.

---

[7] The Australian Commonwealth Ombudsman says that 'ombudsman investigations have customarily focussed on the way decisions are made, and less on the merits of the decisions under investigation'; but he discusses various areas in which this customary limitation cannot easily be maintained: J McMillan, 'The Expanding Ombudsman Role: What Fits? What Doesn't?' <http://www.comb.gov.au/commonwealth/publish.nsf/Content/speeches_2008_02> accessed 22 October 2008. See also A Stuhmcke, 'Ombudsmen and Integrity Review' in L Pearson, C Harlow and M Taggart (eds), *Administrative Law in a Changing State: Essays in Honour of Mark Aronson* (Oxford, Hart Publishing, 2008).

[8] A Abraham, 'The Ombudsman and "Paths to Justice": A Just Alternative or Just an Alternative?' [2008] *Public Law* 1.

[9] ibid 3.

[10] ibid 4.

[11] *R (Bradley) v Secretary of State for Work and Pensions* [2007] EWHC 242 (Admin), [58]. Bean J added, 'A public adversarial hearing is not the only fair way of finding facts'. In this case it was held that although recommendations of the ombudsman are not binding on the agency, findings of fact are unless legally flawed or *Wednesbury* unreasonable.

[12] n 8 above, 4–5.

[13] ibid 9. For an argument that one of the functions of the European Ombudsman is 'quasi-judicial' see RW Davis, 'Quasi-Judicial Review: The European Ombudsman as an Alternative to European Courts' [2000] *Web Journal of Current Legal Issues*, <http://webjcli.ncl.ac.uk/2000/issue1/davis1.html> accessed 2 April 2009.

In Australia, the Commonwealth Ombudsman (CO) has power to refer to the AAT a 'specified question' about the taking of an action or the exercise of a power which is being investigated, and the AAT has power to 'give an advisory opinion on the question'.[14] Note that this provision does not give the AAT power to review a decision which is the subject of an investigation by the CO. In the other direction, there are administrative arrangements for referral of matters by the AAT to the CO in cases where limitations on the powers of the AAT prevent it resolving a case fairly. For instance, unlike the AAT, the CO can recommend payment of *ex gratia* compensation or voluntary waiver of a debt owed to the government in cases where the decision that caused injury or gave rise to the debt is both legal and either correct or preferable on its merits.[15] The AAT may refer a matter to the CO where the conduct complained of was not a decision reviewable by the AAT;[16] or where the application before the AAT reveals a broader systemic problem.[17] The current CO has recently described the customary approach of the CO to individual complaints about administrative decisions as being more analogous to judicial review than merits review.[18] He also says that his office now has more resources for 'own motion' investigations 'because of the more developed system for handling complaints within agencies'.[19] In such investigations, an ombudsman can look into systemic administrative problems that go beyond any single individual's complaint. Moreover, the CO sees the role of the office increasingly in terms of activities other than investigating complaints, such as compliance auditing and human rights protection. For instance, the CO is charged with reviewing the cases of individuals who have been in immigration detention for more than two years.

In the approaches of the English PHSO and the Australian CO respectively we can see two somewhat different understandings of the relationship between tribunals and ombudsmen. According to the former, handling individual complaints (including large numbers of individual complaints about the same or related administrative conduct – group complaints, we might say) is the prime role of the ombudsman; and in fulfilling that role, the ombudsman performs a function essentially similar to that of tribunals (and courts) when engaging in administrative adjudication. Just as tribunals, in the UK model, have long been understood as performing a function essentially similar to that of courts, but performing it better in some respects, so according to this approach, the

---

[14] Ombudsman Act 1976 (Cth) s 10A.
[15] D Pearce, *Administrative Appeals Tribunal*, 2nd edn (LexisNexis Butterworths, Australia, 2007) 185–87. eg, *Re Spencer-White and Secretary, Department of Social Security* (1992) 28 ALD 719; *Re Murray and Repatriation Commission* (1998) 52 ALD 117.
[16] *Re Trustees of the C & M Baldwin Pension Fund and Insurance and Superannuation Commissioner* [1992] *Admin Review* 85; *Re Radge and Commissioner of Taxation* (2007) 95 ALD 711, [29]–[30].
[17] *Re Roberts and Repatriation Commission* (1992) 26 ALD 611; *Re Radge* n 16 above.
[18] See quotation in n 7 above.
[19] n 7 above.

ombudsman performs a function essentially similar to that of courts and tribunals, but better than both in certain respects. Furthermore, just as the traditional way of viewing the relationship between courts and tribunals has led to reforms designed to integrate courts and tribunals, so the current PHSO surmises that a '"Leggatt review of ombudsmen" cannot be that far away'.[20]

By contrast, under the leadership of the current CO, while handling individual complaints is still the core business of the office, more and more of its resources are being devoted to auditing and monitoring the administrative system – fire-watching rather than fire-fighting, managing public administration rather than delivering administrative justice. Neither of these understandings of the office of ombudsman bears much relationship to the visions of the designers of the institution. In England the ombudsman is an officer of Parliament and the office was originally conceived as an institutional reinforcement to assist (Members of) Parliament in holding the government to account. In Australia, the Kerr Committee recommended a 'General Counsel for Grievances' (who would be a 'highly qualified member of the Bar') to complement courts and tribunals by dealing with complaints regardless of whether they fell within the jurisdiction of a court or tribunal and, in appropriate cases, by assisting complainants to bring it before a court or tribunal.[21] The Committee conceived of the ombudsman as an integral component of a set of institutions (including courts and tribunals) for controlling government activity – a vision closer to that of the current PHSO than of the current CO. If that vision took hold and influenced the development of the administrative justice system, it could significantly affect the understanding of the place and role of tribunals (and courts) in that system.

The PHSO, as has been noted, lays some emphasis on the role of ombudsmen in promoting good administration in ways that courts and tribunals cannot. This function is noteworthy in the context of the so-called 'normative function' of tribunals (5.5). Ombudsmen have been active in formulating and publishing general guidance to bureaucrats about good administrative practice and decision-making. Such guidance has no formal status; and as far as I am aware, the impact and effectiveness of such educative activities has not been systematically assessed. A good case could be made, however, for adding to the formal tasks of ombudsmen that of advising upon and monitoring systems established within agencies for controlling the quality of primary decision-making.

7.3 Tribunals and Internal Review

A striking development over the past 20 years or so has been the proliferation of arrangements within government agencies for reviewing decisions and handling

---

[20] n 8 above, 10.
[21] Kerr Committee Report , ch 15.

complaints. Recourse to such an internal mechanism is commonly a de facto or de jure precondition of applying to an external body, such as an ombudsman or tribunal.[22] The creation of multi-tiered systems for handling complaints[23] and reviewing decisions is most commonly understood in terms of efficiency and 'accessibility'. Multi-tiered systems are considered efficient because they allow the bulk of complaints to be resolved at the 'local' level, leaving the external tier to deal with more difficult cases that cannot be resolved locally to the satisfaction of the aggrieved person. The assumption is that internal, local mechanisms will be more accessible than their external counterparts by reason of their relative speediness, cheapness and informality. We lack evidence properly to assess such arguments.[24] However, research has explored possible reasons why relatively few people adversely affected by decisions, about housing the homeless, made by two English local authorities, took advantage of provision for internal review. Possible explanations were found to include ignorance of the existence of the internal review mechanism, scepticism about its integrity, a perception that it was too 'rule bound', and 'applicant fatigue'.[25] Applicant fatigue has also been suggested to explain why people who are dissatisfied with the result of an internal process may be discouraged from proceeding to the external tier.[26]

If applicant fatigue is a significant feature of multi-tiered systems, this not only casts doubt on their supposed practical advantages (from the perspective of the aggrieved person, anyway) but also raises serious issues of principle. A common assumption on which such systems are based is that whereas the internal tier will have the advantage in terms of efficiency, the external tier is more likely to reach the best result in difficult cases. From this perspective, it would count as a disadvantage of such a system that it actually reduced the chance that the best

---

[22] The position in relation to judicial review is tricky. Because of the unique constitutional status of the courts and of judicial review, internal review could probably not be made a mandatory precondition of seeking judicial review. On the other hand, as a result of increasingly active case-management by courts, recourse to internal review procedures may be strongly encouraged.

[23] See eg, *When Citizens Complain*, n 6 above, 18–21; National Audit Office, *Department for Work and Pensions: Handling Customer Complaints*, HC 995 Session 2007–08 (London, TSO, 2008) 1.10–1.11 (describing a system of three internal and two external tiers).

[24] For some relevant data about complaint-handling by agencies of the UK Department of Work and Pensions see *Handling Customer Complaints*, n 23 above, 4.25–4.32.

[25] D Cowan and S Halliday, *The Appeal of Internal Review* (Oxford, Hart Publishing, 2003). For some discussion of why the dissatisfied may not complain see *Handling Customer Complaints*, n 21 above, 2.13–2.17. An Australian report found evidence that fear of retribution may discourage complaints to Centrelink, the social benefits delivery agency: Australian National Audit Office, *Centrelink's Complaints Handling System*, Audit Report No 34 2004–05 (Canberra, Commonwealth of Australia, 2005) ch 4.

[26] Administrative Review Council, Report 44, *Internal Review of Agency Decision Making* (Canberra, 2000) paras 7.3–7.10. Recent reforms in the US to the system of adjudicating disability claims have included elimination of the first tier of review (reconsideration by the original decision-maker) and the internal appeal tier, but the insertion of a form of early assessment between the initial decision and hearing before an ALJ. For assessment see FS Bloch, JS Lubbers and PR Verkuil, 'The Social Security Administration New Disability Adjudication Rules: A Significant and Promising Reform' (2007) 92 *Cornell Law Review* 235.

result would be reached in the most contested cases. This disadvantage is aggravated when it is noted that the external tier(s) may be considered valuable not only in terms of making a contribution to achievement of the best result but also precisely by being *external*. A danger of multi-tiered, mixed internal/external systems is that the less tangible 'legal' values such 'independence' and 'justice' may be sacrificed to the more tangible and, in theory at least, more measurable managerial values such as 'efficiency'.

As a counterweight to such (potential) disadvantages of multi-tiered systems it may be argued, in favour of including an internal tier in arrangements for processing reviews and complaints, that internal mechanisms may be better positioned than external reviewers and complaint-handlers to perform the normative function of improving the quality of primary decision-making.[27] On the other hand, some suggest that compulsory internal review may encourage primary decision-makers to decide in the applicant's favour in cases of doubt in order to avoid internal review;[28] while others think that internal review gives decision-makers an incentive, in cases of doubt, to decide adversely to the applicant and in that way offload the problem onto an internal reviewer. Either way, internal review might be thought to provide decision-makers with an incentive to prefer the 'soft option', casting doubt on the capacity of internal review to improve decision-making standards, especially in situations where decision-makers are inadequately trained and supported to perform an inherently difficult task.[29]

Amongst internal reviews, a distinction can be drawn between review by the original decision-maker (often called 'reconsideration') and review by some other (typically more senior) official within the agency. In the absence of statutory provisions authorising internal review in either of these modes, the default principle is that once an administrative body has made a decision, that decision stands unless and until it is quashed by a judicial reviewer or a tribunal sets it aside, varies it or replaces it with a substitute decision. This finality principle is based on some idea of 'legal certainty', which is explicitly recognised (for instance) in European Community administrative law.[30] However, the principle applies only to lawful (intra vires) decisions. If a decision-maker is asked to reconsider an illegal (ultra vires) decision, the finality principle will not, in theory at least,[31] prevent its reconsideration.[32] Conversely, an agency may, in principle at least, refuse to give effect to a decision which, on examination, is found to be illegal, subject only, perhaps, to some concept of 'estoppel'.

---

[27] *Internal Review of Agency Decision Making*, paras 3.34–3.36.

[28] ibid paras 7.3–7.10.

[29] ibid paras 7.11–7.13.

[30] T Hartley, *The Foundations of European Community Law*, 5th edn (Oxford, OUP, 2003) 146–51.

[31] In practice, it will often not be clear whether the decision is ultra vires or not, and an application for judicial review or merits review may be the only way to have it reconsidered.

[32] eg *Minister for Immigration and Multicultural and Indigenous Affairs v Bhardwaj* (2002) 209 CLR 597.

In the Australian context, both modes of internal review are understood to be analogous to merits review, although the analogy is obviously not exact. For instance, the idea that the reviewer stands in the shoes of the original decision-maker obviously has no application to reconsideration, and the original decision-maker can obviously not remit for reconsideration. When internal review is conducted by another official of the agency, it is perhaps less likely that new material will be considered than if the reviewer were external, if only because of constraints of time and resources.

Be that as it may, the basic point to be emphasised is that in considering the role of tribunals in the administrative justice system it is important to take account not only of how they interact with courts but also how they interact with internal review mechanisms (and ombudsmen). It is only by doing this that we become aware of the striking fact that, in theory, an administrative decision may be reconsidered or reviewed six or seven times: once by the original decision-maker, a second time by an internal reviewer, a third time by an external first-tier tribunal, a fourth time by a second-tier tribunal, a fifth time by a court (either by way of appeal from or judicial review of the tribunal), a sixth time by a first appeal court and a seventh time by a court of final appeal – to which we might add, for good measure, one or two failed attempts at ADR or perhaps the intervention of an ombudsman. In practice, of course, it is unlikely that a decision will be subjected to such repeated scrutiny, although three or four episodes seem within the bounds of realistic possibility. The administrative justice system has become extremely complex, and the bulk of the discussion in this book, focusing as it has on courts and tribunals, judicial review and tribunal review, captures only a part of that complexity.

7.4 Tribunals and Courts

In 5.4 the juridical concepts of merits review and judicial review were compared and contrasted. In the light of that analysis, the aim of this section is to examine the relationship between courts and tribunals as administrative adjudicators. There has long been ambivalence in attitudes towards that relationship. On the one hand, tribunals are celebrated as being better than courts in various respects: expertise, speed, cost, flexibility and so on. On the other hand, these very advantages have been seen by some as providing reason to brand tribunals as purveyors of 'second-class justice' or merely as political expedients rather than the product of genuine concern for the interests of citizens. However, both points of view treat courts as some sort of norm and tribunals as a departure from that norm. Given the fact that the 'modern tribunal' has been in existence for more than a century, and the dramatic growth of the accountability sector in recent decades, the time may have come to reconsider the relationship between courts and tribunals in the wider context of the 'administrative justice system'. However, any such reconsideration must be sensitive to jurisdictional diversity.

7.4.1 Australia

In Australian law, as we have seen, merits review by tribunals is considered to be categorically different from judicial review by courts, at least in procedural and remedial terms. However, in substantive terms there is considerable overlap between the two modes of review, and merits review can be understood as a form of enhanced judicial review. This conclusion poses the question of how best to account for the existence of both side-by-side. Why has judicial review not been rendered redundant by merits review? The obvious answer is constitutional: the High Court of Australia is created by the Australian Constitution and has constitutionally entrenched judicial review jurisdiction. Furthermore, although the AAT can set aside decisions for error of law – in other words, it can decide questions of law – it cannot do so 'conclusively' because conclusive resolution of issues of law is (according to the High Court) a judicial function that only courts can perform. In other words, the AAT (like other merits review tribunals) cannot make law – or, perhaps more precisely, cannot make hard law, although it can (and does) make soft law; and in practice, soft law made by the AAT is generally treated as if it were hard law. Nevertheless, in this respect at least, the AAT is a second-class administrative adjudicator and merits review may be considered a subordinate mode of administrative adjudication. Tribunals may be the biggest show in town but they are not the brightest.

There may be another explanation for the subordination of tribunals to courts. The AAT has jurisdiction to review any particular decision only if legislation (other than the AAT Act) expressly confers on it power to review decisions of that type. By contrast, federal courts have statutory jurisdiction (with only a few exceptions) to review any 'administrative' decision made 'under an enactment' of the Commonwealth Parliament; and the High Court has constitutional jurisdiction to review any decision made by an 'officer of the Commonwealth'. This means that there are classes of decisions amenable (in principle at least) to judicial review but not to merits review. The best explanation for this situation is probably historical (along the lines that courts and judicial review developed organically while tribunals and merits review are creatures of statute). However, a more substantive rationale might be that administrative decisions vary in terms of the appropriate intensity of the external review to which they are subject. Because merits review is in theory, and to some extent in practice, a more intense form of external scrutiny than judicial review, its scope is appropriately narrower than that of judicial review. However, while the abstract principle of variable intensity of review that underpins this rationale is convincing, I doubt that it plausibly explains the categorical distinctions between courts and tribunals and between judicial review and merits review. After all, the distinction between judicial review and merits review is not clear-cut; and as shown by the development of administrative law in the UK in the wake of the Human Rights Act 1998, one and the same institution may apply different standards of scrutiny depending on the nature of the decision under review and the interests affected by it.

This analysis treats judicial review and merits review as mutually exclusive, alternative modes of first-tier external review of administrative decisions. However, many administrative decisions are, in principle, amenable to both judicial review and merits review, and some decisions of first-tier merits review tribunals are technically amenable to both judicial review (sometimes under the guise of a functionally-equivalent 'appeal' on a point of law) and second-tier merits review. In general, courts discourage judicial review when merits review is available as an alternative;[33] and it is a puzzle why an applicant would prefer judicial review to merits review given the less intrusive nature of the former. The higher prestige of courts over tribunals may be part of the explanation; but the question is an empirical one which we lack the evidence to answer. At all events, there is a certain irony in the fact that applicants are strongly discouraged from using what the system considers to be its first-class adjudicatory institutions in favour of their inferior cousins. It is true, of course, that tribunals are commonly considered to be preferable to courts in certain respects (such as greater speed and lower cost); but such supposed advantages have not raised the status of tribunals relative to courts, and if applicants are willing to forego these benefits, it is not clear why they should be prevented from doing so except, perhaps, in order to ration scarce judicial resources.

7.4.2 The US

In the US, the relationship between courts and non-courts as administrative adjudicators is simpler than it is in Australia. ALJs and AJs are embedded within departmental and non-departmental agencies, which are part of the executive branch. Decisions of ALJs and AJs are technically decisions of the agency, and decisions of executive agencies are amenable to judicial review. Judicial review and review by an ALJ or AJ are not alternatives because ALJ/AJ review is part of the internal decision-making process of the agency, not a form of external scrutiny. In this respect, there is a fundamental difference between ALJs and AJs in the US system and tribunals in the English and Australian systems, the latter being understood, like courts, as external review bodies. As we have seen (5.7.2), a complication arises when the agency rejects findings of fact by the adjudicator; but this does not, either in theory or in practice, affect the basic relationship between judicial review and ALJ/AJ review, which is one of superiority (of the

---

[33] See eg, M Allars, 'Federal Courts and Federal Tribunals: Pluraliam and Democratic Values' in B Opeskin and F Wheeler (eds), *The Australian Federal Judicial System* (Melbourne, Melbourne University Press, 2000) 214.

former) and subordination (of the latter). This relationship is to be explained, it seems, by the fact that adjudication by and within agencies is understood to involve the exercise of judicial power delegated by Congress to the agency. In the US system, Article III ('constitutional') courts, Article I ('legislative') courts and agencies can all exercise judicial power. However, Article I courts and agencies, being inferior repositories of such power, are subject to supervision by Article III courts by way of judicial review.

7.4.3 The UK

Institutionally, the position in the English system is similar in one respect to that in Australia. Courts and tribunals are both understood to be external to the agencies whose decisions they have power to review. Moreover, courts strongly discourage applicants who have a choice between review by a tribunal and review by a court from opting for the latter. Judicial review is a last resort. In another respect, however, the English situation is very different from the Australian: whereas Australian law treats tribunals and courts as categorically different types of institution performing categorically different functions, English law treats them as essentially similar institutions performing essentially the same function. Historically, and still, the most common explanation for the existence, side-by-side, of two sets of essentially similar institutions performing essentially the same function is that in various respects, tribunals do the job better than courts. Although the Franks Committee considered that courts should generally be preferred to tribunals as providers of administrative adjudication, it accepted that tribunals had certain 'practical' advantages over courts that gave them the edge in certain types of case. Tribunals – so the argument goes – can provide 'administrative justice' more quickly, cheaply, accessibly, flexibly, informally and expertly. As we have seen (2.3.1), from the 1970s onwards, at least some of these supposed advantages were being called into question, and some of the scepticism was supported by empirical evidence. At the same time, introduction into courts of new techniques of judging coupled with increasing emphasis, in policy-making for the court system, on ADR and precisely the same values that were traditionally associated with tribunals, may be thought to have reduced the comparative advantages of tribunals over courts.

The logic of assimilation that underlay thinking about tribunals at least since the 1950s came to partial fruition with the creation of the First-tier and Upper Tribunals by the TCE Act. As noted earlier (5.7.1), it is unclear what impact this development will have on construction and understanding of the juridical concept of non-judicial review. In particular, it is difficult to predict whether the Upper Tribunal will work towards a unitary concept of the task of tribunals and if it does, what relationship that concept will bear to judicial review. The situation is complicated by the fact that in addition to entertaining appeals on points of law from decisions of the First-tier Tribunal, the Upper Tribunal will also have some first-level review jurisdiction in complex cases and cases raising issues of general significance, as well as limited judicial review jurisdiction.

Australian experience supports the prediction that in England, judicial review and non-judicial review are likely to converge substantively even if they come to be understood as distinctively different modes of administrative adjudication. The area of greatest practical difference between the two Australian concepts is review of fact-finding. Given the differences of constitutional background between Australia and England and the direction in which English judicial review law has developed in recent years, it is perhaps unlikely that any contrast in this respect between the two modes of review will be as great in England as it is in Australia. Another open question is whether the two modes of review will converge remedially and procedurally as a result of the amalgamation of most tribunals into the new general tribunal and the admixture of judicial and non-judicial review in the Upper Tribunal. Once again, given the differences in constitutional background, there is less pressure in England than in Australia to maintain a sharp distinction between the two modes of review.

In Australian law, perhaps the most significant underlying difference between merits review and judicial review is that the latter typically involves only the identification of decision-making errors whereas the latter goes further and involves the correction of those errors. The critical question is whether and to what extent a system that empowers some adjudicatory institutions to correct errors needs to retain other adjudicatory institutions that are limited to identifying errors and leaving administrators to correct them. Limiting review to the identification of errors has traditionally been justified by appeal to some concept of separation of powers. This partly explains why Australian merits review tribunals are technically conceived as part of, or at least aligned with, the executive. In England, by contrast, they are understood as part of the machinery of justice, suggesting that there is no constitutional barrier to conferring on traditional courts the power to correct errors. If that is right, it is even harder to understand why some judicial institutions engaged in administrative adjudication should be limited to error-identification while others engage in error-correction.

One obvious difference between courts and tribunals under present arrangements for administrative adjudication is that courts have residual (common law, inherent) jurisdiction while tribunals have only selected (statutory) jurisdiction. Also, as things currently stand, only courts have power to award compensation against public bodies. So long as these differences persist, courts will be a necessary component of the administrative justice system. Moreover, even if the law develops in such a way that the respective functions of courts and tribunals converge to produce a single concept of administrative adjudication, it seems unlikely that the two types of adjudicatory institution will be completely assimilated. It is more likely that tribunals will be analogised to inferior courts (in the sense of courts lower in the judicial hierarchy) and that the Administrative Court will exercise a mix of original and appellate administrative jurisdiction. The division of original administrative jurisdiction between tribunals and the High Court might be driven by the common and long-held view that in certain areas and on certain issues, only judges of superior courts have the status and kudos to stand up effectively to central government. On the other hand, the fact that High Court judges will sit in the Upper Tribunal may blunt the force of this consideration.

Speculation aside, there is some evidence that senior judges had begun to rethink the relationship between courts and tribunals even before the new arrangements came into operation.[34] Read literally, such evidence only supports a view that courts – when deciding, for instance, whether to grant leave to appeal – should give due weight to the fact that tribunal judges and members tend to specialise in particular areas of the law to a greater degree than court judges, and that there are areas dealt with by tribunals (such as social security) in which courts are very little involved. However, the Senior President of Tribunals, Sir Robert Carnwath, has argued that this approach provides the foundation for re-conceiving the relationship between tribunals (and especially the Upper Tribunal) and the higher courts in 'anti-hierarchical' terms.[35] This suggestion – under which, it seems, decisions of tribunals would be effectively immune from judicial control on substantive grounds – bears striking similarities to the proposals of William Robson for a system of separate administrative courts (2.3.1). To what extent such radical ideas will bear fruit remains to be seen.

7.4.4 Re-conceiving the Relationship Between Courts and Tribunals

Leaving the US aside, the discussion so far suggests three distinctions particularly relevant to thinking about the relationship between tribunals and courts as administrative adjudicators. The first is a distinction between jurisdiction to review specified types of administrative decisions (typical of tribunals) and jurisdiction to review administrative decisions more generally (typical of courts). A second distinction is between power to correct errors in decisions under review (typical of tribunals) and power merely to identify errors (typical of courts). A third distinction is between broader 'merits-based' grounds of review (typical of tribunals) and narrower 'legality-based' grounds of review (typical of courts). These distinctions, I would argue, are now more important than the traditional catalogue of differences between tribunals and courts, focused on membership, access and procedure, not only because the contrast between courts and tribunals

[34] See eg, *Cooke v Secretary of State for Social Security* [2002] 3 All ER 279, [5]–[17] (Hale LJ); *Secretary of State for the Home Department v AH (Sudan)* [2008] 1 AC 678, [30] (Baroness Hale of Richmond); *Secretary of State for the Home Department v Akaeke* [2005] EWCA Civ 947, [26]–[30] (Carnwath LJ).
[35] R Carnwath, 'Tribunal Justice – A New Start' [2009] *Public Law* 48, 56–58.

in these respects is softening but also because of the proliferation of other accountability institutions that purport to offer the sorts of advantages tradition-ally associated with tribunals.

Framing the discussion with these three distinctions raises some fundamental questions: are there good reasons to have two more-or-less distinct sets of institutions, the one having power to review specified types of administrative decisions and to correct 'errors' defined in terms of broad, merits-based criteria and the other having power to review administrative decisions quite generally but only by identifying 'errors' defined in terms of narrower legality-based criteria? Assuming an affirmative answer to this question, a second question is one of institutional design: in what respects should institutions of the first type be different from institutions of the second type? For instance, are different skills needed for respective membership of the two types of institutions? Is it necessary or appropriate for the two types of institutions to follow different procedures? Should the two types of institutions be arranged hierarchically or co-ordinately?

The conditions in which courts and tribunals operate at the beginning of the 21st century are very different from those in which the 'modern tribunal' developed in the 19th and early 20th centuries. Thinking about their relationship in terms of a set of essentially 'practical' differences (such as speed, cost and (informality) gives inadequate weight to the important issues of institutional and constitutional design that are highlighted by the historical and comparative analysis undertaken in this book. This is not to say, of course, that institutional design does not have practical significance – quite the contrary, indeed. For instance, the practical mode of operation of the new UK tribunals and the development of the law of administrative review will depend crucially on the dynamics and interpretation of the set of institutional and relationships estab-lished by the TCE Act and the constitutional principles on which the new system is built. Although traditional thinking about tribunals will, no doubt, continue to play a part it will, one would hope and expect, be progressively supplemented and to a significant extent replaced by much more sophisticated analysis of the theory and practice of administrative adjudication.

7.5 Tribunals and ADR/PDR

The discussion in 6.5.2 concerned tribunal-annexed ADR techniques such as conferencing and mediation. Here we are concerned with the concepts of ADR and PDR as ways of thinking about the relationships between the various components of the 'administrative justice system' surveyed in this chapter. The concept of PDR, in contrast to that of ADR, might be interpreted as displacing courts from the position of fixed point in the system. However, the official understanding of PDR in the UK does not achieve this conceptual breakthrough, instead prescribing that 'disputes should be resolved at a proportionate level, and that the courts should be the dispute resolution method of last resort'.[36] The image this conjures up is of a hierarchically organised set of institutions analogous to the traditional court system. In fact, however, this image does not capture the complexity of the accountability sector or of the relationships between its various components, many of which are not hierarchical.

Moreover, the language of proportionality suggests a scalar relationship between various accountability institutions without providing a clear set of criteria for locating either institutions or 'disputes' at various points on the scale. At its crudest, proportionality seems to mean little more than that all grievances should enter the system at the lowest level, where they can be handled as quickly and cheaply as possible; and that each level should operate as a filter to ensure that the resources available at higher (more time-consuming and expensive) levels are not over-stretched.[37] Such multi-tier structures arguably disadvantage precisely those 'less articulate and less persistent'[38] whom it is the (admirable) aim of reformers to assist.

A different image is used by Boyron who argues that '[a] detailed assessment of all dispute resolution mechanisms would help identify the strengths and weaknesses for each and every one of them and establish their respective "niche markets"'.[39] Whereas the language of proportionality reflects the idea that all the relevant institutions are performing essentially the same function at different levels, the language of 'niche markets' seems to contemplate that various institutions may provide distinctive 'dispute resolution' services. Nevertheless, a similar problem arises: how should we characterise the various modes of 'dispute resolution' provided by the accountability sector and by what criteria should we match 'disputes' to avenues for their 'resolution'. Is it realistic to hope, with Boyron, that 'the competent ministries ... [will] adopt a more global view and ensure that all ... [accountability institutions] fit together in a coherent strategy'?[40] The analysis in this book perhaps suggests that such degree of coherence as the administrative justice system displays in any particular jurisdiction is a product of the rigidity of the constitutional structure within which it operates. On that basis, one might speculate that the relatively informal, flexible and pluralistic nature of the UK constitution may militate against the sort of centrally planned system – complete with a single point of entry and triage facilities[41] – that seems currently to be on the political agenda in that country.

---

[36] See S Boyron, 'The Rise of Mediation in Administrative Law Disputes: Experiences from England, France and Germany' [2006] *Public Law* 320, 325 n 29.
[37] See eg, *When Citizens Complain*, n 6 above, 6–8.
[38] ibid 8.
[39] Boyron, n 35 above, 341.
[40] ibid.
[41] See eg, *When Citizens Complain*, n 6 above, 11–15, 27–29.

7.6 Conclusion

As a result of the rapid growth of the state in the past century, it is meaningful to talk about the 'administrative justice system' in the broad way that we also talk about the 'civil justice system' and the 'criminal justice system'. Understanding the administrative justice system requires careful analysis of the nature and functions of its various components and how they relate to one another. In this book, the focus has been on administrative tribunals. Unlike the literature on judicial review and the role of courts in the administrative justice system, discussion of tribunals is often concerned more with their practical operation than with their position in the constitutional structure or the juridical nature of their functions.[42] A major aim of this book has been to provide a constitutionally-based theoretical account of the nature and role of tribunals and to explore some aspects of the relationship between theory and practice. Historical and comparative analysis has yielded a rich set of comparisons and contrasts that contribute to a deeper understanding of the administrative justice system. In particular, examination of the Australian concept of merits review and the system of merits review tribunals has generated important insights about administrative adjudication. Despite the major role they play in the administrative justice system, tribunals (and other non-judicial accountability institutions) have traditionally lost out to courts in the battle for scholarly attention.[43] My hope is that this book has gone some way to addressing this imbalance, and that it will encourage others to put courts in their place.

---

[42] See, for instance, R Thomas, 'Evaluating Tribunal Adjudication: Administrative Justice and Asylum Appeals' (2005) 25 *Legal Studies* 462, 463: 'The task of evaluating tribunal adjudication systems … requires a different methodology from that of traditional court-centred administrative law scholarship. Rather than analysing the development of legal principles … attention needs to be focused on the management of mass adjudication processes.'

[43] But not only for the attention of scholars. For instance, the UK Treasury Solicitor publishes a guide for civil servants entitled *The Judge Over Your Shoulder* (4th edn, 2006) designed to provide 'a good understanding of the legal environment in which decisions are made and an ability to assess the impact of legal risk on their work' (ibid 3). JOYS (as the publication is 'affectionately known') (ibid) is concerned solely with courts and judicial review, and does not mention tribunals despite the fact that a much larger proportion of bureaucratic decisions is reviewed by tribunals than by courts.

Index

In this Index the following abbreviations are used: